T0129102

"The imperatives of biography are to record, to correct, and to carve out historical significance, and Smith's lively account succeeds on all three fronts." —*Smithsonian*

"Smith never loses the beat." —*Los Angeles Magazine*

"[An] unflinching portrait of the conflicted and contradictory super-star." —Associated Press

"Smith's compelling and detailed portrait of one of our greatest musicians reveals affectionately and honestly the reasons we jump up every time 'I Feel Good' comes on the radio." —*Publishers Weekly*

"Revealing and incisive . . . this bio should be a cornerstone of soul-music-literature collections." —*Booklist*

"With powerful narrative drive, critical insight, and stylistic verve, RJ Smith has written a biography befitting the importance of its subject, one of the most important musicians and icons of the past century."
—Jeff Chang, author of *Can't Stop, Won't Stop*

"In this beautifully written and exhaustively researched monument to the genius that was James Brown, RJ Smith connects James Brown to centuries'-old traditions of protest and resistance, and in the process gives us the portrait of a man who had little choice but to break boundaries and inspire the Rhythm Nation."
—Mark Anthony Neal, author of *New Black Man*

"Unh! Good God! RJ Smith has written a sex machine of a book and it's called *The One: The Life and Music of James Brown.* Get up–get on up!" —Stephen Davis

"Few authors could write so profoundly about Brown's music, and fewer still about the soil from which he sprung; that Smith can do both, with grace and humor, is a monumental achievement."
—Craig Marks, coauthor of *I Want My MTV*

"With a prose style every bit as raw and captivating as the man and the music it chronicles, Smith's book brilliantly captures the roiling con-tradictions of a man and a country in transition."
—Attica Locke, author of *Black Water Rising*

RJ Smith has been a senior editor at *Los Angeles Magazine*, a contributor to *Blender*, a columnist for *The Village Voice*, a staff writer for *Spin*, and has written for *GQ*, *The New York Times Magazine*, and *Men's Vogue*. His first book, *The Great Black Way: L.A. in the 1940s and the Lost African-American Renaissance*, was a *Los Angeles Times* bestseller and recipient of a California Book Award. He lives in Los Angeles.

THE

THE LIFE AND MUSIC OF
JAMES BROWN

ONE

RJ SMITH

AVERY

An imprint of Penguin Random House

New York

FOR JENNY

"It takes two to make it outta sight."

AVERY

an imprint of Penguin Random House
375 Hudson Street
New York, NY 10014

Previously published as a Gotham Books hardcover

First trade paperback printing, November 2012, as Gotham Books

The Library of Congress has catalogued the hardcover edition as follows:
Smith, R. J., 1959–
The life and music of James Brown / R. J. Smith – 1st ed.
p. cm.
Includes bibliographical references and index.
ISBN 978-1-592-40657-9 (HC)   978-1-592-40742-2 (PBK)
1. Brown, James, 1933–2006. 2. Soul musicians–United States–Biography.   I. Title.
ML420.B818S65 2012
[B]
2011028536

Set in Bodoni Twelve ITC Std • Designed by Sabrina Bowers

146122990

CONTENTS

Introduction

GIVE THE DRUMMER SOME

I t was the slaves' day off. About twenty of them got things rolling on Sunday, September 9, 1739, breaking into a warehouse less than twenty miles south of Charlestown, South Carolina, grabbing guns and powder, and shooting sentries who got in their way. They were African born, with memories of life in the Kingdom of Kongo (modern Angola, Cabinda, and the Republic of the Congo). Many were former Angolan soldiers. Now they were soldiers once more.

They marched from the Stono River heading south for Spanish Florida, where other escaped slaves had been granted freedom. Along the way they gathered guns and drums. The cadence they beat on those drums drew more to their ranks, as did their songs and the banners they carried. They shot whites as they found them, spared a tavern owner who had been good to his slaves, and burned plantations. The rebels could not, however, kill all of their tormentors. The lieutenant governor escaped their onslaught and returned with a brigade of planters and militiamen. Outnumbered and having lost the element of surprise, the rebels were defeated by the following Sunday. More than forty blacks and twenty whites were killed in what was called the Stono Rebellion. Stono was the largest slave revolt to shock the colonies in the eighteenth century.

After it was over, the governor of colonial Georgia, expressing his concern over the insurrection next door, filed a formal report to a representative of the Crown:

> On the 9th day of September last being Sunday which is the day the Planters allow them to work for themselves, Some Angola Negroes assembled, to the number of Twenty. . . . Several Negroes joyned them, they calling out Liberty, marched on with Colours displayed, and two Drums beating, pursuing all the white people they met with, and killing Man Woman and Child. . . . They increased every minute by new Negroes coming to them, so that they were above Sixty, some say a hundred, on which they halted in a field, and set to Dancing, Singing and beating Drums, to draw more Negroes to them, thinking they were now victorious over the whole Province, having marched ten miles & burnt all before them without opposition . . .

Dancing, Singing and beating Drums: a unity expressed in performance. The drums communicated beyond the reach of the voice, and beyond sight. They moved bodies to join in brotherhood.

After the Stono Rebellion, South Carolina stopped importing African-born slaves. Too unmanageable. The hiatus lasted ten years, and when the colony again ventured into the trade, it avoided slaves from the Congo-Angolan region. Colonial legislators frantically passed the Slave Code of 1740, banning chattel from using or even owning drums. The overall law forbade drums and swords alike, making clear how South Carolina viewed the instrument: as a weapon.

That was how white colonials valued the drum. They had their own tradition of military percussion, and drawing on it, they understood the slave music as a call to war.

But to black Carolinians, the rhythms of Stono meant war and more. Drumming was a way of representing yourself as an imposing force, a way of demanding respect. As historian Richard Cullen Rath puts it, "The [Congolese] court tradition, which manifested itself in the drumming and dancing that so intimidated planters, was a means of directly representing and displaying power. . . . [It was] perhaps the original form of broadcasting."

South Carolina's ban on drums stayed on the books for over a century, all the way to the Emancipation Proclamation. But, failing to understand the African use of the instrument, the colonial legislature achieved a meaningless goal. The cadence continued by alternate means. One legacy of the Slave Code was that bondsmen found other ways to keep rhythms alive without a drum: Writers of the time record a skill amongst slaves for tapping with different parts of their bodies, hitting the floor and walls with sticks, clicking, banging, and most of all, dancing. That patting, tapping, dancing all flowed into the body as surely as it flowed from it; it was absorbed and passed on to new arrivals. There was a kind of underground flowering after 1740, a sharing of skills that made the drum unnecessary at the same time that it made drumming ubiquitous. Rhythm created community. It brought the news.

It happened again and again, in various places.

Almost eighty years after Stono, the slaves came marching across the Savannah River, heading to Augusta, Georgia. They came from South Carolina, beating on drums and carrying wooden sticks on their shoulders that made it look like they were bearing muskets. It was 1817, and though they had been outlawed, here again were the drums.

From a distance, it must have looked like trouble. Though it was (wink wink) illegal to bring slaves from another state for sale in Georgia, here they came, under the gaze of a slave trader, with "all the pomp and circumstance of illegal triumph," as a letter writer described it in the *Augusta Chronicle*.

Upon arrival in downtown Augusta, the slaves scattered. Somebody reminded the slaver that importing bondsmen was illegal, and he played it deadpan, shocked that anybody thought he was trafficking. The drums, however, did not lie. They scattered, too, going everyplace slave bodies went.

Pass it on: It's 1843, and the editor of the *New York Evening Post*, William Cullen Bryant, is visiting Barnwell, South Carolina. He attends a Negro corn shucking, a merriment conducted by plantation slaves. A bonfire built of longleaf pine logs oozes pitch that makes the flames burst into the air. A pile of corn is gathered in one spot, where slaves will strip the husks as they gather and sing songs that Bryant reports are "probably of African origin."

After work is done, the party moves to an expansive kitchen. Bryant describes that, "One of them took his place as musician, whistling, and beating time with two sticks upon the floor. Several of the men came forward and executed various dances, capering, prancing and drumming with heel and toe upon the floor with astonishing agility and perseverance, though all of them had performed their daily tasks and had worked all the evening."

The corn shuckers then commenced a loopy military parade around the room and performed comic speeches that mocked the oratory of white Southerners. It was whimsy that masked something behind it, something the marchers, dancers, and the tappers were perhaps aware of. Or maybe they were just caught up in the fun of the moment. All the same, the fun and the music represented something, a custom had been passed down over generations to get to this kitchen.

I'm not gonna show you the secret, James Brown would tell people who asked about the One, *but . . .* Then he would start talking.

Brown refused to reveal the mystery because the One was a trade secret. It would remain a puzzle because the more mystique it had, the more mystique *he* had, and mystique was good for business.

The One was a way to find yourself in the music, it was a means for drummers to come together with one another. It was a small element in a life's work, but like the drip was to Jackson Pollock or the footnote to David Foster Wallace, for Brown the One was bigger than it first appeared, a trifling that embodied the world he made.

Maybe most of all, for James Brown, the One was an anchor, an upbeat that put him in touch with his past and who he had become.

As he once explained it: "The 'One' is derived from the Earth itself, the soil, the pine trees of my youth. And most important, it's on the upbeat–ONE two THREE four–not the downbeat, one TWO three FOUR, that most blues are written. Hey, I know what I'm talking about! I was born to the downbeat, and I can tell you without question there is no pride in it. The upbeat is rich, the downbeat is poor. Stepping up proud only happens on the aggressive 'One,' not the passive Two, and never on lowdownbeat. In the end, it's not about music–it's about life."

To Brown it was a heartbeat that connected him to the dancers and singers and timekeepers who came before him. The One put him on a timeline, though the way he talked about the beat, it put him at the end of the line: the ultimate expression of a heritage.

He wasn't gonna show you the secret. But if you listened . . .

Chapter One

A CERTAIN ELEMENTAL WILDNESS

Barnwell, South Carolina, where Bryant viewed the raucous corn shucking, was James Brown's birthplace. The country surrounding Barnwell, in the nineteenth century called the Barnwell District, once grew cotton and vegetables, though both crops were pretty much exhausted by the time Brown came around. There were ponds in the area, and at one of them, euphemistically called the Red Sea, African Americans gathered from all around. They took off their shoes and kicked up the muck from the bottom of the pond. "Muddying for fish," it was called, and as they kicked, they would walk in concentric circles, ever tighter, until the little pond was muddied up, all but the center. There, the stompers finished their work, catching with their hands the fish crowding to the middle. It's a very old practice, which some say points back to Africa.

James Brown's family ripples out from this region in ever larger circles. His father was named Joe Gardner but took *Brown* from a woman who raised him. He was from Elko, ten miles from Barnwell. His family, Joe said, had musicians in it, including an uncle who won a fiddle contest in North Carolina.

James Brown's mother, Susie Behling, was from Fishpond, an area no longer on the map but once about ten miles south of the city of Bamberg. There are many black and white Behlings living in Bamberg and Barnwell, as well as Colleton, Williston, and Smoaks, all small towns in the area. Some whites here trace their roots to a landowning German family from Hanover headed by Lüder Friedrich Behling, born in 1815. Behling inherited the Bella Vista Plantation in Goose Creek, South Carolina, from his wife's family; Bella Vista had twelve slaves. It's possible Susie Behling's family took its name from slave-owning Behlings in the area, but nobody knows for sure.

This is what James Brown wanted us to know about his birth on May 3, 1933: "I wasn't supposed to be alive. You see, I was a stillborn kid." Two aunts delivered the boy in a shack surrounded by pine trees. When he arrived, he was told, he was motionless and quiet. Susie wept, but his aunt Minnie refused to give up, blowing strong breath into his lungs until, after infinite minutes, he came to life.

"I was a stillborn kid." Understand him: James Brown was born dead, and he fought his way into this world. That's a devastating entrance, one that marks him as forever distinct. It is also impossible, because a stillborn infant is dead in the uterus and, by definition, not alive. But Brown *felt* different, and maybe something special did occur at his birth. He saw his stillborn entrance as the moment his specialness first revealed itself.

One good thing about believing you were born dead is you come to feel nothing can kill you. This belief helped keep Brown alive.

The family roots Brown described were conspicuously far-reaching. He claimed he was Cherokee, Japanese, Indian. His daughter, Deanna Brown-Thomas, joked that every time he went to a country and felt the love, he perceived a genetic connection. To a Milwaukee interviewer, he explained, "I'm part Apache and Aztec myself. My daddy's nickname was Coochi, which is called Cochise. And I've got pictures of Geronimo that look identical to all my kids. I didn't pay no attention at first, but that's what it is. I got the head full of hair and I got all that. His [hair] was hangin' down like mine be hangin' down in the mornin'."

Susie told Deanna she had family in Florida. Joe had people in North Carolina and Philadelphia. A few small clues pointing in a few directions. The only recorded lineage, however, never strays from the Barnwell District. It is aunts and uncles and cousins, a web of them, all surrounding the ponds and pines of Barnwell. Brown didn't draw a family tree in his Bible, and he wasn't going to draw one up for his children. "He was a personal person and some things he didn't want out," said Roosevelt Johnson, a longtime personal assistant.

Once, in a relaxed moment, he told a friend who had asked about his ancestors, "I'm not going to ever say what I'm thinking, because it might be disrespectful to my family. Let's just say a long time ago something in the milk may not be clean."

Joe and Susie met in 1929 when she was visiting relatives. Behling was a Baptist, and had long, straight hair that her son said was evidence of her "Geechee" roots. Geechee is how blacks living around the Savannah River referred to their roots in the Gullah culture, a people that flourished on the coastal plain and the Sea Islands of South Carolina and Georgia. Slave descendants, their cultural and geographical isolation allowed the Gullah to maintain an African identity and traditions far more pervasively than other slave communities. Family lore has it that Susie inherited her straight hair and other features from a Native American bloodline, and James said a great grandmother on Susie's side was mostly Native American.

Joe had a second-grade education, Susie left school in the fifth grade. Together they lived in a wooden shack with a small stove for heat and no plumbing. The windows were open and held no glass; when the wind blew or it rained, Joe leaned old doors against the opening. That made the house dark and frightening to James, who spent as much time outside it as he could. Joe might be gone for days at a time, and James would be alone day and night. For company he had what he called his friends, the insects that lived beneath the shack. A sickly child, James contracted rheumatic fever three times before he was eight. With no doctor in the vicinity, his parents treated the illness with folk remedies like sassafras tea.

Barnwell is on the western edge of South Carolina's inner coastal plain, between the Atlantic to the east and the Piedmont highlands. Geologically it is a vast beach, from which the ocean receded east millions of years ago.

In South Carolina, two cultures prevailed. The lowlands, along the coast, were dominated by Charleston and had been colonized from the sea in the late seventeenth century. The uplands were German and Scots-Irish, and were populated from the north in the early eighteenth century. In the lowlands, they dropped their *r*'s and slurred their words; they erected a facade of white columns and easy living, and believed passionately in the charm and manners that honor them to this day. Those in the Piedmont were restive, marinated in a culture of hard work and brawling. Their way of speaking was streaked with Elizabethan pronunciations and archaic words.

In the fertile flatness between these realms was a less populated, and less defined, region, slowly breached from the north. A royal proclamation in 1763 drew a line down the back of the Appalachians, and banned settlement on the western side. Pioneers had been pushing west from Maryland, Pennsylvania, and Virginia, but after the law came down, they instead migrated down the Appalachian valleys, pushing into the unsettled backcountry of the Carolinas and Georgia. This was the empty space between the big cities of Augusta and Savannah, and in those cities, folks were notably dismissive of the recent immigrants. Perhaps because of the sound the newcomers' whips made as they pushed their cattle onward, they were given a name which has stuck ever since: *crackers*. They just naturally set folks off. A representative of the crown thought the newcomers were fixing to do to his beloved Georgia what the Huns had done to Europe. An Anglican missionary passing through the backcountry said the Indians had better manners than this ilk, who were without "the least rudiments of Religion, Learning, Manners of Knowledge (save of Vice) among them."

These are the outsiders who settled the sparsely populated area around Barnwell. And defined it. As the region grew, it became drenched in violence, a lore that is lamented every bit as much as it is embraced. Among those who embraced it was Ben Robertson. In his 1942 book *Red Hills and Cotton*, Robertson presented his Carolina people to the rest of the country in a tone meant to simultaneously shock and disarm. He explained the impact of all that isolation, an insulated existence marking blacks and whites and characterizing the region where Brown was born.

"We live in the fields among the growing cotton and the green corn, and we are face to face with ourselves, with all of eternity and its problems. We try to explain the wind and the sun and life and death, the here and the hereafter. We cannot explain, so we turn from the natural to the supernatural. In solitude we reach our own conclusions. We have arrived at many things alone. So we are personal, we are emotional, we have learned to dream, we are romantic. And because there is pride within us and a certain elemental wildness, we sometimes fly off the handle. Some of our people, before they know it, have shot, have slashed someone with a knife. We must attempt to control ourselves, we must be on our guard."

Matters of honor and respect tilted easily to rage. "We do not as a rule shoot people over property matters; when we shoot we do so because of passion," explained Robertson. "We shoot on the spur of the moment and do not often meditate a murder. Often it is a good way to shoot–to shoot on the spur of the moment; it clears the air like a thunderstorm."

At the end of the nineteenth century, around the time Brown's parents were born, one act of violence among the cypress gums could stand for a great many. A thief had broken into St. Michael's Church. He stole a Bible and, possibly, a piece of furniture. Nobody was charged with the crime, but gradually suspicion fell on Isham Kearse, described in the press as "a young negro of a roving disposition who sought no regular employment, and it is probable that his living was not honestly made." Some white men of Barnwell clamored for confrontation, and on the night of December 2 they got their chance. Kearse, who had been keeping a low profile, was discovered just over the Colleton county line, visiting his mother.

Four Barnwell whites captured him leaving her house, and they tightly bound his hands. Their rope was looped around Kearse's neck and then tied to the rear of a horse-pulled buggy. Those driving the buggy set off at a fast pace for Broxton Bridge, adjacent to a swamp. Kearse ran behind the carriage until roots and rocks tripped him up, and then he was dragged. Others from the party were sent to collect Hannah Walker, Kearse's mother, and his wife, the seventeen-year-old Rosa. For alleged knowledge of the stolen Bible, Rosa was also roped, tied, and dragged across country trails.

At a spot near the Salkehatchie River, the three African Americans were brutally interrogated. Isham Kearse denied the theft and the women said they knew nothing about it. The prisoners were stripped naked, while the whites drank whiskey; they were beaten with a new buggy trace, a stiff piece of leather used to tether horses to a carriage. Kearse was tied to a tree and lashed one hundred and fifty times, until he begged the men to shoot him. The women escaped, Walker running into the swamp, Rosa in the other direction. As Isham fell unconscious, the whites put his ragged coat over him and left for their Barnwell homes. His body was found later that morning. Like her son, Walker died from the beating. She was discovered facedown, arms stretched out, resting in a foot of water. Rosa made it home, where she remained barely alive.

There was no mystery as to the four perpetrators; everybody knew their names and they did not deny the abduction. In two trials, one for each murder, the defendants were found innocent of all charges. A jury in Colleton bought the defense argument that Walker died from drowning, an act she caused herself by falling into the swamp.

A triple lynching was unusual, but not extraordinary. Barnwell had an octuple lynching in 1889; though the victims were taken from the Barnwell jail, they were hanged just outside of town, so the mayor could say the crime wasn't his problem.

That this was a region of astonishing violence is accepted by many who have studied the region, but *why* it was has puzzled historians. Some have scrutinized the particularly high number of lynchings along the Georgia–South Carolina border, as if geography could kill. Others suggest that in places like Barnwell, the mingling of the hell-raising Protestant Piedmont folks and the cavalier, coastal Baptists in the middle of the state created an explosive culture clash. The most likely theory, however, is that racial violence coincided with organized efforts by whites to turn back Negro gains made by Emancipation. If anti-Republican forces were going to succeed in South Carolina, African Americans would have to lose political rights and be beaten into submission.

They couldn't have done it without Barnwell. Republican voters there were chased from polling places, and the few blacks appointed to political office were shot at and otherwise harassed. The same year that Isham Kearse and Hannah Walker were murdered in the swamp, South Carolina passed a revised state constitution, a blueprint for rebuilding white power. Crucial to the new order was a poll tax levied on all registered voters. Registrants had to read and write a paragraph from the Constitution, an effort meant to disenfranchise black majorities. From the constitution of 1895, it was a short sprint to white voting majorities all over South Carolina, and then passage of a spectrum of laws that, together, constructed segregation.

When James was four, he heard his parents fighting. "Take your child," said Joe, fixing Susie with the responsibility. "You keep him, Joe, 'cause I can't *work* for him," she answered. Then she left.

James had few memories of his mother from his early years. After she left, Joe and James moved around the immediate area, as

Joe found and lost work. When he did road work or picked vegetables on a farm, James stayed with aunts or one of Joe's girlfriends.
Later, James would talk about his solitude in the sand hills and
piney swamps of the area as almost a gift. Most people, he explained,
are taught early on what not to do—he was out in the woods by himself, and he missed that lesson. He learned to listen to his own
instincts and trust his own reasoning.

In the early 1930s, Joe was a turpentine man, harvesting the gum
from longleaf and slash pines. This was especially harsh work, dating back to the colonial era, when pitch was used to waterproof sail-
ing ships. It broke down hands, knees, backs; its methods unchanged
since before the Civil War. Overwhelmingly, it was black men's toil.
"Turpentine Negroes," polite whites called them. A worker was
charged with a "drift" of trees, some five thousand or so; as a chip-
per, Joe probably used an axe to scrape the bark off the pines.

Workers were assigned to camps, primitive enclaves of wooden
shacks, dogtrot houses, and lean-tos that sheltered up to several
hundred men. Camp life followed its own rules, which were looked
down on by black city dwellers. Turpentine men burned scars into
the trees with acid that would also eat away their fingerprints, and
in this and other ways, these men were blunt-force individualists
who set themselves apart from society. Self-sufficient and unfree,
they carried a swagger and a desperation; they displayed a revelry
that was earned. Historian I. A. Newby wrote that segregation in
South Carolina was so thoroughly destructive that "black communities in the state were never organized. In fact, they were not communities in the true sense of the word." This was not quite so true in
the turpentine camps, where a sense of identity lifted up its head.

The men built cooperages, stables, and blacksmith sheds in the
camps. There was church for those that wanted it. "Those that
believed in worship service, they would meet around each other's
house, sat and talk the bible or stuff," recalled Anthony Green, a
turpentine man. "The others that didn't, if they were drinking
moonshine, they got together and drank the moonshine. They shot

dice, they done the gambling and all that kind of thing." There was usually a piano around, and guitars, and wandering blues musicians who traveled the region en route to paying gigs and would play for loose change.

It came together on Saturday nights at the juke. These were small venues run by an ambitious camp worker, usually from out of the house he lived in. Fish, hamburgers, and moonshine were for sale, and women might be available. Jukes provided leisure for those who worked fourteen hours a day and were a place to blow off steam. They were also violent places, where men gambled and fought with fists, knives, and guns.

In the camps Joe Brown learned all kinds of ways men can win and lose money with dice, and he would take this knowledge with him when he left. He knew how to make applejack moonshine, which he sold on the side. Joe was good with a knife and was able to play a little harmonica. He sang songs by Sonny Terry and Blind Boy Fuller, North Carolina bluesmen who passed through, and played guitar, perhaps along with Tampa Red, one of the itinerant musicians who frequented the region. A Georgia-born bluesman and one of the great bottleneck guitar players, Red played the camps, and even wrote a song called "Turpentine Blues":

> Turpentine's all right, provided that wages are good
> Turpentine's all right, provided that wages are good
> But I can make more money now, by somewhere choppin'
>   hardwood
>
> Turpentine business ain't like it used to be
> Turpentine business ain't like it used to be
> I can't make enough money now, to even get on a spree . . .

As Red could see, the Carolina forests were being decimated; the ceaseless hacking and scraping weakened the trees, hastening a need to cut them down and send them to mills.

For turpentine men, the season began in April or May and lasted until November. James Brown was born at the beginning of turpentine season, in May. Soon enough, if things followed their usual course, the son would take a job in the camp beside his father. Except that the naval industry was fading, and the Depression was on.

Barnwell thrived on farming, and farming had provided Brown's family sustenance for generations. But now the land itself was sick. Cotton was an important regional crop, and prices had dropped steeply, from thirty-nine cents a pound in 1919 to ten cents by 1930. Worse, the boll weevil was infesting the cotton fields, savaging the plants. Black farmers were put out of business, and the state did little to assist them. In 1938, the Barnwell County Department of Public Welfare filed a report with the state that bared the county's problems. "Proceeds from farming have decreased for the last ten years. . . . Due to the fact that farming has on the whole been a failure for so many years and due to the fact that our county affords very little industrial employment, we have many needy families."

People ate what they found. Corn was husked, the kernels washed and boiled in lye. After a rinse, the whitened hominy was fried with bacon grease and seasoned to taste. Mush or cripple was made by cooking a hog's head, feet, and maybe a jaw, in a salted broth. Corn was added and the mixture then fried to a thickness. This was once what slaves had been fed on the plantation, but in Depression Era South Carolina, the poor white folks were eating it with relish.

Pellagra was widespread in the district. Country people who relied on a diet of corn pone, fatback, and molasses did not get sufficient vitamins, and the state began distributing yeast to the impoverished as a supplement. As the Depression wore on, however, the anti-pellagra program was reduced to handing out cottonseed meal, to be stirred into soup or hot water and eaten.

To one writer, James said he and his father moved to Augusta,

Georgia, in 1938; to another, he declared it was in the second half of 1939. The crops were dying, resin wasn't running like it had, and Susie was gone. For Joe Brown, it was time to leave for something better. Much later, Joe would put a frame around the big picture. "White folks, some young white folks, run *away* from America. They ashamed. Black folks, they run all over, up North, everywhere, tryin' to get *into* America." Joe and his son were leaving Barnwell by foot, walking to America. But before Joe and the son who started calling him "Pops" could try to get there, they had to enter the twentieth century. That meant leaving the pines. They had to break with all of it–the unchanging rural disenfranchisement and stomping for fish and the slavery by another name that was the turpentine camp.

Back there was a medieval poverty and labor that ground you into sawdust. Up ahead was a background to be proud of, the Aztec empire, Geronimo's throne, the warrior clans of the Cherokee.

There was Joe, James, and Minnie Walker, Joe's aunt, who had been there when James was born. They carried what they had, and walked forty miles to Augusta.

Chapter Two

THE TERRY

Georgialina, it is called. A native who knew the place better than most once entered a succinct definition into the Congressional Record: "a region of the Savannah River Valley which includes a number of cities and towns on both sides of the South Carolina and Georgia state line."

The statesman who so crisply defined it, Strom Thurmond, was the elected leader of Georgialina. It defined him as much as he defined it. But, walking a bridge across the Savannah River one unremarkable day around 1939 was someone who would one day be Georgialina's most famous citizen. Save for a few years when he lived in New York City, James Brown never strayed from Georgialina. It was who he was, and he knew every inch of it. He knew what the people there–white and black–thought, and why they did the things they did. He knew where you could get a good T-bone steak and the address of "Caskets & More." He knew the back roads where you could outrun the sheriff. He even knew Strom Thurmond.

Along with golf's Masters Tournament, Brown is what people around the world think of when Augusta is mentioned. He didn't always love it, and as for the people of Augusta, well, many of them didn't love Brown. But, as he said a thousand times easy, Augusta was home.

Augusta looks like a biscuit sitting in a plate of gravy. Rising above everything else is "the Hill," the elite resort settlement of big homes and Old South charm, and surrounding are the flat lowlands fanning out to the Savannah River. The split in altitude accents a split in the city's character. "It is a town with a fascinating case of schizophrenia," wrote Dorothy Kilgallen. "It is beautiful with gambrel roofs and lacy ironwork, creeping vines and colonial porticoes; it is brash with jazz brasses and roulette wheels and chuck-a-luck and slot machines and strip-teasers and a sweet-talkin' disregard for laws that the folks don't like."

Up on the Hill was the Augusta National Golf Club, home of the Masters, and the Partridge Inn, a symbol of Augusta's splendor. James Brown lived down below, where the gravy ran the thinnest.

Pops, Minnie, and James moved into the house of a relative on Twiggs Street. It was in the African American part of Augusta, a neighborhood called "the Terry." Augustans in the 1930s used the term as a shortening of "the Negro Territory," but originally it was an Irish enclave called Verdery's Territory. After the Civil War, when the Freedman's Bureau moved emancipated slaves into the neighborhood, the name changed, but the territory remained much the same. By 1933, the Terry comprised perhaps fifty blocks; here and in the surrounding neighborhoods of the southeastern part of the city lived most of Augusta's 20,000 blacks, composing about 30 percent of the population. There was also a small Chinese community in the Terry, dating to the building of the Augusta canals in the nineteenth century.

The showcase of the community was the Golden Blocks, a corridor at the intersection of Ninth and Gwinnett streets that formed the African American business district. The black-owned Penny Savings and Loan Company, and the Haines Normal and Industrial Institute, a bastion of black education, were both on the Blocks. Nearby was the Del Mar Casino, owned by John "Slow Drag" Crim, gambler, financier, provider. Just off Gwinnett on Ninth Street was the sumptuous Lenox Theatre, built by a quartet of black businessmen tired of the treatment they got in Augusta's white-owned theaters, and designed by G. Lloyd Preacher, one of the finest white architects in the South.

Constructed in 1921, the Lenox was the northern outpost of those nine Golden Blocks, a dignified edifice of Greco-Roman design whose stage displayed the cream of black show business. Ads for the Lenox exclaimed "It is your theater"; from its stage, black soldiers were sent off to World War I with brass band music and hurrahs, and blacks held public meetings there to discuss civil rights. But if it was an inspiration, the Lenox was also within walking distance of the impoverished cottages that also defined the Terry. The streets of the neighborhood were unpaved sand and clay and bisected by tiny lanes with colorful names: Thank God Alley, Electric Light Alley, Slopjar Alley. In the front of the shotgun shacks, morning glories climbed up faded wood fences and across porches. Behind the shacks were outhouses, chicken coops, stacks of wood, and almost certainly a cast iron pot, resting over a fire pit. The day's meals would be cooked here; afterward, lye would be made from wood ashes mixed with animal fat, and with lye the women would do the laundry of the whites that hired them.

Saturday was shopping day in the Terry, and blacks from the countryside came to buy supplies. Farmers hawked produce, and on the streets one could purchase sassafras, raw peanuts, hogshead cheese, sorghum, shoes, magic roots. Sunday was less than a day of rest: Church services started at two in the afternoon so that the women could first make supper for their white employers. Augusta had an abundance of places for African Americans to worship, with five black churches built even before the Civil War had ended.

Near the home on Twiggs was the United House of Prayer for All People, a large plain building with crepe paper hanging from the rafters and a sign over the door proclaiming: "Great Joy! Come to the House of Prayer and forget your troubles." There was also a Moorish Science Temple, a southern expression of fledgling Islamic black nationalism. Members numbered more than three hundred, and were required to wear fezzes and turbans; men sported long beards.

There were able leaders in black Augusta, entrepreneurs and clergymen whom whites felt they had absolutely no reason to acknowledge unless there was an emergency. African American purchasing power was limited, home ownership almost an aberration; in 1940, of the 7,718 homes lodging blacks, fewer than 19 percent were owner-occupied. Only about 2 percent of Augusta's blacks were classified as professionals, and more than 90 percent of those were teachers. African American political power had been made illegal thanks to the white primary system, which kept blacks away from the polls for decades.

In the early 1930s, voting restrictions were working *too* well, in fact, and many whites in this city of 60,342 were complaining that they, too, had been knocked off registration lists for not paying property taxes (one of the restrictions meant to exclude blacks). Barred from the political process, citizens of the Terry had little hope that housing inspectors, say, or the Board of Health, would be of any assistance. Black power was apolitical power, it flowed from those who could raise and spend money in the community. The mark of a respected black businessman was to have set up a recreational center or financed church renovations or a Boys' Club, because here, success meant spreading wealth around the neighborhood.

A hand-tinted photograph, James Brown at nine. He must have just gotten a haircut, his cranium a dome, smooth and hard. His expression is striking for a nine-year-old, eyes slits, mouth unsmiling, the head tilted at an angle that sends a message—got something for me? That orb hunkers down on shoulders, squashes his neck. The boy looks uncomfortable in these clothes, his long-sleeve striped shirt, slacks, a thin belt around a slender waist.

The way Brown remembered it, Joe parked him at the house of a family member he called Aunt Honey. Her name was Hansone

Washington, though many mistakenly heard it as Handsome. Her address was 944 Twiggs Street. The new US Highway 1 passed right by the house, so one could look out a window and watch folks drive from Florida to New York and beyond. On Twiggs there were truck stops and gas stations and boarding houses renting rooms to truckers and travelers. Strangers coming, strangers going. It was a smart place for somebody to set up a whorehouse. Aunt Honey was smart enough.

Prohibition was on and Honey was also selling bootleg whiskey from a hollow space beneath the house's wood floor. Customers called it "scrap iron," because it was made in galvanized drums and had a metallic taste.

There were sometimes as many as fourteen or fifteen men living in the house, and Honey rented out rooms for working girls and their johns. Honey would sometimes cook the boy a potato pone because she knew he loved it, and he'd eat the whole thing by himself. But Honey had a business to run, and a rambunctious relation was an obstacle to profit. Aunt Honey beat James and told him he was ugly, making him hide in the closet when men were over. Honey's brother Melvin Scott was a bootlegger with a temper who was often around. The police raided the place once and Scott thought Brown had tipped them off; he tied the boy in a croaker sack, hung him from the ceiling, and beat him with a belt.

Joe remained a presence, bringing money in when he could, always looking for work. He was around, but not of the household: Aunt Minnie most of all watched over James, as did Honey.

An important part of Brown's story, a detail he told over and over and put in his press material, was that his mother left the family back in Barnwell, and that the son would not see her again for decades.

That was James Brown's recollection. Complicating–and deepening–his memories, however, is evidence strongly suggesting Susie Brown *did* come to Augusta, and that she, Joe, and James lived under the same roof for a period of time. First of all, there is the information found in the annual Augusta city directories.

These books list who lived at every address in town. The 1947–48 and the 1949 directories both list a "colored" Susie Brown living with Joseph in Augusta. The 1947–48 entry records this Joseph's job as a porter at a gas station, and gas station attendant was Joe's regular occupation for many years. Also living at that address, according to the 1947–48 directory, was Minnie Walker, the woman who blew life into the sickly newborn.

In a 2009 memoir, Augusta journalist Don Rhodes cites conversations he had with two longtime associates of Brown who remembered Susie and Joe living together. Susie "did not willingly abandon her family," an Augusta friend of Brown told Rhodes. So what happened to Susie? One source says Joe threw her from a second- or third-story window of the Twiggs house, in the midst of a fight. He threatened to kill her, and Susie moved out.

Perhaps the son picked up the story told by his father; perhaps he even believed it. "Pop had a version of why they didn't stay together, and that had been passed on to Mr. Brown," said Emma Austin, a family friend who grew up in the Terry.

Joe was certainly violent; he regularly beat James, who said his dad was "dangerous." It would have been easier to talk about abandonment than about the beating you took, and witnessed, at the hand of the father who was raising you. As soon as he had a life story others wanted to hear, Brown was crafting it to suit his emotional needs. There's something simpler, cleaner, about being abandoned, than about the violence that Brown experienced and could not stop.

Another inference can be drawn first from Brown's tale. Pop's violence was something his son could forgive. His abandonment by his mother, that was unendurable. What life taught Brown was that men beat people up, and men beat women, and that a beating was to be endured.

Home was where you went when there was absolutely nowhere else to go. In lieu of home, Brown ran wild in the Terry. The finger of the Augusta canal system that flowed behind the house was a landmark, a drain and a sewer out of which he ate fish. He'd jump into the water and hide from cops, and he shot dice under a canal bridge.

On the streets of the Terry, Brown learned all kinds of stuff, like how to fight with knives in the traditional Carolina manner. "People were real bad there," he recalled. "They used to walk up and lock hands with a man and cut it out. He have a knife and you have a knife and y'all lock hands and cut each other. Till one fall." Jeffrey Lockett, who lived nearby on Ninth Street, summed up the mentality of the Terry's streets: "If you want to be a man, you got to fight to get respect. Now people know me, and they know I don't take no shit from nobody. But if anyone bothers me, I'd shoot them in a heartbeat. Just like that, *bam*. Better them dead than me."

Brown learned further from watching his daddy, who presented a brazen face in the Terry. Joe would team up with a cousin and steal guns, using a bluntly effective pitch: They'd walk up to a stranger, request that he either hand over his gun or shoot them, and if the guy didn't shoot, they stripped him of his weapon. The approach had gotten them this far.

Brown joined a gang and was called Little Junior on the streets; his cousin Willie Glenn, who lived with him, was Junior. Soon only fools or blood relations raised a hand to Brown. In the face of violence and insult, he got stronger. He became known around the way. "Stay away from him, people said, because he was always in trouble," said childhood friend Allyn Lee.

He considered himself a thug, and copied the thug style: baseball cap, jeans with pockets on the sides, and a handkerchief tied down one pocket, sneakers turned down real tight. He and his gang wrote words onto their clothes with Clorox bleach.

One day, an aunt saw him behind the house, with a fifteen-cent sack of chicken feed she could use. "Boy you better hand over that feed," she said, "unless you want an ass-whipping." He wanted a quarter for it. She did not give him a quarter, and repeated her threat. Then the boy turned around and poured the whole bag into the levee. She did whip him, too, and he never cried. And when it was over he told her he was ready to take another beating. James Brown was not afraid.

He was pint-size, lacking a formidable build, but Brown compensated with a way of moving that gave off waves of energy. Even as a teenager, he was able to command attention just by skimming along; he communicated he was not to be trifled with, not to be delayed. Here was someone worth measuring.

The brand-new Silas X. Floyd Elementary was a segregated school of 1,600 students and seven grades, a red-brick, Georgian-style building with white pillars out front. Floyd was named after a celebrated local black minister, educator, and poet, who once wrote: "Augusta is a good place to live and Augusta is a good place to die. Living or dying, give me Augusta."

White Augusta did not reciprocate Floyd's enthusiasm. Floyd School, as it was called, had been built against white Augusta's wishes; the city only agreed to erect the much needed facility when New Dealers in Washington gave Augusta money for a Negro school through the National Recovery Act. Augusta spent twenty times on white schools what it did for its black schools, so while the building was substantial, the black community had to raise money to keep it going. Floyd was the largest public school in Richmond County, but it had only thirty teachers and one truant officer. The first-grade class contained 400 students, though few stayed on until seventh grade; they were just too important to families who needed the income that work provided. The average graduating class had fewer than one hundred students.

He quickly made an impression. A student named Henry Stallings first noticed Brown when he caught him stealing his lunch. Stallings's parents sent him to school with lunch packed in a lard bucket, so embarrassing to him that he hid it under a vent. Brown was watching him, though, and took the food. They had a fight over it, but eventually became pals.

Among a poor student body coping with the Depression, Brown stood out. The first day of school, students took off his overalls and threw them in a tree. Another day, he was sent home for "insufficient clothes." "Oh man, he was pitiful," said Stallings. "For me to really tell you what he looked like in the wintertime— the soles coming off his shoes, snot coming out of his nose, I didn't see no jacket on him *ever*. He was always cold.

"He saw me coming to school with those shoes all shined, my parents used to make sure I came there correct. He liked the way they sent us to school all smart, spic and span, pressed clothes. Overalls is what he would wear."

Laura Garvin was a committed Floyd School teacher who took a special interest in Brown. Along with principal Yewston Myers, she kept a sympathetic eye on him. "Neither of us called him James or Brown. It was always James Brown. It just seemed to go like that," Garvin said. She cared about him, giving him the kind of attention he did not get at home. "I knew him as a poor waif on the streets of Augusta and as one who did things which he never should have done, also," she recalled later. But he was not a scary kid; he was respectful, funny—Garvin most of all saw a boy who even then had charisma and affecting openness, so straightforwardly *himself* that it was hard not to smile. "Nothing could make you dislike him," she recalled. She also quickly noticed how much the boy enjoyed singing, and sought to bring that out in him.

School officials had Brown sing the national anthem before classes began. Garvin staged regular performances in her room, charging a dime to see Brown sing. When word spread and crowds filled the room, she moved the shows to the library, which had a piano. Brown would dance and sing "blues things—I was singing the blues kinda heavy at that time." Some students scorned him for his dark skin, and many for his shabby clothes. But Garvin provided him a means for winning respect. Brown called these performances the happiest times of his childhood.

Augusta in the 1940s was famous for its great voices. There was the imperial Swanee Quintet, born in the late 1930s as the

Hallelujah Gospel Quartet. By the time they changed their name
in the mid 1940s, they were filling local churches and arenas and
even had their own radio program, six nights a week on WGAC.
The Swanees took a rural, hard-country quartet sound and wore it
proudly in an age when a more urbane group style, featuring tight,
jazzy harmonies and intricate rhythms, was in vogue. They proudly
stood for old values, with a stubborn resoluteness that Southerners
understood.

They were stars in the Terry, running their own laundry business on Steed Street (decades later, Steed would be renamed
Swanee Quintet Boulevard). In the late 1940s, singer and cofounder
James "Big Red" Anderson befriended a teen shining shoes outside radio station WGAC, on Broad Street downtown. This began
what would be a lifelong friendship between James Brown and the
Swanees. The group would go on the road with Brown in 1966, and
he produced several of their records.

Augusta's most famous voice of the era, Arthur Lee Simpkins,
got his start as a gospel singer; a 1934 write-up in the *Augusta
Chronicle* called him "a lad with a voice mellowed in watermelons,
taters and cotton bolls." Simpkins's voice was courtly, disarming
white listeners, swooping up an octave in a single syllable in his
warm tenor. Augusta was also frequented by street preachers and
shouters Brown would have heard. Itinerant blues singer Blind
Willie McTell traveled through and recorded here. The female
sanctified blues singers the Two Gospel Keys lived in Augusta;
where the Swanees *chose* a rugged simplicity, the Two Gospel Keys
simply *were* raw, and wonderfully so. By the late 1940s, the influen-
tial gospel radio show *Parade of Quartets* began broadcasting. (It's
still around as a weekly TV program on the ABC affiliate.)

A sound that started in the pews was thriving on the streets
of Augusta and elsewhere, a fusion of the church with the barbershop (safe havens where black men could gather), a new vocal style
that melded the sacred and the profane, carrying a spiritual dimension that didn't quite define it. This new sound was apparent

in national harmony groups like the Ink Spots and the Mills Brothers, in the so-called human orchestras and the very first doo-wop
groups. Black gospel music was being programmed on radio in
cities all around the country, and this was one unintended
consequence–once you heard the music during leisure time, gospel became a social sound, not purely of the pulpit. In any case,
gospel was *already* social, for the black church was a part of the
lives of even those who were not churchgoers. This vocal style was
a music of the street–of people for whom church was an understood
part of life, rather than life itself. A music made by folks standing
on corners, congregating in barber shops, hovering at shoeshine
stands. Storefront churches wedged between commercial enter-
prises underscored the way the music pushed into daily life, and so
did the gospel singers standing on a box at a busy intersection.
Brown was circulating in these same streets of 1940s Augusta, listening and learning. He was also going to church and studying
preachers, whom he then imitated, not because he was particularly
religious–as a boy, he was not–but because he admired their command.

He was singing pop songs, and also learning the rudiments of
instrumental music. While employed at a furniture store, Joe was
given a damaged organ with broken wood legs. On a lunch break, he
took it home to the boy, propping it up with a cheese box. The organ
was the instrument Brown best mastered; neighborhood friend
Leon Austin taught him the basics of the keyboard and another
friend, Robert Graham, also gave him lessons. Tampa Red, the itinerant blues musician, was dating one of Aunt Honey's girls. He
befriended Brown and taught him the chord changes to Red's classic "It's Tight Like That" on the guitar. Brown was picking up how
to make music by ear, willy-nilly, but already he had skills and was
bragging about them. He believed in himself, good-naturedly telling his buddies that they were going to know his name. "He always
said, 'You might beat me singing, but when I start dropping records
on you, you won't even be around,'" said Leon Austin.

Soon Brown formed his own vocal group with Graham, mixing that gospel music of the streets with pop and blues, songs by Amos Milburn, Roy Brown, Wynonie Harris, and Red Norvo and Mildred Bailey. They called their group the Cremona Trio, because one of them played a Cremona guitar. The Trio sat in the front row of the Lenox on talent night, charged up to the stage, and sang a version of Louis Jordan's "Caledonia," winning first prize. They lasted about three or four years, getting paid fifty dollars a night to play shows for white officers at the nearby Camp Gordon army base.

In the days after Pearl Harbor was attacked, the city placed armed guards at the bridge that Pops and James had crossed by foot. The Lenox Theatre added the Abbott and Costello feature, *In the Navy*, to their lineup. But a bigger impact World War II had on the Terry, and all of Augusta, was that within forty-eight hours of the attack, Camp Gordon was officially opened. A huge military base, Camp Gordon came about due to the efforts of the mayor of Augusta, the head of the Chamber of Commerce, and a young circuit court judge from South Carolina—Strom Thurmond—who lobbied the Roosevelt Administration to build a base in Augusta for the coming war. Ground was broken in 1941, and soon a blighted area called Tobacco Road—the subject of Erskine Caldwell's novel, its sprawl of poor country whites now a national embarrassment to Augusta—was wiped off the map. In its place was a 56,000-acre training site, home to three divisions in World War II, the 4th Infantry, the 26th Infantry, and the 10th Armored. Camp Gordon transformed the Terry. There were construction jobs for blacks, and suddenly thousands of soldiers were arriving at the train depot on the edge of the neighborhood, with money in their pockets.

Ninth Street lit up with clubs and honky-tonks, giving soldiers a place to drink and be entertained. Aunt Honey and other local entrepreneurs were ready to capitalize. No longer was the Terry a place old white Augusta could afford to ignore, because so many white newcomers were failing to ignore it. Augusta had already been fairly comfortable with vice before the war, and the influx of young men made the city lose its residual inhibitions. To compensate, the city flirted with the French system for controlling rampant venereal disease among soldiers by registering prostitutes and requiring them to undergo checkups. Unfortunately, local leaders chose to register only black prostitutes, the result being a public health emergency and complaints of racial scapegoating.

A report in the *Chicago Defender* in 1941 noted that "White soldiers stationed here by the thousands are said to be following an old southern custom by seeking 'social equality' with colored women 'after sundown,' and the eager desire for commingling on the part of the whites is allegedly causing no end of trouble for those entrusted with the management of the city." Police began arresting African American soldiers seen with women; this led to the detainment of whole families who were innocently strolling the neighborhood. Black soldiers from the North started fighting back against the harassment, and accounts of race riots in the Terry reached the national black press.

Meanwhile, blacks observed how German prisoners housed at Camp Gordon were getting paid to work the grounds of the Augusta National Golf Club, and to pick peanuts, corn, and potatoes across the Savannah River. "They sing and whistle, seem to enjoy work," enthused the *Augusta Chronicle*. "Farmers are delighted." Such news stories left a bitter taste in the mouths of black Augustans, who felt the government was doing more for the enemy than it was willing to do for them.

Southern politicos and the army were concerned enough about unrest, declassified military records show, that a military plan was quietly put in place, should racial troubles overwhelm civil authorities. A report titled "Secret District No. 4 Fourth Service Command Racial Disturbances Plan City of Augusta, GA," written by unnamed army officials at Fort Benning, worried over the stability of elected government in Augusta. Plans included using troops from Camp Gordon and the Georgia State Guard to seal off the Terry.

In the end, all of it–the scapegoating of black Augustans as carriers of venereal disease, the racial brawls, the cordon sanitaire around the ghetto–failed. Curiosity is hard to police, and there was too much money to be made in commingling; the joints kept jumping, whites kept coming to the Terry for companionship. And young James Brown was making what he could off their visitation. He and Willie Glenn were carrying sandwiches and Red Rock cream soda to the troops; on his own he worked as a tout, taking cash from the recruits and steering them to Aunt Honey's brothel.

Some kids learn about the world through reading: This one learned from watching money move around. Here are some of the jobs Brown had before he was sixteen: He picked cotton, cut down sugarcane, collected bottle caps, ran errands, delivered liquor, shined shoes, racked balls at a pool hall, and helped out at a Chinese grocery. None of those jobs taught him anything he didn't already know from living in a whorehouse. Brown came to see there was not too much a stack of greenbacks couldn't buy, and whatever it was, by definition it wasn't worth having.

Brown projected a powerful sense of determination. He could take a punch and come back with another. He believed in himself. As childhood friend Leon Austin put it, "If nobody else loved him, *he* loved him."

When he was young, Brown's Aunt Honey bathed him, and once as she was cleaning his arms, she saw the hairs on them fall in a "crossways" pattern. It excited her, because she saw it as a mystical sign that he was marked. "I'd say, 'What are you talking about?'" Brown remembered. "She'd say, 'See the sign.' She said I was going to be real wealthy."

Good things, bad things, either way, events could feed an impression. When James was seven, Pops and a pal got the boy drunk on mint gin. After about half a bottle, James was so sick the adults stripped him naked and put him in a baptismal font of a small church, "so I could come back to life," Brown said. He looked at his life and what he saw was not suffering or scorn: In his

conscious mind, Brown turned it all into a mark of difference. He
could be tortured, but when he survived it, he would brandish that
survival as a sign that he was special. *You* would have died, but
James Brown did not. He had already been born dead.

He was with his dad one day at the filling station where Pops
worked, hovering in a dirt-floor shed with an old air compressor sitting in the corner. The levee out back kept the ground soaked. While
Joe changed tires and a couple of white guys sat on boxes, jawing,
James, twelve or thirteen, observed. He wanted to hear what the
guys were saying, and as he leaned against the air compressor, first
with one hand and then another, a short circuit in the machine sent
an electrical current coursing through him. His shoes started smoking. He could not let go. It seemed like minutes passed while the men
did nothing. His mind went to a place past agony, and he felt a slack-
ness, a feeling like a balloon was filling up inside him. The feeling he
had wasn't painful; he was flooded with a sense of invulnerability.

Eventually they shut the machine down, and Brown could smell
the burnt hair, his ears ringing. The men tried to take his sneakers
off, but they were stuck to his feet. Four minutes–that's how long
he says he was electrocuted. Four minutes that created a sensation
around the neighborhood, and created in him a sense that nobody
could stop him, that he could not be killed.

He was told he was ugly, he was small, he didn't even own a pair
of store-bought britches. He was not like other folks. He bore a sign,
and early on he learned to read it. Brown took the worst thing that
had happened to him–being electrocuted while a bunch of crackers
sucked on their co' colas –and found in it a blessing.

"I knew one thing–that I was different," is how he put it. "People would pay ten cents to see me dance because I was different."

Chapter Three

THE BLACK SATCHEL

T he Bon Air gazes, like the Sphinx, upon Augusta," Dan Jenkins has written. The hotel was named for the cool breezes that circulated among the sand hills above the city, and had three hundred-plus rooms, riding trails, and a nine-hole pitch-and-putt course. There was Dixieland playing in the entryway, swing playing upstairs, and a piano in the bar. From a balcony the view was incredible.

Inside the ballroom, on a February night in the late 1940s, clusters of men in white jackets sat around tables. This was a classic Southern smoker, and as they waited for the entertainment of the evening, the men chewed on imported cigars and gave the waiters hell with their drink orders.

Tonight's main attraction, ready beneath naked lightbulbs hanging from the ceiling, was a battle royal. An entertainment staple of the South, the battle royal sometimes started or finished a fight card, and sometimes was an event unto itself. The concept was simple: A handful of young black men would enter a boxing ring. Blindfolds would be applied and then everybody came out swinging wildly. The winner was the last one standing. When you won, here is what they gave you: a shower of coins, all you could stuff in your pockets, perhaps a rustle of bills from the man in charge.

Let's hear it for tonight's winner, a bantam Senegambian brawler who makes up with a left hand what he lacks in height: Jimmy Brown!

A dented bell borrowed for the occasion was struck with a hammer, and the fight began. The underlying purpose: to observe a survival-of-the-fittest bloodletting, and to humiliate the young black manhood of the town. Local blacks didn't have to see it that way. "I'd be out there stumbling around, swinging wild, and hearing people *laughing*," Brown said with wonder later. "I didn't know I was being exploited; all I knew I was getting paid a dollar and having fun." Fighters were ushered out of the Bon Air through the hotel's service entrance.

Battle royals were a way to make some pocket money, but an aspiring boxer could also get the attention of promoters. And Brown was a talented boxer just getting started, a man whose fights were recorded in the local paper.

According to an Augusta boxing writer, he was a "nice jabbing welter," who possessed "a fine left, which, after proper tutelage, could be developed into a very damaging weapon." This "left-jabbing specialist" weighed 140 pounds. He started boxing when he was thirteen years old, an up-and-comer who had a trainer and would jump into a car with other kids to drive around Augusta; Aiken, South Carolina; and towns along the Savannah River, staging small-time fights. Augusta promotor Sam Gantt remembered Brown as "a good boxer for his weight. If he'd stayed fighting, he would have been a masterpiece. He had it in him: courage, desire and he'd do whatever you said to do. When he got hit, he'd never get mad. He'd stay calm."

As a teenager, Brown studied those around him. "Mr. Brown liked to have idols," said Emma Austin, who grew up in the Terry. "Somebody *he* could strive to be. He was always looking up." There was, in the 1940s, a vibrant role model for anybody in Augusta who had survived a battle royal. His name was Beau Jack. Brown observed him, and eventually would claim Jack had trained him. It wasn't true, but if you wanted to model yourself after someone, there was nobody better in his field of vision than Beau Jack.

Born in 1921 on a Georgia farm three and a half miles outside Augusta, Sidney Walker was eight months old when his parents abandoned him, leaving him with a grandmother who, for her own reasons, gave him a new name. When he was eight, Beau Jack would get up at five every morning, walk into Augusta, and stake out the downtown corner of Ninth and Broad. It was where the cotton farmers gathered, the best corner a bootblack could have. To work that corner, however, you had to be able to keep it. Early on, a gang beat Jack up and took his money. When he walked home that night, his grandmother stripped him and beat him. "You better fight till the blood runs out their shoes," she told him. Then next day he went back to his corner. He bashed the assailant's head on the sidewalk, and kept coming back every day after.

Later he would pick up a nice reputation for himself as a winner, but in black Augusta, he already had a name, and a core lesson was already established: Life was work and you never stopped fighting.

The small-built Jack developed a taste for brawling, and signed up for battle royals at the Bon Air. After seeing him fight at the Bon Air in 1940, golfer Bobby Jones and other Augusta National regulars bankrolled a trainer to launch him on a boxing career. Within a few years, Jack had become a two-time lightweight champion. His 1944 fight with Bob Montgomery raised more than thirty-five million dollars for war bonds; he sold out Madison Square Garden four times in one month, and was *The Ring* magazine's fighter of the year.

Jack's accomplishments were taught at Silas X. Floyd Elementary school and discussed wherever blacks congregated. Folks knew him when he was shining shoes, and they knew what might happen if you had a ferocious work ethic, and if you fought the right way. "Beau Jack was the first black fighter to make a million dollars at Madison Square Garden," said James Edward Carter III, historian of black Augusta. "He made far more money than people like Jack Johnson. When Beau Jack hit the street, black kids followed him around, we just wanted to be around him and touch him. You'd hear him on fights on the radio, and when Beau Jack was fighting it was like there was a curfew, a silence—there was no crime, no nothing in the streets. Black folks were sitting by the radio. And when he won, folks here would be out in the streets dancing."

Among the celebrants was James Brown. They had a battery-powered radio at Twiggs, where they listened to the fights. He inherited Jack's shoeshine stand at Ninth Street and Broad. Doubtless he had to brawl to keep it, too.

Outside the ring, Jack acted the "good sport," famed for asking after each bout if fans found it a decent fight and liked what they saw. "I'm getting money for this," he told his trainer. "I have to give them my best." It was said he earned much more in the ring than he saw; that his manager would fill a pillowcase with one dollar bills and dump it out on a table—see how rich you are! To blacks everywhere, Jack must have embodied a familiar situation. He was allowed to exhibit a measure of prowess and power, because he didn't fight the powers that be. He fought the "right way," putting all of his violence in one vector. His dilemma was that he also had to keep winning—not just to continue the flow of money, but because it kept the label of Uncle Tom off him. This was the fate of black heroes who stayed alive in the 1940s.

Brown followed him, from shoeshine to battle royals and into the boxing ring. He wanted people to connect him with Jack, an icon. Truthfully, Brown didn't need to try that hard. He, too, learned in Augusta to fight till the blood ran from their shoes.

Beau Jack was one of two black figures who had a decisive influence on James Brown, and on Augusta, in the late 1930s and 1940s. The second role model was, in his own way, also a fighter who found a way to sidestep white rage. It was said he had the power to heal the sick. His fingernails were five inches long, and painted red, white, and blue.

Sweet Daddy Grace was also born with another name. At his birth in 1881 in the Cape Verde Islands, off the coast of West Africa, he was called Marcelino Manuel da Graca. By the time he built his first church, the United House of Prayer for All People, in Massachusetts in 1919, he had Americanized his name to Charles M. Grace. But to his followers, of whom there were thousands, he was known as Sweet Daddy.

He came to Augusta in 1927, intent on establishing a foothold in Georgia. He pitched a tent on Wrightsboro Road, at the edge of the Terry, and staged a revival that lasted for months. The tent held 2,500 followers, but twice as many showed up to hear Grace theatrically attack mainstream black churches and watch him miraculously restore the sick to health. Speaking to those who were new to town, uprooted from the Depression or disconnected by poverty, Grace offered a message of self-help and a sense of community built around social activities, music, and food. Prosperity was his subject and his appeal, and soon he had enough money to buy land in Augusta and build a proper House of Prayer.

Grace's frequent trips to Augusta were front-page news. He was a fascinating, mysterious presence who spoke with an exotic accent and had shoulder-length straight black hair, a wispy mustache, and a dainty goatee. "All together," a local reporter put it, "his countenance is like that of a suave Oriental."

The laborers of the Terry tucked dollar bills in Grace's pockets on his stroll to the dais; his deacons practiced hard sell, soft sell, and in-between salesmanship to separate black Augustans from their hard-earned cash. Grace would walk through the seats and demand churchgoers hand over their jewelry and open their purses to him. The Bishop required members to be baptized once a year and charged a dollar a dip, drenching 2,000 believers at one time. There were concession stands at the back of the House, and Grace sold copies of *Grace*, the magazine, at each service. He also sold face powder, cookies, writing paper, buttons, badges, swords, batons, and walking sticks. Until Augusta's health inspectors stopped him, he even bottled the used baptismal water, claiming it had miraculous powers. Beau Jack measured success by the sweat he shed in the ring; Grace literally sold his perspiration.

If money was elusive in one's daily life, at the United House of Prayer one could get close to someone who had mastered it, and at least bask in its glow. It was a hard-currency faith. "If the angel from heaven comes down and wants an extra pair of wings, don't trust him," said Grace. "Tell him you ain't got no time to keep books today. He have to pay cash." Perhaps his finest accomplishment was taking some of the sting out of the power money held over poor people, by making it, improbably, seem less real.

He said with a calm face, "I have never suffered discrimination or Jim Crow in any form. I don't bother with these things. The white man loves me and so do colored people. I won't talk about prejudice or discrimination, because I am not political. I talk to God. I am God's child. And God is colorless." Grace moved through the South, a man who defined himself and considered the judgments and descriptions, all the things white America might try to put on him, as mere trifling. It was something a poor black Augustan could yearn for.

As his image grew, so did word of the music coming out of the United House of Prayer. Grace brought drums more fully into the Pentecostal scene than anybody had before, and deeply incorporated rhythm into his services. In Augusta there was a string band, a tambourine band, a brass band; groups called the Gold Eagle and the Blue Ribbon played at parades and events.

The parades were attended by white and black Augustans, believers and skeptics alike. They were events. Drum corps and flag bearers, deacons and flower girls were all part of the show, as was music–"actually 'swinging' bands, which might have passed for those of the 'street' jazz era," enthused a writer for the black

Atlanta Daily World on a visit to Augusta. "A loud trombonist in one of the several band units carried the crowd with him as he 'hot lipped' down the avenues. A few sisters and brothers neatly 'trucked on down' to the rhythms."

James Brown loved what da Graca built in Augusta—not as religion per se, but as spectacle, as an expression of doing for yourself, as a lesson in cash-ology, as a stone groove. Decades later, when he was an adult again living in Augusta, Brown was driving with his aide-de-camp, Reverend Al Sharpton. They heard the singing and parked their car in front of the House of Prayer.

"He said, 'I learned rhythm from the band in the House of Prayer'," explained Sharpton. "He absolutely admired Daddy Grace and he fashioned some of his band stuff after Daddy Grace's bands.

"We went there more than one night, sitting in the car for four hours listening to the House of Prayer. He'd hit my knee and say over and over, 'listen to that drum.' He'd go to the church, listen to the services, just to hear the band."

Through the 1930s and into the 1940s, during Brown's youth in Augusta, the city was run by a homegrown political movement with a name that functioned as its calling card: the Cracker Party. The party's supporters were the descendents of those immigrants who had moved down the Appalachians into the Georgia and Carolina backcountry in the colonial era. A century later they were the core of an explosive social movement led by agrarian populist Tom Watson. At the end of the nineteenth century, Watson organized them in Augusta, and almost achieved power, too, with a heady mix of Puritanical moralism, prohibition, and white supremacy—until another part of his platform, anti-Catholicism, cost them too many votes.

By the twentieth century, *their* descendants wore the term "cracker" like a wool hat. The white working class was pouring into Augusta as the Depression and the boll weevil laid waste to the countryside. The pols leading the Cracker Party were smart enough to name themselves after the voters they were chasing and turn a term of scorn into an expression of pride.

For much of the first half of the twentieth century, the Crackers ruled Augusta as a virtual one-party dictatorship. They were affable, loquacious, scheming, hard-edged politicians who thrived by manipulating a ward system that reached into every neighborhood. But most of all, the Cracker legacy was the kind of graft and mismanagement that comes from single-party rule. As historian James C. Cobb has noted, every citizen of Augusta knew about the "black satchel," the fabled coffer into which all city and county employees had to tithe to the party. So assured was their hold on Augusta that, in 1937, the local election was cancelled–all the candidates were Crackers, and thus certain of election, so what was the point? Gambling, bootlegging, and prostitution all existed in Augusta with the blessing of, and kickbacks to, the Crackers. The party successfully kept prohibition in effect even after its federal repeal, not out of a moral objection to booze, but because they would lose a mountain of bribes once the state made booze legal.

They were kept in power by the white primary, which excluded blacks from voting in political primaries and thus shut them out of the political process. There was one crucial way, however, in which the Crackers *did* pay attention to black life, and that was wherever there was a black bootlegger or numbers runner or prostitute in operation. All were under the thumb of the police, collecting from them on behalf of the party. The bootlegging and prostitution that Aunt Honey engaged in would not have lasted long if she hadn't been making her own contribution to the political structure.

The Crackers were riding high, but by World War II an undercurrent of change was dissolving their base. The Supreme Court outlawed the white primary in 1944, and suddenly there was competition from black-supported candidates. Simultaneously, soldiers returning from the battlefields of Europe fed a reform movement. The Crackers were cracking up, and then came sweeping investigations of police and civil commission ties to vice lords, finally laying bare the huge network of bribes. In the spring of 1949, two members of the civil service commission, the police captain, a police sergeant, and a tavern owner were all indicted for funneling gambling profits to local officials. Such purges had happened before, but now the public saw a real possibility for change and was hungry for prosecutions.

A fiery, ambitious solicitor led the case against the officials, the biggest swipe yet against the old political order. In the end, though, the case fizzled, and the only crook remaining in his net was an unknown black teenager named James Brown.

The military had shut down Aunt Honey's brothel, closing off one source of income for Brown. Pops was in the navy serving on a ship in the Pacific from 1943 to 1945, and during that period, James dropped out of Floyd School. He occasionally hopped trains to peek beyond Augusta, he picked cotton and cut sugarcane until his hands bled. But Augusta was what he knew. From Beau Jack's old corner of Broad Street, Brown had the ebb and flow of downtown life under his gaze.

Others had him in *their* gaze; he knew the police were after him. His reputation with them was established, and more than once Brown had robbed an oil company on Twiggs. "He'd steal anything that wasn't tied down," recalled James Carter. He worked when he could and harvested from the streets when he had to. Whatever he got from it was quickly spent. He had nothing.

One friend said Brown told him the police thought he was a suspect in a brutal crime, and when they couldn't get him for it they settled for less. On May 7, 1949, he was caught breaking into four cars, chased around downtown, and cornered in an alley. What sealed his fate were the goods found in his possession. Here was his pitiful bounty, as recorded on a court docket:

1) "one (1) Suitcase of Clothing, of the value of $34.65"

2) "one (1) Trench Coat, of the value of $44.00, and one (1) Man's Brown Suit of Clothes, of the value of $59.00"

3) "two (2) Richmond Academy uniforms of the value of $50."

4) "Dark Blue Suit, Men's Clothes, of the value of $25.00; one (1) Pair Men's Green Gabardine Pants of the value of $5.00"

Perhaps nothing underscores Brown's condition like that sorry sundry of men's clothing. For a boy who grew up wearing under-wear sewn from old flour bags, this was a treasure. A black kid stealing from whites wasn't likely to see much lenience in court, but in the end, Brown's acts weren't what sealed his fate. It was the black satchel.

His arrest was posted in the local paper, the petty act and the race of the suspect relegated to the inside blotter; the front page featured the latest on the big bust-up of the Cracker officials being prosecuted by the ambitious solicitor George Haines. When Haines tried the Crackers, the *Augusta Chronicle* said the court-room would be haunted by "the ghost of Augusta's political past." Soon the paper topped itself, calling the corruption trial "the city's most sensational case in perhaps its entire history."

After numerous delays, on June 13, the corruption trial finally arrived. The court was packed with interested observers who filled the ground floor; blacks filled the balcony. With all the seats taken, members of the local press stood in the aisles. Then a twist. Haines surprised everybody by requesting another delay. Disappointing the whole city, the judge rescheduled the trial.

But with a house full of reporters and observers, perhaps Haines sensed he had to offer a public hungering for retribution *something* for their time. Letting the room empty then and there would have been like letting the air out of a blimp you'd spent weeks blowing up. Before the press exited the courtroom, the prosecutor quickly brought up the next item before the judge. It was the prosecution of four blacks, their picayune cases grouped together for the sake of brevity. When his name was called, Brown stood and pled guilty.

If he expected a deal, he did not get it. Brown said he had no legal representation; court records list the name of a young lawyer, one who specialized in divorces. Before the impatient eyes of the city, Brown was given a sentence of two to four years for each of his four counts, to run consecutively. He was remanded to a state penitentiary, and the punishment Haines demanded called for hard labor.

"Tell daddy, try to get me out," Brown urged his cousin, Willie Glenn, the next day. A certain sum of money to the solicitor, he believed, would secure his freedom. For the next four months, Brown was kept in a grim downtown facility, a teen locked up with adults.

Haines threw hard labor at him, but then let him sit for months in the downtown jail. James felt strongly he was in jail only because Haines was waiting for a pro forma bribe. But Joe didn't even put up bail for James, and he did not offer the solicitor a payment. After months in the Richmond County jail, Brown was finally shipped out–not to some highway crew that the sentence of hard labor would have allowed, but to a juvenile facility, with young men his age and younger.

His dad's failure to act was something Brown never forgot. "He loved his father. His father loved him. His father just made a mistake," said Glenn. "Lot of things he could have did for him and he didn't. Lot of things he could have gave him and didn't give him." He entered as a sixteen-year-old, but when Brown left incarceration, he was on his own, a parent to himself.

Chapter Four

TOCCOA

Eugene Talmadge stopped eating poached eggs. It was just like him to tell his doctors to go to hell. He knew best. The man who once called himself "just as mean as cat shit" had, in 1946, again won the chance to be governor of Georgia, and right then his stomach started hemorrhaging something fierce. Doctors put Talmadge on a strict boiled egg diet and it seemed to be working, too. But then he put his red suspenders on; checked himself out of the Florida hospital; and drove to Georgia for Thanksgiving, where he indulged in turkey, ham, biscuits, red gravy, and grits. A week later the governor dropped dead.

Talmadge had been rough on blacks in Georgia, and tough on convicts, too. Critics in Washington called him "His Chain Gang Excellency," and he had a staunch reputation for ordering shackles and hard labor for blacks, union leaders, and anyone else he did not like. Georgia's practice of chaining convicts together and sending them to rural work camps, Talmadge explained, "kept men out of doors in God's open country where they could enjoy the singing of the birds and the beautiful sunrises and sunsets."

Now the leader was gone, and his son, Herman, wanted the job. He got it, too, taking over for his dad as governor in 1948. But Herman was not a carbon copy of the old man. He was eager to change

44

his state's image. The book *I Am a Fugitive From a Georgia Chain Gang* (and the movie, which dropped "Georgia" from its title) had sullied the state's name in the North, and while Eugene might have been delighted with the portrayal, the son was interested in reforming the system, and thereby gathering federal dollars.

Which was why young Talmadge was standing before a crowd of reporters in Rome, Georgia, stirring up attention for one of his pet projects. Battey State Hospital was a huge medical complex in Rome, with 2,000 beds for tuberculosis patients. Georgia used part of the former army hospital as a facility for nonviolent criminals under the age of eighteen. The Georgia Juvenile Training Institute, it was called, and it mattered a great deal to the governor.

In Rome that day in 1949, the governor, perhaps wearing one of his seersucker suits and letting his Panama hat shield him from the sun, gave a sweeping speech on the grounds of the Institute. He selected this setting to outline his philosophy of crime and punishment, and express his interest in reforming Georgia's juvenile justice system. Right there was something new, for a statewide juvenile justice system until recently had barely existed in Georgia. The larger counties ran their own youth courts and rehabilitation centers, financed by county funds and private charities. Smaller counties made no provisions at all, and sent offenders to state prison with the adult population. An estimated 20 percent of Georgia's prison population was under the age of eighteen, and housed with adult, often violent, criminals.

"It is of course known that crime increases or decreases as our economic conditions vary and that the unemployed and the idle furnish us with a majority of the adult prison population," Talmadge said in Rome. His belief that a lack of work bred criminals had led Talmadge to set up this vocational school where inmates were offered classes and could work on a small farm, producing milk and vegetables for hospital patients. The Juvenile Training Institute was Georgia's first attempt to segregate youth offenders from adults and give them special attention. "I am proud of the part that I have had to play in this program," said the thirty-six-year-old governor.

The backdrop for Talmadge's speech included Battey's long, two-story barracks buildings and those imprisoned within. Among these props was a young black inmate, playing ball maybe, or shadowboxing in the distance. James Brown had been sent to Rome in 1949, as one of Georgia's "honor roll" prisoners housed on the state hospital grounds.

The chain gangs had been outlawed, as had the convicts' striped uniforms and leg manacles. The governor wanted reform, but money had yet to be allocated, and the public was not necessarily on board. There was chaos in the structure, certainly for the juveniles who composed a category the state had barely acknowledged just a few years before. But there was reform in it, too, and Brown reaped the benefits of the change and the chaos.

If he had been found guilty a few years before, Brown might have been sent to the Richmond County facility for Negro youth, a privately run institution, where an average of thirty boys were confined at night to a room with eleven straw beds, barred windows, and a padlocked door. The wood structure, heated by a flimsy stove, was an obvious firetrap.

Though he avoided that and the chain gangs, Brown's years as a prisoner of Georgia could not have been easy. The experience was, however, vastly different from the mental image of Southern prisons that many modern readers hold. At Rome the guards were not armed, and inmates were on their honor and had some freedom of movement. Effort was made to segregate youths from adult criminals kept on the grounds. Punishment could be cruel: When knives were found in a room housing eight blacks in Rome, all eight youths were sent to "the hole," stripped to their underwear, forced to sleep without blankets on a concrete floor, and given nothing but bread and water for ten days. Two were hospitalized for gangrene and had parts of their feet amputated.

Still, Georgia was moving away from its medieval past. The

juvenile institute in Rome was a showcase, but it didn't stay one for long. Having established an ability to separate juvenile offenders from adults and give them special attention, the state began arresting juveniles in ever-larger numbers. A bigger facility was needed. In November 1951, James Brown and the approximately 140 teenagers from the Rome institute were moved to a camp near the town of Toccoa, on the northern border with South Carolina. Called the Boys Industrial Training Institute, the site offered more space and no contact with hardened criminals.

A boy from Augusta who suddenly found himself in Toccoa would think, just from standing outdoors in the middle of the camp, that this place was *very far away.* You could see Currahee Mountain and the foothills that formed the tailbone of the Appalachians; you could smell a chill, fresh air unlike the baked humidity down south. There was green here, and space, and silence. The facility inhabited the remains of a 270-acre former army paratrooper base. Only a fraction of that, an area in the center of the camp, lodged prisoners, and surrounding them were abandoned military barracks, shooting ranges, and storehouses. In Rome, you were squeezed in on all sides; here there was a breeze.

The Industrial Training Institute occupied a group of whitewashed concrete buildings bordered by a ghost town. The camp cafe was rotting away, the post office a shambles. The roads on the perimeter of the base, at neat right angles, were rutted and eerily empty. In buildings farthest from the center, a number of local families tried to homestead. There was less infrastructure than in Rome, no teachers or schoolbooks when the prisoners arrived, and not a lot for them to do. Inmates invented games and wandered around excavating the army ordnance that scattered the grounds. Brown and other boys dug old bullets out of the dirt, stuffed them in lead pipes, and crafted zip guns with them. The Georgia prison system was moving from a malicious negligence, the kind that dressed adolescents in stripes and shackles and sent them to break rocks, toward mere negligence, the kind that let them wear denim and explore a falling down military camp that cost the state nothing to obtain and next to nothing to operate.

The superintendent of both the Rome and Toccoa institutes, Walter Matthews, made an effort to fulfill the training mission of the institution, fighting without much success to get teachers and books. Certainly, Matthews provided the most order Brown had experienced in his life. Brown loved the superintendent; "Really, he's the person that raised me," he said. Matthews only struck Brown once, Brown said by way of explanation, and then with an open hand.

There were no armed guards here, either. Kids from the town of Toccoa, which was six miles away, sometimes visited with church or school groups, or just to explore the empty buildings. "When I first met James . . . we used to go up there and play," said Bobby Byrd, a native of Toccoa. "But there wasn't no fence, it was an imaginary line. Everybody knew just how far they supposed to go." It was an honor system, and what kept prisoners from escaping was the extra time they'd get when they got caught. Of course some *did* escape, and when that happened a group of trustees, Brown among them, would accompany guards on tramps through the woods in search of the runaways. Brown spent more than one night out in the woods, poking around and enjoying his freedom.

A kid from Atlanta named Johnny Terry became Brown's best friend. When Terry was sent a cake or a pie, he shared it with Brown, and Brown never forgot it. He dropped Terry's radio, shattering it into pieces, and his buddy instantly forgave him. According to Bobby Roach, later a member of Brown's band, "Johnny killed a guy, that's what he was in for, killed a guy in the Peacock Ballroom in Atlanta. The guy kept teasing and teasing Johnny. Johnny couldn't fight, but with a knife? Oh man was he fast with it—he even kept a switchblade with a match in it, he could flick it and light the match. They say he hit that boy at the top of the stairs and by the time he hit the bottom, he was gone."

Terry was down-to-earth, relaxed, but he chose his words

carefully; Brown bullied you with words, he used them to overwhelm and disarm you. They made a good team. Meeting in Rome and forming a gospel quartet, they continued singing in Toccoa, building a little reputation for their group that spread beyond the perimeter.

The boys had a nickname for Brown, pegged to the way he glued himself to his radio and made singing the center of his life: Music Box. Toccoa station WLET aired a black gospel program featuring The MelloTones, the top-ranking quartet in the area. Nashville's WLAC was a powerful station with a clear channel signal that carried way beyond the South; it was one of the first to play rhythm and blues. Brown loved the way radio took him out of himself. Being an analytical person, he would have pondered the experience, and understood how radio brought new songs, new voices, new feelings to listeners hundreds of miles away. Radio could inspire you.

When Brown talked about the gospel he sang in prison, he focused on the way performing made him feel. There was something important he learned when his quartet sang "Our Father" to a group of tuberculosis patients in Rome, something electrifying that he couldn't get out of his head. As he performed, he noticed that those around him were moved, crying, and then he surprised himself by breaking into tears, too. You beat an opponent in the ring and people cheered, but *this* was a greater power. Gospel taught him important lessons about songcraft, like how to tell a whole story with his vocal delivery, and how the parts of a song worked. He was a prisoner, and music both secular and sacred came to him the same way—through tunes inmates brought with them, through what came out of his music box. So it was natural to start thinking about what Louis Jordan's "Caledonia" and "Our Father" had in common, to think about them both as influences to be explored, broken down, and absorbed. "Singing gospel's a good way to learn about music in general," he explained. "There's a format for gospel; you learn the different parts, and then you start putting them together . . ."

. . .

Bobby Byrd lived in Toccoa with his mom, grandmother, and five siblings. The Byrds were a prominent black family in town, whose stature didn't have to do with how much they had—they were getting along okay, even after Bobby's dad, who worked for Southern Railroad, was killed on the tracks in Duluth. The accident left his wife, Zarah, in charge, and she took the reins with a drive and optimism that folks all over town admired. She was a motivator who touched those around her. Zarah cleaned for a prominent doctor, was active in the church, and pushed her kids to get a college education. She sang gospel in the shape-note style and took her daughters to singing sessions with her. She passed on a love of music to all her children.

Her son Bobby had graduated valedictorian from the black Whitman Street High School. He was a good athlete and active at Mt. Zion Baptist Church. In fact he was such a joiner that Bobby was the only male member of the New Homemakers Association in all of Georgia. His mother had taught him how to play the piano, and Byrd reckoned he was pretty good at that. He played and sang in a variety of gospel and pop groups he assembled with little plan or organization, with overlapping membership.

Byrd had a group of buddies he played with regularly, singing a never-overlapping repertoire of pop and sacred music, in groups with names including the Avons, the Impalas, the Trimiers, and others—so many groups that locals sometimes just called the lot of them "The Toccoa Band," or "The Bobby Byrd Band." Of all the groups he sang with, the most important, however, and the biggest in Toccoa, was the Gospel Starlighters. They sang at schools and churches and opened for major gospel acts coming through town. The Starlighters were influenced by the Swanee Quintet, who by now were showcasing the raw sugar voice of Ruben Willingham, and by the Five Blind Boys of Alabama.

Groups from Toccoa regularly visited the youth camp, and one day in 1952, the Gospel Starlighters sang for the inmates. After they had finished, somebody there told the Starlighters' leader that he sang nice, but *they* had somebody who sang nice, too. A fella named Music Box. Unfortunately, Music Box must have been in detention and could not come out to meet Byrd. The name, though, stuck in Byrd's head.

That name came up again not long after. Byrd was returning home from a trip to Atlanta with his school glee club, an excursion that had caused him to miss a basketball game in town against inmates of the Institute. But he heard all about the game, oh yes: Not only had one kid stood out on the court with his play, but afterward the guy got up on the piano at the Toccoa rec center and proceeded to entertain the two teams. *Music Box.*

"Now, I was the best piano player in Toccoa, Georgia," Byrd recalled, "and when they said there was another man who I think can outplay you, he's something else . . ." It became imperative to meet this guy, once and for all. Show him how a piano was played.

Finally they collided. The Institute baseball team was playing the county team, and Brown was on the mound. Byrd got a hit and was running to third when the pitcher tried to tag him out as he ran—the collision knocked both of them down. Brown extended his hand, the two laughed, and Byrd finally found out who Music Box was. They struck up a conversation. Brown told Byrd that he would be able leave this place—that the institute would release him to a local family if they would agree to sponsor him.

Around the same time, the owner of a local Oldsmobile dealership, S. C. Lawson, was hauling concrete slabs from the campgrounds for a small lake he was building. Lawson and his son, Howell, were talking to a guard who was overseeing the inmates as they loaded Lawson's truck. The guard gestured in the direction of Brown. "That sure is a good, hard worker," he said. "Matter of fact, he shouldn't even be in prison. If your son had done [Brown's crime], he'd probably have just been given a spanking." Music Box could be paroled if he had employment promised for two years, the guard said. That got Lawson thinking, and very soon he had offered a job to Brown, washing cars and cleaning up at the dealership.

Down in Toccoa, Bobby Byrd had told his mother about this sweet-voiced kid who would be released, if only he had a family to vouch for him. Zarah got her church involved, as well as other black churches in town, and presented a petition with some four hundred signatures to the camp superintendent. The parole agreement declared that Brown not set foot in Augusta for longer than a night for the next ten years and that he maintain a job and go to church on Sunday. On June 14, 1952, he walked out of the camp, down the mountain, and six miles to town. He carried a bag with him, and got directions to the Byrds' house. (Brown later maintained he wrote a dazzling letter that earned the attention of the parole board and thus had secured his own freedom.)

In a limited sense, Brown was walking into Toccoa; really, he was entering a place the poet Frank X. Walker has labeled "Affrilachia." This mountain region was untouched by the plantation system that defined race relations further south, and in Toccoa, while fraught, race relations were viewed by some as less violent than in other parts of the South. Mountain places like Toccoa were where whites learned to play the banjo, an African instrument, by listening to blacks. In Affrilachia banjo and fiddle tunes were the music of most parties, white or black, and when the guitar arrived in the 1920s via railroad work crews, and with it the blues, the sound of the frolics and hog-killings and house parties didn't radically change, it just expanded. Affrilachia was a little different, a place where into the 1920s and '30s banjos and fiddles coexisted with guitars and harmonicas. It did not sound like Augusta.

Upon his release, Brown lived with the Byrds, sleeping in the kitchen behind a curtain. Also in the house were three girls; two boys; Zarah; and a grandmother, Adeline Hickman, who was known as Big Mama. Big Mama was not enamored of the new roomer. "My grandmother, she didn't want that jailbird in the house! She could not stand him," recalled Sarah Byrd Giglio,

Bobby's sister. "But my mother being my mother, she said 'Mama, we're gonna let him stay here for a while.'"

"My mother loved James Brown," said Giglio. "She always called him her son."

He was easy to like, this wide-open youth who talked like he would be running things soon. Brown quickly made a name for himself, and it wasn't always a good one. Friends warned Byrd to watch out for this kid, that he was a dirty con from Augusta and would take advantage of him. Some of them stopped talking to Byrd when he didn't cut Brown loose. But he believed in the guy, and had seen his raw talent, which would sure help any number of groups Byrd was running.

Toccoa was postcard-pretty, and postcard-small: When Clyde McPhatter and the Drifters came through Toccoa—not to play, just stopping to gas up—word got out and a crowd of black fans filled the gas station before the vocal group loaded their car and drove to the next show.

On Sunday afternoons at Boyd Field, groups of boys would gather to play football, and the newcomer was quickly a standout. "James was always there. He was especially good at football," recalls a local. "He could reverse his field about ten or fifteen times, and nobody could ever catch him, he was so fast."

In his daily life, Brown was plowing right into obstacles and people, clueless about how to make his fierce drive work for him. He got into fights and stepped on toes. He didn't understand the dynamics of Toccoa: a hamlet where everybody knew everybody, where what you said in confidence was public knowledge by Thursday, where the heart you broke had a brother working beside you, and the guy you socked had a cousin in your band. Maybe this was what many in Toccoa, including Bobby Byrd's mom, loved about James Brown: He was both clueless and guileless, full of promise and in need of help.

Some accounts have Brown scheming to get into the Gospel Starlighters; others have Byrd desperate to bring the new guy in.

Either way, Byrd introduced him to his boys: Doyle Oglesby, Fred Pulliam, Sylvester Keels, Nashplende Knox, and guitarist Nafloyd Scott. Byrd's guys were all steeped in the music-making ways of the mountain region. They started harmonizing together, with Brown, Keels, and Byrd all sharing keyboards, and everybody but Scott taking turns singing lead.

Brown already knew Bobby's sister Sarah, whom he was dating and singing with by the piano in the Byrds' living room. She sang with the Zioneers, a group out of Mt. Zion Baptist Church. Brown joined her in the group. Sarah also sang with the Community Choir. Brown joined *that* one, too. Sarah and James had all kinds of chemistry.

"James *never* liked nobody to outdo him, even then," she recalled. "He always said, 'Don't try to outsing me.' And after we'd do our little part together, it was 'Sarah, you're trying to outsing me and I don't like that.' In gospel he was like, 'No one can do it better than James Brown.'" Eventually, Big Mama laid down the law, and Sarah and James went their separate ways.

Brown followed Sarah into the Gospel Starlighters, and Bobby Byrd and Brown began a lifetime of making music together. The truth is, if it hadn't been for Bobby Byrd, there might not have been a James Brown.

The Gospel Starlighters became the Avons, started singing pop, and were hired to sing downtown at Collier's Tea Room, a spot for white ladies who lunch. They were black kids flirting from behind a trellis of decorum, now gently folding pop–crooner stuff like "The White Cliffs of Dover" and "Prisoner of Love"–into their spirituals. The ladies loved it, but they didn't have the last word. Bobby and Sarah's mom Zarah *did*, and Zarah did not care for the mixing of gospel with pop. She let them have it.

"My mom was not into it! My mom and my grandma they'd be all 'We don't want to hear that devil's music in here.' They used to embarrass us to death," laughed Sarah.

Further embarrassment came when Byrd and Brown, both members of Mount Zion Baptist Church, were summoned by church leaders for some emergency guidance counseling. Directed into the basement, they were told they could either play the blues or gospel music, but never both. *Choose.* Byrd didn't tip his hand on the spot, but facts were facts–they were getting paid for the pop music and were rising local celebrities. They bowed their heads and, when they escaped the basement, they chose pop.

Now they had to figure out how to fill up a suddenly barren set. A trip to Greenville, South Carolina, stiffened their spines. In the Greenville Textile Center, Byrd, Brown, and cohorts caught a rhythm and blues show featuring the "5" Royales and Hank Ballard and the Midnighters. The "5" Royales were the first great vocal group to take gospel harmonizing into the pop marketplace, and further, they featured the wickedly deft guitar player Lowman "El" Pauling. He sounded great and looked even better, loosening his guitar strap so that his instrument hung at his knees, macking like an outlaw galoot. The rest of the group sang raucous harmonies over hard-edged tunes that were the antithesis of what the gals liked at Collier's Tea Room. Some of these songs sounded suspiciously like church tunes Byrd might have sung, only they were given a new lurid coat of words. The Midnighters, now they were just plain *filthy*, with songs about baby making and booty shaking, acting out gymnastic routines to each number and ending the night with their slacks at their ankles and their voices to the rafters. They, too, sort of sounded like the church, though they pushed thoughts of church far out of mind.

After Greenville, Toccoa remained the town it always was, but Byrd, Sarah, Brown, and gang experienced a cataclysmic pole shift. "We were so, so excited after that show was over, I don't think we sung gospel no more after that," said Bobby. "We wanted to become rhythm and blues singers, and we stayed up and talked about it all night long."

They threw themselves into songs learned from the radio: the Spaniels' "Goodnight Sweetheart, Goodnight," the "5" Royales' "Baby Don't Do It," and the Clovers' "One Mint Julep" was their finale. Each had a star they imitated in their act: For Brown it was

Roy Brown and Wynonie Harris. They passed the lead vocals over from one to the next, and while formally it was Byrd's band, practically speaking, this was a collective in which everybody sang and did some entertaining of their own.

Besides his job at Lawson Motors, Brown was a janitor at the white Toccoa High School. He cleaned the auditorium, and when no one was around, Brown would lay his mop down, get on the stage, and play the piano. Toccoa High had a weekly institution called Friday chapel, where students offered a little entertainment. One Friday the principal told those gathered in the auditorium that he had a special surprise for them this week, and when he pulled the curtain open, there on the stage was Byrd's group, with Toccoa High School's janitor singing lead. "They did seven or eight songs and just had everybody in awe," said M. Tabor, a student at Toccoa High. The group returned to the school, playing Friday chapel for many weeks thereafter.

They were picking up and throwing down shtick as fast as audiences responded. Instrumentation was expanding: Brown built a washtub bass that he thumped in practice, played a little harmonica, and even messed around with a washboard, rubbed with metal to make a rackety percussive sound. It was the wide-open, Affrilachian party way. They moved stuff in and out of their performances, but some staples from the gospel world remained constants—handclapping and foot stomping to assert the beat; Byrd singing the bass parts in the style of gospel quartets; Byrd and Brown vocalizing horn parts, and scatting in the manner of hip gospel groups such as the Golden Gate Quartet.

They had a new name, one that trumped all the earlier ones and that they finally stuck with: the Flames. Some say the inspiration was the West Coast group the Four Blazes, or maybe the crew called the Hollywood Flames. Others suggest it was inspired by gospel's Torches. Guitarist Nafloyd Scott called it like he saw it. When asked why they named themselves the Flames, he said, "Because I thought we were hot!" They were.

A local men's shop let them buy fly outfits on installment. The guys ordered brightly colored zoot suits with pegged pants and baggy-shouldered coats. They were making an unmistakable impression on the locals.

Brown left Lawson Motors, taking a job at another car dealership. He needed the work because Brown was working on a family. He had met Velma Warren, a classmate of Bobby Byrd, at Zion Baptist, and after a six-month courtship they married, on June 27, 1953. She was the daughter of a carpenter from Birmingham, Alabama, and was employed as a maid for a white family. "I could see where he wanted something. He was very ambitious. He wasn't going back to poverty, and he knew with me he wasn't going back to poverty," said Velma. Soon Brown got a job at a thread mill and rented a house on Summer Hill for him and his wife. But there were distractions, and between jobs and shows he was gone a lot of the time. Velma realized it behooved her to come to the Flames' shows not just to see her husband, but to *keep* him. "I was there to keep down a lot of stuff," she said. "He was just like that." Their three sons (Teddy, Terry, and Larry) were born over the next five years.

From a brief stint at a plastics factory, Brown fabricated a cymbal for the Flames; somebody snagged an old marching band bass drum out of Whitman High, and, voila, the Flames had a drum set. Brown was their main drummer, so much so that early on, many thought he was a drummer, not a singer. Their act, meanwhile, was getting more interesting. They'd kill the jukebox and then this stomping herd took the stage. All the singers revolving for their turn at the front, which they *had* to take turns for, seeing as they only had one microphone and one three-tube amp that the mic and guitar were plugged into. Everyone was in constant motion— moving from drums to keyboards, dancing and egging the crowd on. November 13, 1952, the group's name appeared in print for the first time. They were playing intermission at the Ritz movie theater. *The Toccoa Record* announced *House of Dracula* was the featured picture, accompanied by:

"Extra added attraction–Late Show Only.

"The Flames–Local Colored Band–On Our Stage."

They were regulars at the Ritz, where whites sat downstairs and blacks in the balcony. The white kids, remembered Nafloyd Scott, would throw coins at the group. "Had to dodge them dollar and fifty cent [pieces]," he recalled. Brown quickly deduced the advantage of busting out a flamboyant stage-front split at such moments: He'd be there on the ground, picking up loose change without interrupting the act.

Another place they could count on regular gigs was Berry's Recreation Center, a two-story pool hall and cafe run by Berry Trimier. He was an undertaker, ran a taxi company, and at night presided over the venue. Trimier could count on Byrd's group filling his place, and now with Brown stepping up, they were really packing the Rec Center. Trimier began managing the Flames in 1954, booking them into surrounding black "chitlin circuit" clubs in Lavonia and Cornelia, along with white college shows in Athens and Clemson.

The group by now could play country songs and light pop to white audiences as well as R&B. Black Toccoans like Scott had grown up with country and western, which they considered their own music. "That was what we was raised upon–Ernest Tubb, Roy Acuff, stuff like that was all we knew," Scott told historian Fred Hay. The Flames had worked up a kickin' version of Hank Williams's "Hey Good Lookin'." "Oh boy, we could pop that one!" Scott recalled. Their showmanship and versatility had them in demand, and they were playing gigs at white high schools in Toccoa and on the road in Northern Georgia up into the Carolinas. Trimier had booked so many gigs, in fact, that he split them into two or three different groups all billed as the Flames, with other guys Byrd and Brown knew added to the mix. Johnny Terry, Brown's buddy from prison, was now out and added to the group–he couldn't sing but was a terrific dancer, and he had an edge to him that Brown liked.

One more thing had them in demand. According to Byrd, Brown was so eager to decimate the competition, defined as anybody getting gigs he wasn't, that he told club owners the Flames would do a show for less money. It undercut his own group, but Brown figured in the long run it would make them more fans and lead to more employment.

Their zoot suits, their swagger, the way they turned the sound of church into the sound of play–in the small towns the Flames performed in, it all communicated a bigness, an extravagance that audiences appreciated. To a band increasingly featuring a guy who pushed a broom in the white high school, which his fans knew damn well was a good job to have, counting the nickels and quarters thrown at you was a way to count how much freedom you had.

Mostly, image is what the Flames had. With little money and one dicey station wagon or another, they were committed to upholding it. Rolling into town in vehicles without air-conditioning, even on hot summer days, Brown insisted they keep the windows up so that fans *thought* they were cool. They left the same town in cars that often started up with great difficulty; the driver slowly circling the back of the venue shouting to straggling members that they'd better run if they wanted a ride home, because the ignition might not work twice.

One night, on a drive home after a show, the brakes failed and they had a few life-changing moments descending through the mountains. They managed to safely pull off the road, passed a jug around and everybody urinated into it, and the band used that as brake fluid. It got them home. "At the time we didn't really care–it was like, 'Wow, we're going here! We're going there!' To pile into that station wagon was so fun. We all just got on . . ." said Sarah Byrd Giglio.

They were doing great in the smaller towns, but faced a tougher tribunal when they hit Atlanta. James Shaw, a kid from the big city who would grow up to be a singer and songwriter himself, remembers a show performed in the basement of the John Eagan Homes, a large public housing facility. "They didn't have no band, they was just patting their legs. It was fifty cents. But they just was not performers, they just had a guitar player, not even a drummer. Had on green and white suits—green on one side and white down the other side. No band, singing a capella." He chuckled. "Man they thought they were sharp."

Byrd was having the time of his life, but Brown, the family man, was in need of every buck he could apprehend. One night, Byrd got a call at four in the morning. Brown was in trouble again, stripping a car in South Carolina when the owner caught him in the act. The way Byrd saw it, Brown was good at singing, but positively great at stripping a car: He could put it on blocks in twenty minutes, with wheels, fenders, trim—and the perp—all long gone.

But in Carolina that night, a guy had found his fenders, hubcaps, and part of his engine in the rumble seat of Brown's car. Byrd and a group of his friends all drove out to South Carolina to rescue him in the middle of the night. Some combination of verbiage and cash, presumably, freed their friend and got them back to Toccoa.

The guys were familiar with the sheriffs along the Georgia-Carolina border. This knowledge was enhanced by the experience Byrd, Brown, and fellow Flame Doyle Oglesby all had running moonshine from backwoods North Carolina down to Toccoa. Skully, they called it in Toccoa, and there was an endless thirst for it in dry Stephens County. Toccoa was about seventy-five miles from Brevard, North Carolina, driving through the Appalachians. There were closer places to transport from, but the folks in Brevard didn't demand cash up front. Byrd would bring another change of clothes on these overnight runs, and make it straight to school the next morning. They did it twice a week for fifteen months.

The bootleggers had an amazing setup, a veritable "Moonshine City," in Byrd's words. A hamlet was hidden behind a secret entrance, and once you got through the gate there were bars and stores and women—anything you could want. The Flames sometimes even used their shows as cover for their activities. They'd bring the skully to the venue buying it, and then play a gig that wouldn't pay nearly as much as the bootlegging.

. . .

Bill's Rendezvous was a nightclub in a rough part of town that Toccoans called Little Korea. By day it was friendly enough; Whitman High School faced the back of the cafe, and at lunchtime students would climb over a tree branch, enter the back door, and dance to the jukebox. It was a simple, big room with a stage and a cafeteria. At night there was music, and the sidewalk out front got rough. There were stabbings, and Nafloyd Scott's dad killed his second wife there in 1956.

A piano player from Macon was passing through Bill's one night, a young wild man named Little Richard. In a short time he would be famous, but at this moment Bill's reinforced just how far down the road fame was. So when the Flames checked him out and asked Richard from the floor if he would share his stage with them, Richard knew that letting them have his stage was unlikely to help him get to his destination. He said no, but let them play a short set while he went on break. Richard watched them and was big enough to admit he loved what he saw. He asked if they had a manager, and they mentioned Berry Trimier. "Well," said Richard, "*my* agent in Macon is named Clint Brantley, and I think you should give him a call."

Many of the folks they knew spent their whole life in Toccoa. But they'd been to Cornelia, Clemson, and they'd seen *Atlanta*. Screw that, they had seen Moonshine City, and virtually had a key to the place. But close your eyes and listen to Little Richard, just sniff the air around the man, and you got a sense of stimulating, raucous places even farther away from Toccoa.

Richard requested Lucas "Fats" Gonder, his road manager, to make a call. And when Gonder got the Flames on the phone with Brantley, the Macon businessman suggested they come down and audition.

They inhaled the possibility and packed for Macon.

Chapter Five

A NEW ORLEANS
CHOO-CHOO

C lint Brantley was a light-skinned man with a foul mouth and glasses that looked old school even in 1955. Born in Sandersville, Georgia, Brantley was said to have arrived in Macon after World War I with his friend Elijah Poole, who would later change his name to Elijah Muhammad. Brantley opened a barbershop, and by the 1940s was the top black show promoter in town. Tough and practical, Brantley had two huge guys on the payroll to lean against the wall and establish the proper note of seriousness as he conducted business.

It was early in the day when the Flames came to Brantley's club, the Two Spot, for their audition. Way too early. The night before, he had been drinking, and by morning he had no interest in hearing anybody sing a damn song. "You could tell they were country," he snorted. It was probably late 1955. Johnny Terry did the introductions, explaining they were a vocal group looking for a manager, and Brantley sourly waved him off. Not interested. "Well, alright sir," Terry said, all of them heading for the door. Then–aww, *shit*. A tinge of guilt, or maybe he just wanted an amusement before sending them back to Toccoa. Brantley hesitated.

"What do you all sing?" he asked. "We sing rock and roll, we sing blues, we can also sing spirituals."

"Sing me a spiritual–I don't feel good this morning and it might pick me up." Damned if they didn't sing a *bunch* of spirituals, as pretty as they could make them. They finished with a song that had become a set piece in their shows, "Looking for My Mother," a heart tugger with Brown acting out the story of a poor orphan boy finding his long-gone mama in heaven–Brown bawled and crawled around Brantley's joint, under tables and chairs on his hands and knees, he wasn't going to leave until he'd found her. When he was done, he'd found a manager. A couple weeks after that, the Flames relocated to Macon.

Macon was lower to the ground than Toccoa, more humid, and black Macon was more metropolitan and held more money. It was a railroad town, with the Southern, the Georgia Central, the Atlantic Coast, and the Macon, Dublin, and Savannah lines intersecting downtown. Macon was progressive enough to be proud of its Douglass Theatre, a landmark black-owned venue a few blocks from the railroad station. It was reactionary enough that when a black man suspected of murder was pulled off a train and lynched in 1922, whites dragged his body through the street and dumped it in the lobby of the Douglass as a message to the community.

The family owning the Douglass was married into the family that ran the largest traveling black show in the country, Silas Green from New Orleans, which had nobody named Silas Green and was not from Louisiana. Macon became the show's home. The singers, dancers, and comics who played the minstrel circuit lingered in Macon between engagements, and those hoping to work in showbiz flocked to the city. Even the Greyhound station jumped; it was said to have the only restaurant in town where a Negro could get a smothered T-bone steak and sit in air-conditioning. Working in the kitchen, about the time the Flames arrived, was one of the most recognizable people in town. His mama wanted to name him Ricardo, but settled on Richard Penniman; to the extent folks knew his name, they called him Little Richard.

The Flames aspired to be as bold as Richard. He wore astonishing neckties, which his loving mama tied for him, and he drenched himself in Tweed perfume. Richard and his band were wrecking house parties, roadhouses, the American Legion Hall, and even opening at the Douglass, which Brantley booked. Meanwhile Brown had a job at the Greyhound station, and hung out with the showmen in Brantley's barbershop.

Brantley saw promise in the young ex-con. He saw a guy who would work himself to the bone to make it in this world. He was managing Little Richard, and now the Flames, and the acts would sometimes chill at the Two Spot together. On weeknights, Lucas "Fats" Gonder, a piano player whom everybody called "Big Black Luke," threw chili parties. The Flames, Richard's band, and anybody else would come by, eat, and play records all night long.

Commonly, musicians who weren't working would meet up and form a "scrap band," a pickup group playing for whatever. One musician Brown jammed with was Charles Connor, the drummer from Richard's show. Connor was the first real drummer Brown played with. A skinny-tie-wearing, no-necked stud, Connor was born in New Orleans's French Quarter. His father came from the Dominican Republic and had lived in Kingston, Jamaica, before arriving in Louisiana, and his mother was a Louisiana-born Creole. Their house faced Dauphine Street, and often funeral parades passed by. Going toward the funeral, the music was sad and hymnal, but on their way back, revelers fell in with the band, and a rousing festivity prevailed, powered by a battery of drummers that formed what was called a "second line."

Second-line rhythms were loping, loose-hipped, they flowed naturally from the steps the musicians took as they paraded through the streets. And maybe because their bodies were already keeping essential time, their second-line rhythms were about playing off the beat, engaging with it rather than underlining it. Most of all, second-line rhythms turned those walkers into dancers.

"My mother, when she was six months pregnant, said 'Every

time a parade goes by, this baby kicks my stomach! I guess he hears the music,'" said Connor.

His dad told him if he learned to play those drums, they would take him all over the world. Papa also said that if Charles kept practicing the drums, he'd have more women than he could shake a stick at. "And he was right, because I've slept with over 1,500 women in my life, all nationalities."

Connor and saxophonist Wilbert Smith (also known as Lee Diamond) were in Nashville playing with Shirley & Lee when Little Richard invited them to join his new band in Macon. Maybe it was Richard's surreal salesmanship, maybe it was the scent of Tweed, but soon they, too, were in Macon, staying in a hotel full of prostitutes while being molded and shaped by their bandleader. Richard took Connor down to the train station with his drums, and told him to listen—"I want your drumming to sound like a choo-choo train," he said. Connor played along with the locomotives rolling into the station from a half-mile away.

The group settled on a name: The Upsetters. "Our band was like a threat," Connor explained. "We went to your town and upset *everybody*."

Richard wanted them to dress and fix their hair the way he did—sly, parodic outfits, donut curls piled high, a makeup called Pancake #31 on their faces. The guys came around. Partly it was meant to baffle white Southerners who feared black men mixing with their women. Partly it was tradition. Richard was the ultimate product of a little known, extravagant, underground scene. Like a number of other acts, he got his start playing the role of the "tent show queen": cross-dressing song-and-dance acts that played to black audiences. As a teenager Richard performed in drag, billed as "Princess LaVonne," a chair balanced on his chin, in Sugarfoot Sam from Alabam's minstrel show.

Before Richard, there was an even more unhinged figure named SQ Reeder, or Eskew Reeder, or Esquerita, who also performed on the drag circuit. Esquerita and Richard met in the bathroom of the bus station in Greenville, South Carolina, and struck up a friendship. Esquerita taught Richard his hard-driving piano style. That he wore his hair in a tall frizzy pompadour did not go unnoticed by Richard.

Another influence, acknowledged repeatedly by Richard, was the great blues singer Billy Wright. Born in 1932, Wright went on the road with circuses across the South and Midwest, singing and dancing in a cross-dressing chorus line. Richard saw his act at The Royal Peacock in Atlanta, and studied everything about him—how he dressed, how he walked. Richard even got the Pancake #31 from Wright. He called Wright "my idol," and his earliest recordings bear a marked resemblance to his role model's hits.

The tent show culture must have been an amazing thing to behold, and it needs a lot more study. While it was in full frolic, James Brown gave it all the study he could. For while Brown always presented himself as a man's man, he was smart enough to learn a lot about hair and a lot about wild stage personas from the queens of the tent shows.

After hanging out in Macon with Richard, Brown got himself a brand-new hairdo. "I'd sit up in the beauty shop with James Brown, getting our hair curled," remembered Charles Connor. "I'm sitting there with a cigar and there's James. They knew we weren't gay, we were just tired of getting a process—keep that lye in your hair too long and you would burn your scalp." Brown wanted what Wright and Richard had: the ability to command all eyes when they walked into a room. Big hair also added a few inches to a short frame: He did it, he said many times, "so people don't say *where* he is, but *there* he is." Brown took a coif that communicated one thing in the gay carnival shows, and made it a symbol of who he was.

In 1955, however, both of Clint Brantley's acts were strictly local. Richard had made records for RCA Victor and Peacock that flopped. Out of desperation, he speeded up his sound, employing a freight-train rumble and a lurid swagger that he dared not put on vinyl. He urged his drummer to get in front of the band, to push the beat. The band hadn't picked up a bass player yet, and Richard made Connor pound the bass drum on the beat to create a bass line—"almost in a disco style," he said.

Connor was subdividing the good old four-four, turning the whole group into a New Orleans choo-choo. "I had to create a much more powerful, *soulful*, down-home, drivin' beat. Richard wanted 16 and 32nd notes on the sock cymbal or the ride cymbal, and not just a plain backbeat on your rim but 16 and 32nd notes on your snare drum." On the cymbal he was playing a lilting style he says he got from New Orleans and Professor Longhair, a celebrated pianist with whom he had played before Richard. The drumming in those second lines, the complex, shifting beats that flowed out of bodies moving down streets, had long bled into New Orleans music. Now, through Connor, it was changing the sound of Macon.

Richard guaranteed the band gigs four nights a week, Thursday through Sunday, and on other nights Connor and Wilbert Smith, who could play keyboards and saxophones and could sing, would be in a scrap band with Brown at an American Legion club or in some roadhouse. Connor remembers: "One day we were doing this moonlighting thing with James Brown and I'm doing a second line, and James be singing, and James looked around at me and started smiling. What the hell he smiling at me for? He said, 'That sounded good man, do that again!' I was doing a syncopation on my bass drum, a New Orleans second line. I think it was Roy Brown's 'Good Rocking Tonight' we was playing."

The train rumble was getting louder: Late in 1955, a record Little Richard had made, "Tutti Frutti," was rising on the charts. Summoned to Los Angeles for more recording, Richard left his Macon manager holding the bag on several weeks' worth of commitments. Brantley still had the Upsetters around—Richard mostly recorded with studio musicians. He had the venues booked. Now he just needed a front man, and he happened to have somebody under contract who knew Richard's act inside out.

For the next several weeks' worth of Southern shows, Fats

Gonder snatched the microphone and called out in his chesty announcer's voice: "Ladies and gentlemen, introducing the hardest working man in show business: LITTLE RICHARD!" And out jumped James Brown, hair way up high, doing his very best imitation of the wild one.

It could work. It *did* work, often. Richard was on the verge of stardom, but not that many people knew what he looked like. Those who did just became a bigger challenge for Brown to win over, and he liked challenges. Standing before a mix of his Flames and Connor and the Upsetters, he all but asked the audience, "You want Little Richard? I'll give you a show that will make you forget all about that mama's boy." "I've never seen a man work so hard in my life. He would do extra," recalled Byrd. "He just drove himself, driving, driving, driving. We'd say, 'What's wrong with you? By the time it's time for us to try and make a record, you'll be done killed yourself.'"

Sometimes, people whispered, "that don't look like Little Richard, he's too dark." In Alabama, they figured out the ruse and chanted "we want Richard, we want Richard." That did it. Brown held nothing back as he raved through the set, doing backflips, leaps, climbing on top of the piano and landing in splits. By the time he was done, the crowd was cheering the imposter.

The shows taught Brown what it felt like to play with a great band and an ass-kicking drummer. For if Connor wasn't in the league of Earl Palmer, the drummer Richard recorded with, he was mighty fine all the same. (And Connor *did* play the indelible drum part on Richard's "Keep A Knockin'.") He had turned Brown's head around, and years later Brown would say it was Connor who first "put the funk in the music."

A strange word: *funk*. It meant the smell of sex to New Orleans musicians. It was the stench of something filthy–a bum rolling in the gutter, Earl Palmer said. Whatever else it meant, in the music it was a repository for unclean feelings, for stuff proper folks kept locked in their subconscious. Connor had his definition, one that he got from watching dancers. "Funk is imagination. You can see a big fat woman walking down the way, she's got a big booty sliding side to side, doing the jellyroll.

"You look at their behinds, that's where I got my rhythm style. I would look at the dance floor, at some woman shaking her butt, and I would *boom*–do three or four measures of my stuff–then I'd watch her body language." A very old practice, wrenched into the new era. Drummers and dancers passing it back and forth. Conversatin'.

Some time in 1955, Brown and a couple of the Flames went to the radio station WIBB, which was devoting a few afternoon hours to "race music," as it was called. They came to make a demo of a song, something to use as a calling card in hopes of getting a recording contract. The studio was so small that two or three Flames stood out in the waiting area, while Brown sang from the DJ's booth. Recording the song was a WIBB regular named Charles "Big Saul" Green. Noticing how short Brown was, Big Saul pulled the microphone hanging from the ceiling down as low as it would go, then set up a Coke crate for him to stand on–it was the only way Brown could reach the mic.

The song was "Please, Please, Please," a tune they'd been singing since their Toccoa days. All roads to "Please, Please, Please" run through a song called "Baby Please Don't Go," a lament which Delta blues singer Big Joe Williams had a hit with in 1935, but which surely reaches further back than him. *That* song had no discernible impact on the Flames, but it sure shook up Sonny Til and the Orioles, one of the founding R&B vocal groups. They had success with "Baby Please Don't Go" in 1953; the Flames loved the Orioles and knew their version. But a bigger inspiration for "Please, Please, Please" was far closer to home. In 1951, blues belting, former tent show queen Billy Wright recast "Baby Please Don't Go" as "Turn Your Lamp Down Low," a hypnotic moan. The Flames threw out everything but the instrumental hook, which becomes the melody of "Please." They responded to Wright's tune, but what really moved them was a version of the song they encountered on a road trip to Augusta. Visiting there risked a parole violation, but Brown and the Flames went, and heard the hottest local group, Bill Johnson and the Four Steps of Rhythm. The Four Steps of Rhythm were contemporaries of the Flames, and Johnson was from the Terry; they were a singing, dancing, harmony act whose version of "Baby" pointed away from the pretty airs of the Orioles toward something nastier.

This was a tune worth going to jail for. "When we first heard [the Four Steps' version], we said 'Oh man! That's more like it.' I mean, *that's* a song," said Bobby Byrd. "I mean, the song was easy, everybody could sing it." It was almost like that trip to Augusta settled something in all of their minds. The Flames were never going to be a mystique act like the Orioles, they weren't going to win people over with beauty, dignity, and decency. They were a working band, a crawling-on-the-floor, grease-dripping, picking-up-spit live act like the Four Steps of Rhythm. Sometimes it's good to get clarity.

They wrote new words to Johnson's song, which they renamed "Please, Please, Please." This tune was a standalone *emotional* workout, a feature number for Brown that allowed him to evoke the church (in the submission of that *please*) while communicating an abandonment that anybody could understand. Every verse had a different rhythmic delivery, which kept this very simple song interesting while it also communicated a soul in turmoil, trying this, trying that, tramping down every avenue to bring love back. The Flames' tight harmonies glowed in stained-glass hues, while the lead voice started out like a bird accepting capture and ended damned near smashing his head against the bars. "Please, Please, Please" was a straight-up slow burner that sounded old before anybody heard it, built from found parts going back decades and animated by a working band trying to win a crowd, earn another night, get further along the road. A very old cage . . . a strange, new bird.

They recorded it fast at WIBB, in one take. They took it over to WBML, where Hamp Swain, the first black DJ in Macon, spun. Swain had been a bandleader, and Little Richard even sang with his Hamptones for a bit, but the mellow-voiced Swain found greater success at WBML. He started playing "Please, Please, Please" late in 1955, and the response was immediate. "To tell the truth, I didn't think all that much of the song at first," said Swain. "But right away we started getting requests for it, we'd have to play it two or three times in an hour. We were not taking phone requests back then, but the phones would light up and we'd sort of bend the rules and go ahead and play it again." The mail brought more demands for the song.

The first time he heard his song on WBML, Brown said, "I felt I'd been saved." Not saved in the survival sense; he had some money in his pocket, the worst was behind him. He meant *saved* more in the religious sense. He had had a profound experience back at Rome, when he sang gospel to tuberculosis patients and discovered how powerfully he could reach them—their tears gave *him* tears. Seeing himself projected onto others excited Brown, animated him like nothing else in life. Hearing his voice coming out of the radio reignited that chance encounter in Rome, the acceptance of the crowd, projected it across the big city of Macon. It made him feel special, different, and hungry for more. W.E.B. Du Bois: ". . . a sort of seventh son, born with a veil, and gifted with second-sight in this American world—a world which yields him no self-consciousness, but only lets him see himself through the revelation of the other world . . ."

Brantley took Brown under his wing and tried to school him. He got the group to add "Famous" to their name. It stood out more. On days off at the Two Spot, he'd lecture the singer on the importance of punctuality, and how to read a contract. "I'm gonna tell you something important, you better pay attention," Brantley would say. "When a club owner pays you, count along with him. Put out your hand," he'd order, counting fifty single bills into it. "Now, how many dollars you got?" "I done counted it, Mr. Brantley, fifty," Brown would say. And then Brantley would tally them again, slowly this time. It was 49; he showed how he had palmed one bill. "*When you get on the road, you got to watch the hands.*"

Brantley had Brown's back. Driving like a maniac between his family in Toccoa and Macon, Brown ran smack into a tractor one night, driven by a white farmer. Irate, the singer jumped out and slugged the farmer. That landed him in jail for a night, a parole violation that could have put him back in prison. But Brantley knew how to smooth things out. He got on the phone to the jail and pretended to be a white boss who angrily needed "my niggers" back for a big job. Thanks to Brantley, Brown got out of many a fix.

The Famous Flames were waiting for something to happen; James was trying to *make* something happen. He knew a conjure woman named Catherine Thornton who lived outside of Macon. Before a show at the Two Spot, he told Byrd and Johnny Terry that this woman was giving them a chance to have success in music. He was supposed to meet her at a rural clearing on a given night. Brown invited his bandmates to go with him. "Do you want to come with me? They're taking me back tomorrow night." He did not specify who *they* were. "We didn't want to go," Terry remembered with a laugh. Brown drove out of Macon alone with the hoodoo woman, into the woods outside the city, and was gone, Byrd said, for several days. He must have walked back, because when they next saw him, a day or two later, he was sweating profusely, almost hyperventilating and disheveled. "I don't know *what* he met," Terry shrugged, but after his return, Byrd said Brown had a new attitude, a placid new conviction: "Just climb on my back and ride to success." Terry, too, sensed something new. "In a lot of ways," he said. "See, he said he would do anything he could to make us successful. And we were very much successful."

The local success of "Please, Please, Please" and Little Richard's move to Los Angeles made them the biggest act in town. Brantley sent out tapes of the song to some of the biggest independent labels in the country: Specialty in Los Angeles, Chess in Chicago, Peacock in Houston, and Cincinnati's King Records. Other than Specialty, all were interested. Leonard Chess, co-owner of Chess Records, mailed Brantley a contract and said he was flying down to

Macon. King Records knew about the Flames before "Please, Please, Please": Hank Ballard and the Midnighters recorded for King, and Ballard had been telling label owner Syd Nathan that he should sign the Macon boys he'd heard out on the road.

Nathan called the head of King subsidiary DeLuxe, a record man in Miami named Henry Stone. "Henry, you have got to get into your Buick and drive up to Macon–there's a record that's kicking some noise up there and I want you to get it for your label," he told Stone. Unbeknownst to Stone, a King talent scout named Ralph Bass heard the song in King's Atlanta office and decided on the spot he wanted the act for the King subsidiary that *he* ran, Federal. "Please, Please, Please" sounded weird–*different*–to Bass, and that was enough. Talent was cool, but being different–that was what made a hit. The fact that King had two representatives stalking Brown for rival subsidiaries testified to Nathan's huge appetite: When he wanted something, he *really* wanted it, and wasn't going to lose out because somebody couldn't find the road to Macon.

A race was on–none of the contenders knew exactly who was in it, but they had all been aced out of hits countless times, and knew they better jump. Leonard Chess was en route to Macon when a wicked storm grounded his plane. Stone was on the road, but Atlanta is only about eighty miles from Macon, and Bass got there first.

Bass was a tall redheaded hepcat who loved black culture. When he went on the road he stayed in Negro hotels, and when he signed an act it was because *he* liked them–"I didn't give a damn if whites bought it." Once he got to Macon, he knew he had to step lightly, because "an out-of-town white cat could be in trouble in those days," Bass explained. He drove to Macon with a black radio DJ from Atlanta who knew the racial landscape. A meeting with Brantley was quickly arranged. Whites watched for so-called outside agitators talking to "their" Negroes, and Brantley knew all too well that Bass couldn't just walk in and shake hands. He gave the record man instructions: Park in front of the barbershop and wait for the signal. If everything seemed copasetic, at eight o'clock you will see the lights go on and the blinds come down. That was the sign that Bass could enter. Turning to the DJ in his car, Bass said, "Hey man, if I don't come out, if something happens to me, come and get me." Brantley held a strong hand; he waved the contract from Chess, and asked Bass what he was offering. Bass peeled off two hundred dollars and said, "Clint, this is for you. But I want to sign them now." "Deal," Brantley said.

Bass wanted assurance he was signing the group he heard on the tape, and Brantley told him they were singing nearby that night. The show Bass saw might have been good or bad, but what stuck in the talent scout's mind was simply the way the main singer scuttled and crept as he kept shouting the word "please." This cat was way *different*.

A week after that, the Flames were driving to Cincinnati for their first Federal recording session at King's studio. On the morning of February 4, 1956, an engineer for King, Hal Neely, was arriving at work at around eight on a very cold morning. He saw an old Ford station wagon with a bull fiddle tied to the top parked beside the building, and inside six or seven guys asleep. When they woke up, they told Neely they'd driven all night from Macon for their recording date.

Neely gave them a few bills and explained that Syd Nathan, the owner, wouldn't be in until noon. He sent the band to the Manse Hotel, where black acts stayed, and told them to return in the afternoon.

By then, the house rhythm section was in the studio working on something, so the Flames stood in the hallway, waiting to make their record. The seasoned musicians took a break, sticking around to scope out the new act. "I think there was, like, three guys with James when they were singing 'Please, Please, Please,'" said Philip Paul, drummer for King. In the control booth, through thick glass, Nathan stared at the scene. "They were on the floor, and James was hollering, and then I heard Syd Nathan shout, 'What is that piece of shit out there? Oh man, that's terrible.'" He cut them off before they even got through their first song, turning to Bass and cursing his judgment. Nathan was famous for letting you know what he really thought, but the Flames had just now met the guy, and they thought things were over before they finished their big song.

Those who knew Nathan understood his need to vent, but on this occasion many in the room shared his opinion. "Myself and the other musicians said, 'What is *that*?'" recalled Paul. "One of the studio guys said, 'If that's the music to come . . .' We all cracked up. These guys were really good musicians, and when they heard all the hollering and screaming, we all said, 'What is this garbage?'"

It's hard, today, to pinpoint in "Please, Please, Please" the oddness that attracted Bass and which appalled professional musicians like Paul and pianist Sonny Thompson. King, which put out Federal Records, sat on the song for about a month. The way Bass told it, he was back on the road looking for new acts to sign, staying in a Negro hotel in St. Louis, when a regional King salesman told him he had better give Nathan a call. Bass found a payphone and reached the office. Nathan's voice came on the line, no introduction: "You're fired!" (Syd's way of saying hello.) "He's just singing one word!" (Brown repeats *please* twenty-six times.) "It sounds like he's stuttering!" (Popping his P's in the studio, Brown seems to be singing "peas, peas, peas.") At least now Bass knew which record he was talking about. Nathan had just heard the pressing of "Please, Please, Please." Bass started to speak, but Nathan said it all: "You're fired."

Test the record out, Bass urged, just release it in a Southern town like Atlanta and see how it performs. Right about then, Nathan's "I'll show you" bluster asserted itself. Raising Bass's bet, he said, "Fuck it. I'm putting it out cross-country just to prove what a piece of shit it is."

The Flames had recorded three other songs while they were in Cincinnati, and they drove back to Macon wondering if any would ever see the light of day. According to Byrd, some made plans to return to Toccoa. "It took so long for it to finally come out, we were all getting ready to go back to our regular jobs. We said, 'Well, maybe they ain't gonna put the record out. The man didn't like it no way.'"

But they hovered in Macon for a month, and then Nathan issued "Please, Please, Please," on March 3, 1956. Southern radio was slow to pick it up, and two DJs from WLAC in Gallatin, Tennessee, John R. and Hoss Allen, took credit for first playing it.

A response slowly emerged, but really, the guys were just glad *somebody* was playing the thing. There was something funny, though, about the record's label. When the rest of the Famous Flames got a shipment, they held up the disc and noticed the words printed on it: "James Brown with the Famous Flames." They thought it had been a democracy, everyone a Flame. This was news.

A slow-burner, "Please, Please, Please" was listed as a "Buy of the Week" in *Billboard* the first week of April. By the end of the month it was rolling up the R&B charts, peaking at #5. It didn't touch the pop charts, but many a white kid who could hear a powerful station like WLAC would drive out to the country, turn on the car radio, and wait for the song to play. "Please, Please, Please" fell off some charts in September, but two months later it was still riding high in St. Louis.

"Please, Please, Please" became the set piece closer of Brown's show, and he turned it *out*, pantomiming depraved acts of groveling. So much so that when tough blues singer Howlin' Wolf saw the Flames do it, he advised Brown that if he wanted to keep on living in these clubs, he better stop crawling around looking up women's dresses while he sang his song.

Publicly, Nathan began telling people *he* was responsible for "Please, Please, Please." Privately, he admitted he had changed his opinion of the Flames. As Nathan explained to Bass, there were only two kinds of music: the kind that makes the blood rise in your arm, and the kind that doesn't. These guys got the corpuscles running hot.

Another recording session was hastily scheduled, and James Brown with the Famous Flames drove back to Cincinnati.

Chapter Six

TOP BANANA

When King Records moved into its building on Cincinnati's Brewster Avenue, those who worked for the fledgling label immediately found themselves slipping into the funk. It made their feet give out from under them, it stuck to their hands, knees, and hair. The time was the mid 1940s, and they were remodeling a building that had formerly housed Fries & Fries, a Cincinnati manufacturer of edible flavored extracts. When the record people started knocking down walls and drilling holes for plumbing, they uncovered pools and puddles of sticky extracts: banana, cherry, strawberry, brandy, nuts, and Fries & Fries' biggest seller, vanilla.

All the old smells had to go, so that fresh aromas could bubble up. King Records grew on a nondescript strip of industrial and commercial buildings. The owners moved in record stampers and printing presses and built a recording studio that was gloriously good at capturing live sounds. It was a small room with a twenty-five-foot high ceiling that musicians liked. The engineer, the talent scouts, and visitors all sat in a room over the studio, looking down on it like fans seated above a ball field. A bucket of beer and cold cuts were set up on a side table to keep the talent from straying too far.

Presiding over all of it, swiping at the root beer syrup besmudging his thick spectacles, was the man who built King, Syd Nathan. Syd was a wonder, and Syd was a real piece of work. Others who had been where Brown first stood in 1956 instantly formed an image of the man. When Alton Delmore of the country duo the Delmore Brothers came to King, he thought Nathan resembled "a groundhog, just emerging from his hole." To drummer Nelson Burton, he was "a short, chubby Jewish fella, with unshined shoes and chili stains on his tie." Though he was asthmatic he loved his cigars, and even posed with them in his publicity shots. All but blind, Nathan wore glasses as thick and circular as submarine portholes. He was round in the middle and round on top; when smiling, he looked mildly unhinged, and when his mood was otherwise, there was nothing mild about him.

On Brewster Avenue he was building a brand-new model of an independent label, assembled according to his own sense of the right way to do things. King and its affiliates—Queen, Federal, DeLuxe—were self-sustaining under one roof, which no indie had done before. They recorded music, they ran the tape to the room where they pressed the plastic. The art department designed and printed covers, and then the records were boxed and shipped from the loading dock. A King artist could cut a tune in the morning and walk out that night with a stack of singles under his arm. "This was the indie of all indies," said Seymour Stein, who worked at King in the 1950s and went on to form his own record label, Sire. "We all like to think we are independent, but Sydney was the most independent."

He called himself the Big Chief. Throughout the King facility Nathan installed loudspeakers, the better to spread his mandate to the farthest reaches of the plant. One fundamental message: Don't get too comfortable.

He messed with you. The leader of a local rock and roll quartet being courted by King once came in to discuss a contract.

"What do you want to call yourselves?"

The kid thought and said, "Them."

"Eh, that ain't gonna work. How many of you are there?"

"Four, sir."

"Four? Why don't you call yourself the Four Fuckers." That day the young man got a valuable lesson in human relations.

A working-class Jew who had been doing business with Negroes and hillbillies for years, Nathan was an outsider who had no patience for racism. King was probably the only firm hiring blacks and whites together in Cincinnati in the late 1940s; it had integrated Christmas parties and integrated picnics. During World War II, they hired Japanese Americans to run machinery, thereby keeping them out of internment camps. Nathan had hired Henry Glover as an executive, and gave this African American real power in making creative and business decisions. King artists were put up in Nathan's guest room; while Hank Ballard was staying with him, somebody threw a rock through his front window. "He thought it was funny," remembered Stein. "Syd was no racist."

His wasn't an ideological sort of integration, it was a gut thing. Nathan signed hillbilly and R&B acts and scheduled them one after the other in the studio. He had black studio musicians playing with white country stars, and R&B singers covering country songs. "I'm not a genius, and I don't have any geniuses working for me," Nathan said. "We work at it as if it was the coffin business, the machinery business, or any other business. It has to pay for itself." His racial vision, his American vision, was grounded in the ability to make a dollar, and this made Nathan a creative genius and a civil rights trailblazer. With chili stains on his tie.

In the two years after "Please, Please, Please" was made, Brown recorded four more times at King Records, eagerly attempting to repeat the success of that first session. Through his many visits to town, he became extremely familiar with Cincinnati, making it, and the Manse Hotel, his second home.

When Brown wasn't in Cincinnati he was on the road, making as much as he could out of one hit and songs that either sounded like other people's hits or were covers of their hits. He and the Famous Flames were playing the connected assortment of small Southern black venues collectively called the "chitlin circuit." The name came about because, as was true of pig tripe, pleasure was squeezed from hardship. In a segregated land, the chitlin circuit was where the musicians from the black side were able to get paid and gas up for the next town. The chitlin circuit has nothing to do with the big black theaters like the Regal in Chicago or the Apollo in New York. Those were filet mignon. These were roadhouses and chicken shacks, tobacco barns and Quonset huts. Clint Brantley knew a lot of these places from Macon down to Florida, and that was where he sent the Famous Flames in search of a justification for the "Famous" he'd laid on them.

"I knew the struggle, the pinto beans and the bologna sandwiches and the RC Colas, then the no-food period, for two or three days or something," remembered Bobby Byrd. "That's the stuff we all went through together." Most hotels would not give you a room, and at first they couldn't afford the rooms a black hotel offered. You ate what you found, going to the back door of restaurants that would serve you. You might need to buy a whole pie just because you wanted a piece. And there was the sheriff waiting to escort you to the county line.

You took the color line as a given, because that was how you survived. You were probably the only act in town for black folks to see on a given night. Some places let you play to whites if blacks were confined to the balcony, or a separate room, or if in a pinch the races were divided by a line of rope stretched across the dance floor.

Late in 1956, the Famous Flames signed a contract with Universal Attractions, a New York–based agency headed by Ben Bart. Brantley still handled shows in his region for the time being, but the white show business veteran Bart was able to get them dates out West and in the North. As a booker, Bart favored a loaded schedule; he believed in work and loved artists who shared his stamina. His schedule was exciting for Brown, exhausting for others. Not long after he signed on, the Famous Flames were driving from a show in Pensacola to New Mexico. Somewhere in Colorado, in the middle of the night, everybody was asleep except for the driver. While they slept, everybody was coughing, then they were throwing up; carbon monoxide was filling the car at five in the morning. That was it for Nafloyd Scott. "I done been through it," he declared, on the way back to Toccoa.

He was not alone. March of 1957 marked a year since "Please, Please, Please" launched them, and still they had no viable follow-up. They were flailing, listening to King pitch them songs, chasing after a doo-wop tune here, a rock and roll shouter there. What did they want to be?

Bart called off the bookings, summoned them to his Manhattan office. He took Brown aside and they talked for a while, and when Bart then addressed the rest of the group, his message was brutal. Brown was the star of the show. *He* was the one people were paying to see. It made no sense to continue their former arrangement, splitting money evenly and pretending all were equal. The decision was about saving money, but also about admitting the obvious: One guy was leading the way. As Brown hovered silently, Bart offered the Famous Flames a new arrangement: They would get a set rate of thirty-five dollars per show and a straight salary; Brown would take the record royalties. That was the deal, if they didn't like it they could be replaced. Early in March the rest of the Famous Flames said they didn't like it at all. They'd play a string of dates that would send them back to the South and then quit.

Bart shattered whatever illusion remained that the Famous Flames were an egalitarian unit, with Brown first among equals. Bart's declaration sealed the deal, but truly the end had come back in March 1956. The rest of the Flames never recovered from picking up that first copy of "Please, Please, Please" and seeing the strange wording of the Federal label, "JAMES BROWN with the Famous Flames."

"Oh, that was devastating," said Byrd. "All the stuff we had gone through, all the struggles, to *get* to 'Please, Please, Please,' and then to wind up with one person's name on it. That wasn't right, because one person didn't do all of that. All of us did that. Yes indeed."

Brown was not one of them. The Flames had grown up with each other, and to them this was a lark, a moonshine fishtail through the mountains, something to ride until it crashed and you had to go home to your family.

"James was different from us. He didn't hang out with us," Scott recalled later. "James had a mind of his own, he wanted to do something different from everybody else. He wanted to make his own way."

To Byrd, the fun stopped when the arguments over billing and percentages began. "The best time we *ever* had was when we was the Flames and everybody was getting the same amount, whether it was a dollar and a quarter, if it was seventy-five cents. Oh you can't imagine what kind of times it was. Hugely different times, everybody was grinning, and fun. . . . Wasn't like no job to us, we was just having a ball."

The Flames blamed the split on Brown's greed, his sneakiness. Surely, Brown had his share of both. But what broke up the Famous Flames was that they were from Toccoa and he was not. For them it was about having a ball, about a pleasure that was innocent and free. They went home and took care of their families.

No record sales since his debut. No act. No proof he could write a song on his own. Nine singles in a row that nobody wanted to hear. Brown headed out again on the circuit with no wind at his back. He was a solo act in the summer of 1957, accompanied by pianist Fats Gonder on loan from Brantley. He picked up Thomas "Guitar" Gable, who played sitting down with the guitar flat across his lap, for a string of shows. Beyond that, Brown was hiring bassists and drummers as he found them, playing material that they knew, singing his one hit. Traveling light.

That fall, a small miracle happened: Little Richard found God. He had joined the Seventh-day Adventist church and was preaching abstinence and the imminent Second Coming of our Lord on street corners in Los Angeles. A religious booking agency signed him and he announced he was backing out of his secular dates in America. Yet again, Brown was called on, and with so little going for him, he eagerly toured once more with the Upsetters for several weeks. Reminded of the pleasures of playing with a great band and drummer, he itched to get a group of his own together, take them to Cincinnati for a recording session that would establish a new direction. Heck: establish *a* direction.

The problem was, Nathan stood in the doorway. When you had a hit, he would put as many records out on you as he could make, and when you were cold the inverse was true–Syd didn't have nothing for you. After one more session in the fall of 1957, Nathan stopped returning Brown's calls.

One thing was becoming clear, as it would have been to anyone who spent time within the brown brick King enclave. Songs are what mattered to Nathan. He understood as well as anybody in the industry that the real money was in owning the songwriting royalties. "He didn't record anyone's songs unless he got a rate," said Henry Glover. "That's why he had very few outside compositions on his labels." It was a good way to make money, and it was the key reason why Nathan had his white acts covering his black acts and vice versa: because they were taking tunes he had a piece of to black *and* white audiences. "Give me the *song*," Nathan all but shouted at one meeting of his staff. As for the singer that brought in that song, well . . . "If he sings with a harelip, we'll take him, we'll take the song, because goddamnit we can cover him over. If he . . ."–and here Nathan did his garbled interpretation of what a singer with a harelip sounded like–"that suits me, as long as the *material* is good."

He didn't have any particular fondness for music. Nathan liked the business, he liked hustlers cutting deals with other hustlers.

He had worked as a shooting gallery operator and a wrestling promoter, he ran a record store, and had owned a pawn shop. That last
job was particularly salient; King employees recalled Nathan killing time by walking into a local pawnshop, picking out some object
he had no interest in buying, and seeing how low he could get the
pawnbroker to go.

Country music star Hank Penny was one of the first hillbilly acts
on King, in the 1940s. On a visit to the label, he watched Nathan
argue furiously with a music publisher over an eighth-of-a-cent
royalty for a song. "Man, you never heard of such language over
such an actual small amount," said Penny. Afterward, everyone
went out for dinner at a high-priced restaurant, and Nathan paid
for everything. "I asked him how he could fight so hard over an
eighth of a cent and then pick up a big tab. Syd just laughed and
said, 'This morning I was a kike, tonight I'm an elegant Jew.'

"That was Syd in a nutshell," said Penny.

Brown had little ability to induce King to record him. What
Brown *was* in control of were the shows he played, the fringe dates
he was banging out through the fall and winter of 1957. After the
pickup gigs with the Upsetters ended, he kept Richard's vocal
group, the Dominions, with him. They were Louis Madison, Bill
Hollings, J. W. Archer, and now *they* were the Famous Flames. He
had also picked up a new guitar player in Topeka, Kansas, a blues
freak who played with a full-bodied sound, by the name of Bobby
Roach.

This was not a situation where Brown was running the show.
There wasn't all that much of a show, and however the pay was
skewed, nobody bowed to the boss. In Indiana, a couple of women
at the front of the stage were making fun of his looks, and pretty
soon the Famous Flames were laughing with them. In the dressing
room after the show, Roach saw Brown crying. Another night, on
the Carolina coast, the guys were all rolling dice. One of the Flames
was winning and Brown was not. He was a bad loser. A fight erupted
and the singer got thrashed. "We had to tape him up, his eyes were

bleeding bad, he had big sunglasses on. We made the show together, but he was barely able to stand," said Roach.

This group played the West Coast in August, but they rooted in Florida, where Brown spent some nine months. A particularly supportive venue was a wonderland called the Million Dollar Palms of Hallandale, about fifteen miles outside of Miami. The Palms was a former drive-in movie theater and now it was a nightclub where you could hang out stage-side or sit in your car and listen to the likes of Roy Milton, Ray Charles, and Earl Bostic. Palms grew out of the cement, and there was an open-pit barbecue and a 106-foot bar. The white owner ran a Negro motel about a mile away, and another Palms in Jacksonville. The Palms booked you for a solid week, making it an oasis among the garland of one-night joints stretching between Atlanta and New Orleans.

One evening at the Palms, a guy whose name is lost to time sang a song he had written and thought Brown should record. The tune stuck with Brown as he drove across the South and to another West Coast trip. "Stockton, Bakersfield, Fresno, Sacramento, places like that," said Roach. "Didn't draw a fly in none of those places. We drove back to Macon, Georgia, and it was quite a blow to James."

Roach took the wheel, then Brown had a shift, and he drove for a long time, remembered Roach, "Because he was thinking about his career and his songs." They stopped for the night in a small town in Alabama, and Brown told Roach to get his instrument; he had a song he wanted to put a guitar part on.

It was the number Brown had picked up at the Palms, and Roach heard in it a plea to his audience, his label, the world: Give me a chance. *Try* me. He called in the Famous Flames and they started working up harmonies, and the song they created was reminiscent of a hit of the time, "For Your Precious Love." They continued on to Macon, getting in at two in the morning, and headed to WIBB to record it while it was fresh. Roach was there, along with Fats Gonder and the Flames. Brown paid for the session himself, which was looking like the only way he was going to *be* recording. He had

five records made from the tape and sent them out to Southern DJs
he knew. The song was "Try Me," a catchphrase used by young
black men in Georgia, along with some specific body language, to
interest young women. From several angles then, the song had
some urgency to it. But if anybody was ever going to hear the thing,
Brown first had to convince Nathan to let him back into the studio
to record it.

Later, Brown would say Nathan had told him he was off the label
for good, and declared that it was only because the demo of "Try
Me" had started getting some action from Southern jocks that he
relented. But when Nathan finally heard the song he had to acknowledge that he had something, and he bankrolled a session in New
York City with a big-time record producer, Andy Gibson, and good
studio musicians. The song quickly rose on the R&B charts as
Brown and the Famous Flames went back to the West Coast,
appearing at L.A.'s 5-4 Ballroom in November and again in December. By late 1958, the song topped the R&B charts, and it was also
Brown's first song to crease *Billboard*'s Hot 100–reaching 48 on
the pop side. The song was quality, it had a patina, professional
craftsmen had worked on it in the studio; it was the kind of song
Nathan appreciated. Its lachrymose mood, akin to that of "Please,
Please, Please," was not however what Brown wished to sound like,
nor was it the spirit of his shows.

Ever since the first time he played with Charles Connor and the
Upsetters, Brown had wanted a band of his own, musicians he
could take on the road and work on new material with that he could
then record at King. After "Try Me" hit, he could afford something
better than ramshackle, and Brown made a move. He signed up
J. C. Davis, a hard-honking saxophonist who liked bebop, to be his
bandleader. Davis was a North Carolinian who had been stationed
at Camp Gordon in Augusta and played in the Army Signal Corps
Band around 1953. On weekends, Davis would go into the Terry
and sit in with local bands. That's how he met drummer Nat Kendrick, who was a boyhood acquaintance of Brown, and bassist

Hubert Perry, who played with the Four Steps of Rhythm. When he got out of the army, Davis went back home to Greensboro, where he led the house band at the ABA club. He backed up stars when they passed through town, and after he played behind Brown, the singer asked Davis if he wanted to be his bandleader. Soon Davis had brought Perry and Kendrick, the Augusta rhythm section, into the fold. With those three, Fats Gonder playing keyboards, and Bobby Roach on guitar, and with the Famous Flames singing and dancing, Brown was back in business. They were putting "Try Me" at the center of their live show, with the Flames doing steps to show what young Georgia studs did when they asked ladies if they wanted to "try me," and designing other steps and routines, as well.

Immediately, the most important addition was Kendrick. He was coming out of a rhythm and blues background, and did not play the full instrument, preferring to keep a simple driving beat on the snare and a heavy foundation on the bass drum. "He wasn't a great drummer, he just had a lot of feeling, soul," said Davis. "He didn't try to be pretty, didn't try to be cute, he just got on the drums and then, minutes after the show started, his shirt and his clothes was wringing wet. He had a heavy, *heavy* bass foot—he laid down the bass line with that foot and that's what James would dance off."

Kendrick's stamina aided the band in other ways. Brown had been playing pinball in Brantley's club, and while the musicians drove to Savannah to make a gig, Brown was still in Macon, trying to win back what he'd lost. At the club, people were beginning to smash up the tables and throw the chairs around, so the group did their opening set, which Brown wasn't a part of anyway. When he still hadn't arrived, the band pulled down the curtains, and all of a sudden Kendrick came out and played a drum solo, as if this was some weird new way to begin a show. He kept playing and playing, as behind the curtain the guys threw all the gear on the station wagon; he kept playing, as they started up the car; he grabbed his kit and raced to the car and drove away just about the time the audience caught on that Brown wouldn't be there that night.

They picked up horn players here and there, and as the band expanded, so did the show. First, Davis and the musicians would do a handful of jazzy instrumentals as Brown watched and shouted from the audience. Eventually Fats Gonder came out and, with his chesty bluster, pumped up the house for the entry of the Famous Flames, who sang a few hits of the day, and then pumped up the crowd higher, as Brown hit the stage.

When the mood lagged, the group broke out one of their well-rehearsed routines. They did a baseball bit where Davis was the batter who would step up to the "plate" swinging his saxophone as Brown pitched a ball and one of the Flames called strikes or balls. Their song "The Bells" was a soap opera telling the story of a guy who hadn't treated his woman well–she drives off angrily, and the next thing he hears is the police at the door asking for the next of kin. In *that* routine, the Flames were pallbearers pushing a baby carriage with a doll in it across the stage, and when they pass Brown, he falls to his knees and sobs, slowly working his way into "Please, Please, Please."

"We'd be pulling the baby carriage away from him, and he would have actual tears coming out of his eyes," said Davis. It got to where if they came through town again and *didn't* do the bit with the baby carriage, there were those in the crowd ready to start a fight. "He was a guy determined that he was going to be noticed. He was determined that he was going to be the man, he's going to do something to make people remember us, even if it was climb up onto the rafters and fall down and kill himself. He was going to be remembered."

They signified flair and wealth and made a squall. It was how they wanted to be remembered, but being black and representing those qualities could get you killed on the road. It was an art form all its own: tearing it up in the Sportatorium, then slipping away to the next town.

On the road in the South, when they couldn't get a motel room they stayed at "tea houses," whorehouses more or less, said Davis.

All along the way, the police were a presence to avoid, nuance, or outsmart. They pulled the band over on a country road in Waycross, Georgia, telling the driver, Davis, that his rear light was out. "No, it's not," he said—it was his brand-new Kingswood station wagon. "You calling me a liar, boy?" he was asked, and then beaten with a flashlight. Another time, coming out of a show in tobacco country, they were driving to the next gig when flares on the road brought them to a stop. The police arrested the lot and took them to the station. There the musicians' pockets were emptied, and everything they had was taken by the police. Blacks driving in a nice car had to be from the North and had to be taught a lesson. Moments like this showed them that you were unlikely to make it out of town if the gendarmes knew you had a lot of money and were driving a good car with out-of-town plates. From then on, they put the night's take in another car, one that looked more appropriate for blacks to be driving in the eyes of the law.

Sometimes, the sheriffs were funny more than anything else. Alfred Corley was a teenager who had studied saxophone in Florida with Cannonball Adderley. Corley was thoroughly intoxicated the night the police pulled him out of the bus and put him on the grill.

"What's your name, boy?"

"My name is Alfred Corley."

"Boy don't you talk to us like that down here—your name is *Corley.*"

Corley turned around to the guys in the band and said in all drunken innocence, "Now I don't even know my own name!"

It defused the situation, and soon they were on their way.

That was one image of the late 1950s chitlin circuit, an important part, but other flickerings emerged on the periphery of vision. The band was playing a show in Jacksonville, at the Number Two Palms, around 1959. Roach, Davis, and the guys were in the dressing room, joking, waiting to go on, when someone sitting outside the door came in looking nervous. Four or five people really wanted to meet the band, he explained. They came in, saying they were college kids, and then they started laughing, admitting they could have been arrested if they had been caught in this club full of black people.

With that the students pulled off the disguises they were wearing. "They had these natural wigs on and this brown pancake makeup on their faces," said Roach.

"Me and James looked at each other and our mouths flew open. James cried, 'Those are white people!'" They were three girls and two boys, and they said the show was the best they'd ever seen and were committed to following it around. "We played in New Orleans and they was there, then they was in Miami, South Carolina, I saw them in a lot of places, and they did the same thing everywhere we went."

Whites and blacks mingling at venues could bring out the worst in local law officials, and white women and black men mingling was forbidden. Two years before the Freedom Rides, here were white college students who had somehow stumbled on the James Brown show and liked it so much they were willing to travel any way possible to hear him again.

It was a show of many parts, with Gonder, Davis, the Famous Flames, and Brown all getting billing on the posters. The billing on the records, and the size of the checks coming from Universal, established that Brown was the star. But that was different from having control of the entire show, or having the respect of those around you. Fats Gonder called him Monk Brown, and pretty soon the other guys did, too: "Because when he took off his makeup and his clothes, he looked like a little monkey," said Davis. The Flames would be drinking White Satin gin and lemon juice, and they'd needle Brown about how they got more girls than him. There was a lack of esteem on both sides, coming across in fistfights and petty putdowns that showed Brown's ego in full preen. "James started to say 'I'm getting big and you guys ain't gonna be nuthin'. We gonna be walking down the street and people gonna look around and say "There goes James Brown..." They ain't even gonna *speak* to you,'" remembered Davis. "If a girl gave you a banana, Brown's gonna break the biggest piece off real quick. Next day if somebody gave you something, he *still* was gonna break off the biggest piece. He isn't gonna say 'I got it yesterday so it's your turn.' He's gonna get it every day."

Doubtless, there was ego in that, the vanity of a man who believed in himself when nobody else did. But there was more to it. If he was going to build the show he wanted and stamp himself on every aspect of the presentation, he needed to fight his way to the top of his own ticket. "All that tough guy stuff was nothing but a front," Roach believed. "He said 'Bobby, I *got* to act that way, because if I don't the show will walk all over me.'" He was the star, but he wasn't the leader—he didn't tell Davis what to play or how long, the Flames didn't really listen to him, Gonder was his own person. What he admitted to Roach, who roomed with him in Macon, was that, "He was trying to gain control of the leadership."

In March 1959, the group headed again for the West Coast. They had a lot of play in the Bay Area, and there were plenty of places to perform. According to Byrd, Brown had done some last-minute show bookings of his own this trip, without Universal Attractions' knowledge. After one of these off-the-books shows around Oakland, Brown pocketed the promoter's deposit, and the money he was supposed to split with the venue and the band, and drove back to Macon. He left the band stranded in Northern California, without paying them the three weeks' salary they were owed. In his wake, this version of the Flames—Louis Madison, Bill Hollings, J. W. Archer—decamped for good in Northern California. That's one telling of events. Another is that Brown was confronted by one of the Flames on a rainy Oakland street about the money they were owed, got roughed up, and then left town. He lived in the moment, and in that moment he walked out with the money, and without his Flames. At least *them* motherfuckers weren't gonna be calling him Monk Brown to his face any time soon.

"He was not the headliner," said Roach. "He was just part of the show, who was *striving* for leadership. But he wasn't the leader then. When James really became the leader of the show is when the Flames quit and James took over."

Brown had to get back to Macon because his girlfriend, Dessie, was getting a hysterectomy. Dessie's last name was Brown, and between that and the fact that they were living together, folks thought they were married, when in fact James was still married to Velma in Toccoa. "She was a wild young woman, and they were like a sister and brother type deal," recalled Roach. The first ten thousand dollars James saved he sent not to Velma and the boys but to Dessie, to buy themselves a house. Instead she spent it all while they were on the road. "She was not settled," sighed Roach.

There was little time to waste in Georgia, however, for the Flames were scheduled for their debut at Harlem's Apollo Theater on April 24, 1959. Brown had lost his band, which was a challenge, but by this point a pattern was asserting itself: Success came a minute or two after everything seemed to be over. Whether it was winging it on "Try Me" when Nathan wasn't responding, or punching out a white farmer on a country road, things worked out okay. It could lead a guy to think he was invulnerable.

A new set of Famous Flames had to be baptized within days. Looking over the names he could count on, Brown reached out to Johnny Terry, who'd been around the show since the beginning. There was Bobby Bennett, a great dancer who had grown up a block from J. C. Davis in Greensboro, and "Baby" Lloyd Stallworth, a sweet kid the show had picked up at the Million Dollar Palms. "He was a real good guy, and a sensitive guy. He liked girls and he liked boys," said Bennett. "He would mess with men. James took him on the road when he was sixteen years old. His mother sent him on the road to be with James—James said he'll raise him."

Brown still needed to teach these guys the show, and for this task he called up the man he trusted most to understand the needs of his act: Bobby Byrd. Back in Toccoa, Byrd swallowed hard and told Brown he'd meet him in Harlem.

He rented space in the basement of the Cecil Hotel, and Byrd put the new Famous Flames through their paces. Everybody knew what was at stake. The Apollo meant many important things to Bart and Brown: It was the top-ranking black show palace in the country, as unlike the Lenox in Augusta as Harry Belafonte was unlike Butterbeans and Susie. The place signified cosmopolitan splendor, and the lore was that through its doors passed the harshest, most opinionated audience in the country. That was arguable to somebody who played a Southern circuit where they might shoot you if you sang "The Bells" without the baby carriage, but it was true enough. New York was the North. It was where the money was, where business was done, and where Brown would stake his claim.

Coming into their biggest show yet in the big city, everybody felt pressure to look like they belonged. They stayed at a hotel they couldn't afford, and were shocked when doormen opened their cab door, took their bag up, and expected a tip. They couldn't even do their own laundry, because what if somebody saw them? "You had to play the part whether you could afford it or not," recalled Davis.

They wore loud red suits that must have wowed them on the chitlin circuit. Brown and the ten guys on stage with him earned $2,250 for the week, and were listed low on a bill that included Little Willie John. The singer from Macon admired the headliner. He had soft, baby skin, was an amazing conversationalist–he could talk about carpentry, baseball, whatever–and was a "drinks for the house" sort of dude. That was if he cared to; just as likely, Little Willie John was going to fuck with you, messing up your process, undoing the top button of your shirt, trying to make you look bad as you were chatting up a lady at the bar.

John was an inch shorter than Brown's five foot six. Like Brown, he was egotistical and easily wounded, proud and an expert fighter. Only John was handsome, and if Brown admired him, it also meant he envied him, and wanted to replace him.

He was backed by the Upsetters, Little Richard's old band.

Drummer Charles Connor had recently been offered a chance to play with Elvis Presley, but turned it down to tour with John. Soon the Upsetters would back up Sam Cooke—but to Connor, it was all anticlimactic. "Elvis Presley was great but, come on, man. I was with Little Willie John," said Connor. "I'd already reached the mountain."

"Playing behind Sam Cooke was like playin' for people in a convalescent home, for old people," he said. "It was like playin' up in a parade 'second line' band on your way *to* the graveyard, goin' to bury the body." The Upsetters, says Connor, would be muttering on the stage: "Yeah I'm gonna send *you* alright!" ". . . Looks more like a Sam Crook!" . . . and "I'ma *send* this drumstick up his big ugly head!"

There you have it: better than Sam Cooke *and* Elvis Presley. Little Willie John was the guy to beat.

At the Apollo, the Flames' segment underscored how, as Roach described, Brown had to fight to get control of the stage. A *Variety* reviewer said the act "Almost blows out the walls to the obvious delight of audience." But, "It isn't so much a group as collection of performers—singers and musicians—who seem just to have happened onstage at the same time . . . the result is near-anarchy, with each man rocking in his little 'big beat' world." Still, the reviewer said, "Apollo audiences probably couldn't love them more, no matter what."

A legend has prevailed that Brown's first appearance at the Apollo happened earlier, sometime in the mid-1950s, when he supposedly won a talent night competition. Brown, however, always denied it, and so do those who have access to Brown's tour records. There's nothing about it in the Apollo files at the Smithsonian; repeated inquiries made to the Apollo publicity staff have produced no new information.

Davis's band was creating a new matrix for the show, a muscular, rough-edged rocking blues that sounded like Southern country boys roaring through the big city. Coming together on the road and in hastily scheduled recording sessions, it had little to do with doo-wop and vocal groups pitching woo from under the street lamps. "Good Good Lovin'" set the tone, a choogling stop-and-go number with a good-time saxophone solo by Davis. Two other songs underscored this new direction. One the bandleader had brought with him from his Greensboro days, a side-to-side-shuddering arrangement of "Night Train." The band got so good with that they could toy with the groove, dropping stuff like Hal Singer's "Corn Bread" and "Hold It" by Bill Doggett into the song. Brown liked "Night Train" so much, sometimes he'd jump up on stage and shout out, "Hey man, hit that 'Night Train' again for me," and then rap over it as Davis blew a solo.

The other band showpiece was stumbled upon at the Palms of Hallandale, the drive-in that kept laying gifts on the group. During a visit, the group noticed how everybody in the audience was dancing the same step; it was called "the mashed potatoes," they were told, and Miami was crazy for it. Davis created some music to play while the kids danced, and Brown, who was dancing in the crowd, too, jumped onstage shouting "Mashed potatoes, yeah, yeah, yeah" and whatever else kept the moment flowing. They started doing it other places, and Brown got really good at replicating this pigeon-toed stomp.

The time for mashing was now. Nathan said he didn't like the number—oh, *Syd*—and so Brown turned to Henry Stone, the Miami-based record maker who had gotten to Macon almost in time to sign him. They had kept in touch, and now Brown was offering him a record perfectly in synch with the moment. They made it on the sly, with a Miami DJ overdubbed shouting out the nonsense Brown was freestyling live. "(Do the) Mashed Potatoes" came out on Stone's Dade label, under the name of Nat Kendrick and the Swans (to hide how Brown was playing hooky from King). It hit where the dance was popular, while carrying the dance to new towns. The success of "(Do the) Mashed Potatoes" was validation that Brown knew better than Nathan, and it was a concern, too, for if the band was starting to drive the show (Brown's voice was barely on the thing), it might drive over Brown, too—he couldn't play an instrument that well and he didn't read music. He couldn't really *give* musical directions in a way that musicians give to one another. This was a success that he had to stay on top of, and one way he did it was to separate Nat Kendrick from the group. Suddenly he was traveling with his drummer in his car and talking to him alone before or after a show, having Kendrick practice with him rather than with Davis's band. If the band was becoming the engine of the show, Brown was making sure the engine of the band was firmly under his control.

At the end of 1959, control was just about his. Brown had fought his way to the top of the billing, and then he fought to dominate the show. Respect from his band was tolerable. That band was surging in power, and Brown was figuring out how to stay ahead of its power. He had reached the pinnacle of the African American show circuit, with more dates at the Apollo, but he paid his bills in the circuit's trenches. At the onset of a new decade, he was doing the mashed potatoes across the country for another West Coast tour, playing the bigger black venues in California.

They were all riding in cars, passing through Arizona, and it was four o'clock in the morning. "Man, these bright lights come out of nowhere," recalled Bobby Bennett. "There was nothing in the sky and then all of a sudden these lights come out of the air. All around us, and it followed us all the way across the desert."

They were alone on the highway, and the band found itself getting run off the road by the light. "It was scary, everybody ducking and diving all across the desert—you cut the headlights off and it was *still* so bright you could still see. Followed us all night long."

You could drive yourself crazy trying to understand it. To a leader ever more obsessed with his authority, it was a reminder of things beyond anyone's control.

Chapter Seven

THE TRAVELER

The show was passing through Birmingham, Alabama, in May 1961. Brown wanted something to eat and, knowing he would be served in a bus station, in the "colored" section, he and some of the guys headed to the Trailways depot. They ordered and started eating.

Everybody heard the commotion coming from the white side. A short partition separated the races at the cafe, and Brown stood up to peek over it. "All these black people were standing around the door waiting to get a seat on the 'white only' side. Most of 'em looked like they might be college kids, and there were a few whites with them," Brown wrote in his 1986 autobiography, *James Brown: The Godfather of Soul*. He was describing May 14, Mother's Day, when the first "Freedom Ride" pulled into Birmingham. The Supreme Court had decided in 1946 that segregated seating and facilities on interstate bus lines violated federal law. The South had not complied with this ruling, and now civil rights organizations were testing the legality of their refusal by doing what had been unheard-of in the past–sitting down next to whites and requesting service.

A black man settled at the Birmingham lunch counter. The white patron next to him said, "What're you doing sitting here, nigger? You can't sit by me," and punched him to the ground. Another African American took his seat. "Then all hell broke loose," Brown recalled. "People started beating up the kids, throwing things, tearing up the place."

It's a striking description, in part because so little is made of the scene, beyond its momentary oddness. Brown doesn't put any larger meaning in it, which there was: Birmingham was an historic confrontation, and news reports of the violence showed Americans the face of Bull Connor, Birmingham's Public Safety Commissioner and the very image of staunch segregation. Those trying to integrate the station were beaten with bicycle chains, baseball bats, and lead pipes. Connor had given the Klan fifteen minutes to do what they wanted before he sent in his police. "We didn't know what a Freedom Rider was," said Brown. And, understandably, he wasn't going to learn right there in the bus station. The musicians jumped in their car and drove off fast, and so did the demonstrators who could get away from their attackers. Their bus passed Brown's car on the road, and suddenly, Brown found himself sandwiched between the activists in front and racists behind, an approaching convoy of white supremacists in trucks and cars, waving bats and axe handles at the closest blacks they could find. At that moment, he said later, what he felt was something different from any solidarity with the activists. He felt dread that his pursuers would mistake him and his band for Freedom Riders.

Every great autobiography contains passages that work on more than one level, stories that require a reader to step out of the flow of events and ponder what the writer is revealing about himself. In the description of his accidental run-in with civil rights activists and white supremacists in the Birmingham depot, perhaps Brown is showing two aspects of the same thing—how he saw himself and how others saw him. First, he wants us to view him as an individual apart from social forces and categories. He was his own man, and as he once put it, "I do what I want to do and not what anybody—white or black—tells me." That's the guy watching over the divider, and then edging for the door. But the white folks in the room had a different picture: To them he was indistinguishable from a civil rights worker, one more somebody to be chased, and if caught, beaten bloody.

"When we first heard about it," Bobby Roach said of the sit-ins and the Freedom Rides, "well, we didn't get a chance to be getting too involved in it. We was traveling, doing forty-five up to seven-hundred-mile jumps a night." They had a job to do, and a protest, let alone a bloody melee, was an obstacle to fulfilling a contract.

It was getting harder to just hunker down and drive to the next Southern bill. Northern-based agencies were reporting a huge downturn in show bookings, as white parents kept their children away from package tours that featured black and white artists sharing the stage. Black acts were also becoming more reluctant to play the South. After she was insulted by a police officer in Knoxville, Tennessee, singer Ruth Brown vowed to never perform there again. Clyde McPhatter and Sam Cooke had to flee one Southern city when whites saw the out-of-state plates on their tour bus and mistook them for outside agitators. At least they could get on their bus and head North to home.

An age-old system was suddenly being openly contested. Brown, and many of his generation, had resigned themselves to it, and come to a kind of understanding that now was rapidly unraveling. The understanding was that if the Jim Crow system kept blacks apart from whites, there would be a black marketplace *and* a white one, and sometimes an industrious African American could eke out a living by connecting with black consumers. That was how the chitlin circuit worked. Only now there were whites cracking down on it, and there were blacks calling for integration.

Brown was a black Southerner who did not accept his "place" in society, but by temperament he was no joiner, not a candidate for marching in a picket line. He had an individualistic, and fatalistic, streak about what was worth fighting for–any change that he couldn't personally affect, with his powers of persuasion or his fists, he figured probably wasn't worth messing with.

Life had taught him that he could only rely on himself, and he had contempt for the very idea of leaning on others. Others let you down. But after Birmingham, his view of things started to change. Whoever *he* thought he was—apart, independent—he'd gotten a vivid lesson that observers thought otherwise. To them he was just another Negro to chase out of town. Uneasily stuck between Bull Connor and the activists, perhaps he felt he needed to choose up before others chose for him.

"I Don't Mind" was the song Brown was promoting when he left Birmingham, and pushing a hot single meant visiting radio stations and talking up the tune. When he got to Montgomery, Alabama, Brown knew he could count on his childhood friend, Allyn Lee, who was now a DJ in Montgomery, playing records on WAPX.

Lee was a comer on the Southern circuit. Mister Lee, as he called himself on the air, was a businessman through and through, angling to make a profit when a situation presented itself. Wherever he worked, Lee said, he made the same deal with the people who employed him: "Always radio station owners would say, 'I can't pay you but so much . . .' My philosophy was—you can't pay me what I'm *worth*. But I'll work a deal with you. I guarantee you I'll make my time on the air number one if you let me do my thing. 'What is your thing?' Just let me advertise my interest—my record hops, my restaurants."

Disc jockeys, performers, and show promoters all depended on one another, and exploited one another, in an attempt to make a living. For broadcasters like Lee, who were often not paid at all or earned a pittance from station owners, survival meant finding new revenue streams. The largest sources of income were payola and business deals built on the access to black listeners that Lee provided. In Montgomery, Lee drove customers to a restaurant he opened, Mr. Lee's Chickadees, by talking about it on the air. He promoted local appearances of the artists he played. From his access to record companies that supplied him with new product, Lee opened a record store. His friendship with Brown put food on the table, too, as Lee acknowledged.

"Whenever James Brown appeared," he explained, "disc jockeys from within a two-hundred-mile radius came out. And they would never leave until the manager came out and greeted them. Because James Brown always gave out an envelope of money. *Always*. My chauffeur—they once gave *him* an envelope of money. I said, 'James, but he's not a disc jockey.' And he said, 'He might be one next week.' Back then you had fifteen to twenty disc jockeys in the area, and depending on your position there might be fifty to five hundred dollars in the envelope. He would always be appreciating you for you playing his records. 'Play my records man, keep me heard!'"

Brown was exceptionally suited for a life based on money moving around and around. The more he toured, the more folks he met, and the more contacts he maintained. He inherently understood that even when you fell out with someone, it was a mistake to let that disagreement get in the way of putting money through its paces. Brown kept in touch with people from every stage of his life, for many reasons, including his openness to business.

Hit records put bodies in the rooms, and that meant jocks had to be persuaded to play the records. Independent labels had fine-tuned—some say invented—the practice of paying disc jockeys to play a record. When he was called before a senate subcommittee investigating payola, Syd Nathan not only proudly admitted he did it, but even boasted that he kept receipts of his payoffs so he could write off the payments as business expenses on his taxes. To white record people like Nathan, this was just making a profit. To black entrepreneurs it was that and more—if Jim Crow was a conspiracy of whites, it created conspirators on the other side, too.

A black broadcaster in a place like Montgomery was a power broker among people whose power was limited. Lee the promoter would reserve a venue in Montgomery, and pay a deposit of half a guaranteed fee to Brown's booking agency, Universal Attractions. They deducted 10 percent for themselves, and the rest belonged to the performer. After the show was done, the other half would be paid to Brown at the venue by the promoter. Bringing DJs in as promoter was good business—now they had an interest in spinning James Brown's new record, since that would attract more people to the show they had a financial interest in.

Brown didn't invent the practice, he just elevated the game. Whereas a lot of artists played it tawdry, sliding a jock a hundred or two and whispering in his ear, Brown turned it into a legitimate business opportunity. Bob Patton, an ex-DJ who worked for Brown in the mid-1960s, explained: "That's why James Brown became more of a legend than the guy who slipped you something in a handshake. He made you out to be a businessman, not a whore."

His booker, Ben Bart, aided Brown greatly in his understanding of the wants and needs of the gatekeepers. Bart was famous for a black book, compiled and compounded over decades, that he wielded like a Methodist circuit rider's Bible. In it were the names, addresses, and phone numbers of jocks, record distributors, theater owners, and musicians in every city and town. It listed the personal tastes and peccadilloes of such folks, and contained the names of friends on both sides of the law all along the chitlin circuit who, with the proper lubrication, could help one out of a jam.

When James Brown came his way, Bart was among the top bookers of black entertainment in the country. The grandchild of Polish Jews, he grew up in Brooklyn, where he ran a bar called Baloney Ben's in the 1930s, managed boxers, and booked jazz bands for the Gale Agency, one of the biggest theatrical booking concerns. In 1937, he took bandleader Tiny Bradshaw on his first tour of the South, and also represented civil rights cause célèbre the Scottsboro Boys on a series of appearances in the North. A year later, Bart went on what the *Pittsburgh Courier* called a 10,000-mile journey across Dixie, "for the purpose of getting first-hand information about the dance situation in towns throughout the country."

Tenor saxophonist Arnett Cobb gave him his nickname: "The Traveler." Bart formed his own agency, Universal Attractions, in 1945, signing Dinah Washington, Bill Doggett, Wynonie Harris, Foxx and White, and many more. "My dad always said, 'You've got to learn the road,'" said son Jack Bart, who would later run Universal. "So that when you got back into the office and picked up a phone, you knew who you were talking to. When they say, 'I can't pay that much because my hall holds only 300 people,' you could say, politely, 'you mean it holds *1,300* people. And if you want this man you need to pay him the price.'"

The man who managed Elvis Presley, Colonel Tom Parker, was a master of ballyhoo who triumphantly applied his circus background to the higher realms of show business. Ben Bart was the black man's Colonel Tom. He had a knack for getting free press and had absorbed into his bones the credo that there was no such thing as bad publicity. One day in 1947, calls flooded the New York police and newspapers; hundreds of reports of flying saucers were coming in, all of them pegging the source as a bridge near Washington Heights. Squad cars were sent to the scene, where police found four members of the vocal group the Ravens, a recent addition to Bart's roster, hurling copies of their latest release, "Old Man River," into the Harlem River. "They and their press agent"–Bart–"almost landed in jail, via the nut house," reported the *Pittsburgh Courier*.

By the time he signed Brown in 1956, Bart was a formidable figure whom singer Etta James described as "an older white guy who, with a big .45 on his hip, would stomp through Harlem like he wasn't scared of anybody. Ben was a legend among agents and managers, Jewish to the bone." Rhythm and blues was crossing over to white audiences, and promoters were booking package tours of artists, a practice some say he invented in the late '40s. He brought Brown to the North for appearances in December 1956, and had stuck with him through the hungry years after "Please, Please, Please." Building on what Brantley had already taught Brown, Bart gave him a graduate course in reading, and writing, contracts.

What Bart did for his artists was ultimately simple: He kept them on the road, and he made sure they got paid. "He was James's *man*," said Steve Alaimo, a performer and producer. Over time Bart cut back on his other acts and stayed out with Brown. "He was big, gruff–I don't know how honest he was, but he was a guy that James respected highly." The records kept your name out there, they might fill a hall, but you didn't see real money from them. Bart got Brown the money, big boxes of it that Brown carried with him on the road. "It was all about Ben Bart filling the boxes with cash," said Alaimo. "That's how he made a living."

If Brown was in a diner getting loud, Bart was the only guy who could draw the reins in and calm him down. His "Now Jimmie . . ." would be enough to quiet the singer. Introducing himself to others as Brown's father, Bart kept him out of trouble, recognizing what a roughneck he could be.

Bart would have been involved when Brown signed a new five-year deal with Nathan on July 1, 1960, a contract that got Brown off the Federal subsidiary and put him at the top of King Records' roster. King was something Brown and Bart had in common. Nathan had a pit bull lawyer named Jack Pearl, and Pearl just happened to be married to Bart's sister. Along with his legal work for King, Pearl had helped run an independent label, Hub Records, with Bart in the late 1940s. Pearl had his own music publishing company, and did legal work for Universal Attractions as well as King. By the time Brown was making good money for them both, Bart owned a houseboat in Miami, where both he and Nathan spent a chunk of every year. In Miami, Bart was "a real racetrack junkie," remembers Henry Stone, who frequented Gulfstream Park and Hialeah Park Race Track with Bart.

Twice in about a decade Bart had circulated the rumor that bandleader Tiny Bradshaw was dead, the better to get press that in fact Bradshaw was still alive, and coming to a town near you. That proven technique was revived for Brown. "Jimmie is dying!" was the cry *Jet* reported was shouted at Philadelphia's Uptown Theater, where Brown supposedly passed out onstage. He wasn't dying; the story said he was just fatigued and would be back on the road by the time you read this.

The hits flowed: "Bewildered," "I Don't Mind," and "Baby, You're Right" all getting significant airplay in 1961. Success bred publicity; you could plant an item about anything, or almost nothing, with a hit. After a love-struck fan attacked singer Jackie Wilson backstage, the black press reported Brown was picking up extra security to protect him from "another Jackie Wilson incident."

Brown made a major step forward on October 19, 1961, when he got his first national TV exposure, appearing on *American Bandstand*. Airing five times a week from four to five P.M., *Bandstand* had a national teenage audience and offered the possibility of connecting with a white audience. The show introduced viewers to new artists, new dance steps, and its commercials offered teens grooming tips. *Bandstand* was a step-by-step tutorial in how to be cool, and the featured artist was sure to be a topic of conversation the next day in school. In that way, this was a major step forward for Brown. He was taking the music to his largest audience yet, but the moment was tightly governed. *Bandstand* barely had black dancers on camera, and black singers weren't allowed to move the way they did onstage. Given *Bandstand*'s strict policy of lip-synching, Brown wasn't really performing, anyway.

When he looked out at the camera and through the TV screen, what did Brown see? A white audience still beyond his reach. His records were played on pop radio, but few Northern whites had seen his show. In the South, when whites were in the audience, it was at segregated performances. Most of the time, he was still playing for black crowds on a circuit where he felt most at home, yet wanted to transcend. Looking across the divide between his group and the millions of Clearasil kids, this self-confident performer saw an audience he *knew* he could reach, if only he could make his case directly rather than ventriloquizing his latest song. They needed to see the show.

Around this time, Brown was in a Miami studio, watching white singer Steve Alaimo cut a record. The two had known each other for a few years. "He said, 'Steve, I love you like a brother. But I hate you, because you are white. Because you can do the things I can't do. I can't love you because you are white and I'm black.'" The white citizens of Birmingham were still on his tail. As fast as he was going, whatever he did, when they looked at him he was still a black man. He made a gift of anger to his friend.

In early 1961, the band had just played in the Bahamas, and was hanging out in Miami when they heard a familiar song on the radio. It was "Night Train," the instrumental J. C. Davis brought to the group and made into a showstopper. Lots of groups played this staple in the 1950s, and it was probably recorded as an afterthought to fill out the end of a session. Davis said he was told the song would be released under his name. When Davis found it was coming out as a James Brown record, he went berserk. To Davis, it was a repeat of his "(Do the) Mashed Potatoes" experience, where he'd arranged and refined a song only to see it come out under somebody else's name. This time he got his brother, and his brother's gun, and confronted Brown in Tampa. After that, Davis was gone from the group.

Davis went on to play with Etta James and record at Chess Records. Soon after he left, drummer Nat Kendrick also was gone. Brown struggled while he looked for a new band director, eventually picking up St. Clair Pinckney, a tenor saxophonist from Augusta that he knew from Floyd School.

It was the kind of untidiness that Brown felt comfortable with. When they went back to California in the summer of 1962, an event occurred that put Birmingham in vivid relief. They were booked into the 5-4 Ballroom in Los Angeles, one of the key venues along black L.A.'s Central Avenue corridor.

On the same April night that the Famous Flames opened their stand at the 5-4 Ballroom, just a few blocks away, the Los Angeles Police had invaded a Nation of Islam mosque and, after a confrontation, killed one member and wounded six others, all unarmed. Brown seems to have encountered the scene, because two decades later he evoked the experience out of the blue in an interview. "They killed nine Muslims," he said, misremembering the number. "About 50 feet from the 5-4 Ballroom, and they weren't bothering nobody but were lying there dead. I knew then that we must be counted. . . ."

"I knew then that we must be counted": It was something he wouldn't have said a mere year before.

Chapter Eight

STAR TIME

The Apollo Theater was worth fighting for. The first time Brown appeared at the Apollo, April 24, 1959, he argued with owner Frank Schiffman that he and not Little Willie John should be at the top of the bill. The second time he played there, at the end of 1959, Brown refused to go on stage if Reuben Phillips's orchestra played behind him. Using the house band, he knew, would blend him into the overall Apollo experience, the opposite of what he wanted—to stand out from everybody else. The Apollo was where he deserved to be, he understood, needing now to make others understand.

His Apollo debut had been chaotic, rudderless, and it was hard to tell who was in charge. Step by step in repeated visits over the next two years, Brown began to put borders around the anarchy. Over this time a torrent of amusements (singing, dancing, musicians, comedy) was mastered and brought into the mix, chicken shack by chicken shack. Ben Bart probably knew as much about black vaudeville as any Caucasian in the country, and he worked with Brown to tailor tradition for young, more sophisticated audiences. Brown's show was rooted in the old black theatrical circuit, but he streamlined it, took out all the dead spots, and massaged the set pieces and oddball novelties into a flowing, continuous expression of rhythm. The Apollo Theater was the place where all the traditions of black vaudeville came to rest, and with Bart's guidance he would take some of the tradition's anachronistic icons—the rubber-faced clown Pigmeat Markham, the voluminous blues belter TV Mama—on the road with him. He *liked* them. To take his new show to the Apollo was to bring something home.

But if the Apollo was a cradle of tradition, it was equally a destroyer of the past, its pitiless audiences annihilating legacy and lore, putting a flame to anything that hinted of cliché. You had to earn their admiration; you could not sit back and wait for it to roll to you. When Brown first played there, he did the old shtick of tossing his cufflinks and tie into the crowd. Who the hell was this cat? The Apollo crowd threw them *back*.

In 1961, he was a major act, no longer an up-and-comer. At twenty-eight, he had already come, it would seem, taking his place on a shelf just below the elite who had crossed over, like Sam Cooke and Jackie Wilson. They had an urbane presence that made them nationwide. What Brown had, most of all, was an unparalleled work ethic. He was billed as "the hardest working man in show business," playing three hundred-plus shows a year, several performances a night, and he had an understanding of what fans responded to that few could match. Not just an act, now he was a show.

The Apollo was the pinnacle of one staircase, the black circuit Brown ruled. From there, the only place he could go was back to the Apollo, or to somehow cross over. Five months after his last appearance, in the fall of 1962, Brown was coming back. And this time, he wanted to record the show, to get it in front of more people than had experienced it before. Hits were hard to count on, especially when your label didn't shell out for publicity and might let your best work die on the shelf. He knew what his show did to live audiences. If he could get it before new listeners, and make a hit of *that*, well suddenly the Apollo would be a stepping stone, not a terminus.

When he told Nathan he wanted King to record him live, Nathan declined at the top of his lungs. His objections were that live albums had rarely been tried (other than a pair of Ray Charles recordings) and had no record of success. Nathan said no hit single would come from a live recording, not when all the songs were already available, and he declared that he wasn't that interested in albums, anyway. *That* much Brown already knew, as did anybody recording with King. To Nathan albums were an afterthought, a chance to repackage tunes you'd already released as singles. Nathan lived or died with hit singles.

"Didn't nobody believe in us—none of the company executives believed in us," said Byrd. "But see, we were out there. We saw the response as we run our show down." Brown took the money they had saved for an upcoming Southern swing ($5,700) and gambled it on one night. Usually Brown fined his band five or ten dollars for making a mistake, but this time, he put out the word that if you flubbed a note at the Apollo, it would be fifty to a hundred.

By now, he and Syd had a comfortably contentious relationship. Brown would visit Nathan's house to talk business, slipping a mezuzah around his neck in hopes of charming the man into submission, while Syd sat there in his underwear, ready for war. They needed each other. Radio wasn't playing as much of King's raw adult R&B as they used to, and while rock and roll was on the rise, King was painfully lacking in acts that appealed to *American Bandstand* viewers. Syd needed his hitmakers. For Brown, Nathan was an obstacle worth working around, because he provided things Brown wanted: the chance to make the singles that kept him on the road, and money, sometimes from the hits, and sometimes from loans from the boss. Maybe just as importantly, Syd gave Brown a father figure to oppose.

Steve Halper, Nathan's nephew, saw the two argue many times about money. As Syd would point out, he always had James under contract, and one of the terms of their contract was that the contract didn't end as long as Brown owed Nathan money. Brown always owed Nathan twenty-five or thirty thousand dollars.

Chuck Seitz was the lead engineer at King in the early '60s. "I remember James came in one day and he was evidently up against it, needed money. He wanted Syd to give him five thousand dollars," recalled Seitz. "Syd said, 'I'll give you five thousand dollars if you'll sign with me five more years.' And James must have been up against it so he signed for five more years. And in that five-year period, the Apollo thing came around."

For the past year, Brown's shows had featured Yvonne Fair, a singer he first heard with girl group the Chantels. In Brown's show she would come out and sing a few songs with the band, make the audience feel like they were really getting an abundance. A small item in *Jet* magazine in July hinted that Brown was working on something big. "People are talking about . . . James Brown's 'secret' project, which is his writing a full-length rhythm and blues musical production, starring himself and pretty Yvonne Fair, and with plans for presenting it in several of the larger cities next spring." That "full-length rhythm and blues musical" is what Brown unveiled, as the tape rolled, at the Apollo in October 1962. The weeklong stand, in which the group played five shows each day, was to upend rhythm and blues music.

So now ladies and gentlemen it is star time. Are you ready for star time?

When Fats Gonder came to the microphone to get the show rolling, the band had already been playing a while. The ushers stood ready, the crowd was greased.

Thank you and thank you very kindly. It is indeed a great pleasure to present for you at this particular time, nationally and internationally known as the hardest working man in show business, the man who sang "I'll Go Crazy"—

Gonder's palaver radiates from his sternum, it's down-home ballyhoo. The band hits a brassy chord, the crowd goes wild.

"Try Me"!

"You've Got the Power"!

Every line he shouts is accompanied by a blaring chord and then silence. It's like someone is dangling a jewel before you, then snatching it away, over and over.

"Think!"

"If You Want Me"!

"I Don't Mind"!

"BeWILdered"!

"Million-dollar seller 'Lost Someone'!"

"The very latest release, 'Night Train'!"

"Let's everybody 'Shout and Shimmy'!"

"Mister Dynamite, the amazing Mister 'Please, Please, Please' himself, the star of the show, James Brown and the Famous Flames"—

Suddenly the horns count off the beat—wah-wah-wah-wah—and Les Buie's gutbucket guitar yanks us off the curb we've been parked on and into traffic.

Brown: "You know I feel all right." Pause. "I feel all right children, I feel allll riiiiiiight!" He is screaming with a vibrato. That's not easy. The first four songs explore the distance from "don't go" to "please come back."

"I'll Go Crazy": An order—if you leave I will go insane.

"Try Me": A plea—I am so in need.

"Think": A prescription—are you insane? I am the solution to your problems.

"I Don't Mind": The truth—you're gonna miss me when I'm gone.

The first four songs establish a mood. Memories of relationships, or maybe just *that one*, lie shattered into a hundred fragments—a broken mirror across the floor, the singer seeing his solitude wherever he looks. And before his reflection, he poses.

Don't he look good?

The set piece is "Lost Someone," a ballad whose chords rise like a half-filled balloon, they fall almost to the ground, lift a little higher, fall again . . . It is a courtship, with his audience, conducted entirely in screams. "I'll looove you tomorrow," he screams, putting a shimmy on the words. It is an amazing thing to hear a scream vibrate like that, and it shows the control Brown has over a technique most often used to signify a loss of control.

The scream was a transfer from the black church; for the previous one hundred years, where else in public could a black man yell like he could at church? Where else would he not have been whipped, or institutionalized, or shoved to the margins for making the sounds that Brown is luxuriating in making right now at the Apollo? It is a scream activated by the church but not of it, a scream that is an agent of change.

The scream: It is an ugly sound, always has been. Brown was throwing ugly all over the Apollo, and by setting it to the rising and falling spiral of "Lost Someone," and by stretching it across ten minutes, he makes the song a journey in which screams mark our progress. He builds a universe of screams, and it's not his alone: "I'm not singing a song for myself, now/I'm singing it for you, too!" It is an ugliness that he throws out to the crowd and that he wants thrown back. "When I sing that little part that might sting you in your heart, I want to hear you scream," he sings, as he and the audience exchange *oowwws* that are at the same time calm and shattering. This was evidence of the soul, in the old context, and evidence of soul music in the present one, feeling its force at the Apollo: a soul that was not something for poor folks or Southern folks but for anyone in pain, a soul to acknowledge and find room for in your life. At this moment the Apollo Theater was like a jukebox, an Ark, engulfing the country in its light.

Brown was steeped in gospel; he just didn't go to church much. As a boy he studied preachers and aspired to be like them; he just didn't want to be them. The fine line in talking about Brown and gospel is that he was of the music, but not quite of the faith. In his own words, he did not regularly attend services, and when he did, he went to various churches, none winning his affiliation. More than Tom Dorsey or Ray Charles, or anyone but Aretha Franklin, Brown was a musician who inserted the sound and feeling of black faith into the popular arena, showing us that there is no such thing as a simple churchgoing man. He heard gospel and God the way he heard, say, Louis Jordan or Billy Wright, or for that matter, the way he learned about knife fighting and dice–they were vital aspects of life lived on the streets.

Men of the cloth–most of all Reverend Martin Luther King Jr., but many more who stood behind him–were showing the claims black church could make on all of American society. Black artists of the time were doing the same thing. You could identify it most easily in the singers, which is why Brown and Franklin and so many more behind them were rightfully seen to be bringing gospel into the marketplace–even white folks who had never been inside a black church could not avoid the obvious truth of this. They were called "soul" singers. The vocalists got the attention, but in fact a whole performance style was flowing from the pulpit to the Apollo in sanctified rhythms that the best drummers played, in the body moves that signified the presence of greater forces, in the belief that artifice must be lost and that the way ahead was lighted by a direct truth that came from within but did not originate there.

"How do you define soul, James?" talk show host David Frost asked his guest.

Brown: "The truth."

Frost: "The truth?"

Brown: "The truth. The down-to-earth truth. It's from the ghetto, it's a definition of hard knocks, it's a way of explaining yourself. When *other* people don't understand what you're saying, you try to get it across in a song. It's a kind of a frightful thing to avail, so you had to go through a song. Soul explains that, it explains the hard knocks, it explains everyday life, telling it like it is. The truth."

Everybody in exquisite congress, attuned to the moment. Many a writer looking back on the age of soul music would celebrate it as a great expression of blacks and whites working together, a music that would not have lived without the two races overcoming American history to create in tandem. But across this song, and across this landscape, all the faces on stage and virtually all those in the audience are black. This isn't a historic moment for liberalism, but a historic one for African Americanism.

Then, somewhere in the middle of "Lost Someone," bassist Hubert Perry lost his footing and started drifting away from the chords of the song, wandering off. He was not going to slip *that* past the boss. Brown weighed in as the song rolled on, so sweetly the audience could hardly have known what he was talking about; like Adam Clayton Powell Jr., ordering iced tea in the middle of a sermon, he said, "You know we all make mistakes sometimes/And the only way we can correct our mistakes/We got to try one more time." (That and a fine after the show should square the ledger.)

In ways great and fractional, "Lost Someone" is about everybody—the band, Brown, and the audience—in communion with one another, feeling totally open for a moment, for as long as they could forget the clock.

Eventually they played their latest hit, "Night Train," completely unlike the single, released in March 1962. On record it rumbles, you can hear the milk train moving through the night. At the Apollo, drummer Clayton Fillyau's foot kicks a hole in the song, his bass drum reorganizing the beat, horns chitter-chattering around his foot. There's nothing late-night tired about it now, this song roars, "New York City take me home."

In a band fronted by a loud, charismatic singer, it was easy to fade in the background. Indeed, becoming one with the wallpaper was a good way to survive in this band. One of the most important, least-known instrumentalists, and quite possibly the most valuable player of *Live at the Apollo*, was Lewis Hamlin, a trumpet man and the group's musical director. Nobody had as much influence on the sound at this defining moment. "Lewis is the forgotten man in setting the musical course for the band," said Brown's longtime saxophonist St. Clair Pinckney.

Hamlin was raised in Macon's Tindall Heights housing projects (Otis Redding also lived there). Already improvising on the trumpet as a teenager, he took a slot in the jump band led by piano player Gladys Williams. She remains an unsung hero in her own hometown; Otis Redding, Little Richard, and many more passed through her band.

After bandleader J. C. Davis left, Brown was back in Macon, assembling a new group. According to Reppard Stone, who grew up with Hamlin, Brown asked Hamlin to join him as a horn player, and, knowing Hamlin had extensive contacts on the Macon scene, he also asked his help in assembling the new group.

Brown was building more dance into his show, and doing it in the moment; it meant the band had to keep vamping, or had to change the tempo, or follow him in whatever direction he was suddenly taking things. The band of the early 1960s was filling up with musicians able to turn on a heartbeat and thrive in an improvisational moment–a different, more sophisticated cast compared to J. C. Davis's rabble-rousers. Brown did not read music, he could not always talk music to his musicians, but he *knew* music. He quickly grasped the skills new instrumentalists brought to the show. He reacted to them, and used them to challenge himself.

Hamlin was perhaps the first to understand how Brown was weaving songs into a flow that he intended to shape, and reshape, according to his reading of the crowd. As his music director, Hamlin watched Brown's movements, and instructed the band to follow what he was doing. "Lewis, in time, grew to understand his body language," said Stone. "While James was singing, let's say he would do three steps and then stop. Lewis would point out to the other musicians, when he stopped, *you* got to stop, and let him sing his *baby-baby-baby*, and then don't come back in until he says *huh*!

They never wrote anything down, they just learned from each other."

Hamlin was an interpreter fluent in James Brown. "He was a communicator. He could communicate with musicians when James couldn't. James didn't know how to *greet* them. James could tell them something and it would sound like a criticism. Lewis could do it and they'd go, *yeah*, and get right on board."

The Apollo show was one of the first times drummer Clayton Fillyau had recorded with the band. (He is the main drummer on the recording, if not the only one; it's possible a second drummer is also heard on the recording.) A place of combustion like the Apollo was perfect for him. "He was the kind of guy who just liked that atmosphere—if it was jamming and hot in there and you had some good musicians in there, oh, get out of his way. 'Cause he wanted to grab some sticks and get up on stage," said his son, Clayton Fillyau Jr. Fillyau *worked*.

A rugged baller who Brown called Biggun, Fillyau was known to pack a gun under his jacket, which, when things got rockin', sometimes was known to fall out on the stage. Which was not the worst thing that could happen on the chitlin circuit, where letting the guys with guns in the audience know that the drummer was packing, too, could squelch all sorts of stuff.

The family name was French Creole, and he had family in New Orleans, but Fillyau grew up in Tampa, Florida. We don't know a huge amount about him. He died in 2001. Fillyau told Jim Payne, the only person to interview him, that the most important rhythmic lesson of his life was taught by the drummer in Huey "Piano" Smith's band The Clowns. This protean New Orleans block party of a group was traveling with Silas Green From New Orleans's black minstrel show through Jacksonville in the late 1950s. Fillyau happened to be in Jacksonville, and he watched them play on the street there, then caught up with the drummer in his hotel room. "Back then musicians were always in everybody's room playing," said Fill-yau. They started jamming, and the older man, probably Charles "Hungry" Williams, showed him a little lesson in New Orleans drumming, taking him from standard stiff beat-keeping to secrets of the second line. Then he bore down, as if to say it all comes down to this, and told Fillyau, "Now use your imagination. Only thing you got to remember is, 'Where is one?' I don't care where you put it on those drums." Meaning you can hit it on the snare, bass, or cymbal. "Remember where one is and you'll never lose time."

Fillyau joined Brown in 1961, and when he met his new band-mates in Cheyenne, Wyoming, he approached bassist Hubert Perry and declared straight-up, "your days of leanin' on the drummer are over with. You're gonna have to *play*. I'm not carrying no straight time." What he meant—besides HI MY NAME IS CLAYTON—was to convey an ultimatum, a very old one, that the drums had first conveyed to the rest of the musicians in New Orleans parade bands decades before: Don't expect us to hand you the beat on a paper plate, everybody's got to internalize it—you must know where the one is—and everybody's gotta have something to say about the beat. We're rough equals locked in a conversation here, and we better be listening to each other or we'll both be speaking gibberish.

Brown already had one New Orleans drummer play behind him, on those road trips when Charles Connor and the Upsetters backed him up. Now, again, the New Orleans tradition was coming into his music through Clayton Fillyau.

Every time Brown was ready to change the sound and direction of his band, he changed his drummer. Coming into the band in 1961 after Kendrick left, Fillyau played his first show the way Kendrick had played, and Brown could not have been less happy. He called out the group with one of his favorite punishments—a rehearsal immediately after a grueling performance. As they prac-ticed, he asked Fillyau what he thought he was doing. "If I'da wanted Nat Kendrick," he barked, "I'da kept Nat Kendrick." After that, they were cool.

Within a few years, Fillyau wasn't playing the drums for Brown. He was driving the bus. It seems somehow insufficient as an explanation, but the truth is, Fillyau *preferred* driving the bus. And Brown loved having him around; he just couldn't stand having him around. Fillyau did not accept the system of fines Brown laid on the band and would tell the boss to shove it. According to his son, like others in the band, "He was abused by James. But my father would be the one to stand up and say, 'Look here, oh you fixing to give me that money.' See my father has the record for being fired the most."

While he still drove the rhythm section, Fillyau recorded one of the less-known great records of Brown's career, the 1962 B-side "I've Got Money." It's a song whose time has yet to arrive, and it's barely a song. It's like a blueprint of some uncanny object. It's an assemblage of parts: a scimitar guitar chord coming down on the One, a show band horn chorus quoting Judy Garland's "The Trolley Song," and his stampeding drums. The parts are arranged in a line, one beside the next—an incomprehensible rebus. Some folks call this the first funk record, or Brown's first funk track; others say this was the first time a Brown song emphasized the One. It's a fool's argument, because there really isn't anything like a first funk song, anymore than there is one person who invented fried ice cream or the blues. And you don't even need to be on the One to be funky. It should be enough to say, Clayton Fillyau brought the funk.

In the months after recording *Live at the Apollo*, Brown made several important decisions that would affect the show over the next few years. He recorded "Prisoner of Love" in December, with a ten-piece string section and a nine-member choir. The song was a crooner's delight from the Depression, and a set piece at the Avons' tea parties in Toccoa, here delivered as a saloon-singer's lament. "Prisoner of Love" became Brown's first single to enter the pop charts top twenty, peaking at eighteen. He embraced ballads and featured them live even when it was the rhythm stuff that was most powerfully connecting with whites. Ballads moved *him*.

Right after the Apollo dates, singer Yvonne Fair left. She was pregnant with her and Brown's child. Her spot in the show was filled by a young beauty who had turned Brown's head at the Tan Playhouse in Philadelphia. Her name was Tammy Montgomery, and she had a voice every bit as sweet as her looks. Montgomery recorded songs for a label Brown had started, Try Me. They also began dating.

Meanwhile, there was more work to be done on the live album. Nathan remained convinced it was a waste, and when Brown sent the tape to King, nothing he heard changed his mind. Chuck Seitz, chief recording engineer at King, handled the project. "All I know is the tape came in to us . . . and we listened to the damn thing. We listened all the way through and I thought it was terrible." For one thing, you couldn't always tell it was *live*. The trouble was the basic recording approach, which only intermittently picked up the crowd's reaction. If this was going to be a document of a concert, pandemonium had to be reinjected. Seitz went to a sock hop in Cincinnati and recorded throngs of avid white teens enjoying themselves, and then inserted them into the Apollo.

Another problem was editing the tape for the ear. At the Apollo, Brown danced for minutes while the band vamped; his "Please" reaches a theatrical peak that needed to be seen. Such moments would be lost on disc and required careful pruning. When Seitz finished, Nathan still did not like it. King did not have a publicity department, and if ever a record needed special attention to get it played that first time, it was this one. Nathan toyed with the idea of burying it on the DeLuxe subsidiary, and taking a tax write-off on a record he hadn't even funded. Meanwhile Brown was circulating advance copies to key disc jockeys and pressing his case.

Jerry Blavat was a top jock in Philadelphia. Early in 1963, he was working a sock hop in Atlantic City when he saw Brown at the Atlantic City Coliseum. "I went to see James backstage, and he was really down," recalled Blavat. "He told me, 'You have gotta hear this new thing, man. That fucking Syd Nathan, he don't want to release this, he don't have a fucking ear! I'm gonna release it myself.'" He gave Blavat a copy. "I took it home and put it on my own turntable. It was the most exciting live album; this was raw, and it captured what he was onstage, man. Forget it! I busted that fucking thing wide open, just played the hell out of it. The whole fucking thing, because you couldn't really just play one song the way it was put together."

Brown mailed a copy to Allyn Lee in Montgomery. "It hadn't hit the streets yet. I was on the air on Sunday and I played it for the first time," said Lee. "I played it all the way through, and that sort of sealed my fate in Montgomery. A million phone calls came in—see, they didn't really know James Brown in Montgomery; they knew 'Please,' but they had never heard him in *that* form. Now they did."

Nathan was hearing from broadcasters who were asking him when the LP was going to be released. Eventually, he blinked and issued *Live at the Apollo* in May 1963.

Suddenly Brown had the biggest record on the R&B charts, so staggeringly new it scarcely bore any connection to the music *called* rhythm and blues. Here was the new soul music. And, suddenly again, he comes out with a pop record that charges up the white charts. With "Prisoner of Love" pointing the way, *Live at the Apollo* soon crossed over to the pop side that summer, where it spent sixty-six weeks, reaching number two. It certainly would have gone platinum, except that Nathan didn't like to pay the annual fee to the professional organization that certified record sales.

For Brown personally, the moment had special meaning. After you scored at the Apollo you had hit the tar paper ceiling of the chitlin circuit, and there was no venue left—in this league—to pursue. Now, thanks to Bart's tutelage, to his Northern exposure, and to *Live*, a new field stretched before him. He viewed himself in an unaccustomed light. "I started seeing different things and my brain started to intercept new ideas," he said. "I became a big city thinker."

Chapter Nine

KEEP ON FIGHTING

W hen Brown wasn't out on the highway, chances are he was back home in Macon. And when he was in Macon, chances are Brown was shooting up the Club 15.

A squat, gray concrete box on the outskirts of town, Club 15 looked like it could take the abuse. For years, Brown had been living with his loyal but expensive "wife," Dessie Brown, but her money-wasting ways knew no bounds and eventually James and Dessie parted. One night, James was with his latest girlfriend at the Club 15 when who should come in but Dessie and her new beau. The boyfriend confronted Brown, saying he was a dog for ditching a woman who had stuck with him when he was broke, and that he should apologize to his ex for showing off his new lady friend in public.

"Leave me alone," James commanded, "and if you come back, come back shooting."

"I don't have to go away in that case," said the gentleman, drawing down on Brown. Not unarmed, the singer pulled out *his* iron, and suddenly bullets were ricocheting around the club.

In the emergency room, a witness remembered the scene as nothin' but, "Who shot you?" "James Brown."

"Who shot *you*?" "James Brown."

"And who shot you?" "James Brown."

One person came in who was stabbed. "Who cut you?" "James Brown." Still on parole, Brown relied on Clint Brantley and a few thousand dollars to make the situation disappear.

Ex-girlfriends were a sensitive issue. He and soul singer Joe Tex had a shared manager in Ben Bart, and they had a woman in common, too. Her name was Bea Ford, and she was Tex's wife in the late '50s, until she began singing in Brown's show and dating him.

Tex was performing in Raleigh, North Carolina, when he got a hysterical call from Ford. Brown had been hitting her, and she wanted Tex to come down and rescue her. Tex blew off a gig to arrive and tell Brown, "You don't love her and you are going to beat her to death. I'll take her back now if you'll let her go." Brown told an assistant to go get Ford's clothes and things, all the stuff he'd bought for her, and return them to him. She left that night.

In 1963, Brown and Tex were on a bill together in Macon. It was just after *Live at the Apollo* had come out, and Brown was playing a triumphant homecoming date at the City Auditorium. Tex was a bit of a goofball and a good mimic; he'd seen Brown wearing a cape as part of his big nightly finale. So during his opening set, Tex fell down on one knee, à la Brown, and donned a ragged, dirty cape, which he proceeded to get tangled up in and roll around the stage, all the while mocking the headliner: "Please, please, please get me out of this cape!"

This aggression will not stand, Brown declared. He went looking for Tex after the show and found him at the Club 15. Johnny Jenkins and the Pinetoppers were on the stage with their ace singer, Otis Redding. In the crowd was a young white soul fanatic named Wayne Cochran. Brown brought out several shotguns and started firing. Somebody fired back. Soon Tex charged out of the club and ducked behind some shrubs. "James ran outside, and I saw his tour bus pull out of the parking lot with him behind the wheel," recalled Cochran.

"Seven people got shot," said Jenkins. "They were reloading

and coming back in. Me and Otis, we were hiding behind a piano. A guy went around later, and I think he gave each one of the injured one hundred dollars apiece not to carry it no further. And that just quieted it down."

The two had started out as friends, helping and learning from each other. It was common knowledge that Brown carefully studied his peer's stagecraft, refining some of Tex's dance moves and his tricks with the microphone: Tex would push over the stand, do a split to the floor, and then jump up just as the stand bounced upright again. The first time Brown attempted it, he didn't know the secret—a specially made mic stand with a rounded bottom that rocked dependably. Brown almost knocked out his teeth when the microphone hit him in the mouth.

Now, they were enemies. And whether it was because by 1963 his parole was done and he could leave Georgia, or because of events like the shootout at the Club 15, *whatever*: It was time to go. Brown moved to New York, buying a house in St. Albans, Queens, the famous neighborhood that many elite African American entertainers called home. Count Basie lived there, and so did Jackie Robinson. Trumpeter Cootie Williams had once lived in Brown's new house. "James Brown, who is grossing more than a half million this year, bought a 12 room St. Albans home and called in a crew of decorators to perform $65,000 worth of changes in it as he departed on a 21-city concert tour through the US," *Jet* reported. The house on Linden Avenue had castle-like turrets, a guardhouse, and a moat. "It was beautiful," said one of his girlfriends, Betty Jean Newsome. "To get to his house you had to walk over a little bridge. It was a nice house—in the bedroom you had to step up steps to get into his bed because he had it elevated off the floor."

Establishing that he belonged in New York City, Brown entertained friends at his new home and showed it off to the press. In the *New York Herald Tribune*, writer Doon Arbus described the scene. One walked in and entered a cavernous den decorated in black leatherette, a huge bar at one end. The room was sparsely decorated, save for an abundance of pictures of Brown that festooned the walls and shelves around the bar.

Shoes off, house slippers on to make the journey upstairs, passing a trio of large white B's decorating the black upholstered walls. The plastic-covered rug, the slippers, everything, Arbus described, created the impression that this was a place to be seen, not inhabited. "It is as if the whole house were being preserved against the hazards of being lived in, as if it were being prepared for a great future as a museum."

Underground was where it came alive. "It had a beautiful large basement that we used to go down and have our drinks in," said Bobby Roach. "They used to keep white lightning from Toccoa down there. We'd mix in this grape drink called Delaware Punch, that was his drink. Tasted good with that white lightning."

Aboveground he declared who he was: a man of riches who had arrived. Below the surface, if you got there, he was still a Southerner, sipping on Delaware Punch.

The actor Marlon Brando was raised by two alcoholic parents; his father was a mean drunk who beat his mother on many occasions. In a memoir, *Songs My Mother Taught Me*, the actor described how the neglect and abuse he felt as a child fed the emotional intensity of his work.

"When you are a child who is unwanted or unwelcome, and the essence of what you are seems to be unacceptable, you look for an identity that will be acceptable," Brando wrote. "You make a habit of studying people, finding out the way they talk, the answers that they give and their points of view; then, in a form of self-defense, you reflect what's on their faces and how they act because most people like to see reflections of themselves."

Nobody studied the reactions of people around him with more hunger and intelligence than James Brown. He observed the faces in the seats, made instant decisions on how to structure a performance from what he saw. As an aide put it, even when he was onstage singing "please, please, please" with his eyes closed and tears streaming down his cheeks, even *then* Brown was watching everything.

"If you want something from an audience, you give blood to their fantasies," Brando said. "It's the ultimate hustle." Brown wanted plenty from his audience, and he set about figuring how to feed their fever. In the wake of *Live at the Apollo*'s success, he devoted himself to building a bigger, cross-racial audience, methodically making personal choices based on the effect they had on his audience. The clothes and look that had signified flash on the chitlin circuit would get an overhaul. Brown favored cheap suits in gaudy colors, wide shoes, and stretched his money to buy as many things as he could afford. As he played to urban, Northern audiences and identified what worked and what didn't, he began buying suits that complemented his short boxer's build, going for a look that drew attention up high, to his collar and tie and face. He began favoring quality over quantity. He wasn't going to ask associates for advice or help, but when he saw something he liked, he took it. One day he saw his old friend Allyn Lee wearing a new green jacket, and he started asking Lee where he got it and suggesting he take it back, throw it away, the thing was no damn good. Next time Lee ran into Brown, he was wearing the very same jacket.

If he wanted folks to keep their attention tight on him, more changes were necessary. Avid fans might have noticed how little the singer smiled, the reason being he had a gap in his front teeth that all but proclaimed Georgialina. His hair, too, was a problem. He was devoted to a look that had terraced waves and curls on top, a version of the popular "Tony Curtis" style, but a few songs in, when he started sweating, everything drooped, and he looked stringy, soggy.

Together these formed a theme to his life, a subject he returned to throughout his career. "Hair and teeth," he rasped, "a man got those two things he got it all." It sounds so simple, but in African American history, the simplest seeming subjects are often the most elaborate. Booker T. Washington was a fanatic on the subject of the toothbrush. Good grooming was how you first sold yourself to the world, and bad teeth, he felt, reflected lack of self-respect. Richard Carroll was a Barnwell-born black reverend who is often called the Booker T. Washington of South Carolina. Carroll went deep on the subject, declaring, "There is a close relation between bad teeth and dyspepsia, between dyspepsia and religious temperament, and between religious temperament and true spirituality of life." Without good teeth, a man had nothing.

Knowing how tough he could look, and how conventionally un-handsome, Brown set about to invert the effect. In 1961, Brown and assistant Frank McRae stopped on a Los Angeles trip long enough to visit the leading black dentist in Southern California, and have the gap fixed and serious dental work done. For the rest of his life, Brown saw good teeth as a secret of his success. "My mouth," he proclaimed, "is probably the best attribute for me that I've ever had in my business, because with this I can smile."

Soon after the two met in 1961, McRae became something like Brown's personal shopper and all-around fashion consultant. The dapper McRae was a "gentleman's gentleman" who worked in a barbershop behind the Howard Theater in Washington, D.C. McRae saw Brown slide into his chair one day and was so bold as to suggest he could do something about that hair. Bluntly laying out how Brown had a hard face, McRae said that a bouffant style with some croquignole curls would significantly soften his aspect. Soon McRae was on the road with Brown, even sitting on the stage with the band, to be ready when he was needed. From his chair by the horns, said McRae, "I was watching his hair. I loved seeing how it shined in the light, and how people would be screaming."

Expoobident, he proclaimed: hipster lingo that meant tight, neat, *glorious.* McRae made Brown's hair expoobident, and the boss was appreciative. From the early '60s on, Brown would have his hair done in the morning, again before a show, and then again after. And the singer loved to conduct interviews while his hair was being done. Before he left his dressing room and took the stage, Brown would stare in the mirror, examine the man before him. If the hair was right, *he* was right. "James Brown loved his hair better than he loved his women," said McRae.

Further refinements followed. An executive order went out: He was to be called "Mr. Brown," and he addressed others as "Mister" or "Miss." It was a courtly decorum, and a pointed inversion of the disrespectful way white Southerners had always addressed blacks. By making it a rule everyone was expected to follow, he put one straightaway onto his turf.

There were rules at home and rules on the road. The schedule was crushing, and his many rules were meant to make it possible to play five shows a day, five days a week. But there was also an element of imperiousness to it, which came out in the open over time. An element of whimsy, too; some rules might be eccentric, but he was the boss and you were not.

Prison had ordered his life, and he was passing on his need for order to those around him. No tuning up onstage, no getting your chops ready–one arrived set to play. You wore a suit and tie on the bus and getting off it; women wore high heels, stockings, and a dress. Your uniform had better be clean. When Brown spun around two, three times, chances are he was inspecting the troops. When he was being led off the stage at the end of the show by the Flames, in mock exhaustion, Brown took the opportunity to scrutinize the shoes of every musician, looking for Vaseline on leather to fake a good shine. That was a hundred dollars right there.

After a time early on when the band packed up and left, and a stranded Brown was beaten and robbed, a new rule was established: Nobody could leave the venue until Brown left. Everybody was on call. "You got to be like an act, so therefore you cannot mingle, so you have to stay in the dressing room," said Byrd. "The only time you see whoever you need to see is on your way home, after the show is over, but you can't come out of the dressing room. . . . You are an act now, so you have to be in here."

The system of fines has become a part of Brown's image as a tough general. He flashed hand signals to musicians, for missing a cue, for gravy on their collar. Fines were theoretically taken out of one's pay on payday, and put into a pot for parties. But the system was not written in stone. It was according to Brown's whim, and some strong individuals claimed they never paid a single fine. The point, ultimately, was to know that he was watching.

A cordon of helpers flocked to Brown. There was Gertrude Sanders, the only behind-the-scenes female force, who became the uniform mistress. She cut an unforgettable figure, limping down a backstage corridor with an iron in her hand. There were valets for Brown and for the Flames, and valets in waiting who traveled on their own dime hoping for a chance to make themselves indispensable.

A set of knuckleheads was also vying for attention. They helped when it was time to collect the night's receipts. They got stuff for Brown, rustling women and keeping other women away. Chief among them in the early 1960s was a New York hoodlum named Baby James.

"He was a different kind of person, extraordinarily rough. We had to keep him straight," recalled Brown's boyhood friend Henry Stallings, who became one of Brown's hairdressers. "See, you got to give a little and take a little, but Baby was the type of person to take it all. James would give him some money and say, 'Take the man to the door,' but Baby would beat him all the way to the door." When James asked him to do stuff, Baby would be doing it to death, until James had to pay him to stop. Some guys just know how to make themselves useful.

The new security team had the boss's back, though it wasn't, strictly speaking, like the boss was vulnerable. As Reverend Al Sharpton put it, "You notice how many pictures of James Brown, he's got a coat over his arm? Could be 95-degree weather in Miami, you'd see him with an overcoat over his arm. That's because he had his gun under it."

Those who had known Brown awhile were surprised by the new style. Seymour Stein first met him when he worked at King in the 1950s, and had gone on the road with him. In the mid-'60s Stein took the bubblegum act the McCoys up to see Brown at the Apollo. They met Nathan backstage, during a time when he and the singer were particularly at loggerheads. When Brown saw Syd and his party, he pulled a gun on them all and told them to leave.

Live at the Apollo validated notions Brown harbored about his own correctness. Hadn't he just made the bestselling album in the history of King Records—and been forced to pay for it himself? He had just won the biggest argument in his life. The lesson of *Live at the Apollo* was to keep on fighting, to swing like Beau Jack until some stronger force shut you down.

The loudest fight with Nathan was over the new, improved contract Brown wanted and felt he'd earned. That was the tip of it, but then there was other stuff. There was the matter of pride. When Brown went into the studio to record "Oh Baby Don't You Weep," that part of the quarrel came all the way out into the open. "Baby" was a long, blue moan, that took the spiritual "Mary Don't You Weep" out of the church and put it on the cover of a dime novel: "You scream and you holler, your back is soaking wet," he tells a woman who can't forget the man that forgot her. The song is *about* the sweat, its words don't hold together neatly, yet as a performance it is deeply felt. It works.

During the recording, Gene Redd, the tart producer who made some of King's best R&B, stopped the session to tell Brown his piano playing was "musically incorrect." Brown's response couldn't have been clearer: "Does it sound good to me? Then it's not incorrect." Further words were exchanged and Redd stalked out of the booth to complain to Nathan. To his credit, he told Redd to stow it and do it Brown's way, but the damage was already done. Brown was a decent player on a number of instruments, but not by the standards of a professional like Redd. Brown was something rarer than a great musician: He knew when the bad note was the right one, when the noise landed in the right spot. At crucial moments *feel* guided him, and Brown was brave enough to trust it even when the musicians in the room were shaking their heads.

Feel had always been a presence, feel not just in trusting a bad note, but in terms of subtleties, like the way his late '50s and early '60s ballads have a wayward, chambered darkness in the horn parts. Sometimes feel is a superb performance, a scream that pushes out at you inappropriately, a delivery style that overwhelms ordinary material and remakes it. Over time his confidence only grew. It wasn't a passion for rawness, exactly—how could it be, given how hard he rehearsed the band? It was an absolute openness, though, to what was alive in the moment.

"He couldn't read music, but he knew exactly what he wanted," said Fillyau. Taking a seat at the organ, Brown would play a song that Fillyau felt was full of wrong notes, sounds he'd been taught would never work. Then Brown would break down the thing he'd played note by note and tell the band to perform it that way.

It had nothing to do with preconceived ideas or principles. "You don't know why one day you want steak, the next day you want fat-back," Brown explained. "People who plan what they are gonna do, they don't look good."

Brown knew he looked good. Convinced that he was right and mad at Redd for insulting him in front of the band and mad at Syd for being Syd, after "Oh Baby" he stopped making records for King.

While continuing to press for a new contract with King, he formed the Fair Deal Record Corporation in early 1964. Its very name suggests a message to Nathan. Its officers were Brown, his father Joe Brown, and Ben Bart. Together they concluded that, since the current contract was for "James Brown and the Famous Flames," Brown was free to record without the Famous Flames wherever he wanted. Mercury Records had made Fair Deal an offer through subsidiary label Smash, and Brown took the deal. He would produce other acts and record his own music on Smash.

That was just the declaration of war. In the opening skirmish, Fair Deal leased singles by Bobby Byrd and the new female singer in his show, Anna King, to Smash. This was war by proxy. From King: silence. Or at least, the lawyers were silent. Nathan flooded the market with a torrent of inferior Brown product. He re-released "Please, Please, Please" with crowd noises tacked on, hoping to fool the gullible into thinking that it was a new live recording. He put out stuff he had refused to put out before. Back at you, nothing more.

Brown followed the Smash singles he produced with a new album of him singing rhythm and blues classics with a classy big band. *Showtime* was a bizarre sidestep, redoing Mom and Dad's music while the Apollo kids' shouts still hung in the air. One explanation is that *Showtime* was a threat—I *will* record for another label—as much as it was a serious release. Like the singles, *Showtime* tanked, and yet again, Nathan—who knew "it's just business" the way Brown knew "Ain't Nobody Here but Us Chickens"—maintained radio silence. What happened next seemed scripted to get Nathan's attention.

Brown was playing one-nighters, he was stockpiling new recordings that were nothing like the showbiz of *Showtime.* In July 1964, with King still keeping its cool, Brown released one of the new songs he had cut for Smash. "Out of Sight" was really good, and when it started up the R&B charts, and then made it to twenty-four on the pop charts, Nathan finally played his hand. He filed suit, declaring that the Smash releases violated Brown's contract with King.

This was happening at a critical moment for King. Nathan's health was faltering; he'd had two heart attacks and was not around the office much. Two of his hillbilly stars had died in a plane crash, along with singer Patsy Cline, in 1963. Beyond that, King just didn't understand albums, and they didn't understand teenagers—this was the label that slept on "The Twist." They were paying last month's bills with this month's hits, and inferior James Brown product from the vaults was not going to keep the lights on.

In October, a New York appellate judge ordered Brown to stop recording for Smash, while the court puzzled out his arrangement with King. Meanwhile, another loophole had been revealed: The contract was for Brown the singer, not Brown the organ player or producer or anything else. He appealed and the loophole widened. The court said he could not sing for Smash, but otherwise was a free agent.

To Brown, all of this was extremely personal, and Nathan's refusal to give him a new contract was a display, now public, of disrespect. He framed his complaint in terms of an overwhelming force seeking to destroy an individual. As he said while giving a deposition, "I don't think a man should be treated this way in the United States."

There were records coming out that King had no business releasing, and then there were songs like "I Got You (I Feel Good)" that Brown couldn't put on record due to the legal battle. He sang it in a "zany" 1965 American International movie titled *Ski Party*, starring Dwayne Hickman, Frankie Avalon, and a yodeling polar bear. Skiing into a cozy chalet, Brown almost torpedoes any hopes of a film career right there as he struggles to get the words "abominable snow girl" out of his mouth, before he and the Famous Flames, in matching knit sweaters, slam out "I Got You."

In March of 1965, *Billboard* reported that Nathan had decided to sell his label and his publishing company to Mercury. Maybe the story was legit, but this was a guy whose idea of fun was hustling pawnbrokers. If he was truly thinking of selling out, he reversed himself in short order. By June he told Brown he would agree to reconsider a new contract, and that was enough to bring the singer back to Cincinnati.

Who won this brawl depends on which corner you watched it from. But in a fundamental sense, here is what Brown walked away with: Fresh off the biggest victory of his life, *Live at the Apollo*, he was willing to put his momentum, and perhaps his future, at stake for a principle—not even for a principle, for a *fight*. The worst part of his life was the part when he was too small, young, and inexperienced to fight back. Things got better when he battled, and not once had losing really hurt him. If there was ever a plan, it was cryptic; break a contract, shoot up a nightclub. It had gotten him this far, and it was too late to turn back now.

Dizzy from his clashes, Brown was in the market for advice. He called the white owner of a recording studio in Charlotte, and got into a conversation about his problems with King, and about money and music. The man who owned the studio was a musician himself, Arthur Smith, who made the 1948 country hit "Guitar Boogie." Smith was a sympathetic listener, and at the end of the conversation Brown said he didn't exactly know how his troubles would be resolved, but if in a few months he was near Charlotte again, he asked if he could record at Smith's studio. This was the segregated South, and a black man, even one with money, had to ask permission. "You have my number," Smith said. "Love to have you."

In February 1965, as King and Mercury continued their fight, Brown and his band came down to the Charlotte studio. The room was a glorified barn, with a large space for the band, and the control booth up where a hayloft would be.

It was time to record a tricky piece of rhythm Brown had been thinking about for a while. The musicians set up, playing this and that while waiting for the boss to arrive. Finally, Brown's customized white Cadillac with the tinted windows appeared, and the singer swaggered in. "He stopped the place. You just knew that somebody of significance was present," said Clay Smith, Arthur's boy. Constantly in motion and talking so fast he could have used a translator, Brown was not one of the guys. "James was in charge," Arthur Smith remembered later. "I knew I owned the studio, but I knew he was going to do what he wanted to there."

A big chunk of this group had been plucked out of the small town of Kinston, North Carolina: trumpeter Levi Rasbury, saxophonist Maceo Parker and his brother Melvin on drums, and Nat Jones, a saxophonist and music director. For Rasbury, "It was unreal. It was my first time being in a studio, first time I saw how they got records made. How Brown did it was, he would hum the melody of the tune to Nat, pound out the drum rhythm he wanted–'you got it?' hum a bass line to the bass player–'you got that?' So he says, 'Nat, you add a riff to it for the horns . . .'"

Nat's riff had to nest just so with a takeout guitar part, and lining them up was proving difficult. Brown watched a trumpeter struggle for a while, and then exploded.

"Who is this trumpet player?" he said, turning to Jones. "He ain't gonna work out. I want you to fire that nigger."

A moment later, the deed done, Brown again turned to Jones.

"You done fired him. Who you got to replace him?"

"Where am I going to get a trumpeter in Charlotte in the middle of the night?" asked the dumbfounded Jones.

Pointing to the ousted musician, Brown said, "Hire that nigger!"

They ran through the tune with the tape rolling. Brown read lyrics off a sheet of paper. And when they were done, they had "Papa's Got a Brand New Bag." Knowing what he had, and knowing he couldn't put it out on Smash, and knowing that Syd had declared that he would at least *consider* a new contract, Brown announced that he'd made his point to King, and sent the tape to Cincinnati.

When it came out in the summer, "Papa's" seemed to gather together all the implications of "Out of Sight," released the previous July. "Out of Sight" was the scenario–"Papa's" is the whole movie.

Not a bad scenario, though. Brown's voice carries the melody as he colors himself impressed by a femme, and Maceo Parker on baritone sax responds with a sagacious head-bobbing *uh-huh you right*. "Out of Sight" gets loud for kicks then goes hush. The song stops cold at one point and Brown's voice teasingly kick-starts the music again. He was having fun showing how in control and in the groove he was.

Both these records seemed to pull apart the elements of the

band and scatter them around, making their relationships visible, like an exploded-view diagram. The bass was doing things it hadn't done before in pop music, and was perhaps the most active part of either song. It was mobile and so low you had to move in to hear it—a sound carrying information you could only partly absorb. Drummer Melvin Parker knew how hot Fillyau burned. He was smart to go in the other direction, accenting the high end far from the bass—the cymbal, tic-tic on the rim. "I was just trying to be different," Parker said. "Clean, funky, and different."

Coursing through both songs was the playing of Maceo Parker, who had joined in 1964 and was launched into orbit the moment Brown called out his name in the second half of the nearly eight-minute "Papa's," after which Parker and the world simultaneously discovered what a rapport he had with Brown. They sounded like each other, and fed off each other, so much so that Brown later said, "You know, when Maceo plays, it's almost like an extension of me."

These songs were *hip*, and so was Brown. He was taking to New York just fine. He had been the Hardest Working Man in Show Business, the sweatiest guy on Earth, sacrificing himself for your love. When he performed live there was so much moisture on the floor that the band was sliding around in it, so much so that he had to hook up to an intravenous rig after a hot show to restore his fluids. As he put it, "There is nothing so personal as the sweat from your eyebrow," and nightly Brown left his essence on the floor. But with "Out of Sight," hard work became but half of the story. The other part was control, the mastery of a guy who imploded the air around him with a nod, as dominant at rest as he was with his marathon exertions. He wasn't saying "please" here. He was snapping his fingers and making things happen.

"It was the beginning of a new world," Brown said of "Papa's." They stayed on the road as the song came out, and the band could feel the change come over them. Levi Rasbury did bookkeeping for the shows, and he watched the numbers jump. " 'Papa's' had just been released, so we go to Georgia, Alabama–Birmingham,

Mobile–and touched around Pensacola, come up through Lake Charles, Louisiana. By the time we got to New Orleans, James had moved up from $1,750 to about $2,500 or $3,000 a night on dates that had already been booked. We played Shreveport, Dallas, Houston, San Antonio, and he's at $4,500."

The audience, too, was changing. "On my first West Coast trip with James, the audience was basically black," said Rasbury. "We had a few whites, but seventy-five or eighty percent was black." Then "Papa's" drops. "*This* time around, the crowd is changing to like 60/40 black/white in the South, and as you go to Texas, Arizona, it's beginning to go 50/50." It was a new bag, all right, but amazingly, Brown was crossing over more by the day, and he wasn't doing it with ballads or strings, the usual route to white fans. These were feel records, risky business that didn't sound like anything else on the radio.

At the end of 1965, *New York Amsterdam News* reported a raid on a dope den in the Bronx. "Police said when they entered the apartment, there was dancing, gambling, and drinking while James Brown was shouting 'Papa's Got a Brand New Bag' on the record player. Police said knives fell to the floor, a loaded gun, marijuana, cocaine, heroin, and policy slips were also allegedly found in the apartment."

Stark and cinematic, the music created a new kind of space. It was survival rhapsodized as style–and as style it took off. The music floated up from the A train and the diner where they sold cuchifritos, from the Bronx dens and that St. Albans basement where they passed around grape drink and Toccoa moonshine. But Brown belonged to white listeners now, too, and he was taking off– he was becoming a pop star.

Brown's crossover success set its own course, impossible to reproduce by following instructions. In 1965, the great factory for creating black pop music according to plan was Motown. And in that year, the president of Motown signed somebody Brown knew well, Tammy Montgomery. Motown founder Berry Gordy changed her name to Tammi Terrell and began his systematic process of grooming her for stardom, putting her through the Motown finishing school. Meanwhile, Brown had already put her through another kind of school.

Terrell lasted only about a year with Brown, from 1963 to 1964, and in that time, she fell into the rhythm of endless one-nighters, living on the bus and racing to the next stage. She also fell into the natural path of a James Brown featured female singer. Like most of the rest, she was sleeping with him, wearing the wigs he liked his women to have, and being showered with gifts. They played the Apollo, and Brown had her attended by hair stylists, manicurists, and pedicurists. He paid for facials and hair weaves and furs. A little later, they played Grossinger's, the Catskill Mountains resort that had been part of the Borscht Belt but now was struggling to find relevance. The temporary solution was a bill teaming James Brown with comedian Bob Hope.

There had probably been trouble between Brown and Terrell before, but what happened at Grossinger's marked a turning point in their relationship. Backstage, Hope took a liking to her, and invited Terrell to travel with him on a USO tour of Vietnam. Terrell told him she had contractual commitments with Brown she had to fulfill. More important than professional commitments, though, was that Brown could not bear the idea of a woman leaving him. The possibility of anyone—let alone the headliner—"stealing" his woman would not have sat well with him.

His violence went unhidden. "I saw James Brown beat her butt in Atlanta, Georgia, until she was too weak to fall," said Allyn Lee.

David Butts, a dancer with the show, remembered Terrell going onstage after a pummeling from Brown. "She had a tune called 'If You See Bill.' She'd be singing it up there with a black eye."

Butts also recalled doing a show in Virginia, then everybody being told to check out of the hotel and get on the bus. "We were going along on the highway, heading south, when maybe an hour into the ride the bus pulls over. James is driving his car, and James gets out, snatched Tammi out of the car, and commences to smack her. I'd never seen anything like that before. Everybody wondering what it was all about.

"What it was, as they were rushing out of the hotel–see, James likes hot sauce on his chicken wings, and she snatched the bottle up and put it in her mink coat pocket as they left. Later, when he asked for the hot sauce, she pulled it out of the mink and that set him off–'why you put that in your mink coat pocket?'"

Brown's treatment of Tammi Terrell fit a pattern in his relationships with women, and the abuse stemmed from his possessiveness and the dread of being left. Bobby Bennett said he saw Brown hit her three times with a hammer outside of a hotel in Washington, D.C. According to singer Gene Chandler, at her last show with Brown, Terrell made the mistake of not standing in the wings watching everything he did. According to Chandler, interviewed for a syndicated TV show, Brown danced off the stage and beat her all the way down the stairs to the dressing room. Chandler called her mother. The next morning her mother picked her up and took Terrell home.

Her family unpacked her bags. From one they pulled out a blue silk kimono, spattered with blood.

Chapter Ten

THE CAPE ACT

First, she thought she could fly. Then she hoped the fat guy would break her fall.

The woman had come to Rockland Palace in Harlem, to see James Brown in 1961. As the group tore into "Please, Please, Please," something overpowering entered her, a feeling that the world was unreal, and that what she was about to do would connect her with something more infinite. She rose up, planted her feet on the edge of the upper deck, swaying back and forth to the beat, and then . . . she leaped off the planet. Or tried to. She landed on the floor below, and was lucky to survive.

"I saw her body sweep away like she was going up in smoke," Brown told a writer from *Sepia*. "The next thing we knew she had swept and swooned herself to the balcony . . . and leaped over. We didn't dig that action at all."

James Brown put audiences into a trance. On another night in the early 1960s, when the band played a Southern dance, a large woman climbed onto the balcony's lip and flickered there. "No one made a remark—no one approached her, and she never had a moment of unbalance," said a witness. "The whole public was swaying. It was a dance, but no one was dancing. It was like a standing ovation to the singer."

What was happening in the shows of the early 1960s to possess fans to float off like that? The answer is there in the performance of "Please, Please, Please," in a bit of stagecraft Brown had only recently introduced into the show. But to understand this turning point, we have to step back to another era, another dance, and do the mashed potato all the way back to the 1890s.

We are in the area along the Ob River in northwest Siberia, east of the Ural Mountains. It is windy, unspeakably cold, though spring is coming. The people who live here dwell in birch bark tents and hunt with bows and arrows the wolves that stalk the frozen evergreen forest. These people were called the Ostyak or the Ostiak. The eleventh edition of *Encyclopedia Britannica*, 1911: "The Ostiaks are middle-sized, or of low stature, mostly meagre, and not ill made, however clumsy their appearance in winter in their thick fur-clothes. The extremities are fine, and the feet are usually small."

They are one tough crowd, too. Running out of food, they stare at a leader, a hero, who stands before them. They are hungry and wondering if they must again move to a new spot. They are fanatic, obsessed with the hero and demanding answers. They have put him on a platform, and now they surround him, waiting for a sign. They are pleading for a show of prowess, of stamina, of his control over the forces that are ravaging their lives.

They are expecting a performance. Drums play for a long time, then the hero screams in an inhuman tongue, a torrent of words and emotions that touch his followers but which they cannot understand. Eventually he is overcome, inhabited by a spirit that contorts his face, his voice, the movements of his body. He dances.

He sings. The spirit that is in him pours out as he voices a message from the spirit world. He has climbed to heaven and fallen to the underworld, and now he is here, tired on every level. A circle of helpers drop a cloak, like a cape, around him, they attempt to give his body and soul the comfort of mortal hands on his back. A pat, a word, is proffered, but soothing him is beyond them, for only he has the answer to his condition.

After that, the way some folks told it back then, the hero entered his iron hut and fell asleep on a bed of purple clouds. That last part might have been the work of a really good press agent. But the basic, undeniable points are these: Some of the greatest performances originated centuries ago, and sometimes it's the cape that makes the man.

Before we can connect the Ostyak and James Brown, we must make use of a word, an abused word, a cliché, which over the years has become as misrepresented and misunderstood as *funk*. The word is *shaman*. The Ostyak were into shamanism before shamanism was cool. The word was first used to describe people like the communal hero the Ostyak huddled around, coined by Russian anthropologists studying the tribal peoples of Siberia and Central Asia.

But one reason the term *shaman* has come to seem downright corny is that, even before Joseph Campbell went platinum and men's groups, drum circles, and wind-up ravers ripped the stuffing out of the word, shamanism was a global phenomenon. The anthropologists who brought the concept to the masses determined that these people (call them medicine men, call them healers, call them shaman) existed in cultures all over the planet. Their very universality has led us today to spout universal banalities about them.

Crucial to the shaman's shtick wherever he is found is that he must die in front of the community, in a symbolic act that is followed by a back-from-beyond rebirth. The symbolic death and rebirth is repeated over and over, and through this performance he is reborn before all, in a miraculous manner that consolidates his power and prominence.

Shaman, conjurer, bruja . . . American idol. In a charming and thoughtful book published in 1983, the British writer Rogan Taylor argues that our most global performers, the ones who matter most to modern audiences, are working in our own shamanic tradition. In *The Death and Resurrection Show*, Taylor describes a phase in which the hero withdraws from his community and gets his "act" together, and suggests that when a shaman demonstrates his powers to the people, by nature he is putting on a show. A big moment in the shamanic ritual, says Taylor, is when the performer is wracked by the agonies of the underworld as we watch. Taylor calls this a "pantomime of moments in hell." From the banks of the Ob to the buffet at Grossinger's, what ties us to the most powerful entertainers is the same elemental bond humans once had with the shaman.

Taylor calls James Brown "perhaps the most outlandishly shamanistic performer of all." The pinnacle of his show, the event unfolding when the bodies were poised on the edge of the upper balcony, came during "Please, Please, Please," in a bit that quickly was dubbed "the cape act."

The cape act had been a part of his show since 1961. Previously Brown had used a suitcase as a prop during "Please," and into the mid-'60s he sometimes appeared onstage wearing a crown studded with fake baubles. Those were gimmicks, but the cape was in a whole different category. From the first time he used it, the cape altered his show; it made him seem bizarrely and grandly religious. It made him a victim and a champion, running on currents that alternated weakness with raw power. He *said* he gave us his all: The cape act showed it, and showed that his all was bottomless.

Brown had his story of how he first put on the cloak. He was watching wrestling on TV and caught the act of Gorgeous George, another primal performer. George was one of the very first TV stars, and the only wrestler to this day who can fairly be called profound. Maintainer of a flamboyant and demanding hairdo himself, George upped his fame when he began wearing luxuriously beaded, padded, quilted, and studded robes of a feminine nature. Guys who used to scream at him screamed louder when George preened in his dazzling robes. Violently transgressive, he found his gimmick and used it to control events in the ring, define his meaning, and master the audience. He knew exactly what he was doing. "I owe it to my fans to wear nothing but the most costly and resplendent out-fits money can buy," he expounded. "Mink is so mediocre. I will wear nothing less than ermine on my ring robes." He was a sissified brute, and he exerted some influence on Brown.

The cape act, Brown would say, started as an improvised tribute to George, but Brown changed everything about what it meant. On George the robe was a raiment signifying pomp, it oozed prepos-terous self-regard. It feminized him and thereby inspired con-tempt; George's job was to pummel that hatred into respect.

But for Brown the cape signifies . . . what? Nobody hated him when he was draped in it. George *wore* his robes. They established his image. But the cape covers, and conceals, Brown, and keeps us from understanding him. The cape presents us with confusion, and we pull closer to understand.

So, pull closer. Of all the musicians, hairdressers, bodyguards, and aides-de-camp in Brown's traveling party over the years, none lasted longer than Danny Ray. No one could have predicted this back in 1961. Ray was an impeccably dressed drifter and backstage regular at the Apollo looking for a break. "People got to see you around, get to know your face and let your name be Mr. Friendly," he explained. Ray almost got a job with Johnny Mathis before Brown came back to the Apollo.

He started in 1961 as a valet for the Flames, and after Brown saw how sharp they looked, he promoted Ray to his valet. Ray had left Birmingham, Alabama, in 1955 to join the army: "My military training made me be punctual. I guess Brown couldn't find any-body to shine the shoes and clean the five outfit changes he had.

"I used to go up to the very top of the Apollo, to the place they call 'the crow's nest,' and watch the show. To myself I'd say, if I could just get down there . . . I had no ideas how it would come. Then one night . . ." Making himself indispensable kept Ray out of Birmingham and landed him a slot as Brown's announcer. But what gave him fame was the accident of the cape.

Listen to Ray and the talk of Gorgeous George starts to sound concocted, crafted to give meaning to what was actually a fluke. He saw what he saw; he was there when it happened. "Back in the chitlin circuit days, there wasn't no dressing room, there was an outside and an inside, and when you wanted to go off the stage, you went out the door and you were standing outside," said Ray. "I used to catch him coming off singing 'Please' and he'd just be drenched in sweat, and one thing I was supposed to do was hand him a towel. That's all it was. I put the Turkish towel on him. Places were so small, you had to go outside before you come back on the stage. It was, like, our little joke, at first. I put the Turkish towel on him; he'd kick it off and run back in and sing it some more. Folks could see it from their seats. People started noticing and it just became a thing."

The audience saw it, literally out of the corner of their eyes, and it mattered to them. They wanted the bit brought in from outside.

There are three guys who have got the cape, Brown would say: Superman, Batman, and Danny Ray. "You had to be watching him at all times. He would tell me the color of the suits, the color of the capes, only a little before the shows," said the valet. "I kept them safe with me and never let them out of my sight, because I knew what they represented."

The initial James Brown albums released by King conspicuously hid an essential detail: what Brown looked like. His first album featured a gray-suited guy and a skirted lady photographed from the torso. The second non sequitur: a femme fatale holding a pistol. The next, a white baby crying. Brown conveyed his resentment of Nathan's efforts to hide his face. When *Live at the Apollo* did well, Nathan stuck it to him by noting how his most successful album also didn't have a picture of Brown on its cover.

This became a matter of ego, and a matter of conviction, for Brown was sure that if America witnessed him and his act, America would love him. When Brown debuted on national TV on

American Bandstand in 1963, his movements were confined, and the camera shot him from the waist up, his physicality kept in check. That, too, fed his determination.

But in 1964, the America beyond the chitlin circuit was able to see, as well as hear, a James Brown performance. He did eighteen minutes in a movie called *The T.A.M.I. Show*, and it was more than enough time for whole civilizations to leap off the upper deck. The cape act made its national debut on *The T.A.M.I. Show*, and nobody who saw it forgot the moment.

T.A.M.I. stood for Teenage Music International, or maybe it was Teenage Awards Music International, as is sometimes said. Either way, it was an effort to raise scholarship money through a video-taped concert that featured Brown, Chuck Berry, the Beach Boys, Marvin Gaye, the Rolling Stones, and more live onstage at the Santa Monica Civic Auditorium. It would be hard to overhype this lineup, but the producers tried: The ads hyperventilated that it was shot in Electronovision, a legit technology that transferred high-resolution videotape to film for movie theaters.

Much has been made of how Brown upstaged the Rolling Stones, the show closers. How Mick Jagger was petrified as he watched Brown work and needed backstage consoling from Marvin Gaye—"Just go out there and do your best," Gaye told him. He had to tell him *something*. Decades later, Keith Richards told an interviewer the biggest mistake of his life was going on *The T.A.M.I. Show* after Brown.

"I can't even tell you now why I wanted the order that way," said Steve Binder, who directed the film. "But then, I didn't hear any first-person resistance to the idea, other than from James.

"I think how it came down was, he said 'I *am* the final act on the bill, right?' And I said no. And he said, '*Nobody* follows me.'

"'Actually,' I said, 'we've got the Rolling Stones.' He didn't care—he was so confident in himself."

They had four days of rehearsals before the shoot, which was done over two days. Brown was adamant that he did not want to run through what he was going to do. This was for one simple reason: He knew what he had, and he didn't want to tip his hand. On the road, after four days the opening act was liable to be doing your show. When he *did* rehearse for a TV appearance, he practiced something different than what he actually was going to play on the show.

Binder was a polished, forward-thinking director, with a deep feel for music dating back to jazz programs he had worked on in the early '60s. The idea was to have all the T.A.M.I. acts practice all the music so he could plot camera placement and anticipate what shots to use. "The only one who said, 'I don't want to do a rehearsal' was James Brown. I didn't know James Brown from Adam, I had just gotten a bunch of his albums right before we started. He looked at me, nodded, and he just said, 'You'll know what to do when you see me.'"

The director was more than game. His camera seems to move in tighter on Brown the deeper he gets into his set. It's like Binder and viewers are getting to know Brown better as we watch and beginning to think like he thinks.

The audience was gathered from teens on the Santa Monica Pier. Many surely had heard of Brown, but others were won over by what they saw that day. "Here was white America, blond, blue-eyed surfing girls screaming their brains out," said Binder. "One of my camera guys said to me, 'I can't be right but I think I'm hearing "fuck me fuck me fuck me" from the audience.' We couldn't edit it out. Those kids were reacting with honest emotions—there were not applause lights flashing on and off, it was all too real."

There's a swank "Out of Sight" and a devotional "Prisoner of Love," and if Brown's set had ended there, he'd already have been the best thing about the movie. Then he sings "Please, Please, Please," and experiences what at first seems to be a full-scale breakdown, his body and spirit overtaken by a shadow. He falls to his knees, and the Flames, his considerate handlers, drape a cape over him and escort Brown to the side of the stage. They are distressed for his well-being, and though in retrospect a cape is a weird way to express your concern, at the moment it seems like the only possible thing to do.

The Flames–the Bobby Bennett, Bobby Byrd, Baby Lloyd Stallworth version–are wiggling their hips and pumping "raise the roof" hand gestures. They are good-time party boys, big pimpin' next to Brown's morbid corpus. The first time he falls to his knees, the crowd sounds shocked, and Danny Ray drapes a generous frock as he slumps. Bennett comes over, pats him gently on his shoulder, his face a mask of frozen regard.

The second time he falls to his knees, we get a closeup of Brown's face as he is being guided off the stage, the guys now intent on delivering him from this unsafe place. Brown touches his cheek in an almost shocking way, and the crowd is shouting "Don't go!" along with the Flames, but what you notice is how Brown is shaking his head and muttering something. Is he speaking in tongues? So gone he's lost bodily control? He seems barking mad, overwhelmed by emotional forces beyond the capacity of Electronovision.

It becomes easier and easier to notice: The man is falling to the ground on the One. The first beat of the measure. He also throws off the cape each time on the One. He's conducting the band from the depth of his paroxysm. After forces take him down for the third time, and the cape has been administered, a wide shot gives us Ray, his eyes nervously darting back and forth. He was a nervous guy, perfect for this moment–his fear reads as dread for what might be happening to the boss. Brown almost makes it to the wings this time, when he again discards the cloak, waving off his handlers–he can't be handled, not controlled by either his aides or the power of the moment. He will master these forces, and he heads back to the microphone, when . . .

There is one final fall to the earth, the only one that feels mechanical, because the purpose is to break the spell and display his final mastery of spirit forces that have dragged him back and

forth across a stage, worried those poor Flames and Danny Ray
half to death, and caused the audience to move from "fuck me, fuck
me" to sounds more guttural and incomprehensible.

He was a dancer, bandleader, singer. But it is this scene, this bit
of stagecraft out of time and culture, that places him finally on a
plane of pure performer. It focuses our attention on his battle,
makes us care about his life or death and cheer for his existence.

"It's a Holiness feeling–like a Baptist thing. It's a spiritual background thing," is how Brown put it. "You're involved and you don't
want to quit. That's the definition of soul, you know. Being involved
and they try to stop you and you just don't want to stop. The idea of
changing capes came later, 'cause it's good for show business."

That falling-to-the-knees-overcome-with-emotion dramaturgy
is straight out of the Holiness Church, out of a belief system holding, in the charnel heat of the moment, that a person could be over-
powered by a sudden tap from the Holy Ghost. Holy Ghost jumpers
were what they called those filled with the spirit in the earliest days
of Pentecostalism. It was a form of possession, of yielding with
glory to a higher force.

Many figures in the black Pentecostal tradition wore the cape.
There was King Louis Narcisse, a preacher who modeled himself
on Daddy Grace. His church had branches from Oakland to
Orlando. He made gospel recordings and even had a motto: "It's So
Very Nice to be Nice." Narcisse favored ermine. There was Brother
Joe May, one of the major gospel voices of the '50s and '60s, a
barrel-chested, fire-roasted singer who had a million seller with
his very first recording, "Search Me Lord." He rocked a gold one.

Brown knew their work and that of many more behind them,
and in wearing the robe he was surely connecting with their
religious power, trying it on for size. He was religious in ways that
connected with folks who knew the spirit, he just didn't name his
"god." He felt no need to name *any* god, certainly not the one he

was humbled before when he fell to the ground in the act of performance.

But "Please," of course, is a secular tune, tied to teenage things.
So when Brown is on the floor communicating that he is in awe,
humbled by a supreme force, what is the force ruling him? It is the
love he feels for the woman who left him. "Don't go!" he screams.
It is his need. To be in awe of his feelings, though, is another way of
saying he is in awe of himself. A profound and wondrous force has
entered James Brown, and it is James Brownness, the intensity of
being *him*. Here is religion without God, or with but one God, none
other than His Expoobidence. Call it shamanism or showbiz, whatever you name it, this is some powerful secular magic.

In March 1966, Brown made his debut at Madison Square Garden in New York City. In the audience was a showman named Buster
Brown. One of the great tap dancers of the century, he performed
with Duke Ellington's orchestra, and danced for Ethiopia's leader
Haile Selassie, who awarded him the Lion of Judah Coin. After
watching the Garden performance, Buster Brown wrote down
what he felt:

"I am lost for words to speak about this man. When he hits the
stage everything starts happening until he leaves. This man is the
greatest entertainer. He gets his audience like a preacher–like a
Father Divine. He wants to be the Idol, the God one adores. . . .

"He is not trying to put something over. He is not there fooling
around, not for a minute.

"He just wakes them up–no end; and when he goes, they cannot
forget him.

"It does not have a story. It has no message. He promises himself. 'I promise you the best of me,' and then he gives it.

"He leaves them with the impression: 'I belong to you.'"

The tap dancer went to the Garden at the behest of a friend,
dance historian and documentary filmmaker Mura Dehn. Born in
Russia, she was a ballet dancer in her youth. Then she saw Jose-
phine Baker perform in Paris, which changed her thinking about a

great many things. Dehn moved to New York City around 1930, and began visiting the Savoy Ballroom, the home of the swing dance revolution. The jazz dance scene turned Dehn into a pre-server of African American vernacular dance history.

She went with Buster Brown to the Garden, and her own impressions of the singer appeared in *Sounds & Fury* magazine in June 1966. Here is Dehn:

"His emphasis on ego breaks all bounds. He is like a new-born baby in tantrums to enforce his will.

"He leaves you astonished and awed because of the mark of genius and madness."

She reserved special praise for Brown's dancing, but as for the other aspects of the show, "The rest is a tremendous scream for something that he wants more and more of–and gets–and is ready to give his life in order to retain it forever.

"Soul? I don't know what this soul is about. Nothing one could live on or remember when one goes away.

"He is a mythological personage. What he asks for is love–boundless–which can never quite fill his craving. At the end of all that inspiration, talent, sorcery."

Dehn then steps back. Having acknowledged her mistrust of Brown's overwhelming force, and wondering if there is anything spiritual behind the demands he makes, she suggests this plea might be rooted in the black experience.

"Maybe because it was repressed so long, it comes out in this boundless way–in strength and complaint. That may be true, but theatrically speaking, a performer has to produce what our times demand–a monster personality to be sold for 'phantabulous' profits. James Brown is unprecedented. A man touched by divine power. He absorbs. He stuns. And yet you don't feel enriched. You cannot live on what he reveals. You simply experience him, and he is fabulous."

It's some of the most perceptive writing on James Brown. Dehn grasps the depth of Brown's hunger, the need that is there in every great entertainer's act but never, until now, so nakedly the point of the celebration.

What's amazing, finally, is that one of the great black dancers of the time and one of the form's most vibrant scholars go to a James Brown show and they don't even talk about his dancing. Instead they describe what Dehn calls "a completely new theater and, at the same time, an archaic mystery." It holds them, as they struggle to understand.

"The T.A.M.I. Show was the highest energy thing has ever been. I danced so hard my manager cried," Brown later said. "But I really had to. What I was up against was pop artists—I was R&B. I had to show 'em the difference, and believe me, it was hard." First, he had to show them what he looked like. The T.A.M.I. Show put a face on a performer that America knew by sound. It did one other thing, too. It suggested that this Chosen One, the one born dead but not dead, would fall and rise for us all.

Over the next forty years, Brown would signal the end of his show with his cape routine. The color of the garments changed with each fall, the physical moves and gestures might be different, but the ritual of death and resurrection, sacrifice and rebirth, remained a nightly performance he would no more think to forgo than he would forgo perfect hair.

Chapter Eleven

MAN'S WORLD

J ames Meredith was a movement of one. When the Mississippi man set out on Highway 51 in a protest that he called
a march, he was alone. Never much of a joiner, he didn't
mind marching by himself.

Meredith successfully fought to be the first African American
admitted to the University of Mississippi, and his ordeal, the abuse
and threats he weathered, made him national news in 1962. Missis-
sippians viewed him as a black leader as important as Martin
Luther King Jr. In 1966, Meredith announced his "March Against
Fear," proceeding from Memphis to Mississippi's state capital,
Jackson, intended to demonstrate that white supremacists could
not impede the registration of black voters. It began on June 5,
1966. It was halted on June 6, after Meredith was gunned down by
a white man with a shotgun outside Hernando, Mississippi.

In the days that followed, Meredith lay in a Memphis hospital,
recovering from his wounds. Meanwhile the various wings of the
Civil Rights Movement struggled to formulate a unified response.
The march resumed on the spot where Meredith fell, this time with
people gathered from Martin Luther King's Southern Christian
Leadership Conference, the Congress of Racial Equality, and the
Student Nonviolent Coordinating Committee (SNCC). As they

marched Highway 51 to Jackson, the activists camped by the road-side.

Almost as soon as he entered the town of Greenwood, Missis-sippi, Stokely Carmichael was going toe to toe with law officials. Elected chairman of SNCC a month before, he was one of the fiercest leaders of the re-formed march. White locals and law enforcement fringed the marchers, and white assailants were being identified by the crowd. Carmichael drew attention to a vio-lent law officer on the scene. At that point he was arrested and taken to the Greenwood jail.

When he was released, a crowd of perhaps a thousand had gath-ered to hear Carmichael speak. "This is the twenty-seventh time I have been arrested. I ain't going to jail no more," he said. At this moment, he pulled out a new slogan that he had been casually test-ing on those around him. Now would come the big test.

"We want *black power*."

A few voices shout back at him: "That's right!"

"We want black power!"

"That's right!"

"That's right. We want black power, and we don't want to be ashamed of it."

Word that James Brown was coming was passed up and down the line. Appeals had gone out to celebrities to show their support, and a man of the Southern people, a superstar whose music con-noted blackness, could not help but feel the pull. Perhaps Brown felt a personal affinity with Meredith, another bull, another indi-vidualist uneasy with group affiliations. At the end of his first semester at Ole Miss, Meredith had held a press conference announcing that "the 'Negro' should not return." He then added, "However, I have decided that *I*, J. H. Meredith, will register for the second semester." Like Brown, he insisted on being seen as a person, not a category, and was a loner with a streak of grandiosity.

It had been a long, bruising procession, right up to the end. In Canton on June 24, King was addressing the marchers when state troopers fired tear gas into the crowd, and protesters ran in every direction. Many dropped into ditches to suck the air close to the ground; there they were beaten by troopers swinging their rifle butts. The next day, they made it to the edge of Jackson, and pulled up at Tougaloo College, a black institution just outside of town. In the afternoon, King and other leaders gathered at a dean's house to assess the final rally and plan the program marking the finish of the march.

The arguments over who would speak and in what order went on until, finally, King cut things off abruptly. "I'm sorry, y'all," he explained as he made his exit. "James Brown is on. I'm gone."

Harry Belafonte had organized the program, which also featured Sammy Davis Jr. and Marlon Brando, but Brown was indisputably the star. He'd gathered a seven-member version of his band in Cincinnati, put them on his Learjet, and flown to Jackson. In order to take the stage, Brown was guided through the swarming crowd by bearded SNCC activist Cleveland Sellers; *Jet* said it looked like Moses parting the Red Sea. Film images from the day show Brown and the band on a platform at the crest of a hill, a forest behind them. They look small and serious, dwarfed by their surroundings.

Brown peers out at the crowd below him, scanning it for secrets. The stage is cramped; there are people sitting in folding chairs behind him, and high school students crouching on the edge of the stage. There's a podium, too, all of which makes it hard for Brown to dance, yet he tries. Though he typically liked to control his setting and the events around him, the look on his face shows he knows he's part of a bigger story.

The afternoon show began with "Papa's Got a Brand New Bag." It revitalized a crowd that was weary even before the sweltering temperatures rose above ninety degrees, and it also pointed to how Brown's music was being repurposed by a new generation of African Americans. Months before, a group in Canton, Mississippi, many of them domestic workers who had lost their jobs after organizing a voter registration campaign, had formed a sewing cooperative to produce leather coin purses. They named their product "Papa's Brand New Bag." Brown represented a new kind of black self-confidence, and his songs were being turned into expressions of hope and protest by his listeners.

A phrase like "brand new bag" effortlessly became a declaration of a new breed's arrival. Just a few months later, speaking in Newark, New Jersey, Stokely Carmichael would say, "James Brown's got more musical genius than Bach, Beethoven, and Mozart put together."

Another song at Tougaloo might have said as much to the crowd that day as "Papa's." Brown sang his latest single, "It's a Man's Man's Man's World," his plushest ballad yet; an elegy to cold comfort, a slow roll of shrieks and satin. He finished the brief set with "Please, Please, Please"–when he reached the phrase "just hang on," he incanted it over and over as tears streamed down his cheeks. "There was no doubt that he was addressing this plea to the Freedom Marchers who had endured harassment and abuse while marching the 260 miles from Memphis to Jackson," reported *The Philadelphia Tribune*.

At the performance's end, an announcer thanked the crowd: "You have just witnessed the rest of this show. This here's black power, baby." Brown's face looks over the crowd, giving a slight nod of agreement.

Arguments over the meaning of Black Power would divide many African Americans over the next few years. Many of the people who would find themselves at the center of the argument were present at Tougaloo. Many would follow Carmichael and lose their faith in nonviolence and their belief that whites and blacks could work together for equality. King and those behind him would make a moral appeal to America, one based on shared interests. In the space between them stood Brown. He became a cultural politician the moment he stepped off the plane in Jackson. By the time he left town, he found out his portfolio had become exceedingly more complicated.

. . .

"This is a man's world, but it wouldn't be nothing, nothing with-out a woman or a girl," Brown sings. Curiously, the song starts with a boast, and then all broadens a confession. He beats his chest as he sings the title, and from that moment on, doubt seeps into the music. By the final lyrics, the man in this man's world is "lost in the wilderness, he's lost in bitterness, he's lost somewhere in this lone-liness." It's a most peculiar ad for virility: a promise that it will make you alone, depraved, and howling like a jackal.

The song would be nothing without a specific woman, Betty Jean Newsome, who played a large part in writing it, and who then spent many years fighting for her song credit. Brown met Newsome the usual way: He was singing at the Apollo Theater in 1965, saw a pretty face in the crowd, and sent an aide out to bring her back-stage. They began traveling together.

It was a tempestuous relationship. He insisted on having things a certain way, and she was no pushover. Maybe that was part of the attraction. "He wanted his women to carry little dogs in their laps," said Newsome. "I'm not gonna carry no dog of his in my lap. No babies, neither.

"When we were going down South in the limousine, somebody had mentioned how most of his women had babies by him–'Why you ain't gonna have no babies?' I said, 'Why you ask me that–I ain't gonna have none of his monkey-looking babies.' They thought he was gonna knock me out of the limousine after I said that.

"The Flames covered their eyes when he looked like he was gonna hit me. I told them, 'Don't bother closing your eyes because *he* the one that's gonna be getting hit.' I said, 'What kind of men are you that you be so afraid of him?' They were scared stiff. He used to hit them grown men! It was crazy, it was pitiful the way that he treated them. He was something, boy."

As they were traveling by limousine around the South, New-some started humming a song she had come up with, and Brown liked it a lot. He changed some of the words, added strings, and put the song out under his own name. "He added a couple more 'mans' on there so he could try to steal it. But it didn't work," said New-some. "God don't like ugly and he sure don't go along with thieves! They get away with things for a little bit but he catch up with them after a while." Eventually, a judge would grant Newsome co-authorship of the song.

The pace was picking up. A month after the Tougaloo concert, the black press was full of reports that Brown had been beaten up by his hairdresser. Brutalized so badly he might not be able to work due to his injuries, so badly that he filed a suit against the man. Some wondered how a hairdresser could have gotten the drop on an ex-boxer. Others stooped to sarcasm: "Despite his fondness for flowing Batman-type capes, patent-leather shoes, pancake makeup, artificial eyebrows and eye shadow, there is nothing in James Brown's background to indicate he is effeminate," wrote a columnist in *The Philadelphia Tribune*.

Brown was suing his former coiffeur, Frank McRae, for an alleged assault. The precipitating event had occurred several years before, in Los Angeles, after the two had been drinking at Tommy Tucker's Playroom. McRae, Brown, and his girlfriend got into Brown's purple and silver Fleetwood and drove to Dolphin's of Hollywood, a record store off Central Avenue. The singer headed for the shop and McRae was parking the Fleetwood when a police car flagged him down. McRae had liquor on his breath.

One officer called him "nigger" and other things, while his partner kept a hand on his gun. McRae knew the drill from being in the South with Brown, so he just said *yessir.* They gave him a ticket and drove off.

When Brown got back in the car, his girlfriend told him all the things the policeman had called McRae. "You ain't no man, Mac," growled Brown, who proceeded to tell his concierge what *he* would have done had the policemen insulted him, all the way back to the hotel on Sunset where they were staying. In the lobby, up the elevator to the penthouse, Brown continued to describe how McRae had disgraced himself before the police.

McRae had plenty of time to formulate an answer, which when it was delivered was along the lines of, "You wouldn't have done a motherfucking thing." And just like that it was two rights and a left cross from Brown, and McRae was on the floor. He awoke to find Brown "shining his shoes," McRae would say later—kicking him as McRae lay on the ground.

The dapper stylist got up and grabbed Brown, holding him hard against the wall in the hotel hallway. Ben Bart appeared on the scene with a .25 in his hand, and McRae felt sure Bart was going to pop him, "because Ben Bart love him more than he love me." It didn't happen, but moments later McRae left the hotel room, and the employ, of James Brown.

The lawsuit against McRae was a shot across his bow, an effort to get the jump on the suit McRae was fixing to file. Eventually they settled out of court.

The impulse behind Brown's behavior was simple: Make an overwhelming show of his masculine force. He told stories that fed this image, extolling his past as a brawler, his way with women. It was a man's world, that's just the way it was, and he was in control.

At the same time, however, there was a competing image complicating the picture. For Brown wasn't just softening the hard features that McRae noted, he was offsetting them in ways that raised eyebrows. Putting on pancake makeup and elaborate eyeliner, doing his hair in a style popular among black women, in the mid-1960s, Brown made some wonder about his sexuality. His boyhood friend Henry Stallings ran into him on 125th Street around this time, and Stallings's first impression, he said, was that Brown had "gone sissy."

Street corner rumors spread in Detroit and elsewhere that he liked men. Then, in late 1965, came stories that the singer was to undergo corrective surgery. The talk started in Alabama, and then reached Texas and beyond. " 'James Brown is going to change himself to a woman' was the rumor that was circulating as late as last week among the teenagers, and now it has spread among the adults," declared the *Houston Forward Times*. The story was enough of a problem for him in Houston that an emissary was sent to squash it in advance of an appearance. Brown himself would later claim that *he* had spread yet another rumor, that he was marrying Bobby Byrd after Byrd had gotten a sex change. It was all a publicity stunt, he declared. Possibly. But in the black South of 1965, that would have been pushing the "any publicity is good publicity" philosophy beyond convention, if not beyond all likelihood. It sounds like a rumor Bart and Brown were anxious to get in front of.

In March 1966, he made his first visit to England and France. The next month, *Time* said that his "rise in the mass market gives a sign that 'race music' is perhaps at last becoming interracial." Things were happening fast now, and they would for years to come. Time was quickening, and success was like a jewel pressed into the palm of his hand, with so many decisions to be made at once, and so many events he needed to get in front of.

Always he had to assert his will and keep others in check. The competition had to be vanquished—and not just bested, but wasted, that was the idea. In the mid-'60s, no competitor meant more to Brown than Jackie Wilson. A pure singer from Detroit, Wilson had been a good boxer, too, and a fine dancer, and he also was managed by Ben Bart. So they had a lot in common, which was problem enough. But there was a lot that wasn't the same, and maybe that was worse. Wilson was light-skinned, pretty, and had an effortless way with women, and Brown resented him on all counts.

"Being a mulatto, he didn't have the energy or strength I had," Brown later declared. "What got Jackie through was his complexion. During that time, if you were light complexioned, you had it. I was the one who made the dark complexioned people popular."

When Wilson broke through by singing with the Dominoes, Brown went backstage to say hi and was regally dismissed by the star, who called him "Jimmy," a gesture guaranteed to wind him up. After that, it was *on*. As Brown was preparing for an appearance at the Howard Theatre in Washington, D.C., he heard a clamor from out on the street. That's when he saw Wilson, driving a fur-lined Cadillac convertible that just happened to pass by the kids lined up to see Brown. That Wilson didn't even get out and greet him standing there on the sidewalk, Brown felt, stuck it to him all the more.

In retaliation, Brown went to see Wilson's show the same week. The band was playing, getting ready for the singer's big entrance, and here came Brown, fans pushing him up and up toward the stage. The Upsetters, Brown's old cohorts, were Wilson's band that night, and they knew Brown's material–and started playing it, as he sang. The crowd felt like they'd paid for an ice cream cone and been given a double dip.

Then, to rub it in, Brown went backstage to say hi to Wilson. He found him in his dressing room, in red bikini briefs, laying on his stomach and getting a massage. Bart was urging him to get out and do his show. "Why do I need to go out there?" Wilson whined. "*That* guy just did my set."

After the knockout punch came the polishing of shoes. And after the polishing of shoes must come fresh battles. It was the progression upon which a career was built.

In 1966, his contract was finally up, and it came at a time when Nathan felt he *had* to re-sign Brown. Much had changed at King since Brown's aborted leap to Smash. The thirty-three branch offices that had once been essential to King's success, operating across the country and delivering product to stores and radio stations, had become too costly to maintain. In 1964, Nathan shut them down, relying on independent distributors, middlemen who might work with dozens of labels large and small, to put his records in circulation.

Disenchanted, Nathan had come close to selling King when "Papa's" became a huge hit. He was spending more and more time in hospitals and in Miami. Meanwhile, independent record companies everywhere were having a hard time competing with major labels in an increasingly international market. King was a dinosaur, Brown could plainly see that. He could sign with a major label, and be a member of a team, or stay at King and be the only game in town, with complete control. And control, more than money, was always the most important thing to Brown.

In September 1966, Nathan offered him a contract that put in writing the freedom he'd already informally given the singer. King's new contract gave Brown creative control of his music, and the ability to sign and record artists for the label. He was given an office and staff, and King covered a portion of his expenses. It also provided Brown with some 25,000 gratis copies of each single and album he produced.

From this point on, though King might cut a few good songs by other artists, James Brown carried their load. They basically now existed to make James Brown records. In time, many around the label would even believe that Brown *owned* King, though that was never the case. As Henry Glover would put it, "James had his way then. He was selling a few records for [Nathan], and he could do whatever he wanted to."

Brown built a staff of employees who planned his tours, marketing, and publicity. He was a tough boss: One staffer recalled him punching an employee for turning in an expense form without receipts attached. But he was not an insincere boss. Brown ran the office the same way he ran his band, and it was clear going in that hard work and loyalty were necessities. But even with them, a certain randomness kept everybody on their toes.

Watching the store when Brown was out of town was a devoted aide, Bud Hobgood. A tall, skinny redhead from Kentucky who spoke with a backwoods drawl, Hobgood had managed a few local bands before catching on with Brown. Nobody seems to remember him working his way up any ladder. One day he was just *there*, hanging out with the singer in nightclubs, listening as he whispered into his ear. Hobgood did plenty of things for Brown—setting up recording sessions, wrangling new material—but everybody wondered on a more fundamental level exactly why Brown kept him around. He was a man without musical gifts, yet over the next few years Brown gave Hobgood songwriting credits on some of his biggest hits. Hobgood even held the briefcase full of cash for Brown.

"Anything that James had to do with King, Hobgood was in charge of," said David Matthews, a composer and keyboardist.

Rumors flourished—did he know something about Brown? Did Brown feel he owed Hobgood, because he had an eye for his wife? "Nobody could ever figure out what James saw in him," said Matthews. "People were wondering, did James do something illegal that Hobgood knew about? There was never any good answer to this question."

The moneymaker could record what and when he wanted, and his employees had better be ready. Engineer Jim Deak remembered the routine. "Two or three days before they were going to do it, somebody'd come down and say 'James is coming.' And then there'd be a mad scramble to clean the place up . . .

"You didn't have a chance to put up mics, it wasn't like you scheduled a session and knew what was coming. They just walked in and started playing. And while they were playing, you'd walk around and set up the mics in front of them, fiddle with the board."

He could show up and stay in a studio for twenty hours making a single, then pull somebody else's record off the conveyer belt so his new one could be rushed out. Control. Some at King thought Brown was too powerful, and Nathan became one of them. He sought to put Brown's power in check by bringing into the office

Charles Spurling, a talented Cincinnati musician who had also been a teenage gang member and self-professed "knockout artist." Spurling was hired both as black muscle to push back at Brown, and as an A&R man who would draw Bootsy Collins, Marva Wright, and others into the King fold.

The way Spurling explained it, early on he and Brown had a confrontation that clarified many things for both of them. It began one day when Spurling was staring ominously at Brown—"I wanted to eat his ass up" is how he put it—and making his presence felt.

Brown told his bodyguards to watch Spurling, got on the office-wide intercom, and ordered everybody from Nathan on down to a conference in his office. Gesturing to Spurling, Brown said, "I got a man here with death in his eyes. That man right there gonna hurt somebody." Very quickly he had seen the big picture, and deduced why Spurling was hired. He went on a long monologue describing his worth to the company, how Nathan had placated him with Cadillacs and promises; it went on for a long while, a tirade and lecture making the point that he started unappreciated by King and here he was, the man at the top—with King still trying to undermine him. Then he said he wanted Spurling to work for *him*.

It was a brilliant day's work, putting the boss, the hired fist, and everybody in between in their place, and letting them all know he knew what was going on.

"I was going to hurt James Brown," said Spurling. "But see, this is when I started respecting him."

The posse working for him—Hobgood, Alan Leeds, Bob Patton, Charles Bobbit—called themselves the El Dorados, after the pimp car you better drive if you wanted to be a member. They'd go out for dinner together, then maybe over to the Hustler Club or across the river to hear the Dee Felice Trio. They never went together—the idea was a flotilla of El Dorados, all driving in force from spot to spot. They made a gangster-style entrance, beginning with Brown and moving down through the chain of command. The posse settled in and waited for the boss to make the first move. If you saw a girl you felt like chatting up, you didn't do it unless the boss was already chatting somebody up. You weren't supposed to peel off from the pack.

Two concerts in the fall of 1966 suggested the range, and limits, of Brown's gathering power. In November in Kansas City, Missouri, a bottle-throwing melee led to the arrest of thirty concertgoers. Three policemen were hospitalized with injuries. The specifics were murky, though it appeared that the show featured a dance contest in which a local couple did a lurid version of the popular dance called "the Dog," one that the crowd favored. The judges, however, gave the prize to a more dignified dance team, and the house erupted. The show was shut down, and devotees of the Dog went on a window-breaking downtown rampage. Brown at least could note he wasn't even on the stage when that happened.

But a few weeks later, at the Apollo, he was doing his show when he spied several unexpected visitors in the wings, signaling they were about to come onstage. There was jazz bandleader Lionel Hampton, one of the few black Republicans the public knew of, standing beside New York governor Nelson Rockefeller, a Republican who just happened to be up for reelection in a few days, and Republican Senator Jacob Javits. Suddenly they were smiling and walking to him, Brown deftly greeted them, the governor saying hello, there were handshakes, pictures of the handshakes, and the visitors were gone. It might have looked like Brown had brought some buddies out onto the stage to bestow a celebrity endorsement to the Republicans. Later the singer made clear the appearance had not been his idea, and that he had been caught off guard. "The Apollo Theater is non-political. And so is James Brown, the pied piper of the New Breed," helpfully declared the *New York Amsterdam News* in the wake of the bum rush.

People who had never done the Dog wanted a piece of him and wanted to define him for their ends. He may have been polite in letting them commandeer his stage, but the hero of Tougaloo, the rising symbol of the new black manhood, probably walked off the Apollo stage with a fresh awareness of how important it was to control events, and how hard it was, too, the higher you rose above the crowd.

Chapter Twelve

GHOST NOTES

In a show built on rhythm, the drummer was the prime mover. By the mid-'60s, Brown was traveling with several drummers at a time. It made for a fine display of excess, and besides, relying on a single person made him reliant, which was intolerable. Plus, each performance–the band playing a set out front, then the featured female vocalist of the moment, then Bobby Byrd or whoever it was singing *their* new single, then Brown's set–wore down any drummer trying to play all four hours night after night. Brown was deep with drummers in 1965, but he still felt the need to restock.

John "Jabo" Starks was an already established player in 1965, a sturdy stoker of old fires when he joined the James Brown band. Starks was in his early twenties and had been backing Bobby Blue Bland, a profound singer and maybe the last great rhythm and blues performer to thrive in the age of soul. He came in ready to play the *hell* out of the drums, but the men with Bland taught him that the greatest thing he could do was also the humblest–keep the time. Solos and breaks, acrobatics and cowbells, *nothing* was more important than steadiness, because everybody from the singer on down was lost without it. Starks took that lesson to heart, providing something hip and clean that his bandmates could lean on. He became a young man who thought like an old guy.

It would have almost been a crime against nature if Starks had not become a drummer, given the specifics of his Southern upbringing. Like Clayton Fillyau, who had been schooled by a New Orleans master, Starks, too, had his Crescent City mentor. He said the drummer Cornelius "Tenoo" Coleman taught him important lessons when Starks was a young man in Mobile. There was also the influence of the Holiness Church, with its disruptive, soul-fire experience of sanctification. Many African American musicians have credited the influence of sanctification. Trumpeter Dizzy Gillespie said that as a boy, the Methodists did nothing for him, but in the sanctified church he "learned the meaning of rhythm." Bo Diddley said his drummer played "the sanctified rhythm."

Sanctified church music has been praised, but what defines it remains rather unclear. Looking back on his childhood, Starks offered this useful definition: "In the holiness churches they didn't have sets of drums, maybe just a snare drum or a bass drum, but they had tambourines, and they clapped. And the way they clapped, I just loved that feel. It's just a floating feel. They'd clap their rhythm against the songs they were doing—kind of a polyrhythm. One section of folk would be clapping one way, and the other section would be clapping another way, and then the tambourine would be going. I used to go to the 'holiness' church when I was up in the country with my grandmother. I went almost every Sunday because I loved to hear the rhythms they were using. That's basically where a lot of it comes from for me. That sanctified rhythm influenced my playing . . ."

Outside the church, Starks was schooled by marching bands. Mobile, Alabama, his hometown, is a city with a beat of its own, the original capital of French Louisiana, and the first place in America where Carnival was celebrated. "Mardi Gras started in Mobile," Starks told an interviewer. "I used to watch the marching bands. There was a high school drum corps that really just blew my mind and I wanted to play after that."

He took what Tenoo taught him, paired with his sanctified rhythms and his marching band cadences, and burned them down to essences. Light shined through his playing. Drumming for Bland, he became a master of the seemingly simple rhythmic approach called the shuffle. Once you start listening for shuffle rhythms, you can hear them throughout American music. Think of the way triplets—a beat broken into equal thirds—drives "Please, Please, Please." That's a classic shuffle, as is, say, Fats Domino's "Blueberry Hill." Then there's the half-time shuffle, the boom-chica boom-chica that motivates Chuck Berry's "Maybelline" or Bill Doggett's "Honky Tonk" or about a billion other tunes. Then there's the more basic triplet *feeling* nesting in a 4/4 beat and giving jazz its swing feeling. The shuffle is to blues, jazz, and R&B what a *roux* is to New Orleans cooking: a stock that you add to, misleadingly simple and so easy to mess up. In talented hands, the shuffle feels good going on and on and on. And when Brown snatched Starks from Bland in 1965, that's most of all what he brought: a rock-steady foundation tethered to the past, a guy with all the wits to nail it down in the now. He must have given Brown's show comfort and stability.

But first, Starks had to *learn* the show. It was exhausting and long, and once you memorized the song list, you had to be ready to reconfigure it nightly—you had to react to the subtle cues of Brown's hands, his feet, his voice, his eyes. Announce songs? Hah. A-one-two-three-four? Brown's between-song swagger across the stage was his way of counting off the beat, and when he did the splits, *that* was your One. Clayton Fillyau carried the book of James Brown drumming in his head, and though he wasn't playing much by the mid-'60s, he was driving the bus, and he was teaching.

Fillyau took new drummers aside, sat them down after hours in hotel cocktail lounges, and *sang* them the entire show, while beating out the rhythms on the top of the bar. Every once in a while he'd start beating on your arm, hard, and that was part of the education, too—you wanted to learn it right quick before an icepack was required.

Later in 1965, just when Starks was settling in with his new band, Brown hired another drummer, a different type of cat. Clyde

Stubblefield grew up in Chattanooga, Tennessee, and his influences were less specific than Starks's. He, too, talked about marching bands, but Stubblefield described hearing the sounds of Chattanooga–the urban thrum of the foundries and TVA power plants of the "Dynamo of Dixie"–and aimed to convey all that sound on the drums. As a young man he delivered newspapers, and between deliveries he could be found in a club on Chattanooga's east side, playing pinball to pass the time. His hangout was not a large place, and the jukebox was hard beside the pinball machine. From that jukebox, Stubblefield first heard Jabo Starks's playing. As he dropped nickels in and let the balls ring the bells, Stubblefield heard the luminous sound of Bland's perfect hit, "Turn on Your Love Light," and the crazy shuffle beat Starks puts up high on his cymbal.

The totality of that experience was what Brown's band would sound like, a few years down the road, after Stubblefield arrived: the wedding of a pinball machine and the blues, of a gifted shuffle playing against an unpredictable clamor. It sounded damned nice.

After passing a harrowing audition for Brown before a live audience, Stubblefield joined the band. He was told to stand in the wings and watch, for about a month. When Brown finally shot him a signal in the middle of a show, and Stubblefield walked out to where a drum kit was set up next to Starks, he had formally entered the ring.

The records on that Chattanooga jukebox, Bobby Bland and the rest, was music made for adults, African American men and women who dressed up when work was done, held their partners on the dance floor, and grinded out their blues. From the late 1950s on, however, a new music was available under the canopy of *rock and roll*: It skewed to teenagers and to dancers who weren't touching one another. The beat was pushing out the old shuffle in favor of more regular eighth-note patterns, "straight eight," as this rewrite has long been known. Think of Jerry Lee Lewis or Little Richard pounding the piano–they were wailing the straight eight.

Along with the great straight eight, another big thing happened in the late 1950s: New Orleans annexed the United States of America. More or less. New Orleans musicians were in high demand as rock and roll took hold, and the city's numerous studios were cutting numberless hits targeting the children of those who dug Bland. In the Crescent City, drummers were bringing African rhythms, Latin beats, and the street flavors they heard all around them into their recording sessions. Straight eight was a strong, broad back for New Orleans drummers to climb on and take their music beyond city limits. They kept doubling it up, too, playing sixteenth and thirty-second notes—the pulse broken into microns of time, shot through with holes, syncopated so that playing and not playing spun around each other like subatomic particles.

That old swing vibe, the hip knowingness that came from laying a 3/4 feeling over 4/4 time, was challenged by this *new* way of feeling, which allowed more influences into the music, and which, once dancers were educated, spoke more eloquently to the body. Hips don't lie: This was the way ahead.

Meanwhile, the drum section of the James Brown band was starting to look like a midway shooting gallery. The band had *five* drummers when Stubblefield joined, and Clyde made six. He and Starks were restive about getting more playing time and together concocted a plan. They knew they played better than the others, and they found ways to play together and show the boss. One of the others was fired, and then there were five, then four. Brown was listening and liked what he heard enough to keep firing guys until it was down to Clyde and Jabo. "Every time a drummer got knocked off we'd just look at each other and go, 'All right!'," said Stubblefield.

For the next five years, and again later in the 1970s, Starks and Stubblefield played side by side. "We don't get in each other's way, we just groove with it," explained Starks. "And we've got a certain way that we can look at each other, and I know exactly what he wants to do."

You always have to wonder with James Brown, if what happened was really as accidental as it seemed. Did he mean to put one drummer who was the summation of the past several decades together with a guy ready to play the sound of things to come? Or did it just turn out that way? "It's amazing how Jabo and me work," Stubblefield has said. "He plays one type of beat and I come along and play a different groove against what he's playing. And it works."

The band pulled into Cincinnati one May day in 1967, and got off the bus for a scheduled session. They set up in a semicircle at King, with only a single microphone for the lot of them. Brown carried ideas around with him for weeks, months even, until he felt the time was right. This time a bass line had been circulating in his head, one he had already shared with his music director, a good-natured jazzbo named Pee Wee Ellis. Ellis fleshed out the fragment and wrote out charts; *now* the time was right. After the band had worked up something good in the studio, Brown walked in and added lyrics, something about breaking into a cold sweat.

In the middle of the song, for the first time, he says it: "Let's give the drummer some."

Brown was *always* saying guff like that, off-the-top mumbo jumbo, mash notes from the id. Stubblefield didn't know Brown was going to say it, and his response was to keep on doing what he had been doing, as the band dropped out and Stubblefield takes his indelible, unshow-offy solo–a progression of hummingbird dips and sips.

The drummer's sixteenth and soft thirty-second notes drive it. He isn't giving you the time, he doesn't whomp the backbeat, it's there in negative relief as he plays around it, hanging a big wreath around it so you know where it is and can shoot a cannonball clear through it. The two-bar pattern he plays is a constant throughout the song, and when Stubblefield gets to the last beat of the second measure, that final four, he holds off on it . . . hold it . . . hold it . . . When he hits it, it's like the cannonball has landed.

The song they were recording was "Cold Sweat," and the drumming wasn't the only thing that made "Cold Sweat" indelible. Maybe it was also that one-chord-change structure, as visionary and protean as Frida Kahlo's one eyebrow. It was so brutal it made hipsters—the Blue Note records-playing tastemakers Ellis dug–grunt and declare the thing was not music. For sure, it wasn't another pop song.

Instead it was a straight-ahead ride. And here is the deal with that single chord change: If your ride doesn't come to a station, you never have to get off. You are already home. There is a reason why music teachers call the succession of harmonies in a song a *chord progression*. They have a lot invested in the word *progress* nestled in the phrase. Like their assumption that "growth" or history's forward march is tied to a series of chord changes, and the assumption that a proper sequence of chords builds an arc, or a storyline, or somehow creates a sense of getting somewhere. "Cold Sweat" jumps off that train. It moves all right, but it does not travel a route. "Cold Sweat" is about an enduring, dominant present.

Or maybe what made "Cold Sweat" was the smell the title gave off. Nobody ever wrote a hit song about perspiration before. Nobody had ever thought to sing about an uncomfortable ferment of the body caused by the nearness of other-flesh. And when somebody *did* think to sing about this morbid, anxious, and itchy condition, Brown did it in such a way that it did not feel odd. It felt *just*. When the horns go up the scale and Brown exclaims the clamminess is breaking out everywhere, everything stops: You are deep into a clamor of the body and the wanting soul. And then Stubblefield takes a solo.

When he returned to the Apollo to record a new live album in the summer of 1967, Brown had nothing to prove. This was one of his greatest bands, with Maceo Parker back from an army stint and Pee Wee Ellis a new recruit. Perhaps he just felt a need to document the awesomeness he had and could never fully capture on a three-minute 45 rpm recording. He also just liked the Apollo. Who wouldn't?

"Every vice imaginable was on trade at some point each day by that stage door," said Alan Leeds, Brown's onetime road manager. "While you were at the Apollo, backstage was your home–it's small and tight, three or four levels of small rooms, roaches in all of them, and if you're doing six shows a day it was your whole life.

"There was nothing to do but sit back there and observe. If you were booked for a week, after the first or second day you were done with the crossword puzzles. Dope dealers, people selling hot jewelry, prostitutes working the stairwell–you could get a blowjob, hot rings, and heroin all on the stairwell of the Apollo. There were also weird guys waiting around, guys with names like Sparky and Trees, guys who cut hair in case you need a haircut, or who provided security in the wings–you needed security in the wings? But Trees was there. These guys from Georgia weren't gonna pick much cotton in the Apollo, so maybe they'd get into a card game where they could make a few dollars and get over."

You paced yourself when you played there, and you didn't see much of New York, except for the line around the block. "The Apollo was the work place," said Stubblefield. "We'd sometimes do ten shows a day on Saturday. People would be standing in line, waiting on them to get out, so they could get in. Back-to-back shows, some of them. And each show would probably last an hour and forty minutes. I mean, that's a lot of work."

The show Brown recorded as *Live at the Apollo, Volume II* is front-loaded with ballads, and slowly builds to a second-half medley that is among his finest recorded work. Thick in all of it are Clyde and Jabo, Jabo and Clyde.

They challenged each other. Stubblefield was a master of "ghost notes," between-the-beat fractional left-hand flicks on the snare that gave the whole sound a bubbling cauldron feel. Ghost notes were so quiet you might not hear them, and that was when they had their maximum effect–they worked on the listener subconsciously. Starks matched him with what he called "Holy Ghost notes."

They complemented each other. Jabo handled the blues, the

standards, the set tunes, while Clyde tended to play on the jams. But what's great about *Volume II* is that they are side by side in the second half of the record, two approaches to rhythm overlaying a suite of songs, one drummer working a little before the beat, the other a shade behind, and the effect is of time becoming unglued.

Several later tunes on *Volume II* form the piece that's come to be known collectively as "There Was a Time," which is also the name of a song in the medley. Arranger Pee Wee Ellis said of it, "We knew we were putting it down hard and heavy and we knew it was good, but we had no idea that forty years later it would still be important."

This piece begins with "Let Yourself Go," which establishes the choppy midtempo for all that follows. "Let Yourself Go" is meat tenderizer, a way of loosening everybody up, its title as much an order as a suggestion. Follow or be forsaken.

As the rhythm unhitches a few minutes in, the guitar line of "Let Yourself Go" keeps repeating while a new horn riff, the one underlining the song "There Was a Time," insinuates itself. For a tantalizing few moments two songs are grinding against each other, and this is no accident, for it establishes an important idea: The past and the present are colliding, they are exploding together. All becomes now.

Key to it is guitarist Jimmy Nolen–Jimmy Nolen! If having two drummers seemed like extravagance, Nolen was the inverse–he could only play a rarified little bit all over the place, because if Nolen ever played half of what he knew, the knowledge might kill you. He plays from the edges: here a trace of some ancient backwoods dance, there a blues that sounds like rusted iron. His playing is a tincture that gets into everything. His is a really, really old voice, steadying all and pointing the way forward; a guide not strict or harsh, just irresistible and correct.

His approach was overwhelmingly that of a drummer. Nolen said he learned to play his precise sixteenth notes before he joined Brown's band, after doing too many shows with so-so drummers who didn't carry the beat. "I used to just try to play and keep my rhythm going as much like a drum as I possibly could," he said. "So many times I had to just play guitar and drums all at the same time. You know what I mean? By keeping that rhythm going, it kind of keeps the drummer straight."

It was a prolific amount of rhythm for one show, so much that all this talent could easily have pushed the music toward jazz or the avant-garde. (Miles Davis was listening hard; before long, he *was* pushing this music into the jazz avant-garde.) Brown wasn't interested in a dazzling display of technique, he wanted a mass of people dancing. And for this he increasingly made use of the One. For all the genius and dexterity of the drummers, for all the head-spinning polyrhythms that sometimes lock tight and other times subtly pull ahead of and behind the beat, for all of that, Brown made sure that the One was the biggest beat going. Hit that, and the audience could stay with him. The One was many things, and on this record we hear how it is the cash upfront he pays for all the rhythm it buys. Hold on to the One, and then let Clyde and Jabo do their thing. In the studio, he would hear a beat they were working on and, over and over, repeat one unchanging thing: I love it, but you got to put it on the One. You give the audience some, and then you give the drummers some.

Brown had his own special dance number, the ultimate dance number, in "There Was a Time." Jabo Starks struggled to explain what made it special. " 'There Was a Time' was . . . let me see how to use the word, uh, the tune reminded me of what we call hoofers. Dancers, tap dancers and things, you know." The song takes time as its subject. The singer says, "There was a time when I used to dance," striking an elegiac mood and then transporting it to the present, because he's doing all those old steps in front of us. We are not in the past—"Dig me now, don't worry 'bout later," he commands. Then he calls out his move, the Mashed Potato.

"In my hometown, where I used to stay/the name of the place is Augusta G-A," Brown announces. "Down there we have a good time, we don't talk/we all get together in any type of weather and we do the Camel Walk." Augusta isn't invoked as part of his or anyone's literal past. Augusta here is the place we all come from and to which we wish to get back, standing in for Home, or the valley, or wherever our mind goes when we think of sanctuary. And in that place the Camel Walk–like all the other dances conjured–is a shared set of moves through time that bring that place into existence. *We don't talk* because words can be misunderstood, they divide us, and these dances bring us together.

"There Was a Time" is a history of black dance Brown illustrates in sequence. This is the past evoked in the present, every one of the moves a sense memory meant to summon a different set of rooms, moments, lights, and smells. In the middle of the song, Fred Wesley's trombone has peeled off from the rest of the brass, it's offering a salty commentary or parody of the horn riff, a doppler-effect call and response, a theme and variation chasing each other to a beat. It is one more way that the past and the present are in collision.

Then he performs the James Brown. All the steps of the past telescope into this dance with the ultimate name. What *is* the James Brown? He explained it once this way: "Combine the apple-jack, the dolo, which is a slide, almost like the skate, and the scally-hop, which is a takeoff on the lindy hop, add a nerve control technique that makes the whole body tremble, and you got the James Brown." Got it? He preferred to not give away his secrets.

Poet Larry Neal has said that "There Was a Time" does nothing less than "trace . . . the history of a people through their dances." Two drummers pulling at the beat from both ends, unraveling time . . . The history of a people nesting in an ongoing dance called the James Brown . . . Through these means does the performance shake off history and dance us all into a timeless haven.

But the song is not done. Now it's time for *us* to join the dance. Brown talks to the crowd. "Do you feel all right? I feel pretty good myself." The beat comes down to a rustle. He asks the band if they are ready, then the dancers, then the audience. The guitar on top is clacking out an expansive pattern that sounds like a mountain musician playing two bones.

"Building, is you ready? Because we gonna tear you down. I hope the building can stand all this soul 'cause it's sure got a lot coming on . . ." And with that Brown instructs the audience to do what he is doing, to fold in behind him and his steps—he is showing us all how to do the James Brown.

He is taking us back to Augusta in our minds, to a haven as real as any place on Earth. That's a pretty powerful nerve control technique.

A high school student from Sturgis, Michigan, interviewing Brown in the black press in the mid-1960s wanted to know: "Have you ever been embarrassed because of prejudice?" Brown thought quietly, then said, "I better not answer that one." But questions like that kept coming up, and he knew he better have answers. People wanted to know what he thought about the news of the day.

In the fall of 1967, *Jet* covered Brown's return from a tour of Europe. The piece featured a well-crafted quote: "In 12 hours after leaving the US for Europe, I became a man, while I'm still a boy, still growing here where I was born," he said. "I truly felt like a man, not like colored or Negro but like a man—period." In the past Brown had used *Jet* to issue formal statements, and this item has the feel of one. And while he starts by criticizing America's racial shortcomings, his true message follows that setup. "Although we still have problems and regardless of the fact that I was treated so well there, this is still home," he said. "I'm still an American above anything else. It may sound foolish to some people, but I'd rather be a broke man here than a rich man over there."

It was a response to the calls for Black Power, which had only gotten louder since the Mississippi march. Home was home, and for all its flaws America was worth fixing. For Brown, black education would lead to black empowerment, and empowerment to equality; that was his touchstone.

By 1966, Brown was talking about politics with various people, including an independent thinker from the Bay Area named Donald Warden (who later changed his name to Khalid Abdullah Tariq al-Mansour). Warden became a sounding board for the singer and perhaps the biggest influence on his thinking.

Raised in Pittsburgh, Warden studied at Howard University under John Hope Franklin and E. Franklin Frazier, two revered scholars. He did community organizing in Detroit, and then lived in India in the late '50s, where he met Prime Minister Nehru. By the early '60s he was studying at Berkeley, where he joined an African American reading group that included Huey Newton, Bobby Seale, and Ron Dellums, and which was an early intellectual influence on the Black Panthers. Warden hosted a black news radio program that stressed a message of self-help and the need for education.

A quirky local show promoter named Ray Dobard suggested to Warden that putting black performers on his radio program would help publicize his message. Visiting musicians could promote their upcoming appearance, and in return they would endorse his program of "no drop outs, no flunk outs." Aretha Franklin, Joe Tex, and Ike Turner were among Warden's guests.

Dobard told Warden he could interest Brown in publicizing Warden's ideas. They set up a meeting at Dobard's Berkeley office. Brown asked how he could help.

"It was clear to me, of all the entertainers, Otis Redding, Joe Tex, any of them . . . James had the capacity to make a commitment," said Warden. "And when he made a commitment, he was *serious.*"

Warden told Brown, "One or two words from you to stay in school, get honor grades, will make a difference."

And when he simply heard it, James said, "Brother—it's me and you. What do you want me to do?"

They went around Richmond and Oakland, visiting liquor stores, barbershops, walking the streets and chatting with folks. "He was talking to people there and he started telling them, 'You know young man, you ought to stay in school.' He'd say, 'I want you to do this for *me*. We need some doctors and scientists.' I could see it—they'd say 'yes *sir*, Mr. Brown!'

"And I could see him become addicted to this connection. 'Did you see that kid? He *promised* me.' He liked that."

They talked about writing a song to carry the message. "I said 'Mr. Brown, we don't have any musical talent, but we have some people who think they can write some words. We'd like to submit them to you to see if they can be commercialized.'

"Don't get your feelings hurt if I reject them," Brown said. "Because I *will* be in charge."

That's how "Don't Be a Dropout" came to be, as a message and song. Brown debuted it in Washington in 1966 at a National Urban League event, then visited with Hubert Humphrey and got the support of the vice president, who was working on a "Stay in School" program of his own. In Warden, Brown perhaps saw a bit of himself— he was another black man who stubbornly formed his own ideas about progress. A 1963 *New York Times* article described Warden's opposition to integration, based on quirky, nuanced reasoning. Over the next few years the two had regular conversations about politics and black empowerment.

Brown firmly defended America, and had meant "Dropout" to be, besides pro-education, an alternative to black radicalism's standing critique. Don't tear it down, go to school and you can help mend America, he said.

Nobody expected Diana Ross and the Supremes to comment on urban rioting, but people wanted to know what Brown thought. Artists are allowed, even expected, to be ambiguous, contradictory. But spokespeople need a sharply defined message if they seek to be understood. The challenge for Brown over the next few years would be to hold on to his creative freedom—the right to try out and play with ideas and exchange them for new ones—while building his case as an agent of change. He wanted to be both things, at the same time.

When King began closing down its regional offices in the early 1960s, the label lost much of its presence in the hinterlands. Already interested in radio, Brown witnessed the label's waning outreach and become even more interested in using the power of radio. He was still Music Box, and he still depended on the radio to hear what America was listening to. More than before, he pondered what it would be like to present his own programs to listeners.

He yearned to broadcast and already had syndicated a short-lived fifteen-minute show produced by Arthur Smith. On a swing through Texas, he paid an exploratory visit to one of the most powerful independent stations in the world, XERF in Ciudad Acuña, just across the border from Del Rio, Texas. Operating beyond the reach of the Federal Communications Commission, XERF was a so-called border blaster, a renegade signal capable of transmitting at up to a million watts. At peak power, XERF could be heard in distant parts of the planet; it spontaneously turned on lights near the border, and its music was picked up by bedsprings and barbed-wire fences. The programming, too, was powerful, a freewheeling mix of rock and roll, rambunctious preaching, and patent medicine hucksters.

On the day Brown took a cab across the Rio Grande and dropped in on XERF, one of the station's signature voices, an up-and-coming jock calling himself Wolfman Jack, was on duty. A worker had just climbed down from the 300-foot tower when Brown arrived, having replaced a red light that kept aircraft from flying into it. "Would you like to have a job like that?" Jack joked, and quick as that, Brown, in a collarless gray suit and red patent-leather shoes, jumped onto the tower and climbed all the way to the top. When he finished his ascent, he hooked a leg around the last rung of a ladder, leaned out over the Mexican landscape, and waved down at the terrified staff.

Statements to the press indicated he would soon be spinning records on XERF; there's no telling what his fertile mind and a million watts of power might have achieved. But these turned out to be the final days of the border blasters, with the U.S. and Mexican governments jointly cracking down on their signals.

Instead of border blasters, Brown began purchasing regular radio stations, first Knoxville's WJBE in January 1968 for $75,000, and then Augusta's WRDW for $377,000 a month later. Instantly the Augusta station became a symbol of Brown's rise from a ragged boy shining shoes in front of WRDW's building, to the station owner. He changed its Top 40 format to R&B and pledged service to black Augusta. Brown "planned to remedy the problem of one-sided news coverage in Augusta, by complete and objective news reporting." New programming would include "Profiles in Black," segments meant to build racial pride.

Around this time, Brown was separating from manager Ben Bart. Interested in developing business opportunities, he moved his business office out of Universal Attractions' building and hired his own business staff. Bart was getting older, and the protégé felt that he had learned all he could. The elder was a chitlin circuit man, and Brown had outgrown that, too.

His new business office was run by Greg Moses and David McCarthy, African Americans who came on serious and suave and did not look like music industry types. Both wore suits and ties, and both could talk the talk with the TV and movie people Brown was interested in meeting. They oversaw his radio stations; besides movie parts for the boss, they were looking into restaurants, real estate, sports agencies, and more.

While waiting for FCC approval of his stations to come through, Brown relied on older methods of getting out the word. An article planted in the *Amsterdam News* inserted one startling statement into Brown's biography. "His mother died when he was four years old," said the story. "James' missing a mother's love and encouragement are the important factors that resulted in his having so much love and concern for children . . ."

What was noteworthy about the detail was that within the readership area of the *News*, in the Brownsville section of Brooklyn, Brown's mom was very much alive. She had in fact visited him during an Apollo stand around 1959, knocking on his door at the Hotel Theresa. "She had lost all her teeth. I saw her and talked to her. I was just glad to see her," he later recalled. He got her address and kept in touch. For whatever reason, Brown wanted his abandonment and his mother's "death" as part of his biography.

On other occasions, his own health and survival inspired stories he had no trouble planting in the press. When he passed out from dehydration at the Apollo, the news went into heavy rotation, and for months Brown played up the idea that he might not be around long. *Jet* declared the "reports" claiming Brown had a weak heart were false, explaining he just fainted onstage because of exhaustion. A post-concert interview in Los Angeles was conducted with an IV drip in his arm. In New Orleans, Brown announced he was retiring soon. He even declared he was taking a job with the government and that from then on all his shows would be a federally backed public service.

Bart had showed him how spreading rumors that you were sick or retiring was a good way to stir up interest. Now Brown was taking the rumors to a higher level, and they seemed to feed a personal need. He had entered diva territory, evoking Sara Bernhardt morbidly lugging her casket with her from town to town. "Love me now," he was saying, "I might not be around tomorrow."

While he *was* around, he came up with a radical idea for an album cover: a comely bunch of white women casting a hungry look in his direction. The photo was shot, a sleeve made of it, and Brown mailed his cover for the next release down to Syd Nathan in Miami.

Henry Glover was with Nathan when he got the package at the post office and walked with Nathan back to his apartment. "I had to help him sit down when he saw this cover," Glover recalled with a laugh. The boss did not look well.

"What's wrong, Syd?"

"How on earth am I going to sell this to redneck distributors in the South? I don't know what I'm going to do about him, Henry."

"I think they changed the cover," recalled Glover. "But that was the thing that made him really sick."

Nathan was the kind of guy whose tombstone should read "I told you I was ill." He was a hypochondriac with reason for concern, and heart disease and pneumonia felled him on the morning of March 5, 1968, while Nathan was at his Miami condominium. His death came a few months before what would have been the twenty-fifth anniversary of King's first release.

Whether he and Brown liked or just tolerated each other, they formed a marriage that kept a great label afloat. His body came back to Cincinnati for the funeral, where many King employees paid their respects. Glover, Seymour Stein, and Brown were pallbearers. Nathan was buried at Judah Memorial Cemetery in Cincinnati.

"It was a pretty long schlep out there to the cemetery," recalled Stein. "We all ran to the men's room afterward, and I remember Henry Glover was in the stall next to Ben Bart, who was taking a long time to piss. Henry said, 'You know, that's a very bad sign.' I was a kid, what did I know about prostates? But a few months after that, Ben Bart was dead."

Chapter Thirteen

AMERICA

America was the land of a thousand dances, and Brown had done them all in a thousand-and-one places. He'd been everywhere. If in the late '60s white American youth were hitting the backroads and byways in order to reconnect with an untrammeled land, Brown knew the land better than just about anybody, because he'd stomped it from one coast to the other.

His road manager Alan Leeds remembers a typical road trip: They did thirty-seven performances and a recording session covering five cities in eleven days. Brown would get off the airplane at a tiny airport in North Carolina, hop into a rental car, and maneuver sixteen precise corkscrew turns to get to the coliseum where the band would play that night. Ask him how he knew to do that, and he'd say, "I been here before." Brown knew where to get coffee at the airports, where to get fried chicken near the hotel, and the name of the janitor cleaning up the auditorium after the show.

In the neon blur, routine anchored everything. The boss usually went to bed at three A.M. and at eleven A.M. he was calling around, asking his team for answers to all the questions he'd raised the night before.

And when he was on the road, he was never without women. It's all but certain, said folks who have traveled with Brown, that he never once slept alone. There were women who wanted to get near somebody with his level of mojo. There were women who stuffed dirty pictures into your pockets as you left the stage door. There were women Brown shot a look at and signaled an aide to wrangle backstage. There were women.

Big girls: He liked them hearty. "Somebody that's thin they can only be my sister," he said. "When you have a real relationship with a woman, she's supposed to knock you out. It's supposed to drain you, see. Unless you get that kind of feeling, it's a joke. Unless she can put you to sleep."

He might tour with one of his long-term companions or a wife. After that, there was a tier of long-term steadies "trying to become the main woman," said Leeds.

Included in that group was the geechee girl, the conjure woman who he'd known since the mid-'50s in Macon, appearing backstage at a show two or three times a year. "He was afraid of her. He had a relationship with her that I only assume was sexual because that's the only kind of relationship he ever had with women," said Leeds.

Outside that circle, there were casuals he would fly in and out. "You'd get back to the hotel at one in the morning, have a last-minute detail chat with him in his room, and suddenly out of the bedroom in his suite this woman would come out, and it would be one of these women friends he was flying around." Several aides were tasked with picking them up at the airport and getting them to the suite without problems at the hotel desk. "And *then*, on the really bad nights there was somebody in the group. The last resort was always one of the dancers," said Leeds. "And if there was a new dancer, she'd get her chance at first."

All these women—more than one a night, carefully booked on different floors to avoid, you know, complications—were an air-traffic-control nightmare. On a trip to Washington, D.C., Brown discovered his old friend and protégé, Steve Alaimo, was staying at the same hotel. At 2:30 in the morning, Alaimo heard a knock on the door; it was Brown, with his stern-faced wife by his side. "Steve, was I not with you today?" Brown barked. Alaimo sputtered "yes," and then Brown brought his wife into the room and invited her to look. Brown made her look under the bed, in the shower, he even made her pull out the end-table's drawers. "Look behind the drapes! See, ain't nobody here."

The team he moved with was big and diverse. Key to making everything work was an aide who arrived around 1964: Charles Bobbit. He had started as Danny Ray's valet, and worked his way up to being Brown's most trusted adviser and protector. Bobbit was tight-lipped, candid, loyal, and willing to go extra for the Boss.

A background with the Nation of Islam proved useful for working for Brown. "He was one of Elijah Muhammad's main guards," said guitarist Bobby Roach, who came back into the tour in the early '70s. "Bobbit was a collecting artist; he collected money for the Nation and he was good about it. He had a black belt, James always told us. That's how he came to be one of Muhammad's bodyguards."

Bobbit was a soldier, a job description he got the chance to prove time and again while in Brown's employ. Like everybody else, the boss tested Bobbit, to see how much abuse he would absorb. Once, when they were trying to catch a plane, Brown whispered to bassist Tim Drummond, "Watch this, we'll have a little fun." With the rental car's key in his pocket, Brown barked to Bobbit that they couldn't take off until they found the key, which must be locked in the car. "Get it," he commanded. Later Bobbit returned, without the key but with his hands bloody from breaking into the vehicle.

Brown needed his soldiers. In their way, his band members, too, were like troops, and expected to be in uniform and on call round the clock. When they had down time he wanted to know exactly where they were. Hobbies were forbidden, the notion being that the musicians might hurt themselves playing sports and drag the show down. Most of the time this was moot because the pace precluded anything like leisure. But when the group played Vegas, and had only two shows a day, some of the guys took up golf. Pretty soon they were packing golf clubs on the bus.

"James went ballistic," said Levi Rasbury. "Black people don't play golf," he heatedly explained as he threw the clubs off the bus. "Really it was because we were enjoying our lives and having fun, and he couldn't equate with that."

A military force needed to have faith in the general–the leader needed to project an aura of rock-solid confidence. He had that and knew how to project it. Bob Patton was sitting beside the singer in his Learjet when the aircraft lost power and started falling from the sky. "He was stronger than Jesus," said Patton. "I'm grabbing the seat and he's sitting cool, arms folded." Finally the jets fired up and the plane climbed again. "He looks straight at me and says, 'You were scared, weren't you, Mr. Patton?' I said 'Yes.' He said, 'It's not your time. You with me.'"

A video clip of Martin Luther King Jr. and James Brown, standing together in front of the Miami Hilton: King on a step by the hotel entrance, Brown on the sidewalk. Wearing a suit and tie, King drapes his arm around the singer's shoulder, his manner projecting a mellow geniality. He is drawing Brown in.

But Brown does not wish to be included. He has a leather overcoat on, he is all but scowling beside King, and he looks tough, unmoved. King says something to him and Brown pulls back. The reverend wants to keep talking, but the singer moves away quickly, stops in his tracks, then gets behind the wheel of a big car. He throws the camera a forced smile and then drives off.

They knew one another, but they came from radically different places. There were vast cultural differences, rooted in family, education, and economic background. "We are caught in an inescapable network of mutuality," King believed of all Americans. Brown was not so sure. Instinctively the singer responded to obstacles in his path with a display of money and aggression. The idea of a mass movement, of an appeal based on shared beliefs rather than on superior individuality, was not in Brown's makeup. Folks could not be trusted.

"He talked sometimes about King, but not obsessively," said Reverend Al Sharpton. "He was in one world and lived in it. He respected Dr. King, and knew that King had given his life. But he did not believe in nonviolence, he always told me. And he felt that Dr. King was not the grassroots guy he was. He respected him, he just didn't see Dr. King as *him*."

The band had returned from their first trip to Africa, having spent two days in Abidjan, the former capital of Ivory Coast, in the beginning of April 1968. Having arrived in New York, they were getting ready to hit the road when reports came that King had been shot in Memphis. They were supposed to play a big show, their biggest yet in Boston, tomorrow. This was going to take some rethinking.

In the late 1960s, the threat of mass racial violence extended beneath the surface of daily life. "I am afraid of what lies ahead of us," King said. "We could end up with a full-scale race war in this country." The previous summer there were riots in Detroit, Newark, Tampa, Buffalo, and elsewhere. In Orangeburg, South Carolina, in February 1968, twenty-eight African Americans were injured and three killed by police trying to break up a demonstration to integrate a bowling alley. Now it was summer again, and the most important figure in the Civil Rights Movement had just been murdered.

The singer was chatting about his African trip on a New York talk show when the broadcast was interrupted by a bulletin that the minister had been shot. Within hours of King's death on April 4, 1968, Brown was giving statements to black radio stations, urging listeners not to express their anger by burning down their neighborhoods. Then he pondered the Boston performance. A show had long been booked, but reports of fires and mayhem were streaming in from all around the country. The rage beneath the floorboards was out in the open, and the only question that mattered for politicians and performers alike in the days ahead was how their small gestures might shape larger ones.

Unbeknownst to Brown, the managers of Boston Garden had already planned on canceling his show, operating on the belief that canceling all public events was safer and would keep people off the streets. The event's promoter and a black city councilman warned the mayor that this was a terrible idea, bringing thousands of young African Americans into the heart of downtown and then leaving them there disappointed and angrier than before, with nothing to do. How to handle the booking and the crowd with the looming threat of violence was a problem. But even before that was a more immediate question: Who was going to explain to the mayor of Boston who James Brown was?

That's one marker of how segregated the city was, that one of the most famous blacks in America could fill the biggest venue in town and the leading white official, Kevin White, had no reason to know his name.

It was decided that the concert should go forward once the mayor was told how many ticketholders were likely to be downtown, and that any cancellation would be interpreted as preemptively punishing the innocent. Then it was decided at City Hall that the show should be broadcast live on local television, thus giving Bostonians a focus for their grief, and a reason to stay home.

A crisis loomed over how to pay Brown for the show. Because if the artist in him felt a responsibility to honor King and to do what he could to avoid bloodshed, the businessman felt a need to see payment for services rendered. The city had just cost him a lot of money, what with the Garden seating 14,000; that was 14,000 tickets Brown hoped to sell, and now the mayor was giving fans a way to see the show for free on TV.

In his Pulitzer Prize-winning history of Boston in the '60s, *Common Ground*, J. Anthony Lukas cast the negotiations between Brown's people and city leaders in the harshest light: "Martin Luther King had just been killed and here were two black guys putting the squeeze on [Mayor White] for $60,000." That was a familiar media image of black leaders in the 1960s: extortionists and shakedown artists. Lukas inflated the cliché, with reporting that would have been strengthened immeasurably had he spoken to even one key person in Brown's camp, or Brown's Boston promoter, Jimmy Byrd. He did not.

It was ignoble of Brown not to do the show for free. But it's possible to comprehend Brown's perspective, too. Kevin White, who kept calling him *Jim*, pressuring him, telling Brown he owed it to Boston to stick his neck out further than White was willing to. In the end, over a barrel, the city agreed to Brown's $60,000 fee. Then, when the show was over, the city reneged on the agreement, giving him, according to Charles Bobbit, $10,000. "Where the rest of the money went, we'll never know," said Bobbit. Not a bad price for "saving" Boston.

Brown had bigger worries. There were some African Americans who would attack him as an Uncle Tom for urging his people to sit down instead of protesting King's death, as Brown had figured out before the night began. Should there be violence, now that he was cast as peacemaker, he would receive some of the blame. Did he not implore enough, or did the music stir folks up? He understood how carefully he had to choose his words and gestures.

This was an unprecedented show on an uncharted night. Driving in the bus to the Garden, band member Fred Wesley said he was worried he might be shot en route or on stage. Some in the group were praying to just get through things; others were ready to run. Ultimately, they all went into the deepest show-must-go-on trance.

At the beginning of the event, Brown says the hardest words there would be to say all night. A man's name.

"We got to pay our respects to the late, great, incomparable–somebody we love very much, and I have all the admiration in the world for–I got a chance to know him personally–the late, great Dr. Martin Luther King."

Brown brings Mayor White out; he is blinking, groping for air. Like Fred Wesley, he, too, thought he could die this night. Brown reads the moment and rushes in, conferring on the white politico his personal stamp, saying "Just let me say, I had the pleasure of meetin' him and I said, 'Honorable Mayor,' and he said, 'Look, man, just call me Kevin.' And look, this is a swingin' cat. Okay, yeah, give him a big round of applause, ladies and gentlemen. He's a swinging cat." The words were perfect in the moment, Brown establishing authority for himself and for the mayor at the same time.

"The man is together!" raved Brown.

This was nonviolent crowd control, and the master of moving audiences had to take things to a new level. There were perhaps only two thousand people in the Garden, but Brown spoke directly to them, and adeptly measured the folks watching at home, too. Boston was where all those nights on the chitlin circuit–learning how to feel what the house desired, how to make thousands rise up and subdue crowds buggin' for a brawl–had brought him to.

Boston police officers formed a line along the sides of the stage. At the most emotionally charged moment of the show, the cape act, a group of young fans push past white officers onstage. Bodies rush in from both sides.

Down on one knee, he calls for "I Can't Stand Myself (When You Touch Me)," and one, three, five youths break through and jump up, grabbing the singer. The police force them back, and suddenly here was the worst possibility, white cops aggressively confronting black youths on live TV.

The band that could vamp through anything goes stone cold silent, the house lights are up. What else is up? "Let me finish the show," Brown said. "We're all black. Let's respect ourselves. Are we together or are we ain't?"

It worked. "We are," folks yelled back. He signals the drummer–"hit the thing, man!"–and he is back in business. The show continued, and there was no violence in downtown Boston.

The Boston Garden show has become a major chapter in the telling of Brown's life, and an even bigger chapter when Brown described it. As he put it on a TV interview not long afterward, "I was able to speak to the country during the crisis after the assassination of Doctor King and they followed my advice, and that was one of the things that meant most to me . . ."

One problem with this formulation is that, in the absence of a riot, it is hard to prove that any one or one hundred events kept it from happening. In the days after the murder, some 125 cities experienced upheavals, leaving 46 dead and 2,600 injured. Boston did not, but it's impossible to prove a negative. No riot started, but did James Brown stop one?

Indisputably, he kept thousands of angry citizens off the streets that night. News accounts in the days following gave Brown great credit for keeping the peace, and a legend was born. No doubt he recognized King's inability to quell rioting in Watts in 1965, or to control violence during the Memphis garbage workers strike in May 1968. King could not stop a riot, but James Brown could.

He did it because, he would say later, he loved his country and didn't want to see bad things happen. He did it because he loved his people, and thought King's death marked a moment to push forth with his mission, not to ruin it with violence that would be crushed. Though he was hardly a believer in nonviolence, Brown performed the Boston show with King's words in mind. He had sized King up as a sincere man, somebody who believed in what he was saying, and Brown had a Southerner's respect for someone who went the distance for what he believed in. Brown did it out of honor, because it would be wrong to not honor an honest man's memory.

A few days later, en route to a show in Rochester, he got a call from Washington, D.C.'s Mayor Walter Washington, who was facing his own outbreak of violence. He asked Brown to bring to the nation's capital the peace he had delivered to Boston. Brown made appeals on local television calling on looters to stay at home. "Unfortunately the looters were carrying the color sets home and didn't have them plugged in," wrote a columnist in the *Pittsburgh Courier.* Twelve would die, and over a thousand structures went up in flames, in the D.C. riot.

Brown's willingness to stick his neck out earned him notice within the White House. In May, he was invited to a Washington state dinner for the prime minister of Thailand, Thanom Kittikachorn. When he took his seat, the singer found a note at the table: "Thanks much for what you are doing for your country, Lyndon Johnson."

Later on, Brown would say that Vice President Humphrey took him aside and gave him a warning. You are entering deeper waters, the vice president cautioned. Brown was now going to be scrutinized by the mighty. Because anybody with the power to stop a riot also had the power to start one.

At the dinner with President Johnson and his guests, perhaps Brown found a moment to bring up a topic he'd been talking to members of Humphrey's staff about for at least a year: an official visit to Vietnam to entertain the troops. So far this effort had gone nowhere for Brown, but after Boston, the road to Saigon suddenly opened before him.

In the last year of his life, King had reached beyond race and began speaking out against the Vietnam War. At Riverside Church in New York, on April 4, 1967, he delivered a major speech on the conflict, questioning its morality and calling it a burden unfairly borne by the poor. Just as King's critique was being widely reported, other black voices were also being raised. Stokely Carmichael and Cleveland Sellers of the Student Nonviolent Coordinating Committee announced they would ignore their army induction orders. After the rejection of his request for conscientious objector status, boxer Muhammad Ali announced he would go to jail rather than join the army. Suddenly, African American criticism of the war was going pop.

Within a few weeks of King's Riverside speech, Brown went into the studio to record a song meant to address this very moment. The song was called "America Is My Home":

> I am sorry for the man who don't love this land
> Now black and white, they may fight, but if the enemy come
> We'll get together and run 'em out of sight

"America Is My Home" was undeniably daring, and if it had been released at that moment, it would have been understood as a denunciation of black leaders. It wasn't released; Brown kept it under wraps, waiting for a more propitious moment.

In the context of Vietnam, soul music was becoming ever more politicized. Magazines like *Soul* and *Jet* printed letters from African American soldiers noting the absence of music by Brown, Wilson Pickett, or Aretha Franklin on military bases. Black music was played infrequently on Armed Forces Radio, and for all the shows organized for the troops by the United Service Organizations (USO) and the Department of Defense, virtually none featured black performers.

For at least a year, Brown had been expressing to government officials a desire to visit the troops. At one point he even cold-called the Pentagon and was transferred to an uncomprehending colonel who had no idea who the caller was. After that, Brown got in touch with the vice president's office and asked how he could make this happen.

The State Department was sending the likes of Roy Rogers and Dale Evans, Anita Bryant, Wayne Newton, and the Golddiggers on USO tours: Whatever vision of America was described by such entertainment, it was a realm far from the Apollo Theater. In *Jet*, Brown complained, "I've been trying to get to Vietnam for the past 18 months. I think me and my group could take over enough soul to even give the Vietnamese some. I'm past the draft age and so are most of my band members, so we think it our patriotic duty, as Americans, to give a lift to the morale of our guys over there. I get letters saying that they are starving for soul. So far I've contacted all kinds of people trying to get to Vietnam but nothing has come through. I wonder if someone thinks I'll get too much glory by taking so much soul over there."

Ofield Dukes, an African American member of Hubert Humphrey's staff, had spoken to Sammy Davis Jr., about going, and was now talking to Stax Records about an integrated package of the soul label's acts going to Vietnam as part of a "Memorial Tour for

Otis Redding." But Brown was easily the biggest black act there was, and in early 1968, Dukes was working on getting him to Southeast Asia. Humphrey was a dedicated liberal who had stuck his neck out for African Americans since the 1940s; he was also running for president in 1968 and had an elaborate plan to bring black voters on board.

Vietnam mattered to Brown for complicated reasons. He'd read his mail, and was struck by the hunger black soldiers had to hear some soul. A dedicated Huntley-Brinkley viewer, he watched the news every night. He wanted to go to Vietnam because he knew that just by being a famous black man in a war zone, he would be shining a light on brothers who were risking their lives.

Going to Vietnam would make him a designated symbol of his nation, no small thing to someone who could have disappeared in the Georgia penal system. Here was a way to get what he'd always wanted, acceptance on his own terms, projected onto a global drama.

A USO press release dated June 3 read: "JAMES BROWN–AND A SHOW OF 25–WILL SOCK IT TO 'EM ON A USO TOUR OF MILITARY BASES IN THE PACIFIC."

The show was leaving June 5, going to Japan, Korea, Okinawa, and then Vietnam, on a sixteen-day sojourn. The star, of course, was "the one and only JAMES BROWN, dancing and singing soul music, a mixture of gospel singing and blues–with a throbbing beat that is primitive and somewhat savage."

Nobody ever called Wayne Newton "somewhat savage."

Behind the scenes, black antiwar activists were urging entertainers to stay home, arguing that black star power would be used by the government to sell the war at home. In a 1967 *Soul* magazine article, a USO official declared that King himself was telling entertainers not to go.

But if King lobbied Brown to skip the trip, the effort backfired. Brown suggested to the press that antiwar sentiment might be simple cowardice. In any case, he said, it was his responsibility to support his countrymen. "Our black entertainers have been attacked in the white press, giving everybody the impression that they didn't want to go to Vietnam because they were either afraid or didn't like our country being at war in that country," he told *Jet* in June 1968. "Well, I don't like the war, either, but we have soul brothers over there. . . .

"I'm as much opposed to the war in Vietnam as anyone who loves peace. But I can't turn my back on my own black brothers in Vietnam when they call upon me to entertain them. We're going to Vietnam despite the criticisms and despite the risks. We are not afraid of right. We're afraid of wrong."

Brown left on June 5 with his full crew, stopped in Tokyo, and then landed in South Korea for several days of performing. Only when they were in Seoul was he told that taking his full crew to the war zone was too dangerous, that he had to cut his stage show down to seven members. He held a meeting and asked who was with him.

"Everybody was looking at everybody and, heh heh, the ones that didn't go, I think they were happy," remembered singer Marva Whitney. She *did* want to go, she said, because "the soldiers needed to see a sister who wasn't an Oreo cookie." The USO show featured Whitney, bassist Tim Drummond, drummer Clyde Stubblefield, guitarist Jimmy Nolen, saxophonist Maceo Parker, trumpeter Waymon Reed, and Danny Ray, the cape man. If Brown was going to war, damned right he was taking his valet with him.

The fact that Drummond was a white bass player playing in a black group made a statement on bases where racial conflicts had flared. The army appointed them all honorary lieutenant colonels. The band got their shots, were issued thick-soled boots, and given cards saying they were noncombatants, should they fall into Vietcong hands. Then it was showtime.

There were two thousand soldiers at the first stop, Tan Son Nhut Air Base outside of Saigon. The group arrived one day after Vietcong had launched a huge assault on the city, shooting thirty-five rounds of 122 mm rockets into the capital. Danny Ray: "A lot of the soldiers didn't think we were coming. And some of them wondered *why* we'd come. Brown told them, 'I love my country, man. I love America the best, man. That's home.'"

They brought a customized wardrobe with them, clothes suitable for the tropical humidity. "There wasn't a dry spot on me nowhere," Brown declared. The sound system was meager, and it was all but impossible to hear what you were playing. Didn't matter.

"We gave the soldiers a whole new charge," said Stubblefield. "We came over with the funk and the soul."

Drummond: "We went with just pure music and we fucking killed them."

At night they stayed at the Continental Hotel in Saigon, across the street from a presidential palace that was pockmarked by mortar fire. Signs posted in rooms warned guests not to open their drapes or turn on lights at night. That was because the nearby palace guards would think you were a sniper and shoot. At night, the beds shook from the five-hundred-pound bombs American jets were dropping on the countryside.

From Tan Son Nhut they went to Phan Rang Air Base. Typically they did two shows a stop, Brown hooking up to an intravenous saline drip in between. Phan Rang was the only time they flew in an airplane inside Vietnam. It was an aging propeller plane, "like in an old Tarzan movie," said Drummond. They took off and then watched the engine drip oil and start smoking, forcing an emergency landing at the edge of the base they'd just left. Their plane had attracted Vietcong attention, and while waiting in a Quonset hut, the band suddenly heard loud explosions from just past the runway–American bombers dropping weight on the enemy that was closing in.

Time went by, and the air strike ended. Brown sucked his teeth, stuck out his chin, and made an announcement: "We'd like to have a better plane."

As Brown described the experience: "We didn't do like Bob Hope. We went back there where the lizards wore guns! We went back there where the *Apocalypse Now* stuff was going on."

They traveled on converted buses between performances, with the windows wired up so nobody could toss in a grenade. Once, Drummond heard a voice on a walkie-talkie say, "Get 'em out of there, there's a mortar attack coming in." Moments later, they felt it.

At other times, soldiers made Brown and the band get down on the floor, standing over them while waiting for orders.

Once, they were told to jump out of a Chinook helicopter hovering over a marsh, Whitney recalled. "Being a tom girl from when I was small, that helped me because I had to jump four or five feet from the helicopter into the marshes, and I think I took it better than some of the guys did . . ." Another time, moving at night by helicopter, the band watched as red tracer fire chased their aircraft. Charlie, targeting Mr. Please Please Please. As fiery streaks followed the helicopter–some later said they heard pings of metal bouncing off–Whitney looked over at Brown. "He wasn't scared like the other fellas, but he was sad. He was sad."

In the States, Brown rarely socialized with his band. If he came on the bus, it was to inspect it. Otherwise, he kept a distance. He would stay at one hotel, the band would stay at another. But in Vietnam, everyone stayed together, and they were all stuck there after the sun went down and it wasn't safe to move around. Drummond had befriended a veteran, the kind of guy who can get you anything if you have the money, and one night he'd rustled up fried chicken for everybody at the hotel. There was nothing to do after eight o'clock except sit in your room with the lights off, so the band were all hanging out, when suddenly there was a knock on the door.

It was Brown, looking for somebody to talk to. And so he and his band ate chicken and drank and talked. He even did what he almost never did again. He opened up and shared his feelings about the war, and talked to the band about what the soldiers were telling him before shows, about how tough it was for guys over there. They really were in a different country.

The final shows were at Bearcat Base, a large encampment of the 9th Infantry Division built on defoliated rubber and mangrove forests where racial tensions were high. The day after King was shot in Memphis, word had reached this base, and while many black soldiers and a number of whites grieved, a group of white senior noncommissioned officers threw a party in celebration. Racial fighting erupted all around the facility.

At Bearcat they played in an area gulped out of a hillside, which reminded some of the Hollywood Bowl. Brown would claim later that the Vietcong called a ceasefire while he played: "They said, 'Let's get some of this funk for *us*.'" In the States, he had taken to giving the Black Power clenched fist salute from the stage, but Brown wouldn't do it here. "That would have been causing a problem," he said. Thousands of soldiers came to the shows, wearing full field gear in 110-degree heat. At the top of the hillside, tanks were lined up for the performance. "Black and white, they just went wild," said Drummond.

At the end of a song, from behind the stage, the musicians suddenly heard the unmistakable ack-ack-ack of American guns firing on VC to their rear. Everybody was watching the band, and now they were *really* watching, as confusion and then anxiety played across the musicians' faces. Finally, one of the guys sitting cross-legged at the front of the stage spoke to the band: "Aw don't worry. We won't let Charlie get ya!" And then Brown took the microphone and continued the show. "Hit me!"

They taped a program for Armed Forces radio and then stopped in Okinawa, and finally the band returned to the States. Five chartered buses filled with fans from the New York area greeted Brown at Kennedy Airport on June 19. His father was there, too. When he walked down the Pan Am stairs to the tarmac, Brown wore an army field hat and a camouflage jacket.

At an airport press conference, his immediate reaction was to vent indignation: at the "hillbilly" music mostly played over there and at his treatment. He declared that he had drawn more than Bob Hope ever had, and that he should have been able to bring his full band. And another thing: It was an insult that he hadn't been allowed to take his own guns with him to Vietnam.

He came back gruff and reaching for more, though he didn't seem to know exactly what he wanted next. In later days, he would talk about why he had pushed so hard to play Vietnam. He would suggest Muhammad Ali and other conscientious objectors had been afraid, unlike him. And he would say: "A lot of blacks thought they didn't have a real reason to go there because they wasn't getting their rights here. They had mixed emotions on the war. My dad didn't agree 'cause he went into the service. He thought that by going to fight he had more to complain about. That's what I felt. I went in '68 because if you want to demand a hundred percent of your rights you got to give your country a hundred percent of your support." His beliefs were built out of ego, a concern for civil rights, and his Southern-steeped Americanism. Nothing could ever untangle all the strands.

First in Boston and now in the middle of a global conflict, Brown had put himself on the line. He returned home different from the man he had been a few weeks before. As the *Village Voice* put it: "With Dr. King and Senator Kennedy gone . . . James Brown, as spokesman, singer and soul brother had new and heavy duties at the age of thirty-five."

Waiting for Brown when he got to his Queens home was a Western Union Telegram: "WELCOME BACK FROM VIETNAM LOOKING FORWARD TO SEEING YOU AGAIN." It was signed Kevin White, the Boston mayor. It might have been a patrician reflex for politeness. It might have been insurance against the fire next time.

Chapter Fourteen

HOW YOU GONNA
GET RESPECT?

Don't muffle your message. If you're going to tell it, tell it on the mountain. Hubert H. Humphrey stood before the five thousand delegates gathered for the 38th Quadrennial Session of the AME Church, and he told it: "I am a soul brother." Lucky for him there was applause, enough so that he could smile and finish his thought:

"All of us are soul brothers—in the brotherhood of man."

It was early May 1968, just a week after the vice president had announced his candidacy for president, and he was tearing into the campaign trail. Key to this election would be an important demographic Humphrey saw within his reach, the African American vote. And so he came to Philadelphia wearing a green sharkskin suit and a blue shirt.

On the surface, being a middle-aged, snow-complected political insider might preclude membership in the soul brotherhood. But Humphrey had long staked a claim. Back in 1948, when he was a new senator from Minnesota, he led a drive to keep strong civil rights language in the Democratic party platform. His efforts lead a group of Southern Democrats, clinging to segregation and organized by South Carolina Senator Strom Thurmond, to form a breakaway party, the Dixiecrats. Long known as a liberal on race issues, in 1968 Humphrey was banking on black support to lead him to the White House.

In January, he addressed the Organization of African Unity in Addis Ababa and toured Africa with Thurgood Marshall. In the summer he called for a "Marshall Plan" to "get rid of the ghettos," and demonstrated support of the Poor People's Campaign, an economic justice effort King had begun and which was coming to fruition since his death. Humphrey had basketball star Elgin Baylor's endorsement, he was trying to reel in Aretha Franklin, and Motown's Berry Gordy was dangling the possibility of a Diana Ross support.

The veep inspired confidence and obligation from old folks who remembered what he'd done for blacks in the past, but unluckily for Humphrey, New York Senator Robert F. Kennedy was also running, and he inspired love among young black voters. When Martin Luther King Jr. was killed, Kennedy broke it to an Indianapolis audience by saying it felt like a death in the family. Some blacks called him "the blue-eyed soul brother," and unlike with Humphrey, nobody laughed when they said it. Earlier in the summer, Brown was pondering giving Kennedy his endorsement, and had sent his aide, Bob Patton, to Los Angeles to discuss it with Kennedy's people. They met at the Ambassador Hotel just a few hours before Kennedy was shot and killed in the hotel kitchen on June 5.

Brown played Yankee Stadium two weeks later. Outside the ballpark, vendors sold commemorative pics of Kennedy and King together. A dollar for one, $2.50 for three.

In the weeks that followed, Humphrey sought to tap RFK's black support. "What about our negro entertainers such as James Brown, and many others?" he asked in a July 16 memo to his staffer Ofield Dukes. "Can't we get them lined up with us?"

About a week later, as it happened, Brown was calling Dukes. He had troubles of his own. A credit problem had delayed the transfer of ownership of the Augusta radio station to him, so Brown phoned Washington asking for help. During the call, Dukes casually mentioned that Humphrey was going to be in Los Angeles soon, and floated the idea of an endorsement. Brown agreed to a joint appearance in Watts.

Brown had known Humphrey since the Stay in School events of 1966, and the black press had been flooded with pictures of Brown and Humphrey shaking hands. Humphrey had played a part in getting Brown to Vietnam, and the two liked each other on a personal level.

In New Jersey, Dukes says he was approached by LA-based nationalist Ron Karenga, poet-activist Amiri Baraka, and a representative of an urban street gang, who at the time were working to get Kenneth Gibson elected as the first black mayor of Newark. Dukes says the activists suggested that they knew about Humphrey's upcoming appearance in Watts, and that a donation of $25,000 to the Gibson campaign would help ensure its success. Through a complicated route, Dukes said a "contribution" was delivered that April.

The vice president arrived in Los Angeles at the end of the month for several scheduled appearances. At the Elks Auditorium on Central Avenue, he was to speak at a voter registration rally set up by Black Democrats for Humphrey. Before about 500 listeners, Humphrey attempted to discuss his jobs policy, barely getting started before an organized group of hecklers shouted, "Honky go home!" The din drowned him out, and after several tries, Humphrey stepped down. He was quickly smothered by a cloud of Secret Service agents—after Kennedy's assassination in Los Angeles, security wasn't taking any chances. They rushed Humphrey from the auditorium.

This racial static lent additional drama to the meeting of the soul singer and the "soul brother" scheduled for the following day. Humphrey's rally was held on a lot where a grocery store had burned during the Watts Riot in 1966. On the dais that day in Watts were Los Angeles mayor Sam Yorty and labor leader Walter Reuther. Dukes said he saw Amiri Baraka in the crowd, and they nodded meaningfully at each other.

Humphrey was speaking to the crowd when shrieks from several hundred youths suddenly erupted, and all eyes turned to James Brown emerging from the crowd. He popped up next to the veep and opened his mouth. Perhaps Humphrey was expecting a standard "I endorse this man" moment. It went a different way.

"So many times different candidates been elected to different offices, and we haven't got . . . we'd like to know sometimes what's gonna be done for black people." A woman in the crowd shouted: "Right on!"

"I've not come here because I'm a black man. . . . No one could buy me to come out here. I'm here because I have something to say and if at the end of my statement the distinguished gentleman to my right concurs, then I have no choice but to endorse him."

Humphrey suddenly looks wary. He stiffens; his eyes dart.

James Brown was telling it. "First, I'd like to say, the black man wants *ownership*. He wants to be able to own his own things and make up his own mind. Number one in the black community, in the low income areas, we need housing. So we don't have to stay in the dark like I did when I was a kid. Number two, we need hospitals so we don't have to stand around bleeding to death while some other cat gets worked on. I believe in telling it like it is. I don't want no pretty words, I'm gonna tell you just how I feel." Humphrey nods his head, agreeing. Ohh-kay. Let's ride.

"Number three, we need our own banks, so we can get our own money to do things for ourself. We want banks available in the black community. . . . I don't endorse the party, I endorse the *man*."

Brown had come with a more ambitious agenda than Humphrey, and he was aiming to get some political promises on record. He wanted his endorsement to mean something. When he was done, Humphrey looked relieved. That wasn't so bad, his eyes say. I can work with this.

"Let me just say, in the presence of a man that I have grown to respect and admire and a gentleman that I look to as a friend, that what he has said to this audience here today is what I have tried to say but not so well." This was turning out to be a mutual endorsement.

Brown: "I am for Humphrey because he is the better man." This was not the "I love this guy" the pol requested, but something from the heart, unexpectedly real.

The event ended as the band played "I Got You (I Feel Good)," with Humphrey almost losing the endorsement by boogalooing beside Brown.

Brown's name was money. No wonder so many wanted its magic. Black power denizens wanted him on their team, and they tried various methods to get it. There was outright flattery, as when Stokely Carmichael explained "James Brown will be black power" in the *Baltimore Afro-American* that summer. "Muhammad Ali will be black power. All the creative skills of colored individual persons working for the benefit of the masses of 'our people'—that is what I mean by 'black power.'" There was a little quid quo pro, as Brown was clearly hoping for from Humphrey.

In a moment when people across the political spectrum were lobbying him for an audience, in the summer of 1968 he finally released "America is My Home." Musically it wasn't bad, and interestingly, Brown doesn't sing, he speaks the lyrics. And the *way* he speaks them gives them an electric charge. It's not a recitation, it's a guy trying to engage you in conversation, and some have even called it an early rap record. This song was a challenge, with Brown in your face, daring you to criticize the USA. As America was bombing Vietnam and Cambodia and was a magnet for international condemnation, this was an immense argument to pick with his listeners. He knew that.

> America is still the best country, without a doubt
> And if anybody says it ain't you just try to put 'em out

"America," a press release boasted, was mailed to "every governor and mayor." According to Brown's spokesman Bud Hobgood,

"We hope this record, if handled right, will provide a public service and stop any problems that may arise this summer."

Here was the redneck in the man: Even when he was expressing his love, it came out like he was picking a fight. You can hear in "America is My Home" what it must have been like to disagree with Brown.

"He was the most competitive person I ever met—when ordering a meal in a restaurant he was judgmental and competitive and he had to comment on everything," said Alan Leeds.

They went to the Stage Deli in New York, one of Brown's favorite places to hang in town, and he had a point to make about boiled beef. "Mr. Leeds, you're Jewish, you don't eat boiled beef—see, you got all that corned beef, you're gonna get sick. *I'm* gonna get my grease boiled off, *I'm* gonna be healthy . . ." From there he transitioned into Jews and Ben Bart and God and pork. "There was nothing chill about him," said Leeds.

If he could be so opinionated about boiled beef, imagine how intense he could be about the country he loved. The song celebrates a place where a poor shoeshine boy could grow up to shake hands with the president.

"America Is My Home" didn't sound like anything else on the charts; the closest thing to it were country records, provocations like "The Fightin' Side of Me" or "Okie From Muskogee." If it had been a little better musically, it might have been the most dangerous record he ever made.

As it was, "America" was the beginning of a new problem. He probably thought it was an act of charity, but it was heard by many as a putdown of critics of the war, and of black power. It made it to thirteen on the R&B chart, and never landed on the pop chart. It certainly cost him more than he gained, because suddenly Brown sounded like an authority figure, not an ally. The song put cracks in his bond with black fans.

It might have been the single they were pushing, but "America" wasn't on the set list of the Boston Garden show. "Everybody got on us about [the song]," Bobby Byrd said. "We were singing about *America*; black folks didn't want to hear that—we were in a protest situation." The black response was loud and clear: "We have nothing to say to you, because you're with the white man. We're not listening to what you're saying. You're just talking about America and look what they're doing to black folks," recalled Byrd. At the Howard Theatre, members of the Nation of Islam *and* the Congressional Black Caucus came to grill Brown about his little tune.

H. Rap Brown, the minister of justice for the Black Panther Party, called the singer "the Roy Wilkins of the music world," a denigrating reference to the leader of the NAACP who was dismissed by radicals as hopelessly accommodating. In July, *Muhammad Speaks*, newspaper of the Nation of Islam, reported that a James Brown boycott was underway in Cambridge, Massachusetts. The boycott's sponsor quipped, "What record could possibly follow 'America'? May I suggest 'The Star Spangled Banner,' 'America the Beautiful,' or 'My Country 'Tis of Thee' with that up-tight out-of-sight James Brown beat . . .

"If James Brown continues to record this type of material, then all I can say is: Brother Brown, I hope you still remember how to shine shoes."

Tim Drummond was a white Midwestern kid who played bass in the band. Problem. At the Howard Theatre, Brown received a telegram backstage that said, "You got a white man playing with you, a black man needs a job." In Chicago, word circulated that Drummond better not play. Brown didn't get the message, though, and when a worker at the Regal Theater gestured for his bassist to get off, Brown threatened to cancel the show.

He had been a symbol of blackness, and just that quick he was taking flack for being insufficiently black. Critics honed in on one aspect of his image: the hair. "If James Brown is so soulful why does he still wear that konk in his hair?" asked a reader of the *Baltimore Afro-American*. At an Oakland meeting with the Black Panthers, where the group conveyed their judgment of Brown, his hairdo was top of the agenda. The Afro, it had been decided, was the style truest to the race. For a while, Brown would watch his band members one by one getting off the bus with their brand-new naturals, and he would tease them about it, loudly. Then, one day, he came out of his dressing room: with an Afro.

It could not have been easy, for a man who did his hair in a way that would subvert nature, to have to submit to the natural. He did his hair in the morning, then before the show, then again after the show, all so that he would not look like anybody else. Now these guys in their leather jackets were forcing him to look like them.

He tried to sell his new look in the column he wrote for *Soul* magazine: "I don't think I'll ever go back. Even if somebody pointed a gun at me and said they'd shoot me if I didn't go back to a do." He followed that by writing a song for Hank Ballard to record that more forcefully made the case: "How You Gonna Get Respect (When You Haven't Cut Your Process Yet)."

Still, Brown had his own way of doing things, instructing his hairdresser, Henry Stallings, to give him a *processed* Afro.

They must have been quite the sit-downs, those meetings between Brown and the Panthers. Two forces convinced of their rightness, certain they were representing millions. Both voraciously charismatic, pushing out in the world until they met a force that pushed back. All those egos talking past each other, like icebergs passing in the night. The young man who once punched out a white farmer on a rural Southern road might have identified with the guys who had marched into the California State Capitol with rifles in 1967.

They talked of hair, and presumably much besides. Perhaps money was passed to the Panthers; some say it was so. But a simple change of style wasn't enough to ameliorate certain radicals, and once a request was answered, invariably it led to another. Tensions continued between the younger nationalists and the singer. In August the show came to Southern California, and when Brown opened his hotel room door he found a present—a fake bomb, and a letter, the contents of which he never divulged.

"The Black Panthers were putting the heat on us for–*nothing*, really," said Bobbit. He remembered the Southern California visit, and the heat, and watching a TV news report of black-on-black violence with Brown in the hotel, during which the singer became pensive. "Mr. Brown said, 'Black people love each other, why do we have to do this to each other?' I was 'yes . . . yes . . . yes . . . yes.' I was tired." It was the middle of the night.

The aide went to his room. Twenty minutes later, Brown called him back to look at something. When Bobbit got there, Brown showed him a napkin, on which was written, "Say it loud, I'm black and I'm proud."

The words were a reaction to a variety of elements: to the state of black life, to the pressure Brown was receiving from activists who said he wasn't black enough.

"Say It Loud" was a record done fast. Some say it was put together in the studio; Fred Wesley, who was recording with Brown for the first time, remembered the band working out the music over the previous few weeks. They cut it on August 7, in the San Fernando Valley. Brown had the inspired idea to have a children's chorus shout out the song title. He sent Bobbit to find some kids. Their innocent voices took some of the edge out of words that Brown knew might be incendiary. It also put the focus on the future, and made the song feel hopeful rather than critical.

The tape was flown to Cincinnati, where King was able to press anything he wanted when he wanted. For whatever reason, Brown listed his white lieutenant Bud Hobgood as co-writer of "Say It Loud." Within two weeks, the record was in the hands of DJs.

An early pressing was delivered to KGFJ, a powerful black music station in LA, but programmers there said they wouldn't touch it. Brown must have figured that with a song as controversial as "Say It Loud," early resistance could trigger more, because he took out two full-page ads in the *Los Angeles Sentinel*, calling the new song "a message from James Brown to the people of America." His ad urged a boycott of the station.

"The hierarchy of KGFJ has taken it upon themselves to deny James Brown the right to identify himself to his people and to deny the right of his people to hear the message contained in this recording.

"If the Black People are going to stand by and let KGFJ do this then all this fighting that James Brown does for the Black People is wasted."

It was delirious overkill, but there was just too much riding on this single. Soon, the station got on board. And the song began taking off on radio stations across the country.

Within weeks, when the band played shows on the road, Brown would sing "Say it loud" and the audience surprised him by shouting back, "I'm black and I'm proud." It was barely out and everybody knew it by heart. The kids singing the tagline made it feel friendly, but the song also had an edge: "We'd rather die on our feet than be livin' on our knees." (That line seems to pick up on something Stokely Carmichael said in the wake of King's death. He predicted "a violent struggle in which black people would stand up on our feet and die like men.")

Introducing his new record to a Dallas audience in late August, Brown said, "You know, one way of solving a lot of problems that we've got in this country is lettin' a person feel that they're important, feel that they're somebody. And a man can't get himself together until he knows who he is, and be proud of who he is and where he comes from.

"Now, I've just recorded a tune called 'Say It Loud, I'm Black and I'm Proud.' If a man is not proud of who he is and where he comes from, he's not a man. So I want each and everyone to understand: This tune is for the good of what it means and what it can do for a man's self-pride."

Thirty years before, "black" was a fighting word, not so far from the N-word. But in a surge of pride in the 1960s, *black* signified a new unity. Howard Thurman, educator, theologian, and elder statesman of the Civil Rights Movement, declared in the summer that "Now black is a word of power and dignity."

Jet polled its readers on what word they chose to describe themselves. For 37 percent, it was *Afro-American*; 22 percent wanted *black*. The old standard *Negro* came in third, with 18 percent. Of those who went for *black*, 80 percent were under the age of forty. Just to use "black" in a song title was, to some, a provocation.

In Detroit, Reverend C. L. Franklin delivered a sermon titled, "Say it Loud, I am Black and I am Proud." A pastor with a huge following, and the father of Aretha Franklin, Franklin was a civil rights beacon in the city. For this churchman to pick up the phrase didn't just further its circulation, it gave it an important blessing. In the sermon, Franklin strides from the Song of Solomon ("I am black, but comely . . . look not upon me, because I am swarthy, because the sun hath scorched me") to Dr. King to James Brown, who has generated "a new sense of dignity and somebodiness." In a nuanced discussion of separatism and self-love, Franklin wrestles with, and then champions, the song.

"Say It Loud" managed a rare feat: It was an incredibly popular tune that connected with the masses, while scaring the pants off a huge lot of others. According to Byrd, Brown had worked hard to get the racial ratio of his shows to 50/50 white and black. That peaked around "America," and started falling the minute whites heard "Say it Loud." Bassist Charles Sherrell saw it as it happened. "After I heard the words to it, it kind of frightened me," he said. To Sherrell, the problem was that it drove a wedge among his fans—you couldn't sing along if you weren't black. "James realized it, too. Because all of a sudden his crowds started dropping off. He only did that song live maybe three or four times. Five at the most. Then he stopped doing it."

If a Huey Newton or Angela Davis had expressed the idea, it would have been marginalized as an utterance from the black power fringe. But here was the most visible black man in America saying it. Here was the angry fringe and the smiling mainstream coming together.

What made "black power" live as an idea was that it could not be nailed down, that it meant different things to different people. It was a work of art, not politics, and like any work of art it depended on an audience to give it meaning. But for a huge chunk of the populace, the so-called silent majority, black power was static: It meant replacing white supremacy with a different shade, and fighting racism with violence against whites. The silent majority was a bit of an artful creation as well, a demographic label for scared white voters that surfaced around the same time as black power. In the wake of the silent majority's rise, their distortions of simple racial pride gained common currency in white America. "America" made Brown seem like an Uncle Tom to some African Americans. Weeks later, "Say It Loud" made a lot of whites confuse James Brown with H. Rap Brown.

One thing was for sure: The record was a hit, camping out on the R&B charts for three months, rising to ten on the pop charts. Comic Jan Murray presented him with a gold record on national TV.

In what seems suspiciously like a dirty trick from the Republican candidate for president, Richard M. Nixon, a flier showed up on Chicago streets just before the election. It pictured Humphrey, President Johnson, and Chicago mayor Richard Daley dressed like gangsters, holding carbines and saying "Hell naw! You white goats won't get our votes—we are saying it loud we are black and proud." Even Nixon's crew knew the force of the song.

Eventually, a white-power country music version was recorded in Nashville, with a chorus that went "I'm proud and I'm white with a song to sing . . . I'm a white boy lookin' for a place to do my thing."

This was a great pop moment, in the middle of the craziest, most fraught year of James Brown's life. It's possible to see "Say It Loud" as a hasty correction to "America." A righting of the scales. It's also possible to view "Say It Loud" as a response to pressure coming from his left. Maybe it is best to look at these songs not as polar opposites, but as two sides of what would have been the greatest single of 1968, parallel lines running in James Brown's head. This would-be 45 is the greatest, richest expression of Brown's view of civil rights, Americanism, and work. You can play one over the other and hear a messy, blurry atonality. But Brown would have argued that they fit together, and the sound they made was all of him.

On a basic level, both are about the same thing: loving where you came from. And Brown saw no contradiction between loving his country and loving his people. At the same time, the songs have a crucial distinction. "America" is Brown celebrating himself as a modern Horatio Alger, a guy who lifted himself from the muck to the top of the heap. "Name me any other country, where you can start out as a shoeshine boy and shake hands with the president," he raps.

"Say It Loud" patently avoids *me*; it's all about *us*. "We demand a chance to do things for ourselves/We're tired of beatin' our head against the wall/And workin' for someone else." One song says American history has made him free; the other says he's still a slave. Those opposites would define Brown's life in the days ahead.

That fall, Ben Bart suffered a fatal heart attack while playing golf in New Rochelle. Coupled with Syd Nathan's passing five months before, Brown had lost his two most important mentors. At thirty-five, he was feeling powerful and alone.

The relationship with Bart had diminished, and Brown took on more of the booking and promoting of shows himself. The whole concert industry was changing, with major management companies now signing up black acts that would have depended on the chitlin circuit not long before. In Atlanta, a group of thirty-one promoters formed an organization to keep whites from gaining a monopoly on black talent. They enlisted the help of the Southern Christian Leadership Conference's Operation Breadbasket. That organization was using boycotts and other economic pressure to pump money into black businesses.

In Philadelphia, the *Tribune* reported that a group called the

Fair Play Committee was threatening to "eliminate" two DJs engaged in a dispute with Brown. The New York–based committee
was led by Dino "Boom Boom" Washington and producer Johnny
Baylor. They said they were supporters of Brown who had complained that the jocks were not airing a commercial for his upcoming appearance because the jocks promoted competing shows
of their own. Publicity, and a show of police force, calmed the situation.

The black circuit was being dismantled, and entrepreneurs, sometimes using activists with names like Boom Boom, were pushing
back. It made the field more complicated in theory, but in practice,
it was a lucrative time to be James Brown. According to Levi Rasbury, who did bookkeeping for Brown on the road, by employing
his own promotion team, putting his own posters up, and printing
his own tickets, Brown was averaging "anywhere from ten to fifteen
thousand a night on regular nights. And if it's a big promotion like
Madison Square Garden or the Coliseum in Chicago, Braves Stadium in Atlanta, he was making thirty-five or forty-five thousand."

For considerably less than that sum, Brown accepted a booking
that surprised many when it was announced: the inauguration of
Richard Nixon in January 1969. The appearance baffled fans. Having given his blessing to Humphrey, how could he so quickly roll
over and play for the man who beat him? Brown's stated answer was
that he wanted the president to succeed in bringing people together.

Starting off the gala at the National Guard Armory was Lionel
Hampton, the oldest black supporter of Nixon anyone could find–
and people looked. Then came Brown, who did a set that included,
somewhat improbably, a certain recent hit. "Every time the little
dynamo commanded 'Say It Loud,' a little, black cheering section
to the left of stage center in the $100 seats jumped to its feet to
answer back, 'I'm black and I'm proud,'" reported *Jet*. Eventually,
even some of the white guests were singing.

Then Dinah Shore came out in a gold lamé sheath dress, singing
a batch of Negro spirituals that she "heard as a child."

Look magazine put Brown on the cover of the February issue, with these words provocatively across the front: Is he the most important black man in America? Good question. *Look* didn't know the answer any more than Dinah Shore knew Negro spirituals, but as 1969 began, at least it was a question worth asking.

The view from Ninth Street, in downtown Augusta, when James Brown was growing up. An African American man sweeps the street that would one day be renamed James Brown Boulevard.
AUGUSTA MUSEUM OF HISTORY

Beau Jack, the pride of black Augusta, both inspiration and object lesson to James Brown.
AUGUSTA MUSEUM OF HISTORY

A marching band from the United House of Prayer for All People parades down the Terry, sometime in the 1940s. COURTESY OF MILLEDGE MURRAY

Entering the pantheon: an early
King promotional photo.
COURTESY OF STEVE HALPER

JAMES BROWN

Recording Exclusively for
KING RECORDS

Syd Nathan and
Earl Bostic go over the
fine print at King Studios.
COURTESY OF BRIAN POWERS

King Records occupied an unassuming industrial strip on Brewster Avenue in
Cincinnati, Ohio. LEE HAZEN

To the manner made: King James and his court, one night in the early 1960s.
COURTESY OF STEVE HALPER

Brown's manager and confidante, Ben Bart, relaxing at the racetrack.
COURTESY OF JACK BART

Singing at Jackson, Mississippi's Tougaloo College, the endpoint of James Meredith's 1966 "March Against Fear."
JIM PEPPLER; STATE OF ALABAMA, DEPARTMENT OF ARCHIVES AND HISTORY

"**A** *shape with lion body and the head of a man*": *The Cape Act as seen at the Alabama State College Arena in Montgomery, circa 1965, and elsewhere on the road.* COLLECTION OF THE AUTHOR

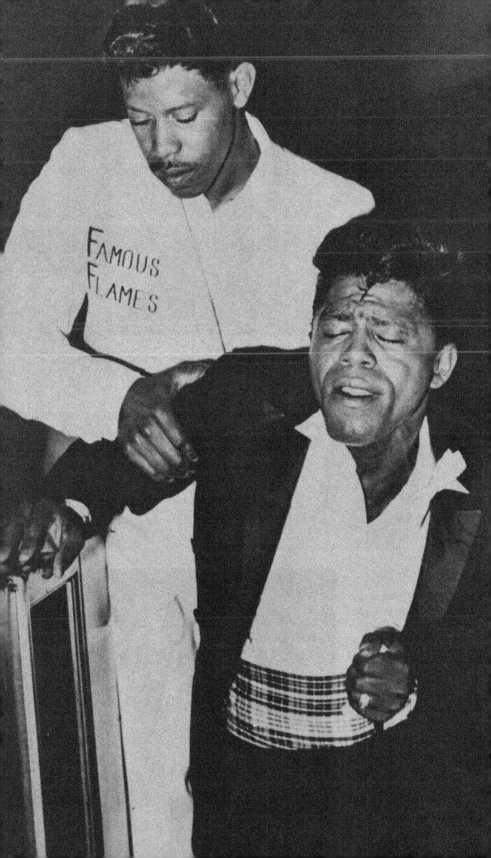

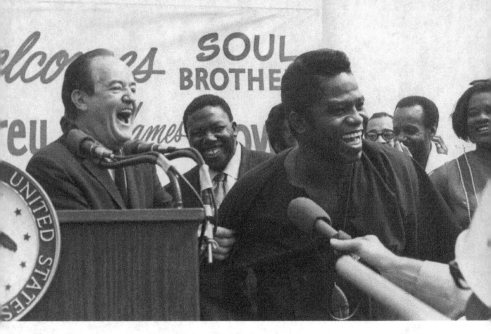

James Brown endorsing Hubert Humphrey for president in Watts, 1968.
COLLECTION OF THE AUTHOR

Brown knew his face was his currency, and he literally made it so when he printed it on the short-lived *Black & Brown Trading Stamp.* COLLECTION OF THE AUTHOR

Enter the mugs: left to right, Robert "Chopper" McCullough, Clayton "Chicken" Gunnels, Phelps "Catfish" Collins, William "Bootsy" Collins, and Charles Spurling. They changed everything.
COURTESY OF PATTI COLLINS

Brown and his wife, Adrienne, celebrating their union. SPECIAL COLLECTIONS UNIT, CLEMSON UNIVERSITY LIBRARIES

Strom Thurmond's house. The senator and Brown were longtime friends. SPECIAL COLLECTIONS UNIT, CLEMSON UNIVERSITY LIBRARIES

The bronze statue of Brown, unveiled in downtown Augusta in 2005. THE RAINIER EHRHARDT/*AUGUSTA CHRONICLE*/ZUMAPRESS.COM

James Brown's final appearance, January 2007. RICK MACKLER/GLOBE PHOTOS/ZUMAPRESS.COM

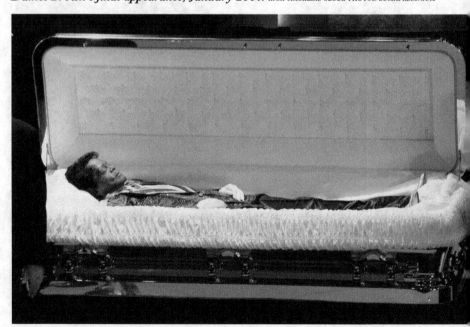

Chapter Fifteen

COLOR TVS
AND DASHIKIS

Two weeks into the Nixon administration and Brown was back in the studio, recording a song that stated his philosophy as clearly as could be. The sui generis celebration of an "us" in "Say It Loud" was replaced with a bracing expression of one man's rights. If you want *your* rights, repeat after Brown: "I Don't Want Nobody to Give Me Nothing (Open Up the Door, I'll Get It Myself)." Give him an even playing field and he can take it from there.

Nixon had campaigned on a domestic policy he called "New Federalism." The idea was to transfer power, money, and responsibility from Washington to states and individuals. He knew how to undermine his predecessor's Great Society and make an evisceration look like a fresh start. Heck, Nixon had enough poetry in his soul to spot the possibilities in a phrase like "black power." There he was, giving a speech on CBS, teasing the possibilities out: "Much of the black militant talk these days is actually in terms far closer to the doctrines of free enterprise than to those of the welfarist '30s–terms of pride, ownership, private enterprise, capital– the same qualities, the same characteristics, the same ideals, the same methods that for two centuries have been at the heart of American success."

With far more dexterity than Humphrey dancing the boogaloo, Nixon sold his urban policy. It was "oriented toward more black ownership, for from this can flow the rest: black pride, black jobs, and, yes, Black Power—in the best sense of that often misapplied term." Dude had *skills*.

Depicting government help as patronizing, celebrating the powers of the individual, Nixon was in tune with the Hardest Working Man. In the years ahead, when Brown was pressed for a statement on his politics, he would quote from "I Don't Want Nobody." No welfare for him. "Don't give me integration, I want true communication," he sang, "don't give me sorrow, I want equal opportunity to live tomorrow." This was a little bit Booker T. Washington and a little bit Pat Moynihan, and the way Brown sang his song, you better get out of the way when the door opened, or else he was coming through *you*. Doing it yourself was an act of manhood. The sentiment was good enough for Cleveland's Carl Stokes, the first black mayor of a large American city, to present Brown the key to the city onstage, and then quote the song to the delight of the singer and his audience.

By 1969, Brown had taken to declaring that he was "25 percent entertainer and 75 percent businessman." He had already established a business office in New York, and owned real estate and radio stations. Nixon had been secretly meeting with black activists Roy Innis of CORE and Floyd McKissick, enlisting their support for his black capitalism initiative. Brown already believed in the position Nixon was trying to steer these activists toward: that the power of the dollar could solve most of black America's problems.

"I Don't Want Nobody" was a vivid illustration of his social ideas, and of his musical ones, too, because the song captures the powers of the One. You can hardly pat your foot to "I Don't Want Nobody" without feeling how hard the whole band leans into that first beat of the measure. The One was a factor in many of his great records of this era, but on "I Don't Want Nobody" it isn't just asserted, it hits like a wrecking ball.

The One might have been a necessity born of Brown's impulsiveness. Reading a crowd perfectly, he could tell when he was losing them and abruptly toss out a just-started tune, extend a bridge for ten minutes, point to a new drummer to take over without losing the beat because the current guy was going nowhere. Brown made his changes on the One, and if the band knew where it was, and used it as their switching yard, then they could keep playing without getting thrown off by his unpredictable changes of direction.

Whatever it was that drew him to the One, he was pushing everybody in the group to respect its power. When singer Marva Whitney joined the group, he changed her vocal style in two big ways: He pushed her to sing higher than she was comfortable with, giving her a deranged, urgent style, and he taught her to sing everything on the downbeat.

"I learned to do . . . what Mr. Brown called 'on the one.' See, I didn't sing on the one and that doesn't come overnight. They had to teach me how to pat my foot," Whitney said. "In church you pat your foot with your toe, but when you're with Mr. Brown, you pat your foot from the heel, which gives you a whole new thing, which they call funk. And if you don't do it like that you don't do the real funk, and that took me a while."

What did patting from your heel do that using your toe did not? It put your ass into motion. It got your body moving to the beat.

Moving asses: *That* he could control. Commercial forces, however, were beyond his powers, and in the wake of "Say It Loud," white-owned radio stations and white programmers turned their backs on him en masse. Just as he was entering a dazzling new period of creativity, he started having trouble with the pop charts. "Say It Loud" scared the gatekeepers, and after it became a pop hit, well, the gatekeepers kept Brown from having another one for seventeen years. He was digging deep into the One, reinventing his sound again, and it came at a moment when white listeners were tuning out. The audience got blacker, and drawing on the One, the music turned to funk.

These factors shaped his life in the years ahead. They were barely visible in 1969, while more pressing matters were at hand. Around this time, Brown was doing a dance on stage called "Bringing Up the Guitar" (the name of a 1968 Brown-produced instrumental by the Dapps featuring Pee Wee Ellis). That dance morphed into a step called the Popcorn round about the time Brown rerecorded "Bringing Up the Guitar" as "The Popcorn" under his own name late in 1968. Early in 1969, Brown cut a devastating bump called "You Got to Have a Mother For Me," in which he shared with the world his taste for booty—"a mother" was his honorific for a big butt, and a mother is what he liked. (Fred Daviss: "That man would fuck a snake if it had an ass on it.") "Mother" was scheduled to come out in March, but then Brown decided to put out "I Don't Want Nobody to Give Me Nothing (Open Up the Door, I'll Get It Myself)" instead. As Douglas Wolk has written, this "had the twin advantages of better politics and a longer title."

Now it becomes complicated. "The Popcorn" was getting traction on the charts, it was a groove dancers loved. So Brown took the lyrics from the still unreleased "You Got to Have a Mother For Me" and retooled the music of "The Popcorn" for yet *another* single: "Mother Popcorn." This was a brilliant piece of lust and rhythm. "Mother Popcorn" was not soul music; it spoke to the body, and it moved the body in ways soul music knew not. This was funk, possibly the moment when Brown fully moved from soul to funk—a music that didn't even have a name yet. It was just James Brown music. It was the sound of the One.

Popcorn itself was another euphemism for booty. Popcorn was something he could not quit. Brown revisited and reinvented tunes throughout his career, and in a month he had gone back in the studio, stripped out most of the rhythm from "Mother Popcorn," and recorded a sibling called "Lowdown Popcorn." Not as great, but it still had enough on it to get to sixteen on the R&B charts.

By late 1969, "popcorn" might have been shorthand for "funk" itself, a magical substance, a kind of *lapis philosophorum* applied to records in carefully calibrated amounts: Too much popcorn and the whole world might explode. He doled it out in prescribed quantities. There was "Answer to Mother Popcorn (I Got a Mother For You)" sung by Vicki Anderson; Charles Spurling cut "Popcorn Charlie"; Hank Ballard essayed "Butter Your Popcorn"; and Brown came back with "Let a Man Come in and Do the Popcorn." This was a commercial craze fronting for an obsession–and in the end it was that obsession for a "mother," for the One, that white radio was really not ready for.

David Susskind had a popular syndicated talk show on which he had interviewed Martin Luther King Jr. and Malcolm X, and so he had come to believe he knew how to bond with black people. One afternoon in the summer of 1969, he was appearing on the daytime chat program *The Mike Douglas Show* along with James Brown. Their conversation went a whole different way.

Quite clearly Susskind viewed Brown as a comparable spokesman for black America. He starts engaging the singer directly, Douglas quickly downgraded to something like a wrestling referee. Susskind saw in Brown's call for black pride the bugaboo of separatism, and he did not approve. The singer responded forcefully that *he's* not separating and that most African Americans won't. But he pointed a finger at rich whites in a position to do a lot more for blacks.

"You have everything you want, you can do anything you want, and I can't right now, and I probably got as much as you, or almost, but I got enough to *buy* anything I want," he tells Susskind with a grimace. "Don't tell me we're going backwards."

"You're going backwards," Susskind baits, jabbing his thumb toward Brown, "if you separate yourself."

"We're *not* separatin'," shouts Brown.

As was often the case with Brown, the issue came down to manhood.

"You call yourself a man, knowing that I pay taxes same as you, stayed right here and used my sweat and blood to help build this country, and *I* got to be a second- or third-class citizen? Do you call that a man? I want to know about my identity–when a flag go up, an American flag at a school, it should have an Afro American flag there with it. Give me an identity–a Negro can't go back nowhere. Let me have an identity!"

Susskind, with a side of smug: "Now Jimmy, should they bring out the flag of Israel for me, or the flag of Poland for somebody else?"

Brown: "Yes." He sees Susskind looking amused. "This is not really a joke. You're laughing at something that's going to be a big problem. Because you got kids out there that can't eat, robbing and stealing, doing what they have to do to make it, and if you don't do something about it, we gonna lose the country internally."

Susskind: "You want to win your objectives by disassociating yourself."

Brown: "We're *not* disassociating. We want to be able to identify *with* something. We've always been asked to identify with you, and what do we get? Nothing!"

The conversation turns to Susskind's show. Brown says black people can't relate to it; Susskind argues that he has a black writer on his staff.

Brown: "I don't want a Negro or a colored man, I want a black man."

Susskind, indignantly: "What's the difference?"

Brown breaks down a fascinating distinction. "A colored man is a man afraid to stand up and face his own convictions. Can't stand up like a man. He sends his wife to the door to pay his bills because he's afraid, he'll do anything somebody tells him. A Negro is a man that wants to be white and don't want to no longer identify with the ghetto. If he identify with the ghetto, then he would know the truth! But, no, he gonna get a job with *you* and try and become white. A black man tells you the truth but he never gets there because a Negro is standing in between. . . ."

Susskind, rolling his eyes: "Jimmy, there's a new survey . . ."

Brown: "We don't want the survey! The survey's out there in the street!"

Susskind can't believe the lack of gratitude for a guy speaking out in favor of integration. How can anybody–a Black Panther or a black capitalist–not want to come to his swingin' party?

After a commercial, they are right back at it.

Brown: "You have a black America and a white America, right?" he asks, poking Susskind's knee.

Susskind: "No–we have an *America*."

But what we've got right now, says Brown, is *two* Americas.

Susskind: "We're trying to integrate it and make it a better . . ."

Brown, with a hell naw look on his face: "Don't integrate it! Seek equal opportunity! Do what the Constitution says."

Susskind rubs his eyes in a theatrical, oh brother way, then says: "Well, *that* would mean integration."

Brown: "No it won't! It would mean America like it's supposed to be! United States, that's what it means! Don't integrate, don't give me that, I don't want that, I want communication! Together. I want to be with you but I want you to give me respect as a man!"

Susskind, excitedly: "You've GOT IT!"

Brown: "The problem is, you can't get [whites] to fight your fight." He's wildly gesturing, bent over, intent on being understood. "You have a fight, you have an obligation to yourself as a man. You see, I don't WANT you to do it for me, I got to do it for myself."

Susskind: "You *can't* do it yourself."

Brown: "I've *got to* do it myself . . . look, for a long time I haven't been a man! And I still don't have the classification as a man. You *say*, 'He's a man'–he's a *colored* man. He's a *Negro* man. Why can't he be just a man?"

This was a great racial debate played out before America's housewives and the unemployed. Brown looks tormented at certain moments, at others he's a gifted actor on his feet, milking the crowd. By the end he appears agitated, unsteady, ready to take Susskind out and then polish his shoes.

A few weeks later, by declaration of the mayor of Los Angeles, it was James Brown Day. Mayor Sam Yorty had signed his proclamation ahead of time, and there was a photo op scheduled in the mayor's office where Brown and Yorty would shake hands. But when Brown arrived at ten A.M., the mayor was nowhere to be found. An aide said he wasn't usually at work that early, and a deputy mayor was enlisted to make the presentation. Brown righteously stormed out and gave an earful to the media.

Dismissing the deputy mayor as "some underling," he said, "I believe in the dignity of man. I'm a busy man. I was here at the appointed time. The mayor has a job to do. So have I. If I can take time to be here, I would assume he could, too."

He *was* a busy man. In 1969, his political adviser in Oakland, Donald Warden, helped him launch a trading-stamp company, Black & Brown. The firm was started with $60,000 invested by the singer, former Oakland Raider football player Art Powell, and a third backer. The idea was straightforward: Black & Brown would make deals with grocery stores and gas stations in black communities. Stores would give customers a stamp each time they spent a set amount of money in the establishment. Black & Brown was bucking several giant national trading-stamp concerns; their ace in the hole was that you didn't have to take your stamps to a redemption center to trade them for prizes, you could bring your filled booklets back to the store that gave them to you and get back three dollars' worth of goods. Each stamp had a picture of Brown on it.

Calling the firm an example of enlightened black capitalism, Warden said Black & Brown was "committed to the struggle and concern of black people."

At the same time, Brown formed a chain of fast-food restaurants,

Gold Platter, specializing in soul food. The firm was based in Macon and drew on a number of Georgia backers, including the car dealer who sold Brown his first auto after he moved to town.

"If you don't like Gold Platter, you ain't got no soul," Brown joked at a press conference. Asked by a reporter about fast-food chains he was competing against, he fired back: "There aren't any. This is pioneer, like Daniel Boone and Davy Crockett. And it's so big that you as an American can't be out of it. You've got to be in."

Sitting before TV cameras at the Beverly Comstock Hotel in Beverly Hills, Brown explained the structure of the Gold Platter operation. A training center in Macon would teach employees skills necessary to work in his restaurants, and franchisees would gain expertise in a business that would reach coast to coast. To buy into a franchise, you needed $25,000. Loans from the Small Business Administration, Brown said hopefully, should make that sum accessible to prospective entrepreneurs.

He also explained his newfound passion for business.

"It's a little like the black capitalism Mr. Nixon is stressing. So we're putting it up to him. We have what he wants, now we'd like his help with some government self-help financing for people who want to go into the business."

Nixon's ideas, Brown said more than once, inspired his nascent entrepreneurialism. Over the next few years, a connection between Brown and the Administration would deepen.

Some observers have noticed an interesting fact about the president's program for black entrepreneurs. Nixon won the White House using what his strategists called the "Southern Strategy"; employing racially coded language and policy to lock up the segregationist vote and steer white Southerners out of the Democratic bloc. It seems a contradiction, therefore, to have a president who is exploiting white fears to be encouraging black empowerment.

Except that Nixon staked black capitalism to black communities; his vision reinvigorated the system that existed North and South in segregated cities where black-owned concerns had a lock on black consumers. This was the capitalism of the chitlin circuit, and it thrived only so long as white-owned businesses weren't forcing out black mom-and-pop concerns. It was dubious economics in the age of multinational corporations, but savvy politics.

On a morning talk show, Brown explained that, "My understanding of black power is of a man owning his own." The interviewer asked, "Are you saying that black people should work just for black people and white people work for white people?" Said Brown, "I didn't say just for black people, but it would be better because a black person will understand me better than you do, and you can understand a white person better than I do." This wasn't segregation, and it wasn't separatism, but it was a philosophy that took the separation of the races as a given. This was Black Power that a Strom Thurmond could support.

He wasn't the only celebrity venturing into economic development; in the fast-food field, Muhammad Ali had invested in a hamburger chain and gospel singer Mahalia Jackson lent her name to a franchise selling "glori-fried" chicken. A letter to a black-owned newspaper, the *Philadelphia Tribune*, struck a note of caution: "Once upon a time if a Negro got out of line, they either put him in jail or made him a Judge. Either way, it shut him up fast.

"The new trick is to lend the guy a million bucks and set him up in business. The president of a corporation doesn't have time to start riots. . . . Will he lose his Soul? Will he desert the Cause? This would indeed be a tragedy."

The writer implied Nixon's black capitalism was co-opting voices of protest, but entrepreneurialism came to Brown long before Nixon did. The idea that accumulating wealth was the best way to improve the community is something Brown learned growing up in the Terry, watching Daddy Grace and the United House of Prayer. To Grace, capitalism *was* Americanism, and he wrapped himself in the flag right down to his red, white, and blue fingernails. He sold food in his houses of prayer, and if fast food had existed then, you could have gotten that there, too.

Grace dangled the prospect of spending yourself into the main-stream. Brown raised the same possibility, while making black business seem vaguely radical. At his shows Brown had taken to giving out color TVs *and* dashikis as prizes, covering several bases at once. Brown made entrepreneurialism groovy, and surely that was noted when the members of the National Business League voted him their Businessman of the Year for 1969. Brown was given the honor in Memphis, at their sixty-ninth annual convention. The venerable organization, founded in 1900 by Booker T. Washington to foster economic development, was older than the U.S. Chamber of Commerce.

In 1969, Brown found new ways to matter to his fans, and to America. He was thirty-six, and when he spoke these days of retiring, the talk was tinged with a desire to settle into the life of a shot-caller. He didn't really mean it, and when he said it, what one took away was that he liked the *image* of a businessman. He didn't look tired, and he didn't seem worried.

He didn't even look weary in photos, taken in the fall of 1969, outside a courthouse in Sacramento. There he was being sued for paternity by Mary Florence Brown, the former president of Brown's Sacramento fan club. The Sacramento trial was widely covered, and Brown was called to testify. But on the stand and outside the courtroom, he projected an air of blessed confidence and hurt that the charge that he had fathered her child had been hurled. When a check he'd written Mary Brown for $2,500 was entered into the record, the singer explained it by saying, "This is what I live for–helping young people." And when he fired his lawyers practically from the witness stand, still he didn't seem worried. In the end Brown settled out of court, wrote her another check, all while insisting "that the agreement include a statement denying that he fathered the child."

He believed in himself, understanding that millions believed in him, too. And when a California Superior Court judge ordered Black & Brown Stamps to stop doing business in the state, and issued an injunction against the company for "failing to file financial reports and letting their business license lapse," barely did he shrug. When, a year after opening its first restaurant, a spokesman for Gold Platter said they were shutting down after taking a "substantial loss" in 1969, Brown lost none of his zeal for business. When there was a wall before him, he knew where to find a door.

Nobody had ever given him anything for free. He had amassed a fortune by running faster than everybody else, and never leaving money on the table. Late one night in Philadelphia, he looked out the window of his car and he saw an image of himself in one of his fans.

Ticketholders had filed out of the huge concrete arena, clutching the programs Brown published and sold at every show. Backstage the local DJs and politicians and the record company folks had come through and gotten a drink and had their pictures taken with the star. Brown's party left through the "secret" exit where as usual a huge cluster of kids waited patiently in the middle of the night for the singer to shake their hand, autograph their ticket stub. He greeted some of them, then climbed into his limo.

They drove off as a huge cloud of fans chased his car, surrounding it at the first red light, tapping on the window. A few more lights and the group dwindled down to three or four, and then it was one or two.

Finally, Brown turned to his driver, pointed to a skinny kid in sneakers and a T-shirt, still racing through the city streets in pursuit of the star. "If that kid is there at the next light, let's pick him up and take him to the airport with us."

At the next light, one of Brown's people opened the car door for a very surprised kid who was expecting to keep on running until he fell. In the car, Brown gave the gasping fan an inspirational talk about how he had made it, and if you stayed in school, you could make it, too. Don't be a dropout. They talked all the way to the airport, and then Brown slipped him a few bills and got into his jet.

Chapter Sixteen

THE OTHER FURTHER

The buildings housing King Records looked pretty ramshackle from the street by the end of the 1960s, and inside, a funk (from the Flemish *fonck*, "disturbance or agitation") hung over the place. Time, and people, moved on. Bud Hobgood, Brown's eyes and ears in Cincinnati, died in July 1970, at the age of thirty-four. His death fed more rumors, some claiming he met foul play, though medical records indicate a naturally caused cerebral hemorrhage.

Syd, too, was gone, though the smell of his cigars hovered in corners of the building. Now Brown was the biggest presence on the block, even when he wasn't around. He had a wall knocked down to give himself a suitable office, and took Nathan's desk as his own: a sizeable semicircle designed to look like half of a 45-rpm record, with the mogul sitting at the center. Its one shortcoming was that, because the desk wrapped around his chair, its drawers banged his legs when they were opened.

Meanwhile, the label was furiously cashing in on its glory days. In October 1968, five months after Nathan's death, King was sold to Starday Records, a small, mostly country and western label based in Nashville. A moment later, King's family jewels, its rich catalog of recordings, was sold to LIN Broadcasting, based in

Nashville. The master tapes of Hank Ballard's "The Twist," Bill Doggett's "Honky Tonk," Little Willie John's "Fever," and the "5" Royales "Dedicated to the One I Love" now no longer belonged to the label that made them.

Nathan had never been sentimental about the past. One knock on King had always been the way its product *sounded*–not how the music was recorded, but that it was pressed onto inferior vinyl that made tone arms wobble. That was because for years, instead of warehousing or selling its old record stock, King just melted down the unsold records and pressed new discs from the molten plastic. The past recycled for the latest product.

Musicians still recorded at King, and in the last years of the decade a crew of barely adolescent locals brought a crazy new energy to the place. They'd started hanging out by the loading dock, then by the front door trying to look like they belonged, maneuvering to get themselves inside the building that locals called *King's*. Finally they got invited all the way in, to play on small-fry sessions. King wasn't paying what it used to and bodies were in demand.

Some of the kids were playing in their own groups, like the guys in the Pacesetters, regulars on the local R&B scene. The Pacesetters were built around the Collins boys. Phelps was the big brother, and he had a nickname stuck on him by his kid brother, who thought he looked like one: *Catfish*. The younger brother, William, who was called Bootsy, also played guitar, a $29.95 puke green Silvertone model his mom had bought for him at Sears. Bootsy played the hell out of it, and even won a competition when he was eight by playing Lonnie Mack's "Memphis," a huge hit recorded at King.

Bootsy could play the guitar, just not as good as Catfish. Eventually he strung the Silvertone with bass strings, and turned it into a bass–it sounded fresh and surprisingly good, and it looked like hell, which probably cinched the deal for him. Bootsy played the bass.

The Pacesetters began performing in 1968, with Frankie "Kash"

Waddy on drums, Philippé Wynne singing, Robert "Chopper" McCullough on saxophone, and Clayton "Chicken" Gunnels and Darryl "Hasaan" Jamison on trumpet. They were odd-jobbing it until eventually they caught the eye of local talent scout Charles Spurling, who got them in the door.

"All the artists and all the hip people hung around King's," said Bootsy Collins. "I was still going to school and so *I* wanted to be hip and cool. I don't think at that time I thought I would actually be a musician that relied on that as my livelihood; I was just looking at my brother and saw how much fun he was having. But the more I hung around King's, I started falling in love with music. From seeing how passionate and how dedicated those musicians were, I realized if I'm going to do this, I can't be joking. It was enough to make me serious."

The local kids scrutinized Brown when he was present–"watched him like a hawk"–but it wasn't like *he* knew who they were. "Forget playing with him, we never thought we could *meet* him," Collins said. "We were just kids hanging out–'get them mothers out of here . . .' But once they heard us playing, and word started getting around, that's when things changed."

Henry Glover started hiring the band on sessions, including an Arthur Prysock record and Bill Doggett's contribution to popcorn-ography, "Honky Tonk Popcorn." Having just vaguely caught Brown's attention, the Pacesetters were promoted to playing on the road for Brown-produced acts Marva Whitney, Bobby Byrd, and Hank Ballard. It wasn't work that paid, but that never mattered. They were playing with *Hank Ballard*, they reasoned, and were now musicians getting dates out of town. They even got to jam with Brown a little in the studio, when he didn't have anything else going on. That was as good as it was likely to get.

"All we knew was music," explained Waddy. "It was a factory, a working man's town. We weren't going nowhere."

In March 1970, Brown was on the road and ass deep in alligators. The band he had painstakingly built, with Maceo Parker,

Fred Wesley, and Pee Wee Ellis at its core, that had collectively or individually shaped "Say It Loud," "Mother Popcorn," "Give It Up or Turnit A Loose," "Funky Drummer," "Ain't It Funky Now," not to mention "Santa Claus Go Straight to the Ghetto," that bunch was history. Ellis had split in late July 1969, Wesley around the beginning of the new year–both tired of the slights, fines, and confrontations that were part of playing in the band. Then, by March, the rest of the painstakingly honed crew were in full mutiny. These were musicians who had established their name in his show–fans knew Clyde Stubblefield, Jimmy Nolen, Maceo Parker. The guys in the band might grumble, but Brown knew how to handle their complaints. This time, though, something more serious was brewing.

They had given him an ultimatum in Jacksonville, literally writing out their grievances and presenting them to him backstage. The stated issue was money, but it wasn't really about that, it was about *Brown*–how he took their musical contributions without giving them credit, how he made them rehearse on their days off, how he made them live an army life they were sick of, how he had thrown their golf clubs off the bus. He knew how to play the revolt: through the old divide and conquer. "He felt that if we had a protest or some kind of grievance, it was better to individually come to him and say, 'Hey Mr. Brown, I think it would be better if it happened this way,'" said Parker. "Not as a group, just maybe individually to solve the problems. He opposed us trying to solve the problems as a group, I suppose, because as a group we were stronger."

They cornered him backstage in Jacksonville, but the hall was packed, and if he'd let them walk out then the crowd would have torn up the place, so Brown heard them out and said he needed time to ponder their demands. Then he sent his jet to Cincinnati.

After the show, he got on the phone to his King office. Bobby Byrd was dispatched on a grave diplomatic mission, and failure was not permissible: Find those cats in the Pacesetters immediately. Drive them to the airport. The next show was in Columbus, Georgia. Bring them to me.

The name of the Cincinnati venue–the Wine Bar–was cruelly misleading. There was not a fern in sight, and the wine options were strictly binary. It was a nothing dive, and the Pacesetters had just finished a paying show there, for fifteen dollars. Total. They planned to do the usual, get in their Dodge Dart station wagon, head on home, take the mattress off the bed, guys sleeping on that *and* the boxspring. When Byrd found them at the Wine Bar, he didn't even say much, just: "We are rolling." He put them in a limo, loaded them and their equipment onto Brown's jet, and they took off for Georgia. None of them had been inside an airport before. "We flew up out of that mug!" said Bootsy with glee. "I had never been in a jet before, let alone a Learjet, which instead of taking off and rising slowly, it felt like it was going straight up in the air. My jaw was over here, my Afro over there . . ."

When they touched down in Columbus, they were whisked directly to the venue, packed and surly, everybody clamoring for the show to start, "James Brown! James Brown!," and now they see a bunch of cats with instruments walking into the place–"There's the musicians!" Great, thought Bootsy, they think it's *our* fault things are running late. Inside, the Pacesetters could tell immediately the vibe was not right. Much of Brown's band was lined up backstage to their left, scowling. To their right was Brown's dressing room. They were ushered in.

Collins: "He says, 'Fellas, I want you. I want you to play my set tonight.' We looked at each other and were like, uh, okay . . . is this mug crazy?' We was drilled for *our* shows–how we gonna do a James Brown show without practice?"

There was no inspirational talk and no explanation. The singer just grunted out a few simple instructions. "Don't worry 'bout it. I'll count it off and when I drop my hand you all just hit it.' That's what he said and that's what we did."

They certainly knew the songs; they'd just never performed them with James Brown.

Before the show could begin, Brown had some unfinished business to attend to. He stomped out into the hallway and addressed the rebels: "I'm forfeiting my conversation with you all. You're fired–everybody!" All of them, except for drummer Jabo Starks, left.

Nobody seemed to remember that first show very well once it was over. It was a nervous sweaty blur. The Pacesetters were so used to playing small stages or no stages that on the biggest platform they'd ever inhabited, they huddled close together like critters in a diorama. But, everybody got through it. They *did* it. Later everybody remembered that.

Brown gathered them all in his dressing room, told them how great they sounded.

"You know, I think I'm gonna give you $225," he said. "Naw, think I'ma give you $275."

Waddy: "Now we really tripping, 'cause we already got a raise!"

Starks was there, observing in the background. When Brown said $275, they all looked to him for some kind of understanding: Was this good? What did it mean?

Starks played his role, and let out a piercing "Whhoooo!" It gave them a special feeling.

"Naw–I'ma give you $350"–and this time Starks exhaled "Oh my goodness."

The band members pulled out pencils and started writing on whatever paper they could find.

"What are y'all doing?"

"Mr. Brown, we're trying to figure out how much $350 divided by five people is. We trying to figure out how much we are getting."

"Naw–that's $350 for *each* of you," Brown said. Starks was surely smiling.

The next day they got into the Golden Eagle bus–no more Dodge Dart station wagon. There were already three uniforms ready for each member. "He had all our sizes already, pretty much," said Waddy. "Never did figure out how he did that." There were three days until the next show, in Fort Wayne, three days of steady rehearsing.

Just one thing, he told Bootsy Collins as they prepared for the first leg of their tour. "Son, I love what you're doing with that bass, but"–he cast a glance at the restrung bluish-green Sears Silvertone–"You can't come in here with that." A new Fender jazz bass was presented to Collins. This was not Cincinnati.

Collins made you sit up and listen. His playing had sap flowing through it, it *moved*. Surely it had something to do with playing the bass like a guitar at first and thus reinventing the fifth wheel, and surely it had something to do with being a skinny, tall kid whose gawky youthfulness stuck out all over the stage–he wasn't going to hide, might as well own it all. If the standard bass player kept the beat, laid down a stout foundation for the other instruments, then Collins was playing something else, because he wanted to play against the beat, and write his name with his playing, not enable someone else's excellence.

Basses sounded different in the early '70s. James Jamerson at Motown was recording the same song twenty or thirty times in one sitting in the studio, striving to shape a different, better bass line with every new take. Bassist Charles Mingus was conducting a big, contentious band *through* his playing. At almost the same time that Collins was joining Brown, the song topping the pop charts was Sly and the Family Stone's "Thank You (Falettinme Be Mice Elf Agin)," a tune that was *made* by bass player Larry Graham and his prehensile thumb. Suddenly thumbs were popping and fans were remembering the names of musicians they'd barely paid attention to before. The guitar was the dominant instrument of blues-based rock, but funk brought the bass to the front.

Always planning ten steps ahead, Brown had mapped out

replacing the old band with the Pacesetters long before either side knew what hit them. Indeed, Waddy thinks Brown had been grooming his group for just this moment months before, when he started focusing his attention on them in the King studio. It was part of Brown's genius, playing three-dimensional chess in the boxing ring. In his music, too, he could see the multiple consequences of a single act. Change a drummer and you changed *everything*. In the past, when a great new drummer entered his band, he found a way to make their gifts the foundation of a new direction. In 1970, he lost everybody *but* the drummer. So what did he do, he still changed the sound 360-degrees, in the words of Jabo Starks, as the new guy–Bootsy Collins–came to prominence. The drummers heard the news before anyone else.

When Collins arrived, said former drummer Melvin Parker, "that's when the funk moved from the drums to the bass. The bass became the funk piece and the drums became the backbone or the stationary part."

Brown was twice as old as Collins; to Bootsy and Catfish, he could seem like a codger from another planet. The brothers had been raised by a single mom. The relationship with their boss was powered by complicated currents, as Bootsy sometimes wanted Brown to be a father figure to him, and at other times saw him as an authority figure to rebel against.

The older musicians, family men, could be bullied and manipulated by his fines and penalties. But the guys from Cincinnati had an almost unthinkable response: They ignored him. It drove Brown nuts, yet he also tried to loosen up. "He was letting us find our way *and* I think he realized early on that we don't have those responsibilities that the older cats had. Didn't nobody ever pay us–it wasn't no big deal. And we had credit at the Wine Bar! 'Take my money, I can still get credit.' So we had that to always fall back on, and I think he knew that."

To Bootsy and his guys, the Wine Bar embodied funk. As much as a bass line or a grunt, to them the word signified making do with your circumstances, turning grease into glory. It was about owning history you couldn't leave behind, and wearing circumstances like a tangerine mohair coat. It was why Bootsy Collins could say this: "Funk was like the way we lived. All of us kids sleeping in one room, it's 105 degrees outside, no air-conditioning. That's funk."

Torn, possibly, between feasting on the atmosphere and keeping the show running, Brown chose his moments for playing a fatherly role, doling out advice that sounded to the newcomers like a foreign language. He would draw near and declare, "Let me tell you something, son. If you ain't on the heel and toe, you *got* to blow." He said that a lot, and Bootsy and Catfish would giggle about it later, trying to puzzle out a meaning. Only eventually did they understand he was saying if you weren't in control of events–on top of things–things would fall apart fast. It was a message of discipline they were not inclined to hear.

Catfish had a couple of bottles of wine stashed in his guitar case on the bus. That was an infraction right there. As for the LSD Collins was gobbling on a recurring basis, well that wasn't even covered in Brown's criminal code. One night he took more than usual; he doesn't recall how or what he played that show. What he does recall is his bass turning into a great serpent, him breaking all the strings, throwing it to the ground, and stomping off the stage.

Afterward, Brown summoned him to his dressing room for a talking to, during which Collins, still tripping, reacted in a way no sideman ever had before. He was rolling on the floor, laughing at the stern father trying to impart his wisdom. Brown gestured to one of his aides, "Get this fool out of here." Collins was kicked out of the dressing room, and Collins said he never called him back to the dressing room again. "I guess he realized he wasn't getting through to this fool . . . this fool's just a lost case."

Call it *continuing education.* Two veterans helped inculcate the inductees into the James Brown show and the James Brown world. Bobby Byrd, who had come in at other eras when newcomers needed to be whipped into shape fast, rejoined the band. And drummer Starks, who knew the show better than anybody currently with Brown, was working closely with Collins. Since Clyde Stubblefield had left with the insurrectionists, Starks was playing most of the show himself. (Young Frankie Waddy, a drummer from the Cincinnati contingent, never won Brown's approval.)

Starks was in the best position to assess how the Ohioans affected the show, saying, "James did a lot of his old material every night but when you heard Bootsy and them do it, it was *different*. They had a different type of fire going." Collins was eased into the flow; for weeks Brown hired other bassists to play the ballads and older songs that needed a more anchored, formal approach. But soon Collins was ripping on, and ripping up, everything. On his own time Collins wasn't listening to Brown's records, he was listening to Black Sabbath and Miles Davis's *Bitches Brew*, and the dark swing of such music entered his own playing. Brown heard it, and let it change him. With Collins's arrival, as Starks put it, "He got a shot of goodness in him and he went into another thing."

The trick for Brown was keeping the young guys busy and constructive without driving them away. Collins recalled: "After the show he would take us to the studio. If it wasn't the studio it was rehearsal. And if wasn't rehearsal, me and Catfish might get called to do a thing we called 'carrying the stick.' That meant hanging out with Mr. Brown on the plane or somewhere, and watching him do his thing. You just had to do it sometimes. All your fun is gone."

In response, the Ohioans came up with a saying that quickly became a philosophy for coping with the boss. Say there was a two-day gap between performances. That was when the schedule got larded with practices and recording sessions. The old guys just took it, staying in the hotel or bus, following the script. Or else they quit. The new guys, though, had a fresh approach. "See ya!" Collins would shout to one and all after a gig, and quicker than Charles Bobbit could get up off of that thing, they'd all be gone, driving back to Cinci until it was next showtime.

"We'd do that to anybody, anybody that would say something we didn't wanna do? 'See ya!' Then we cut it short—it was one word, that's the one James liked. He'd be on the plane, faking like he's asleep, he'd have one eye open and one closed. Then he'd look at you and say 'Seeya!' *That's* when I knew we had him. I knew this was a two-way thing, when he started picking up the street things that we were doing."

Brown's affection for the new guys was demonstrated onstage. It used to work like this: He had his breakout moves, and the sidemen did their simple steps behind him. The two did not intersect. But video from the era shows him watching Bootsy and Catfish as they did their thing and then falling back to line up *with* them, dancing their moves, just one of the guys. The band joined him, and he joined the band.

"He knew this energy we had," said Collins. "He didn't know how to control it but at same time he wanted to grab it and make it his. And it was, for a while. But I guess he knew it wasn't going to be for a long while, because some stuff you can't hold back. We was just wild and crazy and we loved it."

Killin' it, he'd say. *We killed 'em dead,* Brown gleefully told the guys backstage as his knees bled and he hobbled over to have his hair done. But not Collins. If Brown had something to share with the bassist after a show, most likely it was his unwavering parental disapproval. "Son, you just ain't on it," he would grunt, his head sadly shaking with the bad news. "You just ain't on the One." Collins took it for a while, but then he tuned the guy out. "As far as he was concerned, we were never on the One."

These newbies had brought something that hadn't existed in the world before and planted it in his show. They changed stuff. The change was bigger than letting a hot hand rewrite your arrangements, bigger than a new drummer turning the beat around. This was something outside of Brown's experience, something beyond him, and it was making him feel young. It was a magic he labored to keep under his control—and how likely was that?

It was *motivational*. For as Brown could hear, when Collins arrived in the band the One crawled up from the under-muck and popped its gills to breathe air for the first time. With the new band, Brown was taking his investment in the One public. The One leaped from being a way for musicians to not get lost in the flow to an expression of the flow itself. And the brothers Collins and their associates generated a flow that was never before heard, a music that was funnier, dirtier, that was more profoundly in the moment than what had come before.

As the One grew in power and mystique, it became a way for Brown to keep the upper hand with musicians, a buzz kill to apply when necessary. When he couldn't explain what he wanted, or didn't have anything specific to say–"Son, you just ain't on the One." It drove the formally trained musicians around him slightly crazy. "It's really–it's a joke," scowled Fred Wesley. "He didn't know what the One was to him. To him it's the downbeat. But he didn't know what it *was*. The emphasis of the one of the bar . . . his music kind of emulated that, but, as far as it being some kind of a concept–I don't think so." But it was a notion few would debate with Soul Brother Number One.

Signaling this was a new moment. Brown gave his band a new name: the JBs. He liked the way it sounded. They were playing a show in Nashville six weeks after the Ohioans joined up when Brown felt the time was ineffably right to blow out a groove he'd had in his head for months into a record. He had ambitions for a vamp the guys were playing live; there was a phrase that he and Bobby Byrd had been kicking back and forth for weeks. Byrd said he'd heard somebody use the word "sex" in a brazen way on TV, and it stuck in his head. "Machine" they'd come up with themselves; *sex* and *machine* together just seemed an apt pairing, Byrd said.

Brown called his usual engineer, King's Ron Lenhoff, from backstage in Nashville: Come now. Lenhoff couldn't get a flight out of Cincinnati, so he jumped in his car and drove the five hours to the Starday-King studio in Nashville.

A new funk age, a culture beyond sound, was rearing up. You could see its influence in basketball, with the old-school, hold-your-spot, ploddingly pass-the-ball-around method giving way to the improvisational, explosive style of Julius Erving. In comedy, Richard Pryor was performing jokes that were truths, truths that were fictions, fictions without punch lines. James Brown, meanwhile, was in Nashville having a party.

It *sounded* like some kind of party, anyway: "Fellas, I'm ready to get up and do *my* thang/I wanta get *into* it man, you know, like a, like a sex machine man, movin', *doin'* it, you know?" We know.

Byrd grunts "Get on up!" like a hog hot on some truffles, and then the guys enthusiastically second the boss–yes, as a matter of fact, a sex machine sounds like an excellent thing to be in the present situation. The brothers are laying down a whole new sound: Bootsy's bass a flickering, alive thing, Catfish evoking the metallic chank of Nolen but lighter, freer. Brown spontaneously sat and decanted a little aromatic piano. Two takes and they were outta there. Seeya.

"Get Up (I Feel Like Being Like a) Sex Machine (Parts One and Two)" went to #2 on the R&B charts and grazed the pop listings. Two months later Brown got everybody back in the same conducive studio to record "Super Bad (Part 1 & Part 2)."

"Watch me!" he screams at the top, "Watch me!" He could be talking to the band, he could be talking to *us*. No doubt, all over America, teenagers were staring at their transistor radios as he shouted it, imagining the guy right then–his physicality, doing a few steps on a street corner, looking *bad* in the mothy light. The music blowing right past song structure to vamps and monochords and "wrong" harmony; the lyrics blowing past confession and storytelling and all the other songwriters' tricks, going straight to the id, issuing commands to the universe, free associating his love for himself. Brown's "Sometimes I feel so nice–good god!–I jump back wanna kiss myself" is the kind of in-the-moment, off-the-street bravura that would make a legend out of some folks, if it wasn't just a stray inspiration in a session full of them.

There's an exceptionally ill scream, and then an untethered saxophone solo by Robert McCullough. Not the greatest reedman (Starks said the best horn in this band would have been the worst horn in the group that had walked out), McCullough is instructed to overpower whatever shortcomings he had by playing a proudly noisy solo—"Come on Robert... blow me some Trane, brother!" Brown shouts, meaning wail like John Coltrane. It more than works. "Super Bad" must have been what Amiri Baraka meant when, in praising Brown as an icon of the era, he declared his art to be in "combining the free expression of the oldest 'Shouts' with some of the most advanced musical arrangements. Brown's musicians were high tech omni-styled wailers who could drill Coltrane's nuclear sonic colors into James's funk... the sound of the other further!"

On Saturday, May 9, in a black-owned mortuary in Augusta, a woman pulled back the sheet covering a new arrival. The body was that of sixteen-year-old Charles Oatman, an African American incarcerated in the Richmond County jail.

His back was laced with deep gashes, his skull was crushed, and he was covered in what looked to be cigarette burns. Authorities suggested Oatman might have been killed by cellmates, or perhaps died by falling from his bunk.

By Sunday afternoon, it was said nearly every black person in Augusta knew of the condition of the dead boy's body. Some knew that Oatman was mentally disabled, with an IQ of less than sixty. Still, officials had put him with the general adult population of the jail. Talk turned rapidly to police responsibility.

Monday morning, a group of 300 to 500 demonstrated outside the Municipal Building downtown, tearing down the Georgia flag and burning it in front of a line of heavily armored police. Groups formed in the streets, whites were assaulted, businesses looted, and by sunset, billowing clouds of black smoke could be seen over Augusta from miles away.

Charges of police brutality and racial prejudice had fallen on deaf ears in Augusta for years. The heat was rising. Earlier that summer, white Augusta heard rumors that demonstrators were planning to disrupt that most sacred rite, the Masters Tournament; South African golfer Gary Player was given special police protection and the golf course carefully guarded. A week before the riot, a group of blacks had tried to make a statement on police relations at a city council meeting when the mayor abruptly adjourned the session.

By May 12, the second day of the riot, six black men were dead, all shot in the back by the same kind of weapon—the shotguns police were issued to put down the uprising. At least twenty downtown buildings burned. When local officials didn't call in the National Guard and Georgia state troopers, Governor Lester Maddox ordered them in on his own. Troopers patrolled the city with black tape over their nameplates and fixed bayonets. Tanks with mounted machine guns moved through the neighborhood where James Brown had grown up.

Brown flew in from a show in Flint, Michigan, on Tuesday, and went to the radio station he owned, WRDW. The same day, Governor Maddox also arrived in Augusta and came to the station. The singer and the segregationist held a twenty-minute meeting in which Brown both pledged his help to quell the violence and pointedly criticized racism in Augusta. When Maddox said, "I don't know of anyone who is forcing unequal rights on your people," Brown tartly responded, "Governor, I'm from Augusta, Georgia. The black people here don't have equality."

"You don't think it could happen in Augusta," Brown said in one of his public statements. "It happens anywhere when we forget that greed is the master of all wrongdoing. And when you don't divide it—everybody has to have a little piece of the pie. And I think a lot of things came from that kind of frustration."

His words were broadcast on TV and radio, and they presented a message that rioters should stay off the streets—"don't save face–save your city"–along with criticism of the city's oblivious white leadership.

WRDW and the news director Brown had hired, Ralph Stone, had long reported black grievances, and their coverage made them a target. During the Augusta riot, white supremacists circulated a flier calling for Stone's death, and for WRDW–"Where Reds Dare Whites"–to be burned down. Stone responded that neither he nor the station was responsible for the violence in the streets.

"All we do is tell it like it is. The white press generally has never covered our story in Augusta. We tell black people they can do things nonviolently, and we tell both sides of the story. We have run strong editorials saying 'sock it to the establishment'; not advocating riots but saying 'it can happen.'

"Blacks in Augusta are tired of the old black leadership pussyfooting around. We gave them a chance to do their thing. Now we're gonna do ours."

Brown picked up Stone's criticism of the old guard in his comments. He avoided blaming one side or the other and called for mutual respect. He hadn't lived there in decades, but just a year before, Augustans had called Brown their "honored son," and celebrated him with a parade down Broad Street. Now he was watching buildings on Broad Street reduced to ash.

This wasn't the Superman of Boston, 1968. In 1970 Augusta, Brown courageously injected himself into events over which he had no control, and in the end, the results seemed ambiguous at best. His gestures were un-Herculean, his words honed. He seemed like a guy doing what he could, because he needed to help a city he considered his home.

Chapter Seventeen

MASTER OF TIME

B y her own admission, the probate judge of Barnwell, South Carolina, did not watch much TV. When a black couple knocked on her door and asked to be married, the name James Brown did not mean a thing to her.

Early on a November 1970 evening, the judge married the couple. She didn't invite them in. "I got a real nice front porch. I marry most of my colored couples out there unless it is raining," she told a reporter.

His new wife, Deidre Jenkins Brown, was a red-haired beauty from a good Baltimore family. Friends called her Deedee. They had been together for some time, and were waiting for Brown's divorce from Velma, in Toccoa, to come through, so they could get married.

At the wedding, the bride wore a cream-colored, pearl-buttoned dress; the groom, a gray knit suit with a white zipper top trimmed with gray. Bobby Byrd was the best man, and Joe Brown and Danny Ray were also present.

They were visiting Augusta in 1970, when the couple surprised everybody by announcing that they would soon be moving there. Deedee was a smart, stay-at-home sort of woman, and did not like the pace of New York City. "I simply love to keep house," she told a writer from the *Baltimore Afro-American*. "I look forward to our own home soon and keeping my husband as happy as I am."

They bought a $116,000 house, and with an extensive redesign turned it into a two-story modern home, with a pool, three bedrooms, and guest house. It was located in a lavish neighborhood on Walton Way Extension. That was a street on the Hill, the white enclave of old moneyed Augusta. A black family living on the Hill in the civil rights era—and nobody can remember another black family in the vicinity—was an indication of racial progress in the city. But progress was relative. When the African American novelist Frank Yerby, who had grown up in Augusta, visited the town he'd left decades before, he put it this way: "Augusta has gotten a little more civilized since when I was a child, but that's true all over the South. But at least the people of Augusta have reached a stage of kindly hypocrisy, which is a vast improvement."

A group of Brown's new neighbors made a presentation to his real estate agent asking him to move elsewhere, but the singer was set on Walton Way, and there was no drama after he moved in.

In lieu of a honeymoon, weeks after the wedding Deedee accompanied her husband to Africa, where the band was playing shows in Nigeria and Zambia. Though Brown had already performed a private show for the leader of Ivory Coast on a quick visit in 1968, this was in many ways his real introduction to Africa. Black Americans were beginning to celebrate his music as a link to the motherland and celebrating Brown as an exemplar of African culture flourishing on American soil. He represented in America an urge to connect with the source; in Africa, the singer of "Say It Loud" was viewed as the voice of a pan-African spirit.

In Nigeria, a civil war had recently finished, and there was armed militia all over Lagos, first stop on the tour. When the band landed at the airport, thousands were waiting to greet them. Brown had arrived with a twenty-two-piece band, arranger David Matthews, and engineer Ron Lenhoff. At the airport, military forces used clubs to beat a path through the crowds so that the band could get off the plane. Brown saw thousands more lining the road from the airport into the capital city. Everywhere they went, the musicians were doted on. Band members were told that more copies of "Say It Loud" were sold in Nigeria than there were turntables to play it on; fans clutched their copies like prizes. "That's the kind of power James had in Africa," Matthews remembered.

A ceremonial visit was paid to Oba Adeyinka Oyekan II, a sovereign who proclaimed the singer a Freeman of Lagos and made a gift of a scroll depicting Brown's life and global influence. After that, everybody headed to the hotel, where another gift awaited: an invitation to the Nigerian bandleader Fela Kuti's club, the Shrine. Brown's band played in Lagos for three nights, and Bootsy Collins remembers visiting the Shrine two or three times.

Fela was a rising star, speaking for the oppressed, connecting Western jazz and soul with a power source that was profoundly African. A visit by Brown to the Shrine—equal parts Playboy mansion and rebel enclave—might have generated enough enlightenment to float the pyramids.

Two protean messiahs. Fela sometimes proclaimed Brown's influence and other times claimed that Brown had "stolen my music." Said Fela, "James Brown has influenced me in a way, because he had some fantastic bass lines . . . it was like, this guy is an African."

Musically the American was finding his way back to Africa without having *heard* African music. What he heard was the subterranean Africa, fracked by slavery and four hundred years of scrambling and erasure. He heard it through pop music and black drumming traditions in the South. He made it all up himself, his Watts Towers to the stars, and now he was on African soil.

They had offered him the key to the Shrine, but alas, Brown was disinclined to go. Brown didn't visit a peer's stage to pay tribute, he went to rip the mic from their hands and make their audience his. But even James Brown did not have a place called a "shrine," and such a refuge would not have been so easily invaded by a competitor swaggering in from the West. Brown stayed away, while many of the JBs headed out.

When Collins drove to it on his first night, he said he sensed the club long before his driver approached it. "You could be ten miles away and you could hear the drums," he recalled with awe. Inside the perimeter, the experience was even more overpowering. "You could be carrying on a conversation and the next thing you know, your body starts movin' and you can't control it! And you're like, 'Damn, what's wrong with me?'"

The first night at the Shrine made Collins reflect on the all-but religious worship they had received at the Lagos airport. It was nice, but now he felt a need to pay something back. "Man, I told them to take all those praises back, because they was the one that needed to be praised." Comparing Fela's pulse to the groove of the JBs, he said, "When I heard these cats, it was like another dimension . . . a dimension that I had never experienced before. And it had a deeper feeling to me. When I heard them, that was the deepest level you could get."

Brown was disciplined with the press, careful to stick to a chosen message and avoid loose talk. But to a Nigerian journalist, he shared a thought that seemed direct and meaningful. His reflections flickered for a moment on the subject of the difference between blacks in America and Africa. "You have your pride. You possess your culture. The white man couldn't rob you of it."

At a show in Nigeria, a woman was overcome during Brown's cape ritual and performance of "Please, Please, Please," and leaped from an upper tier onto soldiers below. In Zambia, the singer was proclaimed Head of State of Music by president Kenneth Kaunda; Brown reciprocated by singing "It's a Man's Man's Man's World" to the leader.

A long time ago, African music had traveled to the West and places like Brazil, Haiti, and Cuba. It had bonded with local traditions, and then sailors and traders brought the Creole sound back to Africa. Africans liked it–they knew it, even if they hadn't heard it before–and then came James Brown, whom they went nuts for. His music came to Africa through radio and television, and record players in villages where generators hummed and buzzed four hours a day. For everyone involved with this amazing trip, it was a straight line curling back until it formed a circle.

The impression it left on him he didn't feel he could share with the press waiting for him back in the States. To them he expressed appreciation for the response he had received, but his feelings about Africa would remain publicly neutral, mystifyingly bland, expressing little sense of personal connection. Maybe he needed to ponder the experience; maybe the experience was too easily misinterpreted, or too easily distorted by journalists, to simply share with strangers. Maybe "Say It Loud" said it all, as far as he was concerned. But when he returned, Brown was impressively disciplined, even for him.

They played Africa, then they came back through France and played there. The scenery was not lost on the young guys who until now had barely gotten past Dayton. Still, it was hard to forget all the little stuff. The fines rankled.

After a night out in New Orleans, the JBs showed up at the venue, where wardrobe mistress Gertrude Sanders broke it to Collins: "Boss having problems, he gonna dock your pay." Next thing they knew, twenty-five dollars was taken out.

The band balked, and eventually they cornered him. The Ohioans started woofing as they stood on the venue's 360-degree stage before the show, asking why money had been deducted from their pay, acting like this time a message would be sent.

The Boss said nothing. The Boss *did* something. "He did this gymnastic move called a leg circle," said a startled Waddy. "He dropped down to the ground—boom!—with a leg circling around, he spun around down there a full rotation!"

It was Curly Howard in the b-boy circle, a 360 tour de force that made all argument irrelevant. Shut 'em down. "He did that so fast and forcefully, I tell you what, he *levitated*. And whatever we was talking about, we were distracted. We forgot what the hell we *was* talking about. We just walked away.

"Never found out *why* he did it, but that was his answer, and I guess it worked for us."

In time, though, Brown's moves stopped working, and Waddy ejected, to be replaced by a high school buddy from Cincinnati, Don Juan "Tiger" Martin. He had no context for the fast lane he had just entered; one of Martin's most vivid impressions of being in the JBs was the "squooosh" their shoes made when they left the stage at the end of the show, from all the sweat that soaked into their shoes.

Martin compensated for dehydration by swigging diet pills and soda pop. "You can hear it in the music," said Martin. "The stuff would be so fast we'd be killin' James." The leader liked his band's energy, and tried to do his splits and floor show at their rapid fire pace. After the show his knees would be swollen and a needle would be inserted to drain off the fluid.

When they weren't losing bodily fluids they were recording songs like "Get Up, Get Into It, Get Involved" and "Soul Power." When they weren't recording, they lived in dread of hearing the last words any JB wanted to hear: *James wants to see you in his dressing room.* No good could come from that. It either meant you had messed up, or he wanted you to hang out with him for the evening, in which case all you *could* do was screw up between now and the end of the night.

Waddy: "He was like a father figure to us. Don't nobody want to hang with their dad, you know? As a buddy."

New York's luxe Copacabana, a nightclub that all the great singers wanted on their résumé, had booked them for two weeks in March 1971. Brown quarreled with the donnish owner, Jules Podell, when he cut the stand back to a week. Brown told the band they'd have to go on half salary since their booking was now half as long. The guys sent Bootsy in to argue for more money. They'd dispatched him for a raise just weeks before, in Africa, and it worked, because Brown knew better than to let his band walk out on a football stadium full of pumped-up Nigerians. He wasn't so worried about the Copa crowd.

That's one explanation for what happened next. An alternate

take: the Copa had a dress policy. Bands wore jackets and ties. Bootsy and the rest of the Ohio miscreants would do a lot of stuff for Brown, but this was just too damn much. As Brown said, "To put a tie on Bootsy was like to put a bridle on a wild horse."

Whatever the cause, the Cincinnati kids walked out–not just on the Copa, but on Brown, on the penalties, the rehearsals, the squoosh of it all. When it happened, he didn't get upset, he just threw a mountain of dollars on the floor, told them to collect their pay and go. That was it. Almost like he'd anticipated this part of the story, too.

It felt like freedom. Later, Collins thanked Brown for pushing them so hard, saying that all the rigors and rehearsals had made him a far better musician. When he heard it, Brown looked mystified; he didn't realize he *had* been pushing them. Just doing it the only way he knew how.

The Copa fiasco was almost twelve months to the day since Brown had fired his band and hired the mugs. They got to him, and with them he made some of the best music of his life. They changed him by stepping up the pace of songs to rivet-gun velocities. They changed him because they came to funk as adolescents and experienced it not as music but as a culture, a way to live. Their funk was a hole in the wall, and when Brown entered it he came out a different person. According to Waddy, while they were in the group, guitarist Jimi Hendrix approached the Cincinnatians, urging them to leave Brown and join forces with him in a new band. That's one transformation we'll forever have to imagine, because they turned him down.

All in a year: That, too, you could call the One.

In the months that followed, some of the old crew started coming back; St. Clair Pinckney and Clyde Stubblefield, and then Fred Wesley, who Brown made the band director. A big stand at the Apollo was coming up, and it was Wesley's job to get a new band ready.

It was strictly touch and go: Guitarist Hearlon "Cheese" Martin was in, and bassist Fred Thomas; this horn section was no improvement on the last. Starks and Pinckney were in the band, and Bobby Byrd, so there was continuity with the past, but still . . .

They scuffled for two weeks. "We had it shakily together, *kind of* together," said Wesley, and then Brown came to New York and asked if the band was ready. There was only one possible answer: "Yes sir, they're ready."

Really, they weren't. "But he got in front of the band, huffing and puffing and dancing and patting his foot, and something sort of happened," Wesley recalled.

"*Any* band that played behind James Brown becomes a good band, because he will force you to be a good band. You have to do the things right. Just because of his will. He was an extraordinary person. Just because of his will, the band became a good band."

Exerting that will was an art form Brown had honed for years. He had bullied and beaten, coaxed and courted, he had changed the subject by dropping to the floor. Confusion, mystery, and division all helped him maintain influence over his band.

The band was, of course, essential to him. It is impossible to imagine James Brown music without the musicians that played it with him. Never was it lost on him that the band was the crucial way his sound and his voice got across to the masses. He could only agree with what Duke Ellington said about his orchestra: "That's my instrument." The various ensembles he put together were fashioned for the strength and style of the players. For all his world historic ego, Brown was amazingly selfless when it came to giving strong players strong roles to play.

The seemingly candid admission that he was 75 percent businessman and 25 percent entertainer is, ultimately, a clever ruse. *Businessman* was a term he was more comfortable with, a higher calling, perhaps, than *showman* in his mind. There's a term he was most certainly not comfortable with, one that needs to be applied: *artist*. What the Brown bands of the late 1960s and onward do is make a paradoxically freedom-drenched art out of radical acts of discipline. That discipline began in Southern black notions of community building through polish and enterprise, through work that, when exerted, would uplift all. (An idea that was most often expressed in business.) It was built out of the anxiety and dread alive in the mind of the guy gripping the microphone. He *needed* rigor. Left to the misrule of the Terry's alleys, he was transformed by the discipline of the Georgia penal system. The order he demanded from his musicians made it possible for them to play the Apollo and be good so quickly; the order he enforced on himself—the structure and precision needed to move about the country 300-plus days a year—pressed a weight down on things that he did not want to view.

Yet there is, in his late-1960s and onward music, a gift of liberation. Each member or section is playing a pattern, and when the patterns overlap and lock, they have a staggering power. This music pulls you out of your life, out of time—it destroys time—and leaves an impression of being lost in a crowd of pure action. In the way that a great drummer seems to commandeer the space around him, control events for a moment that hangs in the air, with this band full of drummers playing various instruments, there was one guy controlling them all—a drummer's drummer, a master of time.

The big bands of the swing era had disappeared because it was too expensive to keep a large crew intact for long periods of time, and too expensive to move them from town to town. That's what Brown was doing, however, running a big band in the age of the rock-and-roll combo. He wanted it to last as long as possible. Anybody would, but Brown had a swamp of feelings—worthlessness, loneliness—waiting for him whenever he left the stage. To make this pleasure, this salvation, survive, with so many folks coming in and out of the band, he needed to be a leader of rare powers.

Cruel powers. Everybody has a story or ten. One of them is about a young drummer called Turk, which was short for Turkey. Turk came from South Carolina, and would materialize anytime Brown was within 200 miles of his home. He dreamed of playing drums for Brown, and would pack his kit in his car and show up at performances just in case he needed a drummer that night. It was like that for a year.

One night Turk was in the dressing room and Brown sent word for him to put his drums on the truck. What Brown didn't tell Turk was that he would be *driving* that truck for the next two months. A while later, the boss had another message: Tell Turk to put his drums onstage. The show already had two drummers, but now they had three drums set up. Now those two drummers are on their toes, too, wondering what's up.

Turk, whose only goal in life was to play for James Brown, stood in the wings and watched the singer. Waiting for Brown to point at him and signal his entrance. This went on for, perhaps, a month. Then one night Brown pointed at him at the exact single moment when for a second Turk was looking away. He missed the sign. After the show, Brown gave the word: "Send Turk home tonight."

You could not look away, and everybody could be replaced. That was essential knowledge for playing with Brown. Or, as he was known to say: "I've got the Lord in one hand and the devil in the other. You never know where it's going to come from."

He pushed people around because he had to, then he pushed people around because he wanted to. He pushed people around, and in the words of drummer Ron Selico, "he was a black Hitler." He felt he *had* to exert brute control, because if he didn't, they would leave. Nobody abandoned James Brown; if they tried, he wanted them to regret it. But the truth about this management style is that little or none of it was a secret. He did not hide what he was about; he could not. "Control I must have, of everything, of myself. Either that or I can't give you James Brown." If you were with Brown for any length of time, you understood what you would get out of it, and what would never be yours. If you wanted to be a star, this was not the place to be. If you wanted to get rich, or record your own music, or see your name on an album, that was not likely to happen. But if you wanted to see the world and play some amazing music for crowds huge and small, you could not do much better. There were two kinds of people in Brown's band: Those who got it and made their peace, and those who didn't. The latter would spend years cursing the man.

He kept everybody on edge, and he was on edge most of all. Those he shared a bill with were a source of special concern. The opening acts were usually picked by him. He selected those who needed his help, and weren't going to show him up. That wasn't always possible, as when he played Philadelphia, around 1970, and the local promoters insisted on putting the Dells—a very hot vocal group—in the opening slot.

The show was at the Philadelphia Spectrum, a large arena that was holding maybe 12,000 that night. The Dells, Alan Leeds recalls, "were tearing the place apart. Girls were screaming, they were *killing*." Leeds went backstage and found Brown pacing a hole in the carpet, chain smoking, and utterly wrecked. Usually, Brown exhibited a careful mask of confidence before a show. This was a guy Brown's road manager hadn't seen before.

Finally, Brown looked at Leeds and blew up. " 'They're fucking amateurs, *amateurs*; they had them in the palm of their hands and they didn't know when to come off!' " He seemed to want badly for the Dells to exit the stage. Meanwhile, the Dells continued to sing, and the crowd continued to go nuts.

Brown to Danny Ray: "Mr. Ray, they don't know when to come off—get out there and get them off. NOW!" Leeds followed Ray to see how he would handle it.

Brown had once pulled the curtain down himself on gospel group the Mighty Clouds of Joy when *they* were getting too much love from the crowd. God could forgive Danny Ray, but the fans and the Dells most assuredly would not.

Once they got far from Brown's dressing room, Ray turned his

Buster Keaton mien to Leeds and announced, "This is the last time you'll ever talk to Danny Ray, because I'm about to die." He formulated a strategy: "Mr. Leeds, we've got to go up there very slowly, we've got to find the longest staircase there is to get up there." Finally, as Ray made it to the stage, the Dells finished their set.

There was a pause as they changed the stage. The headliner was a frazzled mess. To get to the Spectrum's round stage, Brown had to walk through the audience. Boy did he. "By the time he got to the stage, one shirtsleeve is torn off, his hair is askance, collar was twisted, and he hadn't sang a note. He was on fire that night, and the crowd went berserk!" said Leeds. "If the Dells had them excited, he took it to another level–it was the best show of the year.

"That's what he never understood. That *he* was James Brown and they were just the Dells. They were the opening act."

At King, he was the biggest fish in the lake and could do pretty much whatever he wanted. When King merged with Starday, the company was basically putting out low-budget trucker music and stellar James Brown hits: "Mother Popcorn," "Give It Up or Turnit A Loose," and "Super Bad" all going to the top of the R&B charts. The label may have made a token effort to develop new acts, but pretty quickly the books were getting straightened for another sale, and the lake was being drained.

Having a megastar as your hitmaker was a wonderful thing. But from the Starday-King perspective, having James Brown as their hitmaker was a mixed blessing. "Here was a quarterback who threw nothing but touchdown passes," said Colonel Jim Wilson, general manager at Starday-King. "And his demands were very demanding." Brown was pressuring the label to make deposits to his account on top of his regular check. He even had Starday-King cover the $5,000 lease payment on his Learjet.

Executive Hal Neely, having moved from King to Starday-King, wanted to buy King back, and to do it he needed cash. Selling James

Brown's contract got him the cash he needed. Brown didn't have a recording contract with Starday-King; instead, with great foresight, he had negotiated a personal services deal with Neely, whom he trusted. That meant Starday-King was negotiating from weakness, because Brown could easily leave, and Neely, the only obstacle, would be getting paid either way.

While Brown kept the squeeze on Starday-King, he was fielding bids from other labels. Warner Bros. Records badly wanted him and were probably offering the most money of any label; but Brown was willing to take less money and maintain creative control over his music and recordings, and Warner was reluctant on that point.

Meanwhile, the European Polygram conglomerate had started up the Polydor label in America, and didn't want to build a brand from the ground up—they were hungry for a star who would give them instant credibility. Polygram was especially hungry to enter the black music market, with an audience that was considered more loyal and dependable than white record buyers.

The era of black acts putting out albums with handmade cartoon covers was dead. Making great, all-the-way-through listenable albums had transformed Aretha Franklin's audience. Isaac Hayes was making double-disc opuses for Stax, racking up studio bills for releases that felt like luxury items. Studio technology had left Starday-King behind. Meanwhile Brown was having great success with seven-plus minute songs that were cut up into two or three parts across a 45. His music seemingly was meant for the long form. The early 1970s, he recognized, were a good time to sign a contract with somebody who could underwrite him into the album market.

Polygram offered competitive studio budgets and healthy national distribution. The parent company wanted Brown's back catalog, too, and they ended up paying a lot to Starday-King for the tapes that came with the singer.

Obviously Brown saw how little Starday-King had to offer. But he also knew how much he was worth and bargained hard with his suitors. "James Brown had a seventh-grade education, but there's no telling what his IQ was," said Fred Daviss, who was Brown's banker, and one of his bookkeepers at the time of the Polydor deal. "I remember times when we were sent a thirty-page contract from Polydor, he'd get worked up about something, write a little note in the margin, and everybody in the boardroom would be snickering about it. Two years later, that elementary little side note would bite them in the ass. One little side note cost Polydor four million when it caught up with them."

The bargaining was fierce, and Brown was the kind of stubborn negotiator who would throw it all away if he felt he wasn't getting respect. The discussions foundered, and a spirit of animosity was filling the negotiating room.

Brown called an old friend who also was close to Polydor's Jerry Schoenbaum, and asked him to come in and help. He phoned Henry Stone, the Miami-based record man who had almost signed Brown back in 1955. "I was in New York at the time," remembered Stone. "Got a call from James, saying, 'You've got to help me out. I'm at the American Hotel with the Polydor people and I'm not happy with what's going down.'"

Stone walked into the conference room. "It was *frigid*. James says, 'These guys want to throw me out of the window. They want to kill me.'"

Stone and Brown broke off and talked in a side room, and in that time Brown revealed the sticking point that would make or break the whole deal: He wanted Polydor to pick up the tab on his jet.

He pulled up a chair before Schoenbaum and interpreted Brown to the label. "I said, 'So look, he wants an airplane. You and I both know James is breaking wide open with a new generation of kids. You know that James is huge in the clubs of Europe—all over the world he is breaking out. So why are we arguing about a jet?'"

One more thing: "And look, he wants ten thousand records shipped to me free in Miami." A guy's got to take care of his family. "And do I have to mention what I did with them?" Stone said with a shrug. "It greases the wheel. Because, they did pretty well with him."

The jet was his, and so was a big suite within Polydor's office in New York. He had a lucrative five-year contract that guaranteed he would continue to produce himself. They gave him a pile of cash up front, complete artistic freedom to record what and when he wanted. Polydor would now distribute People and Brownstone, two labels Brown produced for. His last two singles, "Escape-ism" and "Hot Pants," both of them just released by Starday-King, would be his final releases on King.

An early press release put out by Polygram offered an overview of who he was at the onset of the decade. "James Brown will perform 335 days this coming year, losing as much as seven pounds each performance. In an average month, he will give away 5,000 autographed photos and 1,000 pairs of James Brown cufflinks. He will wear 120 freshly laundered shirts and more than eighty pairs of shoes. He will change his performing costume 150 times and will work over eighty hours on the stage, singing, dancing and playing at least 60 songs on one of more than eight instruments."

It could have described Brown early in the *previous* decade. That was how he had long chosen to be viewed, as a steel-driving man who owned lots of stuff. The fact was that even in a new era, with a new label, and with the certain knowledge that albums were the future, his essential image, and his essential method of making records, had become fixed. A letter written to *Jet* in October 1971 complained that he was putting out too many singles, far more than other acts. It was a very good point, if not for the fact that the singles he put out were *killing*. So why change?

In August 1971, he released "Make It Funky," a record that starts with a question.

Ever the straight man, Bobby Byrd puts it on a tee for the Boss: "What you gon' play now?" Brown shrugs and swings, "Bobby, I don't know, but whatsoever I play, it's got to be funky!" The song *starts* with an organ solo, which is the place where many of Brown's songs meander off to when they are winding down. "Make It Funky" was profoundly slack. The horns come in with a thrilling wooziness. They sound like a dance band playing across the Niger River. In the middle, a litany: "Neck bone! Candied yams! Turnips!" Brown shouts. He stumbles over "smothered steak," recovers for "Grits with gravy! Cracklin' bread!" Sometimes a man is just *hungry*.

About six months later, one of the more unlikely hits of his career, "King Heroin," came out. This staunchly anti-drug recitation–spoken from the point of view of the drug–came to Brown one day at the Stage Deli in New York. It was there that counterman Manny Rosen approached with a poem he'd written while incarcerated at Rikers Island for not paying alimony. The ballad, with aptly sepulchral organ, creeps into the subconscious like a public service announcement you're not listening to, until you find yourself riveted.

The hot new team of Rosen & Brown debuted their composition on *The Dick Cavett Show* and then took it to Johnny Carson. A number of other raps recorded by the two remain unreleased. "King Heroin" made Brown an antidrug spokesman. He went to Sacramento to pick up a commendation from Governor Reagan, then to Atlanta, where he donated $5,000 to Georgia governor Jimmy Carter's drug treatment program. Rosen scored, too: A character in *The Poseidon Adventure* was named for him.

In the summer of 1972, a new Jabo Starks drum part seemed tethered directly to the almighty. He showed it off in the studio, and then Fred Thomas affixed an off-kilter bass line to it that slyly sidestepped the One. Brown came into the studio and upon hearing the groove pulled an old Southernism out of the ether–*get on the good foot*, which meant get going. Everybody knew they had something, and Brown bumped his next scheduled single, "I Got Ants in My Pants," to rush out "Get on the Good Foot." It became the summer song of 1972, no doubt, and redirected the lives of countless kids standing within shouting distance of a spewing fire hydrant.

"Good Foot" was his biggest record that year. All told, he was off to a great start with the new label.

Chapter Eighteen

SOUL POWER

I n the early '70s, AM radio was losing listeners to the growing FM market, and programmers were increasingly sorting out their audiences according to musical genres as well as along racial lines. The end result was that the glory days of Top 40 radio playing black and white artists side by side were rapidly on the wane. That was just one more trend Brown had been in front of, ever since the time when jittery white station owners freaked out to "Say it Loud."

All of which might suggest Brown's music was black by default, when of course it was black by acclamation. Changes in personnel and musical direction saw him moving ever further away from the blues, song structures, harmony, and composed lyrics and toward a sound defined by the drum. As the 1970s progressed, his music became less "pop" than ever, pushing more deeply into texture and noise. He produced an astounding string of hits—between 1969 and 1971 Brown had some seventeen singles in the R&B top ten— that resembled little else on the radio and established him to younger listeners as a genre of sound unto himself.

Words like *ghetto* and *funk* were being redefined by the people the words were originally meant to describe. These terms had meant something unsavory, something to be swept under the carpet of respectability. Now, though, both expressions were super bad. They were embraced, held out as mirror opposites of what some imagined them to be.

The music was getting heavier, and so was Brown's persona. You could track his reinterpretation through the work of numerous African American writers in and around the Black Arts Movement, the cultural wing of the black power movement. During the Black Arts heyday, a group of artists and intellectuals increasingly embraced Brown. Citing his "Ain't It Funky Now" from 1969, Stephen E. Henderson exulted that "the obnoxious word ['funky'] had been given a new Black meaning and public respectability." Simultaneously, said Henderson, "another Black word, 'soul,' . . . is on its way out–done in by overexposure and the Man."

Cecil Brown, in a piece from 1971 written for *Black Review*, noted that though you could still find African Americans playing the Rolling Stones at parties, "cutting into James Brown now seems to be the test of one's identity, of one's blackness." Interestingly, the author celebrates a way in which Brown's music isn't *about* something–by now the words are disjointed and used as rhythmic elements themselves–but rather *is* something, powerfully expressing itself as a circumstance, a condition. He focuses on Brown's uncanny use of crudeness and ugliness to turn time into a festival, writing that the rough edges of this funk evoke the hoodoo and root conjuring one still finds in the rural South.

As Bootsy Collins put it: "Funk was like the way we lived." That is-ness of the music, its powerful summoning of a state of existence, was picked up by Larry Neal, a poet and scholar who helped define the role of art in the black power era. In his 1968 essay "And Shine Swam On," Neal wrote: "Listen to James Brown scream. Ask yourself, then: Have you ever heard a Negro poet sing like that? Of course not, because we have been tied to the texts, like most white poets. The text could be destroyed and no one would be hurt in the least by it." Other artists made things, but Brown made experience–he was a verb, and his true medium was us.

In some of the most heartfelt writing about Brown ever published, Neal later declared being in awe of Brown's power, while
also wishing that his music addressed political realities. In a memoir of the Black Arts Movement written in 1987, Neal declared:
"We began to listen to the music of the rhythm and blues people,
soul music . . . the big hero for the poets was James Brown. We all
thought that James Brown was a magnificent poet, and we all
envied him and wished we could do what he did. If the poets could
do that, we would just take over America. Suppose James Brown
had consciousness. We used to have big arguments like that. It was
like saying, 'suppose James Brown read Fanon.'"

But of all the writers of the era seeking to put Brown on a pedes-
tal, it's Amiri Baraka who listened most deeply to the music. His
poem "In the Funk World" asked "If Elvis Presley is/king/who is
James Brown . . . /GOD?" As far back as 1966, Baraka heard the
noise in Brown, and in that squall sought to locate the heart of
his blackness. In "The Changing Same (R&B and the New
Black Music)," Baraka–then LeRoi Jones–wrote: "James Brown's
screams, etc., are more 'radical' than most jazz musicians sound,
etc. Certainly his sound is 'further out' than Ornette's. And that
sound has been a part of Black music, even out in them backwoods
churches since the year one. . . . The hard, driving shouting of
James Brown identifies a place and image in America. A people and
an energy harnessed and not harnessed by America."

Beyond a few lines scattered across a career, Brown did not con-
fess anything in his lyrics, he didn't write out words to tell his story.
Rather, the words fit the music and the words seemed to flow from
him in a state of connection not to personal experience but to a
shared moment. That made him a representative figure in the early
1970s black literary circles, where ethics and aesthetics were
viewed as one. When the writers and musicians in the New York
group The Last Poets recorded a poem called "James Brown" in
1970, Brown was called a "witch doctor," channeling the distant
past into the concrete present. In African American arts journal

Amistad 2, Mel Watkins threw all the cards down and flat said it: "James Brown is the personification of Blackness, the embodiment of the Black life style."

For these performers and critics, to discuss Brown was to discuss race and politics and, then, life and magic. Brown represented an intersection of a great many things.

When he spoke for himself outside of the music, the starting point was extreme protectiveness. And yet Brown loved to talk; along with the privacy was that Southern love of speechifying. That, together with his Carolina accent, his frayed voice, and intermittent dental disasters that left it hard for him to articulate, could make his conversation a strange meander through sound and subject.

In interviews, Brown cut a broken field path through his thoughts, racing to one side of an argument, and then darting to the seemingly opposite position. If you were prodding him to talk about his views on a dangerous issue like racism, he might not give you much. But to a writer for *Jet* in December 1971, Brown was unusually candid.

"I'm a racist when it comes to freedom," he declared. "I can't rest until the Black man in America is let out of jail, until his dollar is as good as the next man's. This country's going to blow up in two years unless the white man wakes up. The Black man's got to be free. He's got to be treated like a man. This country is like a crap game. I'll lose my money to any man as long as the game is fair. But if I find the dice are crooked, I'll turn over the table."

He believed that racism was a product of economic inequality, and that the solution to the nation's most vexing problem was fiscal opportunity. He had it with the black radicals: When "Talkin' Loud and Saying Nothin'" came out (recorded in 1970, sat on until the time was right, in 1972), it was an open criticism of self-styled arbiters of racial justice. His "Soul Power" may have been a rebuttal to those shouting for "black power," declaring that he had something better to offer.

"What we need are programs that are so out of sight, they'll leave the militants with their mouths open," Brown enthused. "A militant is just a cat that's never been allowed to be a man."

He looked at himself as a master of exchange, a salesman, and he felt that being one, he understood America in a way the nationalists never could. Life was about the hustle; that was America's story, too, and why would somebody on the outside not want to buy his way in? Here was his definition of a child—someone who did not enter the game. That was his thinking, and Brown was about to express it, publicly, to a degree he never had before.

Soul City was a real place. It existed on the map of North Carolina, in the Piedmont a bit south of Virginia. Warren County, which contained it, was a poor, rural part of the state, and Soul City was in just about the poorest part of the county. Soul City existed. But where it lived most of all was in the mind of Floyd McKissick.

On the map, it was a plot of scrub pines and a scattering of trailer homes. McKissick was developer of the municipality, but in the early 1970s, he was seeing beyond the pines, to a future for America. Soul City was meant to be the first of a great many black-led communities, attracting businesses and drawing the country's poorest urban citizens to North Carolina.

Many were searching for the next step forward in the civil rights struggle, and black capitalism seemed a viable platform for consolidating progress. McKissick illustrated how complicated and contradictory the era's fervor for black entrepreneurship was. In the 1960s, he had steered civil rights group the Congress of Racial Equality away from its long-standing philosophy of nonviolence and toward militance; by 1972, he was endorsing Republican president Richard Nixon for reelection.

Soul City spotlights the ambiguous position of the black businessman. As its developer he stood to gain from any success. McKissick's endorsement of Nixon was followed in the fall of 1972 by his creation of a group dedicated to steering African Americans to the Republican Party. Like dominos falling, *that* was followed by a $14 million pledge from Nixon's administration to help build Soul City. As is often the case with black business, the question rises: Is there a line between self-interest and helping the community?

It's a question no one asks of white businessmen, of course. Without self-interest, lifting anyone else up was far harder. As Brown said, "I can't throw you a rope until I save myself. It's slippery around the edge of the bank."

How slippery it was, McKissick quickly found out. After his relationship with Nixon became public, syndicated newspaper columnist Carl Rowan, an African American, wrote, "This black man who used to style himself a super-militant could not possibly be regarded as a Republican. But put $14 million worth of 'black capitalism' within his grasp and he'll call Spiro Agnew godfather." Georgia state representative Julian Bond angrily criticized blacks receiving money from the administration as "political prostitutes," who were set to "deliver lambs to slaughter."

Sammy Davis Jr. was next to wade in the water. While McKissick raised funds from Republicans for Soul City, the song and dance man was appearing at the 1972 Republican Convention in Miami. He had been on the stage at Marine Stadium for several hours already, emceeing a Young Voters for Nixon rally, and was about to introduce a rock band. Protocol was that the president did not appear in public at a convention until he had formally received the nomination. But in Miami, a Secret Serviceman whispered to the entertainer that Nixon was heading to the stage for a surprise appearance. And that's how it happened, one of the most famous images of the year, and of Nixon's entire presidency: a stone-gas Davis mugging and hugging an aghast Richard Nixon.

Wire services ate it up. The impact was instant. Robert Johnson, executive editor of *Jet*, said the picture inspired the biggest response in *Jet*'s history (and *Jet* had published pictures of the mutilated body of lynching victim Emmett Till). The feedback was not positive. Davis got booed weeks later at the National Black Expo in Chicago, and then came the death threats from angry African Americans who could not believe Davis was supporting a president who, to their eyes, was no friend at all.

The vice president, Spiro Agnew, was out on the trail making appeals to whites with statements like, "If you've seen one city slum, you've seen them all," and "There are people in our society who should be separated and discarded." Nixon knew he wasn't going to win more black votes than George McGovern, his Democratic opponent, but he knew the value of peeling off a few percentage points.

So he launched what could be called his Soul Initiative, a courting of prominent figures who spoke to the hopes and dreams of black Americans. McKissick was part of it, and so was Davis. Football superstar Jim Brown and basketballer Wilt Chamberlain got on board. So, too, did James Brown.

Crucial to reeling Brown in to the Nixon camp was the president's special assistant, Robert Brown, a public relations man who had worked behind the scenes in Washington for years. By one estimate, he had been responsible for channeling almost a billion dollars of federal aid to black colleges, businesses, and towns in the South. Nixon's strategy was to appease white voters by not challenging segregation, and funding separate black institutions was a savvy way of doing it—if he picked up some black votes as well, even better.

Robert Brown had been in contact with the singer since 1971, when he paid a visit to his radio station in Baltimore, WEBB. The two began a dialog, and the special assistant drew him in. He visited him down in Augusta, and when the singer was in Washington, he lunched several times with members of Nixon's staff in the White House lunch room. "He felt some of the things Mr. Nixon was doing were good things he believed in," the aide explained. "He was leaving the door open. I just kept talking to him and calling, had him in there to meet with the president, you know."

Early in 1972, a roster of black celebrities threw a tribute dinner for Robert Brown in Washington, a party that was also a recruitment event for the Soul Initiative. Davis emceed the night. In attendance were CORE's Roy Innis, McKissick, Republican Senator Edward Brooke, Jackie Robinson, and the Hardest Working Man in Show Business. The politico went out of his way that evening to make the singer feel important.

Also making Brown feel important was that the aide set up a meeting between Brown and the president in the fall of 1972. From secret recordings Nixon made of conversations in the White House, we know what was said during their October encounter. A few hours before their appointment, Nixon is heard complaining about how many meetings he'd already had with African Americans. "I've *done* the blacks!" he vented. "I don't want to continue to do them." Questioning the value of such sessions, Nixon declared, "I don't want any more blacks, and I don't want any more Jews, between now and the election." Unfortunately for Nixon, just as he was saying this, James Brown was heading for the White House. To bring him up to speed, an assistant told the president about the singer: "James Brown apparently is popular with young people, he's *black . . .*"

"What am I supposed to do, sit and talk to him?" Nixon asked.

Robert Brown ushered the entertainer's party into the Oval Office: the singer, his father, Charles Bobbit, and federal marshal James F. Palmer. "He has a fantastic string of hits," Robert Brown tells Nixon by way of introduction, and a game president responds, "Oh, I know." Nixon keeps the plates spinning, offering the visitors a tour of the room.

In about ten minutes Nixon signals it's time for the party to go, but right then James Brown steps forward with something he wants to express. His voice lost the laughter it was full of a moment before, and the room goes silent. Brown speaks slowly and measures his words precisely, and there is a visceral anguish in his voice. He tells the president how important it is to a great many people that the nation make Martin Luther King's birthday a national holiday.

A movement to honor King's birthday had begun days after his murder, and it would be many years before it was finally signed into law by Ronald Reagan. Commemorating the day mattered to Brown; he'd taken out a two-page ad in *Jet* calling for legislators to put it on the calendar.

Nixon nervously agrees that he wants to do something "appropriate."

"I knew him, of course not well," the president adds, before looking at Robert Brown for a hand. The aide steps in to say that the current time was not right for the president to declare a new national holiday, that it would look like pandering right now. Perhaps after the election.

Now it really was time to go. "Good luck and much success . . ." Nixon says. Brown, though, doesn't budge, and brings up King again. Nixon acts like he doesn't hear him, continuing to the door "–and keep working those kids!"

From the White House the singer went directly to the headquarters of the Committee to Reelect the President, where he told a group of assembled reporters that Nixon was his guy. "You know, in Georgia we look folks in the eye, and I kept my eyes on the eyes of the president and he's saying something." Acknowledging Robert Brown's influence, he said, "Seeing blacks in high places and realizing that they're taking care of business, I began to change my mind about the course of this administration."

Nixon, Brown explained, had "done a lot of things [for blacks]," and then named federal funding for the study of sickle cell anemia.

He talked a bit more, finishing with, "I'm not a sellout artist. I never got no government grant, I never asked for one, don't want one. I'm not selling out I'm selling in, dig it?"

Events followed quickly. He was playing Baltimore October 15, and Troy Brailey, a black state delegate, called for a boycott of the show. "Soul Brother Number One has sold out," Brailey said, predicting the Nixon endorsement "will bring his image to a very low ebb, especially among the young people who look up to him." The concert was picketed, and only 2,500 tickets were sold for the 13,000-seat venue. Howard University's student radio station broadcast a scathing attack. The Congressional Black Caucus released a statement criticizing all the black celebrities who were backing Nixon, singling out Brown by name.

"The emotionalism and division are so intense that some blacks fear that the disunity may leave damaging scars that would take years to heal," said *The New York Times*. The *Times* also reported on a strong suspicion "that the President is buying black support through the Administration's black capitalism programs."

No way would he change his mind, especially once the protests started in. At least one adviser had urged him not to make the endorsement, worried about his fans' response. But Brown was a man of his word, and he was set to ride the endorsement all down the line. Days after his press conference, he released a telegram in which he again publicly declared his support. In Augusta he continued campaigning for Nixon, taking officials from the Department of Health, Education, and Welfare and a rep from the Small Business Administration on a tour of local drug and alcohol treatment facilities.

With singer Hank Ballard by his side, Brown held a press conference to explain himself and yet again bestow his blessing on the president. He dismissed the Baltimore boycott, which he declared, "didn't hurt us." A letter from Nixon was passed out to reporters, in which the president said, "The mark of a man" was standing firm in the face of "recent unjust pressure." Brown repeated that he had lobbied Nixon to make King's birthday a national holiday; when he did that, special assistant Robert Brown hastily seized the microphone to make sure everybody understood the president hadn't taken any position on the subject.

From then until the election in November, Brown was responding to attacks. In the Newark *Afro-American*, a columnist said he had an application to buy a Newark radio station pending before the Federal Communications Commission, and suggested he supported Nixon in order to obtain the station. In Cleveland, activist Angela Davis told an audience, "There is no way Sammy Davis Jr., or James Brown, or any of the others could have been thinking of the needs of their people. They were simply interested in getting into that game for themselves."

Charles Bobbit, Brown's lieutenant, threw himself into damage control. He could see how badly it was all playing out. "Brown is not supporting President Nixon in order to give or receive money to or from the reelection campaign committee," he said. "He is not supporting Nixon, the man, but his program and what it has done for blacks." Brown took out a four-page advertisement in *Jet* to further explain, saying he was a black businessman with dozens of employees, and that Nixon's policies were good for entrepreneurs around the country.

At the election night party in Washington's Shoreham Hotel, Sammy Davis Jr. sang "The Candy Man" to Republican supporters. Later, he was interviewed by CBS's Daniel Schorr and Michele Clark, who grilled him about the black community's criticism and the hug that went around the world. Tenuously, Davis offered that he "hoped this would make the President more responsive to blacks."

Just beyond the camera's view, Brown was studying the interview. A reporter asked how he felt about Davis's ambition to shape Nixon's civil rights policies. No way, Brown said. "He doesn't have enough clout. I wish Jesse Jackson had come on over. He could deal with the man. It all falls on me. I'm the one he's gonna be talking to. If I didn't believe that he was going to be coming through, I wouldn't be coming down straight. I don't shuck and jive when it comes to what's best for my people." After that, Brown, Floyd McKissick, and other black supporters of the president moved to Robert Brown's hotel suite and watched election results come in.

Brown could have predicted a harsh reaction to his support of Nixon *before* the election, but the growing intensity of criticism *after* Nixon was reelected had to be a surprise. In December, a columnist for the *Pittsburgh Courier* wrote, "It will take more than someone yelping 'I'm black and I'm Proud' five minutes before he gives it up to the oppressor to fool Black folks." That was only the beginning.

Near year's end, Brown played a show in Knoxville, Tennessee. The scene afterward was utterly familiar: handshakes with local celebs, smiles and autographs for fans. An off-duty police officer working security brusquely told Brown to get out. It was time to close the hall.

The conversation with fans continued and the officer returned with more guards, again demanding that Brown leave. The singer responded, "That's no way to tell a man to get out," but, soon, everybody did leave. Brown and two aides were standing in a parking lot when they were attacked by Knoxville police responding to a call from the guards. Two Brown employees were arrested for assaulting officers, and the singer was booked for disorderly conduct. When they returned to Augusta the next morning, they were bloodied and their clothing was ripped.

The next day, Brown told reporters his men were jumped from behind while he was counseling a group of young blacks to keep off drugs and stay in school. He announced he was filing a $1 million civil rights suit against the Knoxville police. The radio station he owned in Knoxville, WJBE, stopped playing music and went open mic on the event, airing calls from listeners who shared stories of their own interactions with local law enforcement. The pressure led to a march on city hall and then reforms in Knoxville police policies. The city dropped its charges against him; two years later, his suit was dismissed in U.S. District Court.

A letter to the editor of *Jet* raised a telling point. "I saw where James Brown made a statement that he supported President Nixon because this is a free country. But I guess after the incident of Sunday night, Dec. 19, he found out this country is not as free as he thought. And I would like to know how he feels about this country now and how free he thinks it is."

The subsequent inaugural festivities for Nixon promised to be the most integrated yet, by Washington's standards. Word went out that Sammy Davis Jr. would be singing at one ball, and Brown, along with The Mike Curb Congregation and Tommy Roe, at another.

In the end, both were no-shows. Davis begged off, saying he had the flu. As for Brown's absence, *Jet* said that he was tired.

At least in spirit, though, the star was present. "Let us remember that America was built not by government, but by people–not by welfare, but by work," the president said in his second inaugural address. "Government must learn to take less from people so that people can do more for themselves." It was gospel to the man who had sung, "I don't want nobody to give me nothing, open up the door, I'll get it myself."

He knew firsthand how white patrons expected great shows of gratitude for every black they let in the door, as if fair access was a privilege. He didn't want to be on the *Ed Sullivan Show* because he was black; he knew he deserved his slot.

Face and pride drove him; the idea of a government or a court "giving" him his rights never sat well with Brown. "Don't *make* me equal," he once said. "I can't survive on equality." He had fought for the right to be accepted as special, and he wasn't ready to settle for mere equality. He had earned more.

Having been born with nothing, a big part of him could never grasp the idea of "birth rights." Blacks and everyone else had to earn rights, by working and fighting for them, his experience had taught him. "Unless you do something for yourself, it won't get done," he said. "How are we going to have equal opportunity until we had equal minds?"

Strangely enough, all the criticism he took over his endorsement of Nixon validated the decision, as far as he was concerned. He had fought for it, and he didn't waver. He'd earned his right to say what he wanted.

No wonder he was tired.

Chapter Nineteen

FOLLOW THE MONEY

S ettling into Augusta life, Brown was one day standing on a corner in a black neighborhood, talking to a friend. As he looked around, he evoked the scene in a way that encompassed his past *and* present. "There's a lot of money here. This ain't the ghetto; this is the *mint*. For crime and corruption." Folks with money call it crime, he explained. Those who lived here call it survival.

Now that he was again in town, Brown sought to inspire those around him. A teen basketball team bore his name, he owned the radio station, and was looking for other business opportunities. In the summer of 1973, he opened the Third World, a roomy nightclub that booked Ray Charles, Aretha Franklin, and even the comedy team of Amos 'n' Andy. (Brown never lost his love for old-school showbiz.) It was a unique place. In the front of the club was a takeout restaurant that only sold chicken wings. There were uniformed doormen, and inside, a color scheme and decor Brown himself picked out. The bathroom fixtures were gold-plated.

The word *can't*, Brown said, forced people into poverty and crime. Nobody said *can't* anymore to Brown. On a whim, he might pull up at a corner, pop out of his limo, and start handing five-dollar bills to startled teens who nodded as he told them to stay in school. He would send Danny Ray into a bank to make a mass with-drawal, and then have his valet throw handfuls of cash out his car window.

Scholars of black business history note how wealth-building points far beyond personal success. Individual accomplishment reflected the whole community and, conversely, one's own fortune meant little unless it left a mark on the neighborhood. In his own flawed way, Brown fit into this historical dynamic.

Money was for circulating. "You never seen a Brink's truck fol-low a hearse to the graveyard, have you?" he'd say with a cackle. While he owned some stock, on a basic level, he didn't believe in investing. When you could work one night and make tens of thou-sands of dollars, the idea of accumulating interest lost its appeal.

With cash filling cardboard boxes every night, Brown didn't feel a need to open a bank account until the early 1960s. One day in Atlanta, he got off a plane, entered a bank in the airport in order to cash a check. He liked to carry stacks of royalty checks and other notes on him as a cushion against crisis. The teller, Fred Daviss, suggested he open an account; it might have been his first. Brown handed a pile of greenbacks to Daviss saying, "Here's a thousand." Daviss counted eleven hundred-dollar bills, and after he passed the test by handing a hundred back, Brown knew here was a guy he could do business with. In the next few months, Brown flew in with suitcases full of cash to deposit. He would take off his boot, pull out a roll of dollars, and deposit that, too. The women at the bank would spend hours counting his wadded, filthy bills. In no time he had six million in his account, said Daviss.

The Southern circuit that raised him was a cash-only business, and Brown accumulated quite a lot of the stuff. "He took boxes of money out of the shows each night, we don't know where it went," said Fred Wesley. "He told me, 'If they ever want to mess me up, all the government has to do is change the color of money.'"

He always carried what he called his FU Money, what he paid out to people when he wanted them to look away, or join him, or when he wanted them to go. Cash was many things to Brown, but perhaps most of all it was a way to keep people out of his way.

Investing in black business, Brown believed, would empower his people. This was his intent, but his inability to delegate, his mistrust of even his closest aides, and his desire to pay bills only when absolutely necessary, all made reaching that goal difficult. He was a bit like Marcus Garvey, the pan-African nationalist of the early twentieth century who inspired thousands with his dream of building a black-owned global shipping line. Both men shared an amazing ability to give heart to their followers. Their weakness was in successfully following through on their business model.

In 1970, Brown purchased a two-hundred-room hotel in Baltimore for $5 million, renaming it the James Brown Motor Inn. Business was solid for months, but then there was a fire, and then, in early 1971, came an FBI raid and the arrest of several bank robbery suspects at the Inn. Soon after, Brown disassociated himself from the venue and closed it down.

His club, the Third World, had a solid launch, but within a few months checks started to bounce. Then, in October 1973, the club burned down. Arson was suspected, said the *Augusta Chronicle*, and a jar of gasoline was discovered near the front door. Arriving at the smoldering site, Brown was asked by a reporter what might have happened. "I don't know, I don't know. I've been kicked in the teeth, I've been kicked in the pants, but this I don't know about," he said. "Is it wrong to build the finest nightclub in Augusta so the people can have a fine place of entertainment? Is it wrong to want the best things out of life?"

Nobody was ever arrested for starting the fire, which caused an estimated $125,000 in damages. The Third World never reopened.

A performer as riveting as Brown would seem an intriguing investment for Hollywood. For years, his name had been linked to various projects—it was said he would play the boxer Henry

Armstrong. Then that he had a part in a movie produced by Ossie Davis and directed by Senegalese filmmaker Johnny Sekka. Then he was going to be in a movie about a pool hustler, or was set to play himself in a biopic produced by Dick Clark. None of these projects came to fruition. He had an aversion to supporting roles, and Hollywood wasn't exactly brimming with good lead parts for black actors.

Old Hollywood had little inkling of what to do with a presence like Brown. But in the early '70s, a slew of independently made films starring black performers was achieving startling success. These dramas harmonized with the essence of Brown's persona. The first of them was released in 1971, *Sweet Sweetback's Baadas-ssss Song*. Whereas most movies premiered in Hollywood, this one debuted in Detroit, and then played a circuit of ghetto theaters and porn houses. Its soundtrack, rejected by A&M Records, featured a new group called Earth, Wind & Fire, and when Stax picked it up they had a hit.

Later that year came *Shaft*, with a studio budget and a likeable lead actor. A columnist in the *Amsterdam News* declared that "Nightly, as late as 11 pm lines of fans waiting at the *Shaft* box-office resemble those waiting for James Brown at the Apollo," which made sense because the audiences were much the same. *Shaft*'s soundtrack was even more successful than the picture, guided by a composer who was as cool as Brown was agitated, turned inward where Brown was ready to explode. Isaac Hayes was a new breed of star, and with *Shaft* he was having a breakaway moment. His "Theme From Shaft" won three Grammies that year, and the Oscar for best original song. Its evocation of ghetto cool reached far beyond the inner city. Stax, Hayes's label, distributed the music free of charge to marching bands around the country, and within months, Sammy Davis Jr. recorded *his* astonishing cover of the tune.

If violence was as American as cherry pie (H. Rap Brown), these movies laid out a new national zeitgeist: here was the pie, everybody fighting for a piece, and there was the pie fight, mayhem and laughs and raw sensation hurled all over a bogus-looking set that felt a lot like America. Blaxploitation flicks, as these films were called, became an all-American cinema of sensation.

Shaft was an outlier, a *detective*, a visitor to the underworld. But the strongest of these movies embodied the underworld, and in 1972, when *Superfly* presented a drug dealer as hero, the underworld was the place to be. *Superfly*'s soundtrack was a set of eloquent Curtis Mayfield music that was more judgmental than the images were. Observers argued about the morality of these movies, but the box office, and the audience, had settled the argument. As *Soul* magazine's review of *Superfly* put it, "In this case where a man deals in dope and comes up a winner, morality could be argued on and on and on . . . ad infinitum. We shall forget morality and grade this on effort and Blackness—it passes the test in both departments."

During a stand at the Apollo that fall, Brown admitted he had enjoyed *Blacula*, but said he had reservations about the genre; he *was* grading on morality. The genre, clearly, had no reservations about him. When it was announced that he had signed on to an upcoming blaxploitation movie, the only real question was, *Is he providing the soundtrack or the storyline*?

The movie was *Black Caesar*, and the studio first approached Stevie Wonder to compose the music. "He watched the footage, if you can believe it, and I think he felt it was too violent," said director Larry Cohen. "I think James Brown liked the idea of doing a gangster picture." This would be his first movie score.

When they screened it for Brown, he reportedly exclaimed that *Black Caesar* was *his* life story, and it's easy to see why. It depicts the rise of Harlem hoodlum Tommy Gibbs, a street urchin with a chip on his shoulder, shining shoes and studying how the world works. Gibbs builds a crime empire, and he's "top of the world" until he fatefully overreaches. *Black Caesar*'s harsh message was that anybody could make it in America, if they didn't mind the bloodstains.

Having signed a profitable contract with American International Pictures (AIP), Brown planned to simply recycle his old hits—"Try Me" for one scene, "I'll Go Crazy" for another. The studio had an original score in mind, and eventually Brown asked Wesley to compose much of it. AIP also handed Brown a song that the studio insisted he sing as the first single off the soundtrack, "Down and Out in New York City." It was a country tune, of all things, and Wesley labored mightily to smear some funk on. He did that, and he did one other very smart thing, arranging it in a key that was not the singer's usual. Brown ended up screaming at the top of his range, and it gives the song a desperation in synch with the movie.

Deeper still was "Mama's Dead," a ballad with special meaning to Brown. The day he recorded the vocal he called the studio in Augusta and said he didn't want anybody present, just him and engineer Lowell Dorn playing back the already-recorded music. "He said, 'I want just one light on the microphone in the studio, and that's all I want,'" Dorn said. "I went to put the tape on, and he said, 'Just roll it.' He started on the emotional vocal part and got choked up and that got me crying, too. It took several takes until we got the vocals down. He cried a good bit."

There were two fine vocals, and Brown felt he was done, but the soundtrack was far from complete. When the studio started asking where the rest of the score was, it fell to Wesley to write instrumental music. Nobody wanted to tell the boss about it, though. When the movie was screened and Brown heard Wesley's fine music for the first time, the singer scoured the room, spotted Wesley, and fired him. (Brown hired his music director back after his "point" had been made.)

"I saw James at the screening in New York of *Black Caesar*," said Cohen. "James was always on—you never knew who he really was, he always gave you the smile and talked the talk, but you never knew what was going on in his head."

The soundtrack did not reach the sales levels of *Shaft* or

Superfly, but between Brown's vocals and Wesley's big band funk, it was memorable work. The movie did one further thing for the star: It established a new nickname. "Hail Caesar, Godfather of Harlem," went an advertising line for the picture. Charles Bobbit saw possibilities in that, and experimented with the slogan "Hail James Brown, godfather of music," before he ultimately suggested Brown simply bill himself as "The Godfather of Soul." Danny Ray began working that handle from the stage, and the appellation stuck.

Black Caesar was followed in mid-1973 by the soundtrack to *Slaughter's Big Rip-Off,* another urban action film, this one starring former football star Jim Brown. Again much of the work was delegated to Wesley, who assembled some impressive studio musicians for the recording. Though the picture was not a hit, like most of the films in the blaxploitation genre, it was inexpensive to make, and did not require a lot of homework to understand its plot.

Months after *Black Caesar* came out, a kid from a Bogotá barrio is watching a badly dubbed copy of the film with his guys, projected on a sheet in a garbage-strewn park. There's a scene where the ambitious black gangster comes down hard on a white hood, and then drops his severed ear into a plate of pasta being eaten by his Mob boss. "I thought you could use some more meat in your sauce," he wisecracks. The kid in Bogotá smiles a wide grin.

All over the world, poor people were watching movies like this, with scenes of revenge exacted by dark-skinned people, of blacks outwitting whites, and minds were set churning. With its abundance of action and afterthought dialogue, blaxploitation traveled freely around the world. It circulated at a moment when funk, and the image of people like Pelé, Muhammad Ali, Angela Davis, Tommie Smith, and John Carlos were all spinning in the same high orbit. Black aggression was entering the pop mainstream, and doing so not via Hollywood or London so much as from barrios and shantytowns and ghettos. Black aggression was becoming the text of a global pop culture.

"The world is a ghetto," the funk band War proclaimed, and if it was true, then James Brown was a transnational potentate representing favelas, *ashwaiyyat*, migrant zones, and arrival cities all over the planet. A borderless Creole culture, the lump sum of funk and soul and fringe cinema–blaxploitation, Kung Fu, Italian spaghetti westerns, and Indian musicals–forged a sense of identity among peripheral people.

Bob Marley called reggae "the music of the ghetto." In Kingston, Jamaica, the young singer asked record producer Lee "Scratch" Perry to help make him sound like Brown, and on an early song by Marley and the Wailers, "Black Progress," you can hear him shout out, "I'm black and I'm proud." Brown's influence on reggae music would be a lengthy essay indeed; let a seed be planted by noting that after King Records was sold to Nashville interests, the label's record presses were disassembled in Cincinnati and shipped off to Jamaican buyers. Poetic justice: The very hardware that stamped out James Brown's music was now pressing hits by Toots and the Maytals, the Wailers, or Culture, all of them knowing their James Brown records by heart.

In the working-class precincts of São Paulo and Rio, black Brazilians were coming together in the early '70s to dance to the music of Brown and other soul stars. Brazil was a polyglot nation that officially squelched racial pride in order to hold together a complicated national unity, but the Black Soul movement fed a hunger for identity among the poor. In the Liberdade district, soul devotees built their houses with small bedrooms and large living rooms so that they had the space to fully work out their James Brown steps. In Bahia, a new term came into currency to categorize the working-class youth who were expressing themselves through soul: *brau*, derived from Brown. According to one writer, *brau* meant "modern, sensual, and black."

Wherever African people and traditions scattered was where

Brown mattered most. Unsurprisingly, his impact on the African continent was substantial.

A few indications: In the music bars of Addis Ababa, Alemayehu Eshete vied with Tlahoun Gèssèssè for the title of "the James Brown of Ethiopia." In Benin, the great jam band Orchestre Poly-Rythmo drew heavily from Brown's drummers. "He had more influence on our music than Fela," said singer Vincent Ahehehinnou. "Back in the days, there was no band from Benin who didn't have something in their repertoire influenced by James Brown."

All over the continent, rock and roll and soul music connected with independence movements in a generational call for new possibilities. When student leaders heard "Say It Loud," Brown became the focus of all such hope. In Tanzania, " 'Sex machine' was scribbled on high school walls, motor bikes, and necklaces," said writer May Joseph; in Bamako, Mali, young hipsters copied the swagger of his album covers and the clothes he wore.

One more example of this international township culture flourished in the South Bronx, where a subculture was organized in the summer of 1972 by the sound of "Get on the Good Foot." Dancers created a step called the Good Foot, pedal action à la Brown, and participants calling themselves b-boys assembled in crews to practice and, if need be, wage war with opponents through dancing. The very way Brown started his song–"Que pasa, people, que pasa, hit me!"–was an evocation of black and brown sympatico, and in the South Bronx, African Americans and Puerto Rican kids *were* uneasily coming together to the sounds of records that neighborhood DJs played at block parties. Spinning records on the Bronx's Sedgwick Avenue, Kool Herc was among the first to seize on Brown's latest music as a harbinger of something new. He chopped it up, switching from one turntable to another the choice part of the jam, extending it as long as the crowd responded. Brown drew the moment out one way, Herc in another. The DJ calls Brown "the king, the A-1 b-boy." In the Bronx and elsewhere, music and dance were laying the groundwork for the hip-hop revolution.

"James was the ultimate god of the funk," said Afrika Bambaataa, DJ and leader of the Zulu Kings, a pioneering b-boying crew in the Bronx. When fights broke out at dances where Bam was spinning, he would throw on "Good Foot." "Certain songs make people get their vibe on. You still have to talk and calm them down, but certain James Brown music just seems to chill the mess out."

It was uncanny, like an ear in your spaghetti. All over the world, Brown was being embraced as a symbol of identity for young people who identified with very little. He was the coming thing.

But far from places where "Good Foot" held sway, an extended drama was unfolding, one in which Brown had a less-exalted role. The lead in this tragicomedy was a powerful wheeler-dealer from California, pulling so many strings he forgot what they all connected to. Richard Nixon was still in power, and Brown was still catching hell for it.

At what was billed as the *"Black Caesar* Show" at the Apollo Theater, picketers carried signs decrying "James Brown Nixon's Clown." One demonstrator said Brown was doing more for the president than "for the black folks who made him a millionaire." It was worrisome enough that Brown quickly met with demonstrators inside the Apollo, and stood on the corners around the theater to get his own message out. His became "a desperate effort . . . to persuade his Brothers and Sisters that it is quite possible for him to operate in both the Nixon and the black bag without his being adversely affected by either," the *Baltimore Afro-American* reported. "He affirmed his innocence of any kind of sellout and reassured them of his blackness."

It was as if even incidental contact with Nixon could suck the pigmentation right out of you. Those around Brown had to wonder what he was getting from his connection to the president. Nixon had channeled aid to his other major black supporters; what did he do for the Godfather of Soul? Brown still owned three radio stations, and they were causing him problems with the Federal Communications Commission. Fred Daviss said he spoke directly to Nixon about the FCC scrutiny of the stations. According to Daviss, Nixon offered to fix the problems, "And he did, too, he called them off of us for a while." Around this same time, the Internal Revenue Service was stepping up an investigation of Brown's tax returns. On this matter the president was less helpful, said Daviss, though the president was involved in getting the IRS's legal proceedings against Brown transferred from criminal to civil court.

According to Alan Leeds, Nixon "might have helped" with the FCC. However, "James thought he was going to get help on his tax stuff, and he didn't get any help."

Brown had several channels to the White House. There was his friend Bob Brown, the Nixon aide, and his friendship with some legislators. There was, as well, the odd matter of James Palmer, a federal marshal who logged serious time traveling with Brown and his band in the late '60s and early '70s. Nobody seems to know exactly what Palmer was doing on the road with the singer, or whom he was working for. But he sure made himself a presence.

Martha High, a singer with the show, said that Palmer was sent by the feds to oversee Brown's cash flow and insure he kept up payments to the IRS. But Palmer did more than just observe; he worked as a security official for the singer, and was delivering other services, too. "I saw him every now and then, a U.S. Marshal would come around the show and would do things for James. I don't know exactly who he was, but he was a big cat," said Fred Wesley.

Alan Leeds describes the marshal as a handsome, light-skinned man who always wore a suit, tie, and trench coat. He also said that Palmer was able to work his governmental connections to keep Clyde Stubblefield, Frankie Waddy, and Leeds himself out of the army when they got their induction notices. Keeping Stubblefield seated in the Brown band counts as one of the great unsung patriotic acts of the era.

"[He] was, in fact, at least officially, simply a U.S. Marshal. Some-where along the line, circa 1967-68, he befriended James Brown," said Leeds. "His relationship with JB, fostered during those volatile times, was hardly a coincidence–I'm convinced he was 'assigned' by somebody to keep an eye and ear on good old JB. Brown certainly seemed to accept him into the entourage, rather openly–whatever skepticism JB may have had about Palmer's motives, he kept to himself."

That fall of 1973, Brown released "You Can Have Watergate Just Gimme Some Bucks and I'll Be Straight." By the time it came out, the breadth of the Watergate scandal was coming to light, and the televised Senate hearings had just finished. The lyrics match the song title, a cold dismissal of the affair chanted by Brown and the band. It would have stood as his kiss-off to the whole Nixon ride, if he hadn't followed it up with a revelatory interview in the *Augusta News-Review*, early in 1974.

In this interview he is more forthcoming on race than usual, comfortable at home talking to a black Augusta newspaper. The reporter asks him if the Watergate disclosures made him wish he rethink his support for the president.

Absolutely not, Brown said. "If I turn against the President then I may as well turn against everybody walking the streets. Because we're sure everybody's got skeletons in their closets. . . . Black peo-ple got to remember, the positions that were handed out by this president in four years hadn't been handed out by all of the presi-dents since Reconstruction.

"It's bad that I know these things and would be skeptical whether I should say them. But, you see, I'm not going to be skeptical. Whether I sell a record tomorrow or not, whether I have a person come to my shows or not. That's not important. It's important that I tell them the truth. Maybe Nixon did take the money out of the street. But what he did was make the white man come down to his size, to the same size as the Black man. You see, before, with all the other administrations, the white man was in the air and the Black man was on the ground. But now, the Black and the white man is scuffling like hell."

You had to give it up to Watergate, he said, for finally bringing the white man down to the level of the black man.

He continued. "I want to remind the Blacks, I'm not Democrat or Republican. But it was under a Republican administration that Black people were freed. I'm not Democrat or Republican. But the Republican states in slavery were never enslaved. It was always the Democratic states that were in slavery. You see, I know they don't know that. See, these are things they need to know. It was under Republicans, a simple thing as a water fountain was integrated under the republicans. The Democrats put two water fountains there.... Black people can't vote Democrat or Republican. They got to vote for the man who will do something for them. Who would've thought that [Lester] Maddox would've done more for us than anybody else?"

The interview might have hurt him as much as did endorsing Nixon, if anyone beyond Augusta city limits had ever found out about it.

A year after Nixon left the White House in 1974, the Senate Select Committee on Intelligence revealed that the Administration had misused IRS files between 1969 and 1973, passing to the FBI and other government agencies copies of tax returns and information gathered on people and organizations as varied as the John Birch Society; Sammy Davis Jr.; the NAACP; the Conservative Book Club; and James Brown. Later the singer and others would point to this finding as proof that the government was out to get him any way it could.

It certainly showed they took him seriously enough to spy on. But few around Brown accept the depiction of unalloyed victimhood. According to Fred Daviss, the singer was not filing tax returns until 1967, when he opened his business office in New York. About a year later, the IRS notified Brown that he owed substantial sums to the government.

"He couldn't understand why other people were getting money back from their return," said Daviss. "He'd say, 'With all this money I put in, they should be sending *me* money back.' I'd have to say, 'Mr. Brown you didn't do no withholding . . . this is not your money you're paying in.' He got it, but he didn't want to admit it. I told him no, you're deducting that money from your employee's paycheck, and though you are matching it, that's part of doing business."

The IRS investigation came to a head in the early 1970s, and the government had him on the hook for millions—for the tax period ending on the last day of 1974 alone, he was told he owed $2,231,817.77. He didn't trust the people who worked for him to make important decisions, and he often hired layers of employees with similar job descriptions so that exactly who was responsible for what remained unclear. By the mid-1970s, the hash he'd made of his books was finally catching up with him as the IRS confiscated a truck full of records covering Brown's taxes, his publishing companies, businesses, the road show, and more.

Of all Brown's children, Teddy was the one who looked the most like his dad. He was born in Toccoa, and stayed with Velma, his mother, after Brown moved to Macon. Like his dad, Teddy was a terrific dancer, and he wanted to pursue a music career, with his band Teddy Brown and the Torches.

One day in June 1973, Teddy and his dad got into a fight while he was staying at the house on Walton Way. It was probably over money. "James told me, 'Mr. Daviss, he's gonna have to learn,'" said Daviss.

"Teddy was just an average teenager. Teddy was always smiling. He always had a smile on his face."

After they quarreled, Teddy angrily grabbed some money and flew to New York. The nineteen-year-old was hanging out there in Brown's office with Alan Leeds and his brother Eric, Bob Patton, and aide Buddy Nolan. They talked about going to a Harold Melvin show at the Copa, Teddy took some pictures, kibbitzed, and suggested Eric drive with him to Montreal, where he was going to see some girls he knew. "He loved his dad," said Leeds. "He groveled for acceptance and approval from his dad, and his dad loved him. That was clear. His dad was so strict–getting out of the house successfully was a real emancipation for him."

From New York, he jumped into a car with two pals and headed North.

"He was protective of his dad, but the same way a lot of us employees were–when dad was out of sight, he got it, he didn't drink the Kool-Aid. Teddy understood the effect his dad had not just on audiences but on the employees. He watched how we got by while getting fired two times a day. He watched and developed some of the same tactics. We all looked at him and thought, with what we go through, we can only imagine what *he* goes through."

The singer was getting his hair reset at home when the phone on the kitchen wall rang. Bobby Roach took the call, and a New York state trooper told him, "An accident happened up north near Elizabethtown. We think his brother was in an accident. Please let us speak to Mr. Brown."

Confused, Brown told the troopers, "I don't have a brother." The car had gone off the highway and smashed into a bridge abutment, he was told. All three passengers were instantly killed.

Brown called his pilots and told them to get the plane ready, they were flying–Brown, his wife, his father, Roach, and Danny Ray–to New York City to see what the situation was. They drove to Elizabethtown in the afternoon. Roach recalled, "It was a very warm, wonderful town, people were very friendly. They asked for autographs, but we told them we were on very important business and we'd like some privacy right now."

Strangers directed them to a funeral home. Joe Brown started crying. James was taking nitroglycerine pills for a heart condition at the time; "I told him it might be good for me to view the body for

FOLLOW THE MONEY

him," said Roach. Even with a puffy face and broken neck, he looked like his father.

"Just a crowd of people in an old country church," said Daviss of the funeral in Toccoa. "Some people say Aretha Franklin was there; I didn't see Aretha there."

Brown fell to his knees while going down the aisle at the church, screaming. It was the only time anybody saw him lose his composure that day, and it was brief. Standing with his inner circle at the cemetery, Brown busied himself making business decisions—who was going back to Augusta, who would head to Atlanta, when everybody would see each other again.

"This was a guy whose whole motto in life was 'Never show weakness,'" said Leeds. "And to him mourning *was* a weakness, wallowing in something out of your control. He didn't bat much of an eyelash getting back to what he knew how to do. But that's who he was—a guy who totally could not imagine himself just going back home and sitting and crying. I'm not saying he didn't do any of that, but he didn't sit shiva and think about it."

The day after the funeral, to the shock of those around him, he was back on the road. Contracts had been signed, money had gone out. "James Brown was a hardworking man, and after the funeral he told me he cried, he got over it, and he put it behind him," said Daviss. "Later, there was times Brown would get melancholy late at night and he'd start talking about it. 'Yes, my son would have been such and such age now.'

"Brown said the reason he went back to work was, 'We all got a job. Life goes on. I gotta make a living.' Like it was his last dollar. But he shut it out—that was his way of dealing with it. He got over it and went on about his business."

In late August, AIP released *Slaughter's Big Rip-off.* When Brown heard that the studio was going to shoot a sequel to *Black Caesar,* again directed by Larry Cohen, he said he wanted to do that soundtrack, too.

There were complications. According to Cohen, the studio was irked by the singer's having sent over a pile of random tapes for his previous two soundtracks, music that was not composed to the length of the scenes. After directors twice were stuck editing the music to fit, said Cohen, AIP had vowed they would never do it again. Cohen said he heard from Bobbit that Brown wanted to record, and he had to relay to Bobbit that the studio considered him "persona non grata." Bobbit didn't give up, saying, "The man accepts a challenge." So Cohen agreed to take a soundtrack on spec. When the music came in, Cohen played it for producers who told him, "It's the same old James Brown stuff." They hired Motown composers and singer Edwin Starr to compose for the sequel, *Hell Up in Harlem.*

A widely repeated story is that Cohen rejected Brown's score by telling Wesley, "It's not funky enough, babe." The director denies it.

"First of all I wouldn't have known what that meant," said Cohen. "For me to tell James Brown what his music was about, that was just not me. But to the people at AIP, it was 'the same old James Brown stuff,' that's how they put it. I told them they were never going to get any better from anybody else, and they didn't."

The song that was intended to set the tone early in the picture, "The Payback," was recorded August 1973. According to Jabo Starks, who worked on it with Fred Wesley, "We sat and watched the movie, wrote it out. Fred had the words." They recorded an instrumental track, and then Brown came into the Augusta studio and listened. "James completely changed everything. We got caught in the middle of an ocean without a paddle. It was do or die—James had to make the record *then.* All we had was the rhythm. I just tried to hold it and make it *solid.*"

"It's never a tune until James Brown come in and do it. I mean it sounded all right," said Wesley, "but then James came in sweatin' and humpin' and screamin' and it fired everybody up. Only when he came into the studio did it instantly become a hit."

Brown arrived in a terrible mood, and as he sang words he had written, he kept shouting *damn* over and over. That was a problem, and the engineer spent hours carefully cutting them all out of the tape.

If the song didn't make it onto the movie soundtrack, the fact remains: "The Payback" *is* a blaxploitation movie that makes its own soundtrack. "Revenge! I'm mad," Brown shrieks over a guitar scratching like a razor on a rock. "I can do wheeling, I can do dealing, I just don't do no squealing," he shouts, several decades before *Stop Snitchin'*. A chorus of curb girls sass and second him throughout, while Martha High's triple-tracked keening moan keys the moment when all the pigeons abruptly fly off and the action jumps.

Brown's words and delivery are so focused, so obsessive, that folks ever since have wondered exactly what wrong he was fixing to pay back. Some suggest it was the arson of the Third World. Couldn't be; though the song came out after it, "Payback" was recorded before the fire.

Byrd thought he was paying back the white man, and counseled Brown to choose his words carefully: "*We* know what you're talking about, trying to pay people back—I understand that, but some things you just can't straight out say." Wesley believed Brown had found out a woman who worked for him was dating with Harold Melvin, and he wanted revenge on that.

In the end, it's pointless trying to figure out what inspired "Payback." He's *mad*, deal with it, and the song is a funny, wicked, 360-degree sweep of the streets circa 1973 that sums up an era. Hail Caesar: he may not know karate, but he knows ka-*razor*.

Chapter Twenty

EMULSIFIED

From the street, the house in Augusta looked like just another fortress for people who had made it, either recently or in the ancestral past. Beyond the front door, though, life was more freewheeling than elsewhere in the neighborhood. Musicians and associates from New York or Atlanta came and went. So did James and Deidre's children–daughters Deanna (born in 1969) and Yamma (born in 1972)–and also coming, going, and frequently staying were the boys from Toccoa, Larry (born in 1958) and Terry (1955). Then there were other children, like Darryl (born in 1960), whose mother was Bea Ford, a singer with Brown and Joe Tex early in the 1960s, and Venisha (1965), whose mother was singer Yvonne Fair. There was a bit of the feeling of the house he had grown up in, full of family and strangers.

At the same time, there was an established order, an awareness that power pointed straight to the chief. The foundation of family life wasn't a delineation of right and wrong. No, the true foundation was an oft-repeated credo, one the kids commemorated on a plaque hanging in the kitchen.

"THE GOLDEN RULE," it declared, "Is as follows:

Who ever has the gold makes the rules.

Who has the gold?

DADDY

Everyone is in agreement that DADDY sets the rules in this home."

Signed: "all the little Brown rats: Deidre, Daryl, Venisha, Deanna & Yamma. We Love you Daddy"

According to Deanna, Deidre was a homemaker who was hands-on with the kids. "And when he was home, he was hands-on, too. He was a very strict father, very strict. Very strict."

A few doors down lived Carl Sanders, former governor of Georgia. The community was wealthy, it was white, and it could not have been easy for the Browns to make Walton Way their home. Brown never spoke of any hostility. But perhaps he got a measure of revenge at Christmas, when he put up lavish lights and decorations on the front lawn, a large Santa Claus and wise men tableau—all of them, including Santa, black. Folks from all over Augusta—poor folks, black folks—drove up the Hill to view this display of exuberance in an otherwise reserved enclave of antebellum heaps, where anything beyond a Georgia football pennant was beyond the pale.

Nouveau riche African Americans in an antebellum paradise, the Masters Tournament down the road. A dad who ruled firmly, but infrequently. It wasn't simple, but it wasn't boring.

One morning Brown was lounging in his robe, feeding bits to the family poodle, Poojie, at the dining-room table. There was a swinging door to the kitchen, and on this morning the maid opened it briskly, cracking the animal's head. "You done killed Poojie!" Brown exclaimed. That was not quite true: It took a week for Poojie to expire.

Brown loved that dog, and laid the poor thing to rest in a lavish white casket with hand-painted nails. Then he staged a full-scale funeral at the house. The family was all there, and aides and

employees of his radio station, everybody careful to dress appro-
priately for a state ceremony. Danny Ray was there, and when
Brown broke down, inconsolable before the dog lying in his sar-
cophagus in the kitchen, it was Ray who tenderly placed a hand on
Brown's shoulder, whispering in his ear, finally dropping a cloak
over Brown's back.

He did not know what to do with his kids. "Common sense dic-
tates this was a guy who grew up without anything like intimacy
around him," said Leeds. "Affection was a commodity, something
the soldiers bought. He knew what was expected of him, and knew
to hammer on the fatherly points—'stay in school,' 'do your homework.' But it was a role to him."

He enjoyed taking the family on long drives to the South Carolina countryside where he was born, but they were not so interested
in that. Then, in the summer of 1973, he met a young man who was
burning with obvious talent. The teenager was not just skilled in
motivating strangers, but hungry for it. The teenager worshipped
Brown, and did whatever he was told. He *liked* driving to South
Carolina with him, or at least he didn't complain.

The young man was Alfred Sharpton, a New York friend of Teddy's, and after Teddy was buried, mutual friends brought him to
the Newark Symphony Hall for a backstage meeting with Teddy's
father. Brown stared at the chubby eighteen-year-old street
preacher a long moment, then said, "Are you the reverend?"

"Yessir."

"If you listen to me, I'll make you the biggest one out there."

Flummoxed, Sharpton stammered out a "Nossir," explaining
he wasn't interested in music, he was in civil rights.

"That's what I mean—you listen to me and go whole hog and
you'll be the biggest."

Sharpton's father had run out on the family when the boy was
nine, and Alfred was hungry for the interest the singer displayed.
They appeared on *Soul Train* together, Sharpton presenting his
mentor with an award from his organization, the National Youth

Movement, praising "The Payback" as "the theme song of young black America in 1974."

The teenager began promoting Brown's concerts around New York, and then went with him on the road. Brown was sculpting him, teaching Sharpton to be an outspoken, never-back-down rabble-rouser in his own image. "Just like he said, 'I'm going to make Maceo my star saxophone player,' and 'Fred will be my featured trombone,' I was meant to be his civil rights leader," said Sharpton.

Brown convinced him to shorten the name to Al–too many syllables in Alfred–and he made his protégé promise that he would style his hair in his fashion, and keep it so for as long as the singer was alive. "I'm telling you, he handled me like I was his act," Sharpton said.

In Vegas on an assignment, Sharpton once ran into Reverend Jesse Jackson, a rabble-rouser from an earlier time. Sharpton brought Jackson back to the hotel with him to see Brown, and the singer was fully holding court, taking the conversation where *he* wanted it to go. Finally, Brown turned to Jackson and said, "Jesse, you're a Motown act. You're a Motown act–you are black, but you are accepted." He thrust a finger at Sharpton. "He's a James Brown act. He's raw and authentic, and he's going to outrun you in the end."

They would talk–of many things, but only of certain things, because Brown was careful to keep the strands of his life separate. Still, by the terms of Brown's life they were "close," and it did not escape the singer how voracious the youth was in absorbing lessons from his adopted dad.

The two drove out of Augusta one day, across the Savannah River toward Bamberg, to see Brown's aunt Jettie. "Pull over," Brown suddenly rasped. Between the beveled sunlight and swamp oaks, their car off the blacktop, there was something he wanted the young man to understand. "I was born out here," the singer said, and then he talked about how his dad used to leave him at home all day while he was out tapping the trees for turpentine. "Look out for my boy," Joe Brown would tell a neighbor, but no one did, not really.

"I been hurt all my life," Brown said, opening up. "I learned how to turn the pain around and get energy, and I learned *how* to be alone."

There was one thing he wanted to make sure that Sharpton heard him on, out in the quiet Georgialina sunset. "Whatever you do, do not follow the crowd. You got to stand alone and have your own style, your own way of doing things." That was the lesson he all but pounded into Sharpton over and again through the years.

Surrounding Brown in the 1970s was his family, and the friends he took an interest in, like Sharpton. There was his band, which he labored to keep in line and apart from himself.

Beyond the band there was the circle of protectors on the periphery of the show, controlling access to Brown, carrying the gun or the curling iron. Henry Stallings, Brown's boyhood friend, was back in the mix. A short guy whom Brown labeled "'*Do*," as in "hairdo," Stallings sometimes styled Brown's coif and all the time watched his back. In Los Angeles, Fred Daviss saw a roadie named Kenny Hull get into a tussle with 'Do. Hull busted a Budweiser bottle on a coffee table and moved in on him. "Do you think you are gonna cut me with that?" Stallings asked. "Put the bottle down . . ."

Hull did set it down. While his hand was flat on the table, Stallings pulled out a stiletto and plunged it through his palm and three inches into the table. "Then he kicked his ass all around the table," said Daviss. "Oh, Kenny was about to cry."

Probably the hardest, and definitely the most devoted, of this group was Charles Bobbit. He looked like a Secret Service man, blank and alert, his eyes expressing a mission, his fingers gripping an attaché case. He *did* know karate. A guy got in his face in a crowded concession area, bothering him about some trifling matter. Bobbit told him he didn't have time for it and kept gliding, but the fellow blocked his motion. Two slashes of his briefcase, two piston pumps of an elbow, and "it looked like somebody stuck a damn 220-volt plug up his ass," recalled Daviss. "Looked like a bolt of lightning hit him." The guy slunk away, everyone in the crowd looking every which way trying to figure out what had happened, and Bobbit, well, he continued on his mission.

Also in this circle was Clayton Fillyau, the drummer. He worked on and off stage and sold cans of beans and meat to the musicians on the side. Playing drums was cool, but to Fillyau, making shit happen was the most fun. He was gifted at mapping a route to take the money from the box office to the backstage at places like the Howard Theatre, where you had to be crafty and change your path every show or be robbed. They were playing a gig at a baseball park in Florence, South Carolina, and afterward Brown directed Fillyau, whose son was with him, to pick up the money and bring it back to the hotel. Then he left. *Everyone* had left, except Fillyau and his son, sitting with the four white guys in the baseball clubhouse counting receipts.

The Fillyaus tallied twelve thousand tickets sold. The white guys counted only six thousand. "Oh no, look–" Fillyau commenced, and one of the promoters slammed a pistol down on the table in front of him. "Goddamit, I *said* it was six thousand."

"I was so scared, I couldn't move," said Clayton Jr. "But my dad was so cool, he just said, 'You know what? You are right, my mistake,' and swept the money into the bag.

"We walked away, across this baseball field with the lights turned off. I said, 'Dad, I am so scared right now.' He said, 'You know what, Clay, don't look back, don't say nothing, just let us get to the car.' It was the longest walk of my life."

That was hardly the end of the night, however. They had to give Brown the bad news. "Mmmm," Brown said meaningfully. "Well, you got to go back to that field and get the other six thousand."

After that, everybody was mad at everybody else. The bringers didn't bring the money, Brown didn't get his, nobody was going to get paid.

Recriminations flew back and forth. "You ain't nothing but a thug in a fine suit," Bobbit said, which might have had some truth to it but still wasn't very nice. Fillyau responded, "All *you* got is that suitcase, and I know what's in that suitcase. Just a peanut butter sandwich and a pair of drawers." It was a fight over who had more usefulness to the singer, just the kind of internecine jujitsu Brown loved to stir up.

On a night soon after, Brown, Fillyau and son, Bobbit, and Stallings were all shooting the shit, and talk turned to how Fillyau was due some money from Brown and he felt very much that he wanted it now. That's when the three adults started teaming up against him. "You better leave now," he told his son. "It's about to get ugly." Stallings said something to raise the heat, and nobody moved.

"Talk like that again, and I'll throw you through the window," he told Stallings. "I'd like to see you try," was the answer.

Fillyau moved toward Stallings, and Brown jumped on his back. Brown might have been a boxer, but Fillyau stood nearly a foot taller, and within seconds he had the singer in a headlock. Stallings pulled out a pistol and aimed it at Fillyau. He didn't act too concerned: "Now, talk to me like that *again*," Fillyau said, "and I will pop this little nigger's head off." It took a little time to get sorted out, but Fillyau didn't just end up with his money, according to his son, he got a $2,000 bonus.

Note it: Brown rewarded initiative. When the band Mandrill was opening and played five minutes over their contracted half hour, Fillyau walked out on the stage while they were mid-song and pulled all their plugs out. Then he moved Brown's equipment onstage, while Mandrill was still standing there. "That's what James liked about him," Anthony Fillyau said. "He was bold."

Boldness was good; boldness turned against boldness was even

better. Brown competed with everyone, and as the decade rolled
on, it might be that his maneuvers and plots were becoming ever
more preposterous.

He had a gift for simultaneously extracting your loyalty
and making you feel like a jackass for handing it over. He once
described to the guys how he had seen government spy submarines
in the Savannah River, their nuclear reactors emitting an eerie
green light. He must be kidding, but he wasn't smiling. Turning to
the one guy in the room not nodding and laughing at his story, he
said: "*You* believe me, don't you?" That's when things would get so
quiet you could hear a rat piss on an electric car.

On a drive to see big band jazzman Woody Herman play in Milwaukee, Brown rode in the limo with Danny Ray, a bodyguard, a
hairdresser, and Daviss, the only white guy. "He didn't want anybody ganging up on him, so he had a way of keeping folks from
being too tight with one another," said Daviss. They were riding up
the road and Brown looked over at Daviss, who was half asleep.
"Fellas," Brown began, in a good mood, "I'm going to tell you
about Mr. Daviss. Mr. Daviss is not a lover of niggers . . ." And he
laughed his raspy *heh heh heh heh heh*. "Do you *hear* me, fellas?"
he said again, laughing louder, his hands gesturing intensely.

"Everybody is laughing with him. Finally he leans back and
says, 'Mr. Daviss'—I crack one eye open—'You don't like niggers, do
you?' How the hell I'm gonna answer that? I'm not gonna say, 'No I
sure don't.' Not gonna say, 'Hell yes I do!'"

Leaning on his suitcase, Daviss made a reference to a notorious
neighborhood in Atlanta, saying "Naw, I don't like those Ninth
Street niggers. But y'all . . . y'all are regular guys to me." Everybody got real quiet, waiting to hear how Brown would respond. He
stayed in Daviss's face. About thirty seconds passed, then it was
heh heh heh heh . . .

That cut the tension. "Guys, here's what I want to tell you,"
Brown said. "You all *think* Mr. Daviss is your friend and he's real
tight with you and he holds your money and all . . . but look at this.

He's a Southern white guy. He's *never* gonna be tight with *you*. But, see, here's what I'm trying to tell you right now. *I* can pull out my wallet"– and right then he did–"and here's pictures of his two little daughters right here. And I can guarantee you in *his* wallet, he has my daughters' pictures, too. What I'm trying to tell you guys is, you can't ever get tight with Mr. Daviss like I can . . ." And then he leaned over and stared them all down as it became totally quiet. *"Because I'm a different kind of nigger!* Heh heh heh heh . . ."

It was a master rap, creating more fissures than there were people in the car on a leisurely trip to Milwaukee to hear some progressive jazz.

Brown again visited Africa in 1972, when the band played Zaire that June. The continent meant many things to him: It was a chromosomal connection, though he continued to keep his personal feelings about it to himself. Africa was a lucrative market, and a place where he really felt the love. "Everywhere I went there were thousands of people just waiting to see and touch me, it was frightening, their respect was like reverence, it was like they were looking up to me like a god," he told *Black Stars* magazine after the '72 Zaire trip. Despite a case of food poisoning, he took a victory lap around a soccer stadium while thousands screamed.

Two years later, in 1974, came the big one. A heavyweight championship boxing match between Muhammad Ali and George Foreman was coming to Kinshasa, Zaire, through the joint ambition of promoter Don King and Zaire's president Mobutu Sese Seko, who posted $10 million to bring the boxers to his country. Knowing the "Rumble in the Jungle" would direct the eyes of the world to his nation, the dictator aimed to keep festivities going in the capital for as long as possible. Thus, a music festival was scheduled for the week before the fight. Then, due to circumstances still debated today, the match was postponed for a month, and the carnival atmosphere extended, with reporters and tourists all celebrating an extended party in the capital.

The three-day festival was a jam-up of music with African roots. There was blues guitarist B. B. King, songwriter Bill Withers, and *salseros* Celia Cruz, Johnny Pacheco, Ray Barretto, and the Fania All Stars. A roster of African artists was present, including Hugh Masekela, Miriam Makeba, Tabu Ley Rochereau, and Franco & T.P. O.K. Jazz. The festival might have been even bigger: Promoter Masekela wanted Miles Davis's free-jazz funk band, but alas, Don King did not. Stevie Wonder flat turned them down. Even so, with Brown as the headliner, the festival was a once-in-a-lifetime event.

It was a conference of international icons, of athletes and pan-Africanists and soul brothers and sisters, with Brown fixed to declare his position in the order. In the chartered jet carrying the musicians and boxers to Kinshasa, he insisted on first-class seating for himself. His demand that the plane be loaded with his huge volume of equipment almost kept them from being able to take off. The pilot asked him to move back to coach to balance the aircraft, but Brown demurred. According to Masekela, during a stopover in Madrid, Bill Withers bought a dagger and held it to Brown's throat, suggesting he sit in economy with the rest of the folks.

When they landed in the capital they were greeted by drummers and dancers, a forest pygmy ensemble, and a women's traditional healing group all lining the tarmac. "I looked out the window and saw scores of natives dressed in their skins and feathers, waving their spears, and shouting those guttural chants–'hunga! hunga! hunga!',", said singer Etta James. Don King had control of a microphone, and when the door opened, he delivered a tried-and-true announcement: "And now, ladies and gentlemen, this is the moment you've been waiting for . . . the hardest working man in show business . . . Mr. James Brown." First out of the aircraft, Brown hit the ground with beauty-pageant winners Miss Ali and Miss Foreman on either arm.

Mobutu's prowess was at its peak in the fall of 1974. The Zairean soccer team had won the African Cup of Nations and qualified for the World Cup finals, the first sub-Saharan team to do so. The international copper market had crested, and the mineral-rich nation was flush with cash. The Rumble in the Jungle put the dictator on a world stage, and together with its festival, showed off Mobutu as a visionary able to gather the scattered forces of the diaspora.

In Zaire, Brown wore a blue denim jumpsuit with studs that spelled out GFOS–God Father of Soul–on a cummerbund-like piece that wrapped a spreading mid-section. He had a thick mustache and flowing, shiny waves of hair: Strength and the good life were on display for Africa to see. Stripped to the waist and sweat rolling off him, he shouted, "Say it loud, I'm black and I'm proud" to tens of thousands of fans.

Brown and Ali were twin brothers in the motherland, the two most famous black people on Earth, basking in the shared glow. They were more than acquaintances, less than buddies, and the only people, perhaps, who understood what it was like to be them. From time to time the understanding they shared led them to seek one another out. "James was always boasting and Ali was always boasting, they kind of just boasted in each other's face," said Fred Wesley. " 'I'm the king of the world,' 'I'm the best entertainer'– they never got together and just *talked* to each other."

They had people who talked, though, and back in 1967 they had settled on a multimillion-dollar deal–Brown would play a show, followed by a championship bout. But then came Ali's Vietnam protest, and the idea was shelved. Later they competed in Times Square, seeing who could stop the most traffic by stepping out of a limo. Neither could put away the other, and that led to a mutual fascination. Ali once presented a gift to Brown, a lengthy poem he had written in tribute. The first letter of each line, when read down, spelled KING JAMES BROWN.

Ali, of course, whipped Foreman in Zaire and regained his title.

He used a strategy that acknowledged his ebbing physical powers and the greater size and strength of his opponent. To compensate, Ali emphasized craft and motion, his body giving and flowing with the action, courageously absorbing punches without falling. It was the wisdom of a guy who had peaked, finding new skills and fresh ways to thrive.

From Zaire, Brown returned to the States, but then flew to Senegal in January 1975. A British documentary of his Senegal visit hints at how open he really was to the continent. As he freestyles on "Man's World," Brown breaks into an extended melismatic invention, chanting "Senegal soul" and then building to a passage that sounds uncannily like a muezzin's call to prayer. Brown went to Goree Island, once a dispatch point for the slave trade in Dakar. As he and the crew took wooden boats from the mainland to Goree, local boys swam out in murky water to greet him. They reached up out of the ocean to shake his hand, and with each encounter neither said anything: Their eyes simply took each other in.

They saw holding pens where slaves were stacked atop one another, the holes where the sick and feeble were thrown into the Atlantic. According to Wesley, "Mr. Brown was so affected by these stories that he broke down and sobbed uncontrollably." Then a tour guide whispered to him that one should never cry in front of Africans because they will take it as a sign of weakness. Brown immediately straightened up.

After Senegal they were booked to play a birthday party for Omar Bongo, president of Gabon. But something went awry as the band left Senegal; a scheduling problem, or maybe the money from Gabon had not arrived. In any case, Brown decided to skip the party and fly back to the United States.

While his plane was en route, the pilot received a message that President Bongo was in a jet now following Brown's jet, and was pleading for Brown to fly back to Gabon. They landed briefly in the States, transferred luggage from one plane to another. The money was all taken care of.

Omar Bongo was a *fan*. "He loved James Brown," said Lola Love, a dancer with the show. "He and James had the same body type. I think he was probably a pygmy. He wanted to do everything James did. He wanted his barber to shave him and make his hair look like James's." Bongo spent $160,000 to bring Brown to Libreville, where Brown serenaded him on his thirty-ninth birthday. Gabon's president was quoted in the *News-Review*, a black newspaper in Augusta, saying that he identified "with every aspect of [Brown's] career," and that he wanted Brown to come back to Gabon to work with him on business ventures. For his part, the singer hinted an interest in Gabon's considerable oil reserves. When Brown left, Bongo presented him with numerous gifts, including African robes and an ivory elephant tusk.

A few months later, Ali and Brown both took a victory lap. They were in Cleveland: the boxer to defend his title against Chuck Wepner; the singer to offer an extended, off-the-rails invention on the theme of the national anthem from the boxing ring. When he got to "the land of the free . . ." Brown took a detour, singing "I wanna be free! We gotta be free! Come on, all of you, free! Free! Free!" Out so far beyond a limb he didn't dare look down, Brown sang the words like they had meaning.

He knew of the Senegalese villagers who walked miles into town to stand in a line of hundreds, everybody carrying their copy of "Say It Loud" to play on a hand-cranked record player. Rulers wanted to *be* him. Loved in Africa, at home Brown found times were getting considerably tougher.

In 1975, Maceo Parker, Wesley, and trumpeter Kush Griffin all left to play with George Clinton. They'd had it. After years of discipline and fines, of drinking that James Brown Kool-Aid and making sure the bells of their horns hit the same compass point when the boss was watching, now they were getting paid to play funky music for a much looser boss. You drank Clinton's Kool-Aid, and you didn't remember the next forty-eight hours.

George Clinton was a creative genius whose greatest talents were manifest outside the spotlight. He was a conceptualist and a ringmaster who was no slouch at keeping bedlam rolling down the road. Like Brown, he had a gift for giving space to quirky talent. With roots in gospel and doo-wop, he had knocked around the lower rungs of the black circuit that Brown ruled in the 1960s. Clinton once believed, like Brown, in the importance of "hair and teeth"; his first group, the Parliaments, had formed in a barbershop he operated in New Jersey. Eventually, though, Clinton's hair came down.

Born less than a decade after Brown, he nonetheless seemed to germinate in some remote pod of history. Clinton loved the Beatles, and then, by the late 1960s, was in Detroit and holding his own among the feedback freaks in rock bands like the Stooges and MC5. His vision was broader than Brown's, or perhaps it was that his attention span was narrower. Whatever the distinction, by the mid-'70s Clinton had assembled—amassed might be the better word—an underground empire of sound. There was Parliament, a soulful harmony act with a swinging horn section. There was Funkadelic, acid washed, unclean-thought-smooching vanguardists who wanted to be the black Beatles. There was Bootsy's Rubber Band, a get-out-of-jail-free card for the bass player who had felt constricted in the JBs. Operating under the collective title of P-Funk, Clinton had illustrators and girl groups and theorists and a string of badass guitar players, all of whom could be plugged into last night's great idea.

Going from the James Brown band to P-Funk was like running away from the army to join the submarine races. Bootsy was in, and now that Brown's horn section and institutional memory had gone, too, Clinton had many steady hands to balance the crazies. Early in 1976, Parliament released *Mothership Connection*,

Clinton's first gold record. Then he went on tour with a $250,000 set that included a flying saucer and singers launched over the crowd shooting "bop guns." Ties, no; diapers, yes. P-Funk was obnoxious and indefinable, a new language, a sect, a sensation. It scared folks.

America had known Brown for two decades. He was a Great Man, and his every record was the latest end of a historical process. P-Funk was counterculture, it was a conspiracy unleashed in the marketplace. Which is another way of saying that Brown seemed old and Clinton did not. He was not above rubbing it in. Grabbing his nuts in a 1976 interview, Clinton said, "We call him the Grandfather of Soul—only as a joke but it holds him back, just the fact that we even say it as a joke. He really should go just a little contemporary."

A listener arrived at Brown's funk through work, by manning up and accepting his challenge. One got to Clinton's funk through play. It was not all that much of a contest.

There's that word again. *Funk* had meant a stench, the smell of sex in a room, and in the mid-'70s it still had a bouquet—you could not even say its name on some radio stations. That was the only place you couldn't say it, though, and by the time Clinton emerged *funk* was in flower, and to say it was to evoke overpowering sense memory: the brine dripping off a pickled peach, the curve of Pam Grier's nose. It is something that you can't get rid of once you are in it; funk was environmental, and funk was an emulsion. Wayward, sticky, a slather: all describe the music Clinton made.

In one of history's biggest cases of industrial espionage, Bootsy had brought Brown's prime directive, the One, with him to the P-Funk camp, and Clinton delighted in the secrets it unlocked. The One became for him less of a way to structure rhythm and more like the Masonic secret of how everything worked. It was the deal he presented to the audience. If you accepted the One into your life, you were one of us.

Describing what he liked most about Brown, Clinton told an

interviewer, "His music has primal rhythm, the basic One. You can get sophisticated, but you have to come back to that primal rhythm. If you can do that, it's next to fucking. If a James Brown record comes on, whether you like him or not, you'll be on your feet . . ."

It came from New Orleans, from the slaves' quarters and from marching and dancing to drums playing in parades. It came through the drummers in James Brown's band, and through the mind of the man who put himself at their service and made damn sure they were at *his*. He brought it out of the dirt and gave it to America. And now, in the mid-1970s, America was taking it away from him.

That is how it worked. You could not copyright a beat, a smell, the One. You made it and then a younger man in an ass-length blond wig marked it up and made it new.

From the mid-'70s until the mid-'80s, funk hovered over the American mainstream. It was a subculture that emulsified mass culture, through acts like Earth, Wind & Fire, the Meters, the Ohio Players, Kool & the Gang, Zapp, Rick James, Mandrill, Slave, the Gap Band, the Junk Yard Band, the Fatback Band, Cameo . . . Brown was the signal, Clinton was the amplifier, and these acts were the noise coming out of the speaker. When he heard them, Brown could have felt gratified for having disciples in so many places, proud to see ideas he tossed off influence so many lives. But, naw: It probably just made him mad.

Brown crossed paths with the P-Funk menagerie one night, some place on the road in the '70s. He cornered the bass player who got away, now with a whole group Clinton had named after him— Bootsy's Rubber Band. Brown began talking, and as he did, time seemed to flow backward. "Son, how you gonna call it a Rubber *Band* when you don't wear uniforms?" he lectured. "You don't even look like a band!"

Chapter Twenty-one

THE HUSTLE

There was, however, one cultural force capable of uniting Brown and P-Funk. From the mid-1970s until the end of the decade, disco pushed aside funk, punk, polka, and anything else that stood in the path of the rolling mirror ball. As a force, disco was broad. It changed the music industry and reached out to marginalized audiences. As music, disco flowed from Brown's body of work and then moved far, far away from anything he had known.

In his own story, Brown found a durable explanation of how the world worked, and in his music, he saw an expression of raw, uncut reality. In summary, then, he was the light and the truth. Disco was something other than that. Disco basked in fragmented light, embracing artifice and unreality. If this was a "Man's World," then where was his place in a pop movement that empowered gays, lesbians, and straight women? After years of pushing deeper and deeper into a music that signified "blackness," and carrying blackness as a banner around the world, now came a wave that seemed, to many coming out of soul music, capable of washing blackness away.

Disco was a rhythm-based music that made people want to dance, and it's impossible to string those words together without evoking James Brown. He was a parental figure. He used grit and noise, tension and release, to build to a transportive state of repetition. Meanwhile, disco, with its less syncopated, simpler, 4/4 underpinning, established repetition from the jump, and by doing so threw the doors wide open to everyone who cared to join the party.

Having fought his way to the top, having proved that he could turn a segregated system into a meritocracy through the force of his personality, he wasn't going to accept the slide from funk's meritocracy to disco's faceless egalitarianism. Life had taught him, and many in his generation, that the only way to get credit and reward from white America was to work twice as hard, and be twice as good, as the white man. You did that and you lifted yourself up from the masses. You got noticed, you got your due, and you ate.

In a jarring comment, Brown once said he looked at all the disco dancers and saw "a cottonfield"; here was all the anonymity he worked to escape, "all the things I got tired of doing," being embraced by America. It wasn't the toil he minded, it was the repetition, and most of all the reward: losing yourself in the crowd. A long time ago he had escaped invisibility, and if he had anything to say about it, he wasn't ever going to be lost again in the fields.

In the summer of 1975, under a headline asking "Is James Brown Obsolete?" writer Vernon Gibbs lamented that "in the middle of the biggest dance explosion in recent history, James Brown is being left out and he feels it." Gibbs tracked Brown's decline to 1973, when a dance called "the Hustle" was sweeping New York's dance clubs. If the Twist had taken dancers out of each other's arms and opened the door to Brown's revolution—movement as a solo, a bravura display of one's essence—what was Brown going to do now that a new movement had dancers working together again? What could he do when dance became a social movement, not an expression of individual identity?

Take credit for all of it, was one answer. His 1975 album *Sex Machine Today* was marketed as "the world's hottest disco album." The song "(It's Not the Express) It's the J.B.'s Monaurail" rewrote B.T. Express's disco hit "Express" while lobbing snark at the group. Soon he'd be billing himself, desperately, as "The Original Disco Man."

Another possibility was to enter the studio and match disco's chart success with your own. Hollie Farris was a white trumpet player from Nashville who had just joined the band in 1975. He was at Criteria Studios in Miami, doing his first session with Brown, "Get Up Offa That Thing." The band set up together in the room: horns, drums, everything. Brown entered, huddling with different musicians, telling the drummer to play the part from one hit, the guitar to trace the riff from another one, the bass to tweak the line from still another of his songs, humming the part he wanted the horns to play. It seemed strange to Farris; by the mid-1970s, the standard approach to recording a mainstream release was to tape the different instruments separately over many takes, and then piece together the cleanest performances, layer by layer. Recording live in the studio was way out of favor.

The musicians were standing there with their orders, having never yet played the song, and then Brown said, "Okay, roll the tape."

"I just looked at everybody like, 'What? Are you kidding me?'"

The engineer at Criteria later told Farris this was *his* first big recording session, too, and he was sweating out how to set proper sound levels on his mixing board when the band hadn't yet attempted the song. He was fiddling with the knobs, guessing where the levels should be, and then Brown stepped up to the microphone and shrieked one of his classic screams, a wail that knocked every needle into red and had him resetting the knobs for the rest of the session. They played it twice; Brown liked the first version better. That became the hit.

"He didn't care if it had 'mistakes.' All he cared about was the feel," said Farris. "If the song felt good, that was his song. That really taught me a lot. If you don't have the feel you got nothing."

He had something, no question. "Get Up Offa That Thing" reached number four on the R&B charts. He took shots at Barry White on the song, and comes out in favor of dancing. Still, Brown's approach felt anachronistic alongside contemporary music by Earth, Wind & Fire, Isaac Hayes, the O'Jays, and Stevie Wonder, whose hits stressed multitracks and sonic precision. Trying to recreate a live sound on his singles, Brown palpably did not fit in with what was being played on the radio.

He sounds detached on the records of the era, the drumming less surprising. According to Fred Wesley, Brown wanted him to write knockoffs of other people's hits. He wanted a copy of David Bowie's "Fame," which is a head-scratcher because "Fame" itself is a pale version of Brown's 1970s sound. Returning from a trip to Africa, Brown dropped a bunch of African records on Wesley and told him to copy the lot. That was the last straw for Wesley, who took the job with P-Funk. The tightlipped veterans who knew how to make the most of his "feel" approach and who could apply polished nuance on the fly, statesmen like Maceo Parker and Wesley, were gone. The way Byrd saw it, "He was stumbling through the dark" in the disco era, with "no direction then. Everybody had lost interest. When all the money is going one way, then it's easy to lose interest."

The state of his personal affairs tended to color his outlook on the world. When he was doing well, America was a land of opportunity. Now that he was losing his footing, Brown viewed the status of black Americans as slipping backwards. Which doesn't make him wrong, because in numerous ways, the momentum of the Civil Rights Movement had slowed to a shudder step in the disco era, and many on the right sought to roll advances back further. Just because he was egotistical didn't make him any less prophetic.

In a freewheeling interview with a Detroit public-TV show host, Brown was asked to share thoughts on the state of black America in the late 1970s.

"Total repeat, everything's a repeat," said Brown. "If I had to go to work today, I would have *no* job.

"It's worse now than it ever was. Because at one point, you were being *heard*. Today you're not anymore. . . . The struggle is not over, but the success of it has ceased. And ceased because we do not have our direction together." James Brown, disco, the fate of black America in the post-civil rights era: He was talking about it all.

The concert business was floundering, and disco, valuing technology at the expense of live musicians, made it worse. Brown could no longer reliably fill an arena. "When I first got with him, he had a lean year there," said Farris. "We played one time in Gary, Indiana, for fifty people. He did a two-and-a-half-hour show! I couldn't believe it. If he did ten minutes they would have been happy, but he did two and a half hours. It's what kept him alive."

A propensity to not pay his bills added an extra urgency. The band played Miami Stadium, and then did several small dates at a Florida marina. The night of the last show, Brown left on the jet, stranding the musicians. When bassist "Sweet" Charles Sherrell found out, he pondered his options. From his hotel room, Sherrell spotted the tour bus and equipment truck still parked outside, and he hatched a plot.

Phoning the truck driver, Sherrell explained he needed to get a keyboard out to write a song, James wanted him to. "Sorry I woke you up, man; just loan me the key and I'll bring it right back." Then he tracked down the bus driver and said he needed to retrieve some, oh yeah, *books* from the bus to give to a DJ. James had asked him to do it. The bus driver delivered the key, and Sherrell urged him to go on back to bed.

Now it would be necessary to phone the boss and explain the situation. Sherrell was in possession of Brown's bus and truck; Brown was in possession of the band's pay. Perhaps they could work something out.

What came next was no surprise to Sherrell. Brown sent down three big guys, "goons," to set things straight. But Sherrell had notified local law enforcement, and the ensuing standoff forced Brown's heavies into retreat. Having hijacked Brown's equipment and vehicles, now Sherrell hijacked his *band*, giving them a new name, the Nuclear Explosions, and booking shows for them first in Miami, and then on the island of Guadeloupe. An island in the

French Antilles, Guadeloupe is far from Augusta. "It's a nice place. They have a Club Med," said Sherrell.

Finally, Brown sent the money, and brought them home. "We didn't have no argument about it at all. No bad words," said Sherrell. "He walked up, 'Sweets! How you doing?' I said, 'I'm fine, how you doing? Good to see you.'" James Brown rewarded initiative.

One year into his contract with Polydor, Brown began having second thoughts. In an angry letter to label brass, he complained about their lack of success in getting his records onto the pop charts. The note was addressed "To all white people this may concern," and declared, "Goddamit, I'm tired. It's been a racist thing ever since I have been here."

Someone at the label had complained about the number of Brown's people who were coming in and out of the Polygram office in New York. He heard about that, and in response wrote: "LEAVE ME THE FUCK ALONE. I AM NOT A BOY BUT A MAN, TO YOU A BLACK MAN."

In the old days, Brown could thrash it out with Nathan. It would get ugly, and when they were done he'd make another hit. But now Brown was a corporation, and Polydor even more so, with one layer of record company guys in New York reporting to another layer of sophisticated Europeans across the ocean. Later, Brown would sum up his problem by saying, "I got in a fight with the Jews and the Germans. The Jews wanted me to make it and the Germans didn't."

Over the next few years, an assortment of folks he owed money attempted to get it by billing Polydor. At the same time, the company became increasingly interested in recouping loans and advances they had extended him. By the end of 1976, the balance on his loans was $1,514,154, and Polydor wanted him to move on it.

Late in 1977, Brown wrote that he had a sure hit record coming and wanted $25,000 for Christmas. Polydor scotched that and soon indicated they were impounding his plane. Do that, his lawyer seethed, and Brown would do "everything in his power to make life miserable for you."

Polydor was pressing him for new hits. Since the King days, Brown was in the habit of holding records hostage until he got money up front, but by 1977, Polydor was unwilling to go further down that road, with their books showing him to be in debt to them. In 1978, Brown demanded a new ten-year contract, one that would wipe the slate clean of his debts. The Germans demurred. By 1979, the label was tagged for $700,000 in debts Brown owed to others. It was a hellish standoff.

For decades he'd been running ahead, from last month's Learjet bill to the latest big concert, from the previous business opportunity to the next cardboard box of cash. From the Jews to the Germans. As long as he kept running, he had the possibility of making more, and Brown was good at outracing those he owed, mostly. Then the IRS entered the picture and screwed it all up. In 1968, they started examining his books and describing the huge sums they felt they were owed. By the early 1970s, said Daviss, the IRS claimed Brown was $4 million in arrears on back taxes. By the end of the decade, Daviss had gotten the case moved from criminal to civil court, a victory, but by then the government said he owed $17.3 million.

That, not to mention all that he owed creditors, was more than he had in the bank. It was time to tap the strategic reserves he'd stored around the house in places known only to him. Brown had hundreds of thousands of dollars buried in his backyard. When an airport refused to release his jet until he'd paid a bill, he told his Atlanta-based CPA to go to the Walton Way house and start digging near the pool. There were boxes of cash in the house, too. The kids found them and played Monopoly with real money. According to another story, Marva Whitney once witnessed a wall in the house collapse because of all the holes knocked in it to retrieve stowed cash.

Bobby Roach said Brown paid him to fly around the country in his jet in the late-1970s, taking money out of accounts one step ahead of the IRS. Roach converted much of it into cashier's checks, and was carrying $4.5 million in cashier's checks for Brown on at least one occasion.

The IRS was fixing to put a padlock on the Walton Way home until he paid up $40,000. He told Daviss to meet him in downtown Augusta. Together they sat in Brown's van for a long time before anybody said anything. "I've never seen him that focused for that long. He'd usually run things up to the hilt, right to the edge, even when he *had* the money in his pocket to pay you. But that night he was setting there, working up a sweat, and he didn't look as spiffy as he usually looked, hair was roughed up . . .

"We sat on the street corner in the dark. I wondered why the hell did he call me here." Finally, he reached under the seat and pulled out a sack of money, like he was extracting a molar.

"Hold on to it as long as you can," he told Daviss, "but then pay 'em."

There was a new man in the White House, a Georgian, no less. Brown had shaken hands with Governor Jimmy Carter, and donated to his antidrug effort. Carter had remained aloof, however, and Brown decided to see if he could make a friend. On January 24, 1977, Brown sat down and composed a lengthy epistle to Carter, in which he sought to explain himself to the new president. Brown shares with Carter his first sexual encounter and then his incarceration, very slowly meandering to the real purpose of the note: a request to refile his taxes and clear up his financial problems.

The president never responded. He did forward the singer's plea for help to his deputy chief counsel, who somewhat alarmingly wrote Brown back suggesting that the singer start listening to the advice of his own lawyers.

Back when Carter was campaigning for president, Brown had met with him in an airplane hangar in Georgia. It was then that the ambitious governor told him, "James Brown will have a friend in the White House." Since he had gotten elected, Carter wanted nothing to do with the singer.

Brown hated Jimmy Carter.

. . .

Frankie Crocker was a New York landmark. He was the most important black DJ in the world, and to hear his voice on the radio was to realize that, whoever the mayor was at the time, this guy truly was running things. Frankie Crocker *knew*. He coined the phrase "urban contemporary"; he had great ears and a stash of panache. "There was a time when five guys on the radio controlled the music business," said Al Sharpton. "Frankie Crocker was one of the five. If he went on your record, he made you a hit in the biggest market in the country. And if Frankie went on your record, the other four guys were going to get on it."

In the mid-'70s, record bizzers were whispering rumors of a government investigation of payola in black radio. When an indictment finally came down on the biggest name on the feds, list, Crocker told the FBI he had never taken money to play records. One day the government brought a surprise witness into the courtroom who testified to personally giving Crocker money to play records: This was Charles Bobbit, Brown's most trusted lieutenant. He had been pressured and admitted to giving Crocker $6,500 over eight years. Eventually Brown took the stand, claiming that he had no knowledge of Bobbit paying DJs to play his music, declaring it an act he did not condone.

"Mr. Bobbit took a bullet for Mr. Brown," said Sharpton. But it was Crocker who ended up going to jail for a year on perjury charges. Brown's relationship with Bobbit suffered, and eventually Bobbit left Brown.

That happened on a late-'70s trip to Gabon. There are several versions of what happened. The way Bob Patton told it, Brown had been given a million-dollar loan from President Bongo. Then Brown asked for another, and dispatched Bobbit to pick up the money. Bongo balked, but he liked Brown, and sent Bobbit off with a few hundred thousand for the Godfather.

But Bobbit was tired of carrying messages and cash for Brown. According to Patton, Bobbit pocketed the cash and then wrote out a letter of resignation, climbed onto the jet, which was parked on a Libreville runway, and handed his note to Leon Austin to give to the Boss. Then he climbed off. The note told Brown he was staying in Libreville and going to work for Bongo. For the next decade, Bobbit was a chief adviser to the president of Gabon. He even applied his time with Brown to produce a 1978 funk album on which Bongo's son Alain sang songs arranged by Fred Wesley.

Paying DJs to spin your song was one tried-and-true way to get a new record played. Brown, of course, had even better ways: his own radio stations. Here, too, the heat was on. In 1972, J. B. Broadcasting, owner of the three stations, was taken to court for failing to air thousands of commercials that had been paid for. Two years later, the IRS filed a tax lien against the stations, declaring they owed a total of $94,000 in payroll taxes from 1969 to 1973.

Running a station, let alone three of them, was a full-time job, and Brown was doing it from rotary phones on the road. In Baltimore, WEBB went into receivership after creditors charged that the station owed them more than $500,000. In a separate action, the FCC gave evidence in circuit court that WEBB had violated broadcast regulations more than one hundred times.

In 1975, the American Society of Composers, Authors and Publishers, or ASCAP, took WEBB to court for not paying fees after it played music by ASCAP artists. In court, it came out that WEBB lacked the proper license to broadcast *any* copyrighted music. By 1978, the FCC ordered the Baltimore station shut down over repeat violations, but the order was delayed because of the station's ongoing bankruptcy proceedings. That probably wasn't even the biggest crisis in Baltimore: Lawsuits filed by WEBB's previous owners claimed Brown had not yet paid them for the station he'd bought in 1969, and that therefore they were still the owners.

"I don't know that Mr. Brown ever paid any money on that station," sniped Percy Sutton, head of New York–based Inner City Broadcasting. Brown's problem, he said, was "not his failure to get advertising, but to manage the money he got."

A district court in Baltimore ordered Brown to turn over
WEBB's records. Brown failed to do so, and a bench warrant was
issued for his arrest. Thus it was that on the night of July 16, 1978,
Brown was arrested in the most humiliating way: during a performance at the Apollo Theater. A U.S. Marshal permitted him to perform his show and then transported the singer to Baltimore. When
he arrived, Brown was put in shackles and spent two nights in jail.
Charged with contempt of court, he had to surrender his passport
before being released on bail.

The litigation over the sale of WEBB continued into the fall.
Brown added to his troubles by playing a show in Zambia without the okay of the court. Apologizing to the judge, he sought to
explain his overall predicament: "When I was a kid, I never had
any education. I was put into a juvenile institution which was more
like a prison. After I made it big, I employed people who do know
about things. I put myself in my lawyer's hand. I'm just a dumb
nigger."

At that, the judge interrupted, saying, "Now Mr. Brown, dumb
you're not."

The Knoxville radio station was quietly sold in early 1979.
Brown focused on salvaging his Augusta anchor, WRDW, and to
do so he teamed up with high-profile New York lawyer William
Kunstler. A celebrated champion of civil rights causes, the lawyer
for Angela Davis, Harry Belafonte, and others, Kunstler held a
press conference with Brown in New York in November 1979,
where he slammed Polydor for not giving him a new contract, and
attacked the IRS and the FBI for persecuting the singer. "They
cannot permit a black messiah to arise," Kunstler thundered.

The lawyer said he had taken on Brown's case after meeting him
in Augusta and discovering that the singer was interested in lend-
ing his name to Kunstler's political battles. Brown, he announced,
would soon visit the St. Regis Indian Reservation in upstate New
York, where Mohawk Indians were barricaded against law enforcement agencies from both the United States and Canada. There was

talk as well of a joint political action involving Brown and Native American activist Russell Means, as well as JoAnne Chesimard, a Black Liberation Army member who was currently on the lam.

It suddenly seemed like Brown was getting back into politics, and this time for the far left. After the press conference, Sharpton, Brown, and a few of the guys had dinner with the lawyer in Greenwich Village.

"Mr. Brown says, 'Mr. Kunstler, you've done a lot of famous cases. Tell us about them,'" recalled Sharpton. "He told us about the Chicago Seven, and about this and that one.

"'Chicago Seven?' said Mr. Brown. 'I remember that one.'

"Then he said, 'How many of them did you win?'

"'None of them,'" Kunstler said.

"He looked at me and said—'Mister Sharpton, this man wants a martyr, not a client. I don't need to be nobody's cause, brother.' And that's why pretty fast he dropped Kunstler."

The Augusta station was sold at public auction, after owners defaulted on a $268,000 loan. The Baltimore situation dragged on until early 1980, when Brown was forced to sell WEBB to pay debts. "I haven't seen no money in a lot of years," he told the judge. "Sometimes I just work to pay the band, because I hope that one day it will all come back."

Even on the stand, he gave until it hurt, a delivery that seemed highly theatrical. Having transcended a boyhood where literally nobody cared what he felt, communicating basic emotional information to human beings was something he only learned later, after he found a way to make people care. The one place he *did* get emotionally heard, and fed, was on stage. That lesson led him to think that emotion should be expressed as a performance. It could make him seem false—when he sobbed at Goree Island, Fred Wesley thought he was pretending—and he certainly had depths of falseness in him. But the way he communicated fear, love, *anything*, was like he was onstage at the Apollo, trying to get those in the balcony to see what he saw. So when he told the judge presiding over the fate of his radio station he hoped one day his empire would all come back, Brown was being shameless, but it didn't mean he was lying.

Deedee had left him. She wanted domestic bliss; he wanted the road and was emotionally unavailable when he was home. She packed Deanna and Yamma into her 500 Mercedes Coupe in front of the Walton Way home and tried to say good-bye. He came running out, reaching into the car and pulling her hair.

Deedee hit the button to the window. Up it went on his hand. According to Daviss she drove away about one hundred yards with Brown's hand caught in the window, dragging him down the driveway. "Tore his knees *up*!" said Daviss.

Troubles with the IRS, Polydor, a divorce on the way. During a visit with his boyhood buddy Leon Austin, Brown said he was ready to give it all up. "He said, 'I can't keep fighting this thing. I can't make any money, everybody's against me . . . I can't do it.'

"No, you're not going to quit now, you are *not* gonna quit," Austin told him. "What you talking about now?

"You *have* to go to work. You the one that can *make* some money. Got too many people depending on you." They argued back and forth, and Austin, raising his voice, reaffirmed that Brown needed to get himself to the airport, get onto a plane, and take care of his business. Austin hopped in his car to follow his friend and make sure he got to the Augusta airport.

"People gave me a chance to live three or four times, to their once not-living. I owe that to the people," Brown said. "Especially I owe it to the poor people. I owe it to the ghetto. And I even owe it to the rich, ignorant people that don't know truth. . . . If I had gotten everything I should have gotten, I'd be an old man and I'd be throwin' *down*. But I'm still trying to get the recognition that you're fighting for each and every day; that the poor people, the farmers, and everybody are trying to get across. And that keeps me going."

. . .

By decade's end, Brown had been to Africa many times and played Europe more than that. Now it was time to try to win over a truly remote ethnic enclave, a culturally isolated island-state where strangers were easy to spot. The Godfather was heading to Nashville.

Even in a place as set in its ways as Music City, the 1970s had showed the necessity of change. A once-vaunted tourist attraction, country singer Webb Pierce's iconic guitar-shaped swimming pool was closing down in the face of mass indifference. That was bad enough, but then, in February 1979, Porter Wagoner sang disco. Though the country and western hitmaker wore a reassuring purple rhinestone suit with wagon wheels on the legs as he did the hustle in a local club, his new direction appalled the country music hierarchy. "A John Travolta he ain't," tutted the *Nashville Banner*.

Wagoner was just getting started. A month later, he announced he was bringing James Brown to the Grand Ole Opry, where country music elites performed each week on a nationally broadcast radio program. Disco was bad enough, the Opry having only recently accepted *drums*; they had showcased a few black country acts before, but sweating, screaming negroes had yet to breach their perimeter.

Wagoner's keyboardist knew Hollie Farris from Brown's band, and through him sent Brown an invite. "He asked me what did I think of the idea," said the trumpeter. "I said it sounds crazy. James would sure go for it!"

When the booking was announced, esteemed singer Jean Shepard complained on the air. "It's a slap in the face. The Grand Ole Opry is supposed to be a mainstay in country music and it's fighting for its life. We are fighting to keep what identity we've got left," she declared. In case anybody thought the critics were fighting to preserve racial purity or something, pianist Del Wood clarified. "It's not an anti-black issue. . . . But I'm against James Brown's music on the stage of the Opry because I love the Opry and what it stands for. I could throw up. The next thing you know we'll be doing the strip out there."

The bill Brown played on featured an array of country star power: Hank Snow, Roy Acuff, Skeeter Davis, and Stonewall Jackson. By the March date, the scorn was rising high. "What's he going to do, sing 'Papa's Got a Brand New Bag'? I don't understand it, none of us do," complained songwriter Justin Tubb. "If it was Ray Charles, I'd be standing in the wings waiting to hug him when he came off the stage. But it's not."

That was certainly true–James Brown was no Ray Charles. When he released *Modern Sounds in Country and Western Music* in 1962, Charles bent over backward to include white listeners, adding blindingly white chorus singers and orchestrations as toothache inducing as Georgia sweet tea. He hid the drums. He made a bold declaration that country music was *his* music, too, and he made his point by meeting the listener at least half way. Charles was a genius at disarming an audience and sneaking his way into their hearts.

James Brown craved America's love even more than Charles, but he needed it to be on his terms. He reached out to America–and then yanked America over to where he was standing. When asked who his favorite musicians were, he'd give out names like Perry Como, Frank Sinatra, or Jimmy Durante along with more obvious names. He didn't want their act; he wanted their audience. Brown did not believe black music had to be confined to the chitlin circuit, and he knew that there wasn't an audience in the world he couldn't bag if he stood before them and worked.

Everywhere he went, Brown made sure *he* was at home. That's why he could sit down with presidents and capos and crackers and cons and always own the room. State dinner or war zone mess hall, he settled in and got comfortable, turning every inch of it into his space.

How he handled the Grand Ole Opry says much about who he

was. Damn right he did "Papa's." And he did the cape routine. *Twice.* He sang two country tunes–three if you consider "Georgia" country, which it was when Ray Charles did it but wasn't after Brown turned it into gospel step aerobics.

It didn't matter how big you were, you could be Conway Twitty with a hot new record: When you did the Opry, you got three songs. That was chiseled in stone from the days of the Pharaohs, and nobody challenged it. James Brown did four. And then he wouldn't leave. He was up there for half an hour, making sure everybody knew who they had just seen.

The Nashville *Tennessean*, which a week before had lavished attention on Senator Robert Byrd's fiddle playing at the Opry, neglected to cover Brown's historic appearance. The *Banner* headlined their story "Brown Fails to Stir Audience," and said ticket holders "sat and watched somberly" while Brown was "receiving only smatterings of polite applause and raising a few eyebrows of Opry regulars."

Afterward, Wagoner threw a cocktail party at the Opryland Hotel. Clearly having heard the words uttered backstage by a glowering Roy Acuff–the superstar muttered, "I wish I could go out there and speak my mind, but I won't"–Wagoner gave Brown a soul handshake and declared, "He is to soul music what Roy Acuff is to country music." Together they hadn't just brought funk to the Opry; they'd peed in Webb Pierce's pool.

Brown always said he was grateful for the treatment Opry listeners had given him. "This is my miracle night," he said. "It's a miracle I'm here. I haven't slept good in two weeks knowing I was going to play the Opry."

After being pushed to the periphery of the pop marketplace, after struggling to simply talk to his audience, it must have felt great to come into Nashville. At the Opry he could meet the gaze of the whites who filled up the seats, and do his best to put on a show for them. They didn't love him, but they watched him work. He let them know he was at home.

Chapter Twenty-two

I CAN SEE THE LIGHT!

A ugusta was home. How much he loved it there was clear to those around him. Or maybe it wasn't so much love, as it was that Augusta was a place where he felt anchored. Deidre had pushed him to leave New York, but with her and the kids gone, he had no plans to leave. When he lost the Walton Way house in September 1979, in a dispute over unpaid property taxes, even then he wouldn't leave. He found a new home nearby, a house across the Savannah River in Beech Island, South Carolina, about ten miles from downtown Augusta.

It was a Southern ranch house that Brown would build up over the years. The property covered forty acres, and where Walton Way was tied to the ebb and flow of Augusta life, the new address suggested Brown was pulling back. The area, said one writer, was "a quiet rural community full of mobile homes and curvy roads where people sell hay and antiques."

To get to his home in Beech Island (not really an island), you drove down a dirt road, stopping at a wrought-iron gate modeled on one from Buckingham Palace, and then headed through pine woods, past a pond. Nobody would be bopping by to view the Christmas decorations, and few would even get past the gate. "You had a certain status to get inside the gate," said Sharpton. "But then you had to have superstatus to get from the road to the front of the house–or inside."

The life of the spirit began to concern him; for a while Brown studied the Koran with Bobbit. In the end, he went with the god he had known his whole life. The month after losing the Augusta house, Brown got in his car, drove out to Williston, South Carolina, near where he was born and where some of his mother's people still lived, and was baptized at St. Peter's Baptist Church. He would attend services and play a role in church affairs in the years ahead.

Otherwise, in his leisure time Brown pulled on pointy-toed cowboy boots so tight they made his toenails curl into a barrel shape, donned a straw hat, grabbed a shotgun, and hopped into his customized Dodge van. He loved that van, with its deeply upholstered swivel seats and mud flaps, shag carpeting, bar, sink, and loaded with chrome. At home, James Brown was Soul Bubba Number One.

He never slacked, but closing in on fifty, Brown was hungry to have a place to relax without feeling he had to be *on* all the time. He tried to chill, and key to that was owning a plot he could call his own. Maybe nothing marked Brown as a Southerner more than his attachment to land. It was the most important thing a man could have. Always measuring himself against his daddy, who got his hands dirty working on other people's land, Brown *owned* his plot. It was forty acres, sans mule.

Southern pride, he would say, is a hell of a thing. Those people in New York, they'd serve you food while they were fooling you, have you thinking you're entering their front door when you were coming through the back. All those Northerners, he sensed, talking all that mess about race, were the same people calling you "nigger" behind your back. In the South, he explained, that was beneath them. The Southern white was going to tell you to your face. "You can trust a Southern white man, you are always gonna know where he's coming from," Brown declared.

"There are some horrible white people there in Augusta," said

Alan Leeds, "but they pray to the same Baptist god and eat the same grits and gravy and worship the same red clay as the blacks. They even talk with the same drawl, use some of the same colloquialisms. There is a commonality that most Northerners never get; we just never have that experience."

To understand James Brown, Leeds explained, you have to understand that he was a Southerner, as much as he was anything. "He *was* a good old boy. We'd get off his Learjet when he went home and get into his pickup truck."

Forces were gathering behind the Beech Island gate, and family was gathering, too. In the 1980s, Brown brought his mother down to live with him. She was an independent, somewhat irascible presence, who gave as good as she got. Susie would declare he didn't respect his mother; he'd tell Mom to go to her room. "She looked like him," said guitarist Ron Laster. "James gave her hell when he was raised, and now she didn't give a damn. She used to say, 'I don't give no damn about no Sex Machine.' She was not impressed by all the TV shows."

Her behavior, however, was erratic, and Brown decided he couldn't leave her at the house by herself. Susie muttered even when there was nobody to talk to and engaged in obsessive behavior, like making the bed three or more times in a day, plucking off invisible objects. Deanna Brown said she had water on the brain, and after undergoing surgery, "she wasn't all the way there." Eventually Brown sent Susie to live with her sister in Smoaks, South Carolina. Brown would send a car to pick her up for visits, but she would turn it down, preferring to take the bus.

Joe Brown was living in Augusta, but he, too, regularly came out to the house. Pops wore smudged glasses, a felt hat, and overalls. He called his son Junior, and spoke with a speech impediment. "He worked with his hands, loved his son, was not well educated," said Sharpton. "He was the only one I ever saw Mr. Brown give some deference to. He'd argue with him but he would always end up saying, 'That's my dad.' He loved his father."

Pops fancied himself a fix-it man, and was always ready to help James at Beech Island. "He was a funny guy and he could fuck up a junkyard," said Daviss. One time Pops was mowing the lawn with a tractor, coming down a steep hill, and the tractor started sliding, until it slipped into a pond. All the way under, bubbles coming up. James ran down and started shouting at his dad. Joe was indignant: "Now J-J-J-Junior, y'all can k-k-kiss my ass!"

An Albanian American and a Canuck drove from New York to Los Angeles in a vintage Oldsmobile 88. They had nothing to do but play music and talk, and by the time they got to the coast, they had sprung an idea. The two men were John Belushi and Dan Aykroyd, and the concept was for a skit on *Saturday Night Live*, the hit show on which they were regulars. They would play siblings, the Blues Brothers, dress like Jack Webb, and play great rhythm and blues music. Precisely where the gag *was* in the Blues Brothers act was a bit elusive, one big reason why it lasted so long. People didn't get tired of it. The humor was in the exuberant silliness of these dark-suited stiffs bursting into black music with abandon.

The songs Belushi and Aykroyd covered were expertly selected. They were cool and humorous and not the usual oldies, pre-rock styles curated for white baby boomers. The brothers opened for Steve Martin in the summer of 1978 in Los Angeles and, having established that they were some sort of "real" act, they released *Briefcase Full of Blues* that year, an album that sold two million copies.

When the inevitable movie came out in June, 1980, *The Blues Brothers* ran over two hours, cost $30 million, and had more car chases and explosions than any twenty comedies are likely to feature. So full of gags and booms, the movie was almost formless.

The story involved brothers trying to get their old band together to make money for the orphanage they were raised in. Aykroyd and Belushi really loved the musicians they emulated, and cast some of their heroes in the film. Cab Calloway was a cleaning man; Aretha Franklin a waitress in a hash house; and James Brown was a palpitating preacher who tears the church apart with his sermonizing and dancing. The critic Pauline Kael called such casting "somewhat patronizing," which was somewhat understated. The script left you wondering if they understood the culture they professed to admire.

Brown played the Reverend Cleophus James, pastor of the Triple Rock Baptist Church. Aykroyd and Belushi stand in the back of his church while a service gets underway. The reverend seems to be speaking directly to them when he tells the congregation about "lost souls seeking the divine light," and then he points at Belushi, who looks nervously at his watch. "Do you see the light?" he barks, and after resubmitting the question a few times, Belushi *does* begin to see it, finally shouting, "Yes! Yes! Jesus H. tap-dancing Christ, I have seen the light!"

Behind Brown, James Cleveland's Southern California Community Choir sing a gospel number, and the church erupts into dance. The original script makes a racial point more strongly, with the reverend referring to Belushi as "my little lost, white lamb," but it comes through loudly all the same. Brown, and all the performers in the movie, will lead white America to the promised land.

"Praise God," says the reverend; "And God praise the United States of America," Aykroyd shouts back, as *he* now dances down the aisle. For all the stereotypes in this movie, the Blues Brothers tries to evoke the civil rights era's vision—blacks and whites together, united by God and song.

The film was released in the summer of 1980, and that December, Brown was a guest on *Saturday Night Live*, where he sang his new single, "Rapp Payback," and a medley of older hits. Both the movie and the appearance on a hip, youth-oriented TV show did much to introduce Brown to young whites who were making the leap from the Police and Talking Heads to the artists who had inspired them.

Attention was being redirected. Older black audiences hadn't just moved on from the blues and soul the Blues Brothers messed with, by 1980 they had moved away from Brown. Which was funny, because at the same time, younger audiences were getting a huge taste of Brown through hip-hop. In the late '70s, DJs at block parties would loop break beats—choice moments from songs like "Mother Popcorn" and "Funky President," extracted and then extended—and by the early '80s, as performers began making rap records, James Brown was on his way to being the most sampled artist in hip-hop history. In Washington, D.C., go-go music was flourishing, using Brown's hardest funk numbers as a template. "When it's got a thump to it that makes you wanna move your ass and stir around and get some exercise, *that's* funk," said Chuck Brown, godfather of go-go. "James Brown, that's where I got a lot of my inspiration from." Hip-hop, go-go: In circles beyond the mainstream, he was the light. That meant something, but it wasn't going to pay the bills. Standing there in his bare-chested jumpsuit on *Saturday Night Live*, looking into the TV camera, he was a landmark acquainting himself with those who would sustain him through the decade: white folks, young and old.

There were more reasons for optimism. As he told a columnist for the *Los Angeles Sentinel*, he was free of Polydor and America had a new president, both giving him "a new lease on life." Brown called Reagan "My number one cowboy." He just *liked* Reagan, he explained. "The man looks great. He could still act if he wanted to. But he's put his life on the line to help the country get back. Think of your grandfather coming back and running the country—you got to take your hat off to him."

Unlike the dour Carter, Reagan responded when Brown contacted him. After Brown sent a note congratulating the new president, Reagan wrote him back, on White House stationery. With a wink he praises a God that has given us Brown, a man who knows "soul" in all its meanings. Reagan finishes by thanking Brown for his contribution to the nation.

Like the new president, Brown had a near-magical faith in the power of the individual; both had come up from nothing and believed that their success was America's—they'd made it, so anybody could. Garry Wills has a term for Reagan which applies equally well to Brown: He had become a "rabble-soother," an ex-insurgent now using that rhetoric to cheerlead for mass values. Brown carefully told white journalists he was through with politics, a message that could only help him connect with his new fans. Now he stressed the greatness of the nation, and let the music say the rest.

Those in the band could see the audience change before their eyes. "You noticed it. It became more white," said Hollie Farris. "When I first started with him in 1975, it was ninety-nine percent black audiences. And then it started to change, and before you knew it, it was mostly white. They were discovering him; the blacks had already discovered him. Whites knew who he was, but then they saw him in that movie and decided they wanted to see more of him."

Ron Laster was a guitar player who joined the group at the end of 1979, just before they got a bounce from *The Blues Brothers*. He remembered playing the Beacon Theatre in New York for forty-four people before the film's release. Afterward, you could fill up a small venue. "It was like an advanced chitlin circuit. We would do the best little clubs in town: the Lone Star in New York, the Sugar Shack in Boston, Lupo's in Providence, First Avenue in Minneapolis, Front Row in Cleveland, Park West in Chicago. . . . We would destroy these places because they were packed, and the girls so close to you. We used to love it, I said *love* it," said Laster.

The show focused on his most recent record and the oldies, because Brown thought that's what his white fans wanted. He mostly was right, though sometimes, when a crowd wanted the funk and he hadn't brought any, things could get messy. "They threw shoes and sneakers at us in Switzerland—they wanted 'Hot

Pants' and 'Soul Power,' and he had us doing this little Holiday Inn show.

"How big the house was, it didn't matter to him, he was gonna keep playing," said Laster. "If they come, they come. It took a long time for them to come back."

It was a comedown, and Brown did what his ego needed to cushion the fall. When arriving at a hotel, he'd send Henry Stallings first, to check in at the front desk. Then he'd charge in and start barking orders at his assistant from the entrance, making sure everyone knew a player had arrived.

Women still threw themselves at him. "I was with him one night when he had about six at the hotel," recalled Laster. "We used to run interference. He'd give us money to entertain them, tell them jokes while they were waiting for him. He'd laugh and come up to me and say, 'Mr. Laster—tonight I did a nickel.' That was five. Another night it was 'I did a trey.' 'I'm free, single, and I like to mingle.' That was his thing."

These club shows were not the marathon sessions of a decade before. The stagecraft was scaled down to the venue, but it wasn't like he avoided the moves that made him famous. "Singer James Brown has found he can no longer perform those wild athletic leaps he did as of yore," reported the *Los Angeles Sentinel* in 1981. At New York's Lone Star, the *Sentinel* columnist wrote, he attempted a split that "left him prone, and reputedly too injured to open a slated concert at Ripley Music Hall in Philadelphia." Another time he did a split, lost his balance, and landed sprawling in the drum kit.

The performances were never, however, cautious or sleepy, and where some detected a slippage others saw a crafty adjustment to age and stage. Reviewing a show in the San Fernando Valley in 1982, the *Los Angeles Times'* Robert Hilburn sized up the "mostly white audience, both young fans wanting to sample their pop history and older ones wishing to relive some memories. . . .

"Brown uses his years of stage savvy to maximize his more

limited movement, building a slow, steady tension through the show. . . . He really did give *more*, unleashing a series of inspired moves that made you feel for an intoxicating few minutes that you were back in the '60s. . . . You only need one word to describe this performer–in 1982 or 1962–and it's great."

It was at this moment, when his finances were in shambles and his ability to make money severely disabled, that Brown began using the synthetic drug PCP regularly. Also called angel dust, it had once been used as an animal tranquilizer and was tested as a human anesthetic decades earlier, though it was discarded because of the psychotic effects it triggered. Brown broke up chartreuse crumbs of the drug and sprinkled them over marijuana. For years he talked about it as if it was only marijuana he was smoking, and he almost seemed to believe it himself. Bob Patton, a booker and aide to Brown, accidentally shared a joint dosed with PCP in the mid-1970s and hallucinated for hours. Vicki Anderson, a singer with the show, told writer Barney Hoskyns that Brown was smoking PCP before 1982. His usage became well known in Brown's inner circle by the mid-1980s, and it affected how business was done.

"One time we was in Augusta and we got to get paid," recalled Clayton Fillyau Jr. "My dad was under a tree drinking his liquor. He calls Danny Ray, asking if James Brown was home; 'Man he's home, but I don't know if you wanna go, he's on that stuff,' Danny told Dad.

"Dad thought we got to go get paid before he gets too crazy. We were driving fast when all of a sudden this black Seville comes passing us going the other way at 130 miles per hour. It was James Brown. My dad turns around and pulls him over, but before we can get to him he hops around the car, does some little dance or something, then just jumps in and is flying back into South Carolina. We couldn't keep up with him."

Angel dust makes the legs wobbly, triggers nausea and dizziness; mental effects include a sense of disassociation from one's body. It is sometimes grouped with anesthetics, but unlike most anesthetics PCP isn't a depressant—it speeds up the heart and can foster great physical feats. The singer had scorned intoxicants his whole career, rarely going so far as to have two drinks before bed. What led him, in his fifties, to pursue PCP? Perhaps Brown was drawn to it because, after a lifetime of exerting rigorous discipline over every aspect of his life, abandoning himself to its loss of control had a strong attraction.

Maybe it was all the things that he used to do but wouldn't anymore. Levi Rasbury thinks Brown struggled with the diminishment of his gifts. "You are a perfectionist and you honed your ability to the point that you became uniquely successful. And then, through no fault of your own, it's not there anymore. [The drug use] was a result, I think, of not being able to handle the outcome of what happened.

"Falling from grace is one thing. But to be a perfectionist who has to face failure? That's an ordeal. Those are suicidal situations, there."

On Groundhog Day in 1982, he was taping an appearance on the syndicated TV show *Solid Gold*. Brown would sing "I Got You (I Feel Good)" and perform a comedy routine with ventriloquist Wayland Flowers and his puppet, Madame. Walking down a hallway before the taping, Brown saw the show's hairstylist through an open door. "Good God," he said, "look at the *spank* on that woman." He told Sharpton to get her number and ask her out for him.

The two began spending a lot of time together. Adrienne Lois Rodriguez, thirty-two, was an exotic-looking woman who had once dated Elvis Presley. She was Italian, black, Jewish, and Latina, and in some pictures she looked like a modern-day Cleopatra with heavy eye shadow and straight black hair. She was raised in South Central Los Angeles, living in foster homes and then with a grandmother who made Adrienne and her two siblings pay for the food she fed them.

They married in 1984. Brown felt their special bond from the beginning, believing they shared a connection with a land far away–that they were both outsiders, genetically distant from where they called home. "Our souls met a long time ago. We met visually on *Solid Gold*. But we was already really together because we're Third World people. Nothing in this country is like us," he said. "All of our likenesses is in the Mideast and the Far East and then some drifted to South America. We got that other look . . ."

That was how Brown and Adrienne viewed it: As far as many white Augustans were concerned, he was black and she was the opposite. "He got a lot of flack," remembered Sharpton. "He told me people would say things to her–they'd call her 'nigger lover.'"

Deidre savored a house full of kids and the good life of Walton Way. Adrienne–Alfie, as she was called–loved show business, and wanted to go on the road, maybe as a backup singer–just *something* that put her in the lights, too. Brown's life had driven more than one wife to distraction, but Alfie was equipped to share it with him.

The Blues Brothers had handed Brown a new audience, and he also appeared as himself in the 1983 Dan Aykroyd movie *Doctor Detroit*. Money in, money out. The IRS continued to shadow him, auctioning off three of his cars, including his beloved Dodge van, in 1983. That same year, he left the band stranded in Sacramento at Thanksgiving, stuck without gas money to get home.

There was a ruckus of clean breaks. In this climate of unexpected change, fate handed him one more distraction. Jimmy Nolen's heart wore out.

Nolen had auditioned for Brown's band on the West Coast in 1965, and he laid down the "chanka-chanka," or chicken scratch, as it was called, that motivated countless Brown records. Nolen was skinny and quiet and survived in the band longer than anybody but the even quieter St. Clair Pinckney. Over the years he got to know Brown's ways so well that he could tell when the boss was about to forget a lyric and would rustle up a wave of chicken scratch to fill the gap. Brown would take him aside and rehearse with him for hours. He wasn't a rhythm guitarist, he was *rhythm*, nearly as much as the drummers.

Knowing what he had, Brown insisted that Nolen move with him when he went from New York to Augusta, and Nolen found a place in Atlanta. Being near Brown made it easier to rehearse; being where Brown could keep an eye on him kept Nolen from accepting other offers. Though his contribution was immense, Nolen quietly complained about how Brown left his name off the album covers. In Macon, Brown pulled a gun on him and slapped him. He would fine him for broken guitar strings. Nolen was the most famous secret guitar star in the world: When Eric Clapton came through Atlanta, he would call Jimmy to get together. Nolen might even do it, though he'd beg Clapton to keep it quiet, or else Brown would think somebody was trying to steal him.

A couple heart attacks on the road; Brown and the band kept the news from his wife, though she found out when she discovered his blood pressure pills.

He loved children, and sometimes when he was home, he'd round up neighborhood kids and head to Adams Park. They'd cross a bridge, stop near a huge boulder that looked like it had rolled off a mountain. Nolen would climb on the rock, carefully set down his thermos of Manischewitz white. Then he'd get out his guitar and play "Popcorn with a Feeling."

He died at home, having skipped a trip to Canada because he wasn't feeling up to it. Lunetha, his wife, told the band it was a heart attack; then she had to find somebody to tell Brown. This would not be easy. Danny Ray gave him the news after his show that night, and Brown called Lunetha. The first thing he wanted to know: Was there anybody else in the room when he died? Brown thought maybe somebody had killed his guitarist, but Lunetha told him no, nobody murdered her husband.

Just before he died, Nolen took Ron Laster aside and taught him the secrets, saying, "Now *you've* got to lead the band." He asked Lunetha to deliver a message once he was in the ground. As they say, it was like he knew what was coming. He watched a TV show about rock and roll greats and noticed how many had died before they were fifty. The life just ground them down.

She carried her husband's words to Brown. "You had to be strong and look James right in his eyes—you had to let him know, 'James, I do not fear you. . . . You need to hear this,'" Lunetha recalled. "He was curious—he wanted to hear this and he *didn't* want to hear this."

St. Clair Pinckney knew what was coming and did not want Lunetha to meet with Brown. But what could she do? Jimmy had made it his last request. " 'You tell James,' Jimmy said to me, 'the next person you get to work for you, I hope you treat them better than you did us.' I said, 'I don't hold it against you, that's what Jimmy said.'"

When she told Brown, he put his arm around her and apologized. "I'm sorry I hurt him like that," Brown said. "He hugged me and said he was sorry, that he was afraid someone was gonna take Jimmy away from him."

Caught between a "can't change me" rebelliousness and a desire for a hit, Brown displayed a new interest in taking creative risks, in making records in fresh ways. The Polydor deal was history, and he had signed an agreement with Island Records, home of Bob Marley. In 1982, he went down to Nassau to record with the brilliant Jamaican producers Sly and Robbie. They cut some material, but not enough to make an album before Brown had wandered off. More fruitful was a 1984 single with Afrika Bambaataa, "Unity," on Tommy Boy. Bambaataa was a South Bronx medicine ball of a man who, as a DJ, producer, and dispute settler, had played an important role in the birth of hip-hop. By linking with Brown, this hot artist popular with indie rockers was publicly paying tribute. His futuristic electro-funk, and the call for "peace, unity, love, and having fun!" in "Unity" built bridges across generations and subcultures. Punk rockers and new wavers were getting into hip-hop through Bambaataa's records, and they were also identifying with Brown's rawness and immediacy. "Unity" symbolized a moment when, at the edges of marginal communities and at the places where neighborhoods touched, folks were crossing borders.

Like Aykroyd and Belushi before him, Sylvester Stallone had a vision in the desert. The actor and director had a scene in mind for his upcoming *Rocky IV*, a demented, patriotic scene, a production number set in the heart of Las Vegas. In his wildest dreams, Stallone imagined James Brown singing a new song, and his black boxer Apollo Creed dancing to it in an Uncle Sam costume. There'd be Vegas showgirls and flags flapping, a chorus line, and dancers in top hats and tails. Stallone saw it all quite vividly, and now he needed others to see it.

Rocky III had set the bar high for heart-pounding, artery-clogging anthems, with its scene built around Survivor's "Eye of the Tiger." The hit song sold the hit movie, and the hit movie sold the hit song. Stallone took his notion for a new song to Dan Hartman, a studio veteran who could make good records in hard rock, metal, disco, or mainstream pop, and who had specialized in planting bombast in big-budget Hollywood movies.

Stallone's pitch couldn't have been more direct: He wanted a top-ten hit, sung by James Brown, with a strong patriotic undercurrent. *Rocky IV* pitted Stallone's fighter against a heartless, cheating Moscow mule named Ivan Drago. President Reagan had ramped up the Cold War and made it a patriotic touchstone; Stallone aimed to make a hit movie that would sell the conflict that would sell the hit movie. Hartman balked at the patriotic part, probably not because of his politics but because his hits typically created a sense of "us," and a flag-waver would divide the potential market. He wondered, too, about Brown's ability to deliver a million-seller. "I think James Brown has made a lot of good records, but it was that purist James Brown thing that he was doing in the beginning, and people won't let him do that anymore because time marches on. That stuff is classic to me, but other people get bored with it," Hartman told the *Los Angeles Times*.

"I said that if I write something for James Brown, it would be too organic ever to be in the top ten. I had too much respect for him to water down his style." There the vision paused, until Hartman and songwriting partner Charlie Midnight came up with a notion for a song that would have elements of Loverboy's "Working for the Weekend" and Springsteen's "Born in the USA": the patriotism came across in a whoop for American pop culture, while noting "everybody's working overtime" trying to "make the prime." With Brown as the image of American toil, the song in effect said, "We're all in this together, now get to work."

Brown was game, so much so that he asked Hartman to sit beside him in the studio, telling him, "When I do it, I'm going to do it like James Brown, but you must have had something in mind when you wrote it and I want to know what it was." Together they came up with just enough grunts and asides to make it James and more than enough of Hartman's marching band melodies to make "Living in America" the top-ten hit Brown, no less than Stallone, craved. The song was on the pop charts for eleven weeks in the winter of 1986 and made it to number four; it was his first pop hit in ten years. "Living" earned Brown his first appearance on the British top ten. It received the tribute of a "Weird Al" Yankovic parody, "Living With a Hernia," and won a Grammy in 1987 for Best Male R&B vocal performance. Most of all, the song replanted Brown in the American mainstream.

He wore his cowboy boots in his *Rocky IV* scene: He symbolized America, its Reagan-era celebration of the survivor. It was an astounding transformation for a figure that many in the country had never before viewed as *American*.

With *The Blues Brothers* and now *Rocky IV*, whites celebrated him as an icon. During the subsequent tour, *Rocky IV*'s mechanical robot Sico introduced the Godfather of Soul to the crowd. As for the hit, with no emphasis on the One and no rhythmic tension, it was a challenge for the band to weave it into his show. "We used to open up with it every night because, whether he liked it or not, it is what brought the crowd out," said Laster. "We tried like twelve different versions of it to put some kind of funky groove on it. We got some versions that were more James Brownish—you'd say, 'Damn, is that "Living in America"?' But he needed his face back in the public and *Rocky IV* did it."

He followed it up with a new label, Scotti Brothers, and an album, 1987's *Gravity*, that had "Living in America" on it, produced by Hartman. He said his career was climbing again, telling one writer, "Coke and Pepsi are fighting over James Brown. All the car companies want me." His finances might have been improving, but not too much. Brown lost his Beech Island house in 1987, but then his lawyer, Albert "Buddy" Dallas, bought it and gave it back to him.

It was a time of clean breaks and fresh starts, punctuated by crazy drives into the pines. His first autobiography, *The Godfather of Soul*, by Brown and Bruce Tucker, came out in 1986. With "Living in America" still booming out of the radio, Brown was in the first class of inductees into the Rock and Roll Hall of Fame. Joining him in the Hall were Elvis Presley, Little Richard, Ray Charles, Sam Cooke, Buddy Holly, Fats Domino, Jerry Lee Lewis, and the Everly Brothers. These were his peers, some of them old acquaintances. Unlike any of them, Brown had a hit record at the time of his induction.

At the ceremony at New York's Waldorf Astoria, he wore a crimson silk shirt, chartreuse scarf, and a black coat. After he picked up his award, with an evening and a celebrity-studded performance before them, Brown turned to Sharpton and said: "Let's go." Surrounded by stars and industry elites, even then he drew on a lesson he learned long ago. Never be regular. Don't ever let them get tired of you.

They ducked out.

Chapter Twenty-three

AN UPROAR
ALL THE TIME

He opened car doors for her.

She did his hair better than anybody.

He explored the holy sites in Jerusalem with his Jewish wife.

She got baptized knowing it would please him.

They called each other "Suga Wooga."

James and Adrienne had been in love with others before, but this was different. It was wilder, and it was more unpredictable. The singer was fiercely protective of his wife. He interrupted a recording session with Dan Hartman to pointedly ask why his producer was looking at Adrienne. She had a spot of jealousy, too, and quickly became a gatekeeper, exerting control over who got to see her husband. Those in the inner circle had to make sure they didn't offend her. James had been married twice before and brought numerous women on the road with him, but this one, quite possibly, was a first: When you pushed her, she knew where to push back.

Meanwhile, Brown's recreational PCP use was escalating into addiction, and Alfie was using, too. Many addicts have described how the drug makes time seem to speed up, and makes hours and days seem to flutter in an instant. For James and Adrienne, at any rate, events were rocketing forward, and the drugs created a whole new kind of rhythm in their lives, oscillating between crazy rage and operatic displays of affection.

She called 911 to report domestic violence once in 1984.

Three times in 1985.

Once in 1987.

At least seven times in 1988.

Some of it was swallowed up behind Beech Island's gates, but on the road incidents were harder to hide. When the couple were staying at the Plaza Hotel in New York, Adrienne became convinced that James had been with another woman, and she confronted that woman, stabbing her in the rear. Brown's attorney Buddy Dallas dealt with the hotel, and said later, "I was able to settle that matter out for a small compensation to the ladyfriend who took scissors in the buttocks."

On another occasion, Brown was playing Las Vegas, and Adrienne was with him. They arrived at the airport together with Dallas, who remembered, "Being a Southern boy, my mother always taught me to be polite to ladies, and the then-Mrs. Brown had two big, heavy bags. I reached down to pick up her bags and when I picked them up I said, 'My God, these must weigh fifty pounds apiece.' Mr. Brown came over and *demanded* that I put the bags down.

"'Mr. Dallas,' he said, 'what you don't know about those bags can get you arrested. She insisted on bringing those bags, so *she* can carry them.'"

They might have contained tableware—Dallas said Adrienne had an impressive, and ever-growing, silverware collection. Or it might have been a controlled substance. Whatever was in those bags, Dallas did as he was advised.

"I had to rethink my gentlemanly upbringing. From that point on, it was 'Yes, Mrs. Brown,' 'No, Mrs. Brown...' I didn't even open a car door for her."

PCP had come into his life before Adrienne, but it wasn't until after he met her that his drug use hit the public record. Probably, he was smoking more than ever, and, probably, her control of who got to be around her husband kept a few of his protectors at bay. These are unknown variables, but one thing was a certainty: Both of them liked to get high and then go for a drive. In September 1987, Brown led police on a high-speed tour around downtown Augusta, including breathtaking shortcuts through an IHOP parking lot. That same month, Adrienne was pulled over in a Lincoln Town Car at four in the morning for doing seventy in a forty-five-mile zone. When the police put Alfie in a squad car, she tried kicking the doors out. That November, Brown struck cars at two different Todd's Shop N Go's, then drove away. He was jailed for resisting arrest and leaving the scene of an accident. Twice.

Things seemed to take a turn for the worse the following spring. On Easter weekend, 1988, Adrienne called 911 and reported Brown had beaten and threatened to kill her. He disappeared, turning himself in the next day. She told reporters she wanted a divorce. A week later she was arrested at Augusta's Bush Field airport after a PCP-soaked cigarette and four nasal spray bottles of the stuff were found on her and a friend. A month after that, she was arrested for setting Brown's clothes on fire in a Bedford, New Hampshire, hotel room, and for possessing seven ounces of PCP.

In an interview with the *Augusta Chronicle*, he sounded strangely at peace: "Everybody loves the Godfather of Soul," he said. "America is concerned about the Godfather of Soul because America *is* the Godfather of Soul."

He also sounded lost: "My faith in God is the only thing that brings me through. Faith is the only actual thing that keeps me going."

Most of all he sounded certain, convinced that the story of James and Adrienne Brown was a tale of two complex people who cared deeply for each other. "Love's a funny thing," he said.

The flutterings between rage and romance were happening so quickly now, it was hard to tell which extreme they were visiting at a given moment. In May, he spent the night in jail after she phoned the police and he fled—when he was finally arrested, it was for possession of PCP, assault and battery, failing to stop for police, and possession of an unlicensed pistol. Now *he* said he wanted a divorce. Soon after, Alfie's lawyer was in court trying to get a drug charge dropped with a novel defense: Augusta had once officially designated James Brown an "ambassador of soul," ergo he had diplomatic immunity—which per the norms of statecraft should carry over to a diplomat's spouse.

To anyone brave enough to venture the question, Brown denied he even used drugs, let alone was an addict. No way would he poison the flesh that had given him so many gifts. "My nose, my ears, my eyes, my rectum, my privates, those are parts of my body that I don't want to fool with. And my arm."

And then he went for a drive.

It started at his business office in Augusta on September 24, after Brown had determined somebody had used his bathroom without permission. Toting a shotgun, he walked into an insurance seminar next door. He appeared very mad. Folks chose their words carefully when he inquired who had used his toilet. Brown departed—leaving his gun (for the record, unloaded) leaning against a wall when he exited the room—and seems to have inspired confusion as much as fear among the attendees.

By the time an off-duty sheriff at the seminar called law enforcement, Brown was already in his red and white Ford pickup. When he observed officers arriving, he did a U-turn in the parking lot and raced off.

Thus began a heated pursuit along the dotted line of Georgialina, with Brown driving across the Savannah into South Carolina, and then doubling back into Georgia and ultimately grinding to a halt on rims—his front tires shot out, sparks flying, the pickup riddled with bullets—as a line of police officers finally stopped his forward motion. It was said by a Georgia Highway Patrol officer that when he came to rest, Brown sang "Georgia" and did the Good Foot dance.

He was found guilty of failing to stop for a blue light (South

Carolina parlance for running from the police, a felony) and attempting to run down two state safety officers. A weapons charge was thrown out on insufficient evidence. He was sentenced to six years in Georgia and six and a half in South Carolina, to serve concurrently.

When describing his situation to those who reached him in prison, inmate #155413 sounded baffled, indignant, bitter. "I've been in slavery all my life, ain't nothing new," he said of his prison term. "It just means I don't have to answer a whole lot of phone calls. Ain't nothing changed for me but the address."

All he wanted was to go home, put on some denim, and play with his dogs. He could have been doing those things, too, if only he had pled guilty to the drug charges, he claimed. But that he would not do because that would be a lie. Over and over he declared he did not have a substance abuse problem. Alan Leeds: "In James Brown's somewhat distorted sense of what it is to be a man, he thinks his fans would have seen it as a greater weakness to admit he has a drug problem. In his mind, to go to prison makes him a martyr; to go to a hospital makes him a weak man."

All these complications, Brown explained, came from a very simple event. "God said, 'Boy, go home.' I got in my truck and tried to go home. Then the police began to chase me."

He tried to go home, but he could not.

A year after Brown went to prison, there was another hot pursuit: in Beverly Hills, California, Zsa Zsa Gabor drove away after a police car signaled her to pull over. When she finally stopped, she slapped an officer who leaned into her car. Gabor was driving without a license, and an open flask of Jack Daniel's was espied in her $215,000 Rolls-Royce. The actress got three days in jail. Brown was convicted of fleeing from the police and assaulting two safety officers by attempting to run them over—he said he was driving around a roadblock to get away from a frightening situation.

Brown's stiff sentence fed a faith among many of his fans that his conviction amounted to a textbook case of Driving While Black. Some even called him a political prisoner. Others noted how he had avoided jail time for beating his wife and driving while high on PCP numerous times before. "We wondered what took them so long, if you want to know the truth," said guitarist Ron Laster.

At the South Carolina facility, it must have frustrated him to be surrounded by a large number of young men with little or no interest in who he was. On the outside he couldn't grab a bite at TBonz in Augusta without locals and older folks coming up and saying hello, pressing a paper napkin in his hand to sign. Now he was the old dude with the crazy hair who moved through the halls like a ghost ship.

He wanted to be left alone. In April 1989, a Columbia, South Carolina, judge trying to impress friends had the singer sprung from prison for a few hours so he could sign autographs in the judge's chamber. Three months later, the world-famous marching band from the historically black school Florida A&M University received an unprecedented honor. They were selected to be the sole representative of the United States at a celebration in Paris of the Bicentennial of the French Revolution. The only music they played as they marched down the Champs-Elysées and stood before the Arc de Triomphe? The works of James Brown.

That's where he was in 1989: a global symbol of American art; a trophy to be displayed by a South Carolina judge.

A "Free James Brown Movement" was hatched, publicized on MTV and in the music press. DJs distributed buttons, and rappers spoke out against his arrest. Mike Tyson was photographed wearing a "Free James Brown" T-shirt. Maceo Parker cut a song together with Bobby Byrd and Bootsy titled "Let 'Em Out."

Assigned to work in the kitchen, Brown cooked breakfast for several hundred inmates at a minimum security facility. That changed after $48,000 in cashier's checks was found in his room. In punishment, he was moved to a minimum-maximum security prison in Columbia. The IRS impounded the checks, along with seven hundred dollars in cash.

Being alone was okay, he told people, they need not feel sorry for him. When Herb Kent, a DJ from Chicago, visited, Brown flashed him a gold card, explaining that with it he could get the president on the telephone. He was lucky, was the message. Not like the rest of the guys here.

At other times, he looked at his situation with mellow rumination, a slow shake of the head for what had been done to him. "They went way back with this, before civil rights, before Martin Luther King," he told Bruce Tucker.

"To your childhood?" Tucker asked.

"I think so," Brown answered. "I think so."

Alfie grieved, lamenting her situation and his. She wrote to him in jail, working on him to sever his ties with his staff, guys like Danny Ray and costume chief Gertrude Sanders, folks who had been with Brown for decades.

Love's a funny thing. Just months before his incarceration, Adrienne had given the *National Enquirer* photographs of her bruises. Now she was calling the FBI, alleging her husband's arrest was a racially motivated frame-up.

She visited him regularly, as did Sharpton. Little Richard called, but, according to Sharpton, not one artist who professed the influence of James Brown came to see him in prison.

Band members and everybody else mostly stayed away. "Where are his friends?" asked Bobby Byrd. "They're as far away as they can get."

Among the few who did visit: Republican strategist Lee Atwater. Raised in Aiken, South Carolina, just across the Savannah from Augusta, Atwater was an essential asset of the Republican party. As a youth, he trick-or-treated at a neighbor's house and made a connection that would last his whole life. The neighbor was South Carolina Senator Strom Thurmond (he passed out Snickers bars). Atwater became a protégé of Thurmond, a roguish dirty trickster and an architect of the "Southern Strategy," which vilified African Americans in order to scare white voters into the Republican fold.

Atwater explained the Southern Strategy in a 1981 interview, sketching the history of an idea he inherited but made his own. "You start out in 1954 by saying 'Nigger, nigger, nigger.' By 1968 you can't say 'nigger'–that hurts you. Backfires. So you say stuff like 'forced busing,' 'states' rights,' and all that stuff. You're getting so abstract now [that] you're talking about cutting taxes, and all these things you're talking about are totally economic things and a by-product of them is [that] blacks get hurt worse than whites. And subconsciously maybe that is part of it. I'm not saying that. But I'm saying that if it is getting that abstract, and that coded, that we are doing away with the racial problem one way or the other. You follow me–because obviously sitting around saying 'we want to cut this' is much more abstract than even the busing thing *and* a hell of a lot more abstract than 'Nigger, nigger.'"

A fan since he first heard the captivating squall of "Please, Please, Please," Atwater was a rhythm and blues lover and a James Brown fanatic. In sixth grade, he sat in a segregated balcony to watch Brown perform, using binoculars to study the guitar parts. In no time Atwater would become a quality Brown imitator on the South Carolina beach and frat circuit, in a series of earnest white R&B bands.

Like Brown, Atwater looked at the South not as it might one day be but as it was–and he found a way to exploit the *wasness* of his state all the way to the capital. Atwater appreciated Brown's art and empathized with his troubles. He may even have used his political ties to protect Brown in this period. The singer appreciated his patronage. When Atwater collapsed while giving a speech in 1990 and was diagnosed with a brain tumor, Brown sent him a telegram: "Hang in there my wife and I are pulling for you there is no one greater than God he'll give you peace." When the presidential aide died in 1991, Brown attended his funeral.

He was even better acquainted with Atwater's mentor, Strom Thurmond. Brown once said, in a letter to Senator Phil Gramm, that his father had worked for the former governor and then senator from South Carolina, and Brown said of Thurmond that "He knew my father's father and knew me before I knew myself." The redheaded segregationist was in the audience when Brown was granted a furlough to perform two free shows in early 1991 for army troops at Fort Jackson, South Carolina. He opened with "I've Got You (I Feel Good)" and finished with "Living in America," and according to *Jet*, "He told the soldiers he was proud of them and proud to be in America." Backstage at Fort Jackson, Brown and his wife were warmly greeted by Thurmond and military brass.

After serving two years and two months, he had his first parole board hearing early in 1991. Addressing the South Carolina panel, Brown's attorney, Buddy Dallas, introduced him to the board by announcing, "It is my distinct pleasure to introduce you to James Brown; a man that is known locally, nationally, and internationally." The inmate and his representatives spoke to the state panel, and in twenty minutes Brown was paroled, on February 27, 1991.

"I think your future, your entire future, your career, is going to overshadow your past tremendously," enthused the parole board chairman.

"We'll do more bonding now," Alfie told *Jet*, "and I'm gonna just eat his face."

Upon his release Brown held a press conference and then headed to Washington to thank a few people who had helped him. He visited the Congressional Black Caucus, whose members had signed a petition calling for his freedom. "Then he told Sharpton, "I gotta visit Senator Thurmond."

"Why you gotta do that?" the reverend asked.

"Can't do all black. He's a friend of mine."

So they went to see the senator—Sharpton, Brown, and Adrienne, and the politician insisted they take pictures of the party standing behind his desk.

Both were defined by Georgialina, which was part of what made them friends. But their ties were tactical, too. "James had been beaten by these crackers; he had made money with these crackers. He had all kinds of relations with these crackers," said Leeds. "And he had enough confidence in himself to pick out the good ones from the bad ones and play them like a violin. He knew he was a commodity to these guys."

That month a summer tour was announced. Polydor released *Star Time*, a four-CD, seventy-one-track compilation spanning his entire career. It was the most comprehensive overview of his vast body of work available. Along with a wave of enthusiasm tied to his parole, and a series of vigorous performances, *Star Time* went a long way to presenting Brown's art to many who might only have known him from recent news reports.

In the weeks and months after his release, Brown must have said "I feel good" more times than in all the years before. The song became his gleaming show-business smile, his mask. By now he was an icon and a curio, a figure Americans had grown up with and now smiled over. Late-night comics made fun of the idea of him as a "political prisoner." Eddie Murphy played Brown as a grunting funky papa with a hot tub. A Kenneth Cole billboard on view around the country showed a photograph of the singer beside a picture of a Cole shoe: "Two great things with sole under lock and key," read a caption. (Those Northerners: The Southern racists thought that sort of thing was beneath them.) He had reached an apogee of American show business: He had become larger than life, and less than real.

Brown celebrated his release with a June 10 pay-per-view concert, promoted by boxing impresario Butch Lewis, and featuring MC Hammer, Kool Moe Dee, En Vogue, and others testifying to Brown's influence. "Every star you could think of was in the audience," said Sharpton. The reverend was in the dressing room, fielding notes passed up from those arriving in limousines. This star wanted to come back and see him: Brown shook his head no. Another, and another: no, no, no. Finally, Brown said, "Reverend, tell them I'll see whoever came to see me in jail."

Dan Aykroyd was getting ready to do a hellzapoppin' intro when Brown sent Sharpton to retrieve one of the producers of the show. He asked the producer if there was a room off the side of the stage, and a camera, so that the reverend, he, and his family could be seen on the broadcast praying to God in gratitude for his freedom. The band was starting to play Brown's first song; "No time for that now," said the producer.

"Do you know how to sing 'Get on the Good Foot'?" Brown asked.

The producer looked baffled.

"Do you know how to sing 'Get on the Good Foot'? Because you're gonna sing it tonight unless you let this man lead us in prayer."

He got his wish. He and Alfie prayed. Then Brown put on a leather coat and took the stage. All the way back.

On the road that summer, many band members said Brown was more relaxed and fun to be around than he had been in a long time. He was moving better and looked healthier. But he was still married to Adrienne, and the two of them were battling for control, for revenge. They were using PCP again, too, which made it all burn hotter.

One night, after they'd brawled and Brown had thrown her out, Fred Daviss was sent to make sure Alfie found a place to stay that night, somewhere that wasn't Beech Island. He found her walking by the roadside, and as he slowed down and opened his car door, she muttered to him through clenched teeth: "I'm gonna get back in that house. And when I do–I'm gonna bring that nigger to his knees."

Somebody who worked in Brown's kitchen told Daviss that Adrienne was secretly putting PCP in his coffee ice cream and his cream corn. "He loved cream corn. And I do believe Alfie did it."

She went in for liposuction in a Beverly Hills clinic early in 1996. The eight-hour procedure exhausted her, and she spent the following two days at home recovering, helped by prescriptions of Demerol, Valium, Vicodin, and morphine. She became unconscious, and paramedics took her to a Century City hospital, where she was declared dead. A coroner's report indicated that a heart condition, as well as the PCP found in her system, contributed to her death. Adrienne Brown was forty-five. "She probably knew him better than any women he was ever with," said Daviss.

Little Richard, Dan Aykroyd, and Casey Kasem attended her funeral. Part of the service was in Hebrew, because Adrienne was Jewish. A message from Brown appeared in the funeral program: "Dear Adrienne, Honey my life will never be the same, wait for me. I want to be the first guest on your TV show in heaven. Yours always, James."

After the service, Brown, Sharpton, and others went out to eat. "Ten minutes in, he was smiling and holding court with the gang," said Leeds. "Brown was through with the morbidity of the situation and it was time to move on. Those of us who knew him knew he was hurting badly, but this was a kid who was forced at elementary school age if not kindergarten age to learn how to compartmentalize pain. His very survival as a child depended on it. He had a place to put that pain."

In Washington, Strom Thurmond had a tribute to Alfie inserted into the congressional record.

Two years later, up all night smoking angel dust and thinking about his dead wife, Brown walked onto his front lawn in his underwear. He fired a .22 caliber semiautomatic handgun and a .30 caliber rifle in the general direction of heaven.

His daughter Deanna called the police, and they had him committed to a facility for observation. Brown put out a press release saying the hospitalization was due to an addiction to painkillers, while his lawyer Buddy Dallas spun it that he was simply tired from too much touring. "He's been on the road for six years and he's just exhausted," declared Dallas. "He is keeping the faith and he'll be back strong."

Journalist Barney Hoskyns caught up with him, asking if it was hard to reach out for help. Brown took it as a hypothetical question. "Well, you reach out for help if you need it. If I needed it, I'd probably reach out for it. I can't fight rhetoric, you know what I'm sayin'?"

The writer tried again, and Brown got mad, saying, "When you see me, look in my eyes and look at the way I act. . . . I'm sixty-five years old and I can do all my dances. I can even do the splits if I want. Most people *twenty-five* years old can't do it. I'm in good shape, and anything that I do, drugs will not allow you to do it, so that'll let you know right away whether I use drugs or not."

Meanwhile, the IRS still wanted $9 million. On this matter, he was willing to reach out for help to at least one person: the president of the United States.

The news media was giving major play to Bill Clinton visiting Africa, where he had expressed official regret for America's history of slavery. Whatever else he saw in the news, in March 1998, Brown saw an opening. He wrote the man at the top.

"I want to say congratulations to you. Congratulations . . . Congratulations. I see Dr. Martin Luther King's story is brought back. It's going to be an uproar all the time," Brown declares of Clinton's statement. The letter goes on for pages, about the teaching of music in school and the idiocy of teaching opera, about captured animals and the state of black America. He praises Clinton, mentions he's been in Little Rock before, and that he had performed for the president. Slowly, he comes around to the subject at hand: Now that Clinton had acknowledged America's past, he should enlarge on his statement at home, and establish a form of reparations to African Americans. Brown provides just the sort of thing he has in mind: Clinton could declare that African Americans did not have to pay taxes. As he reminds the president, "taxation without representation" is against the law.

It's a stunning tour de force, one more elliptical, devastating groove. There is no record that Clinton ever responded.

The president was unable to help, so Brown turned to Wall Street for assistance. A young investment banker named David Pullman had a sexy idea: to create bonds that were securitized by a musician's future royalties. In 1997, David Bowie became Pullman's big catch, and "Bowie Bonds" were all the rage. Two years later, Brown came knocking. He received $30 million up front in the form of a loan (untaxable earnings). The financial institution investing in his future earnings got a bond that presumably reaped more than old-fashioned bonds.

Jeff Allen, a booking agent working with the singer, accompanied him when he signed the Pullman deal. Allen said Brown asked a startled Pullman at the meeting if he would like to try PCP. "You ever smoke gorilla?" Brown asked. That was what he called angel dust: gorilla, pronounced go-rilla. "The president smokes gorilla. Everybody should smoke gorilla." He signed the contract. After the meeting, Brown jumped into a white limousine with Allen and had himself a celebratory smoke.

Pullman had provided him with a sudden sense of financial stability that he had never in his life known before. He was diagnosed with diabetes. Then, late in 1999, Brown had successful surgery on his prostate.

All the while, he remained addicted to a substance that wears down men half his age. Two female employees took him to court, one claiming sexual harassment and wrongful termination and the other rape (only the wrongful termination claim prevailed). In 2002, his daughters Deanna and Yamma sued him over record royalties. He had put their names on songs when they were children, doing it perhaps to hide money from the IRS. Still, their names were on the songs, and they insisted on getting their due.

He was not in jail, but where was he?

Appearing before the South Carolina Department of Probation, Parole and Pardon Services in May 2003, Brown was granted a pardon for the crimes dating to the 1988 car chase and for a 1998 drug charge. After the decision was announced, from his seat he sang "God Bless America."

"I'm getting very tired, and I'd love to quit yesterday. I've got diabetes, I've almost broken my feet, did something to my tendons, hurt all in my back–but I work. I don't tell [fans] how bad it is. I smile when I see them," he said. Talking to a reporter about his upbringing, Brown was asked: How much did his childhood shape him?

"If I had been free, totally free, I wouldn't have been this," he answered.

Chapter Twenty-four

THE DANCER

James Brown got his start when he was waist-high and egging on soldiers, daring them to throw coins while he did buck and wing steps. "I started dancing as a necessity back in 1941. I was living in Augusta, Georgia," he once said. There was a modest concrete-and-brick bridge over the third level of the Augusta canal, next to the gasworks. That's where he got maybe the biggest idea of his life. There were plenty of soldiers lingering, not far from the train depot. He danced, and seeing all the nickels, dimes, and quarters tossed at his feet made his mind up for him: "I realized dancing was gonna be a way of life for me."

In a flash there by the bridge, dancing was no longer a mere necessity. Move your body the right way and people threw the most coins at you, and what made it the right way was moving to an appreciated rhythm—sung or clapped as you danced, or one you carried in your head. You figured out that the more ways you punctuated the rhythm and played with it, the more it delighted the faces surrounding you. And the more they spent. From an early age—he would have been eight in 1941–Brown was teaching himself that rhythm meant attention; it meant lulling hostile adults into a reverie, bringing them over to your side. It meant nourishment, in every sense of the word. Born dead: Now came rebirth.

The buck dance was done flat-footed and low to the ground. So much of Brown's dance was performed with his feet. He was a shoeshine, a boxer who studied at the feet of Beau Jack who danced across the ring, a man who tended to hold his upper body in check–not frozen, but coolly reserved, letting a little sway or shoulder dip telegraph a wealth of insinuation. He lived down low.

The men who watched him were the same ones he directed to Aunt Honey's for the sex and the bootleg whiskey. He was an escort to the illicit; obvious enough in terms of the brothel, but to what unauthorized place was he escorting folks when he danced on the banks of the Third Canal? To a place more captivating and powerful than Aunt Honey's pussy and scrap iron. Leading them there on the banks–the bamboozled so foolishly certain that they were directing *him*–Brown must have felt enormous, connected to something outside himself, a force that made him feel more powerful than anything did the rest of the day.

So, he watched the older boys and copied some of their steps. Watched the soldiers, too. Funny thing is, when people are giving you their charity, their patronage, they believe themselves free to inspect and scrutinize you. The little roughneck was the object, they were the actors. But Brown was the most watchful of all: He studied and learned what made the money rain, what choked it off. He was good at it, he could *feel* it, sense when hands were going into pockets even before the GIs knew what they were reaching for. He learned another step.

James Brown had many guises, many names: Crip, Music Box, the Hardest Working Man in Show Business, Mr. Please Please Please, Butane James, Soul Brother Number One, Skates, the Godfather of Soul–Johnny Carson once introduced him as "The Godfather of Soil." He was His Own Bad Self, the Sex Machine, Black Elvis, the Minister of New New Super Heavy Funk, the Original Disco Man, Universal James. But before any of them, he was, simply, a dancer, doing the James Brown.

You couldn't tell him anything, not directly. But if he heard you say it to somebody else, or if he could *watch* you do it, then he learned the thing better than you knew it yourself. He watched the showmen on the stage at the Lenox. He watched the minstrel hoofers get off the train and set up a cigar box in front of the Douglass Theatre in Macon. He learned another step.

It is 1959, and the band is getting louder as they work their way through the first part of the show. J. C. Davis's crew is playing arrangements of songs by Thin Man Watts and Bill Doggett, stomping shuffle blues with the horns scrapping for attention, everybody eyeing the dancers on the floor. If the dancers like it, they play it some more. The Davis band was establishing that this was no sit-down concert, and everything that happened for the rest of the night was meant to keep you moving. Moving with the audience was Brown, in the guise of reveler. As they made their way through the South–where they mostly played, and all the best dances came from–Brown made mental note of the steps they were doing in one town that they weren't doing in the last one. When he finally jumped on stage, he would show how well he'd assumed the local moves, putting on a proud demonstration and bonding with the crowd.

James Brown was a Johnny Appleseed of dance. "He was taking the steps right out of the audience, going town to town," said Davis. "By going around that circuit every six months or a year, we would take stuff from one city to the next–people in Washington didn't know what a mashed potato was and we were doing it for them, when maybe *we* didn't know it six months before that. It would kill the house is why."

The steps inspired the music–you wanted to inspire the people on the floor so you played music meant to feed the flux. Contrarily, when you got back to the hotel room you might knock out a song meant to coin the motion you'd observed in the house just an hour before. A song inspired by an action, a way to put your little thing over on what they did. But first came the dance.

"The mashed potato was popular in Florida, that's where it was.

But like in Washington they might be doing the horse, or the watusi, a different dance. So we'd learn how to do the watusi, the watermelon man, the horse, the mashed potato, the chicken scratch, and actually his dancing became a part of the horse, the chicken scratch, the watermelon man," said Davis. "When you go from town to town doing those things every day, what we learn in Washington is brand-new to the people in Miami, and what we took to New Jersey or New York is brand-new, different, to them there. You do it from day to day and you are perfecting it. Mix 'em all together and now we're doing some of everybody's dance together."

It is 1959, and late at night en route to the next show, a red light pulls the bus over and everybody gets out along the deserted highway. One of the sheriffs asks who's in charge, and Brown steps forward to be asked, just who does he think he is and what does he think he is doing in Yazoo City? Brown says he's a showman, he works in front of these musicians every night. They were just playing at the Pythian Hall and are heading now to Jackson.

"Is that a fact? You a hambone? Let's see what you can do." Right there over the gravel the sheriffs have him working, keeping it simple with a flat-footed shuffle suited for the grit beneath him. They provide their own rhythm on the oiled road, five pistol cracks sending sparks that light up Brown's face. It's the kind of intimate performance he used to give at the Augusta canal. These two sheriffs, though, they didn't throw any money. They start out looking excited, and end with bored expressions and telling everybody to get the hell in the bus and get on down the road.

Dancing was a declaration of who he was. He went from town to town.

The five minutes are surrealism's finest hour. A skinny young man staggers out onto a stage like a spasmodic robot–a robot with a sports bag on his head. He falls, twitching, then rolls around trying to pull the satchel off his head, all the while moving to a James Brown song. He gets up, frees himself, and ... possibly ... is ... dancing or wrenching his body in and out of tempo. Or something. One minute he is Don Knotts, and the next, one of the greatest street dancers you've ever seen. He dives on his belly across the floor, sliding completely out of view as the fixed camera shows nothing but white floor for a long time. When we find him again he's running around the stage, almost knocking a dancer off his stand, then striking a bizarre GQ pose, all the while throwing crazy-cool moves in every direction.

In 1976, Brown produced, directed, and hosted *Future Shock*, a dance show shot in Atlanta, airing on a UHF TV station owned by the young Ted Turner. It was Brown's idea, but the stars of *Future Shock* are the amazing roster of dancers, culled from Atlanta-area colleges, high schools, and parties, that perform in an astonishing spectrum of styles.

Never mind that: Let's get back to our spastic robot. Brown calls him "Bojangles," and awards him first prize in the contest that Bojangles just destroyed. The award inspires him to throw himself on the floor again, wriggle over and kiss Brown's foot, then pop up, do splits, jump up, and throw out a whole lost language of hand signals. The scene is as unfathomable as any five minutes of *Un Chien Andalou* or a film by David Lynch. *Future Shock* was the best dance show on TV, ever. It ruled because though Brown was constantly a presence, he had the wisdom to pull back and give it up to the dancers. He lets the astonishing mix of popping, locking, early break dancing, and vintage disco carry the program. He calls the shots, and dance is in all of them.

Brown's idea was to syndicate *Future Shock* to American and then African markets; he saw it as a show where black people could be themselves, instead of performing for white TV audiences. He saw it as building on *Soul Train*, which it sort of did, in the way that John Wilkes Booth built on Abraham Lincoln. *Future Shock* was a short-lived, riotous, no-retake spectacle.

The program's dancers don't ride the beat, they express a new rhythm on top of the one we hear. "When you are dancing against the grain, it makes it more dynamic. But if you float, then you're not doing anything," Brown once said. Looking at the old clips of *Future Shock* floating around the Internet is like peering through a bathysphere window at an unseen world at play. Who are these amazing dancers, and what are they doing today? Pumping gas? Hydroponic gardening on Eurydome? Anything is possible.

Everything starts with the dancer. The music came out of him.

Toni Basil was a dancer and choreographer on *The T.A.M.I. Show*, the movie that let America see Brown move. "Nowadays, we have to choreograph to a record or a song," said Basil. She means professional choreographers get handed a piece of music and are paid to design a routine around it. "Whereas, what he did is what Astaire and all the old stars did. They created a dance, with a drummer and a pianist, and then they scored it musically." The dance was what the music was *about*.

Brown had a capacity for expressing different rhythms through his form. "Every part of his body had a beat, had a rhythm going on–his feet, his head, his neck, his chest, his ass," said Lola Love, a dancer in the show. "And all those beats were different and were what made him funky."

He was not a virtuoso. What we respond to is not what he does, but what he promises. The man was a master at holding himself in reserve, and in making a display of his work–he is gesturing in everything he does, a gesture that needs us to complete it.

He is more than good enough, an embodiment of what Zora Neale Hurston called "dynamic suggestion," a quality she considered the essence of black dance. However explosively or fiercely he moved, Brown telegraphs that there's more we *don't* get to see–his actions exert maximum impact with a minimum of exertion (coolness), a withholding that compels the viewer to follow the gesture through in the imagination. His dance wasn't supposed to be appreciated with detachment. It was meant to pull you over to where he was, to engage you in the act. You can't sit still.

Asked to demonstrate the boogaloo by a TV show host, Brown danced around a Hollywood soundstage in a way that looked exactly like a boxer throwing punches and owning the ring. To Brown, dancing was competition–"Can *you* jerk? Watch *me* work/ Can *you* do the slide? Then watch *me* glide . . ." His idea of dancing against the grain a way of imposing himself on the rhythm–a way of fighting his way into the flow, of fighting his way into existence. "Rhythm is everything in boxing," said Sugar Ray Robinson, who liked to train to Brown's music. "Every move you make starts with your heart, and that's in rhythm or you're in trouble."

Dancer . . . drummer . . . fighter. Here is the spirit of the Stono Rebellion, where musicians, dancers, and warriors marched off the South Carolina plantation.

Chapter Twenty-five

HIT IT AND QUIT IT

omi Rae Hynie was working the Vegas lounges in 1998, throwing her long hair around, singing a tribute to Janis Joplin in the "Dead Legends Live Revue." When they met, after one of her shows, here is what Brown saw: a stunning redhead, shapely, her face almost as carefully put together as his. He invited her to join his show. They soon were a couple, and young James II was six months old when in 2001, the two were married at Beech Island. He was sixty-eight, she was thirty-two. At their wedding reception, the newlyweds teamed up to sing Brook Benton and Dinah Washington's "Baby (You've Got What It Takes)." As the couple danced, one of his daughters was heard to say of her new stepmother: "I hate her. I hate her. I hate her." Everyone was still getting to know one another.

They lived together at Beech Island. She saw him in a complicated light: both as employer and husband, mentor and lover. "He had no one to take care of him. Nobody wanted to be around him because he was so ornery, but I loved him and understood him and devoted myself to him," she said. "The things he could teach me I could never learn on my own. At first I felt it could benefit me so much if I could just listen—and then I ended up falling in love with him."

Tomi Rae was capable of theatricality herself, and her presence was greeted with suspicion by some of those around Brown. With difficulty she sought to fit into the entourage and establish a home life. She made him dinner and massaged his legs five times a day with oil, to abate the pain of his diabetes. "I cooked liver and onions for him, that was what he craved. And he liked collard and turnip greens and sweet potato pie and ice cream, but with the diabetes, I had to start making him sugar-free pies. And every Sunday we went to visit his mother in Bamberg and I would brush her hair. Then we would go to church and after that to the best chicken place in the South, this little convenience place called Quick Stop that served catfish and chicken. Every Sunday we looked forward to that. We'd drive out in a limousine to his church and then we'd go out for chicken."

At Beech Island he stayed up watching Westerns and the Playboy Channel, or sitting out back of the house at night, where he could fire off a shotgun and not bother anybody. Popping Viagra, Brown had no problem gathering women to keep up all night and the next day. He did not want to be alone.

"What did he do at home?" declared Gloria Daniel, a mistress since 1968. "*Nothing.* Fuck fuck fuck fuck fuck fuck. He operated the remote–only cowboys. And you ate what he wanted you to eat."

The PCP use did not slacken. Always paranoid, Brown became intensely so in his last years. "If we passed some trees while traveling in the car, he'd say 'See those trees? Watch them move, that's the government watching me,'" said Daniel. He told interviewers that the TV was watching him, and that government satellites monitored his thoughts. For that matter, Tomi Rae believes that unnamed people put cameras in the Beech Island estate and spied on her and her husband.

In older times, Brown called himself Santa Claus, a bringer of joy to the masses. Now he was identifying intensely with Moses, telling visitors that God spoke to him, and that he was chosen to lead the people of the world.

The drug was isolating out aspects of his character and making them immense and wrenching. According to Tomi Rae, he used to sit on his bed and talk about being a slave all his life. Then he would weep that he would never escape it.

When the writer of a book on Tiger Woods asked Brown what advice he would give the golfer, the singer gave him more than he expected. "Get him to understand how vicious this world is," Brown advised. "Everything in this world disappears and vacates."

He was also turning increasingly spiritual, reading the Bible at home, quoting scripture, and discussing it with a reverend in Augusta. His faith, said Buddy Dallas, "was not feigned, it was not lip service. Mr. Brown was a sincere, deep believer in God the father. He failed to have an understanding of the trinity, because, as Mr. Brown would often say, 'I got to go to the head man, Mr. Dallas. The son is *not* the head man. The student can never be greater than the teacher.' That's just the way he was."

But while students he could at least acknowledge, Brown recognized exceedingly few peers on the scene. When one of the rare voices that could give him pause asked Brown to sing with him in 2002, it must have seemed like an irresistible opportunity. Luciano Pavarotti was sixty-seven, two years younger than Brown. The tenor had lost both his parents earlier that year, so when it was time to produce his annual Pavarotti & Friends summer concert in his hometown of Modena, perhaps the chance to sing for friends and family was a special balm.

Sting, Lou Reed, and the classical crossover musician Andrea Bocelli were all on the bill, performing duets with their host. For his song with Pavarotti, Brown selected "Man's World." The moment was rich, the music huge. A large orchestra provided backing, singers interpolating "Ave Maria" with the pop song.

The day of the concert, Brown was told that the arrangement of the song for the massed strings and voices was based on the hit version from three and a half decades before. With age, however, Brown's vocal range had moved down a bit, and he'd moved his arrangement down a half step to keep it easy to sing. The festival planners played their arrangement for Brown, and he said, "That's fantastic, but we got a whole new arrangement now that's really hip," and proceeded to insist the orchestra use his version, as if new music could be written up on the spot. It was about to become a confrontation, but Brown's young music director, guitar player Keith Jenkins, very gently suggested to Brown that it would be a lot easier for the band to adapt to the orchestra than the other way around.

In the duet, Pavarotti does more than simply sing the original words, he presents meditative new verses, sung in Italian, suggesting that a man who reaches for power all his life will ultimately be lost. Sitting on a stool, Pavarotti looks out with sorrowful eyes that seem to burn through the thousands before him. The stars' voices don't mesh, nor are they supposed to. These are grand pillars side by side holding up the sky. The song's over-the-top mannishness is more over than ever here, recast by old guys who have seen too much to treat it as a boast. Now, it's a tribute to the dead.

"The horns weren't playing on that one, we stepped off the stage," said Hollie Farris. "I stood out in front and I actually cried. Man, what he sang, the level that Pavarotti pushed him to. . . . They went to a whole other level."

Backstage, Brown ran into Lou Reed, who he had met years before. Treating Reed as a fellow veteran, Brown said pointedly, "You know, Lou . . ." The New York rocker responded, "Yes, Mr. Brown?"

"Well, Lou, you know what the difference is?"

Interested and a bit baffled, Reed said, "No, I don't, Mr. Brown, what is the difference?"

"The difference is, now we know why we're doing what we're doing."

The man was seventy. A crew of Southern California digital effects geniuses watched him dance in their studio, scanned and animated him, using 3-D modeling and motion capture technology to synthesize his mobile essence for a museum installation. When finished, his image would jump off a billboard at the Experience Music Project in Seattle and teach kids the meaning of funk.

A James Brown doll was new on the market. It maniacally shook and shouted "I Feel Good" over and over. His cape and a crown were preserved in the Hard Rock Cafe in Las Vegas. As a personality, Brown was larger than life, a force that deserved preservation. As an entertainer, he had been handed that most horrible of designations: *legacy act.* A Jell-O salad from olden times, which it was the duty of every person at the party to sample. The specific irony for Brown was that he could never coast and feel the love the way a legacy act is supposed to. He was still convinced that he had to win people over with an exhibition that exhausted him. He could see no laurels to rest on.

The tour continued, a looped groove unto itself. He did it because it was what he did. He'd done this most of his life, and if he stopped now his life would, too. "He was a very lonely person," said Emma Austin, who had grown up in the Terry. "And, in his loneliness, there was only one thing that relieved him. And that was, when he got on stage before a big crowd."

Asked when he was going to stop, Brown was flatly defiant: "I'm gonna stop when George Burns comes back and be born again. I'm gonna stop when Bob Hope starts buck-dancin'. I'm gonna stop when Sinatra bring the Rat Pack back, and all of them gone. I'm not gonna stop."

The man was seventy, and people wanted to pay tribute. At the Black Entertainment Television awards in 2003, Brown was presented a lifetime achievement prize. Just as he was wrapping up "Sex Machine," a figure came over to drape the cape on him as he expectantly bent over, and when Brown looked up he saw Michael Jackson as a surprise guest-star valet. He smiled broadly and the two danced a bit. Jackson, the King of Pop, shimmying on the tips of his toes across the stage; Brown—when was the last time he needed a new nickname?–earthbound by comparison. If it had stopped there the caption would have read: "Young icon upstages old guy on his special day." But Brown signaled to Danny Ray, who took Brown's cape as Brown ordered, "Put it on him!" and now Michael had the cape. The meaning of the moment changed; it became Brown benevolently bestowing his gift onto a kid. Now *he* owned the moment.

Though by that time Jackson had developed his own innate style, to get there, he had studied and absorbed Brown's moves: the splits, the one-legged glide, the essence of the moonwalk. In a 1970 interview, Jackson described Brown taking him aside and demonstrating tricks with the microphone. At the Jackson 5's audition for Motown Records, the first song they did was Brown's "I Got the Feelin'," and young Michael performed his very best tribute for the talent scouts.

They knew each other well, and in later days, when Jackson was down or in trouble, he would call Brown in search of advice or reassurance. For all that, they were superstars, competitive and alone, and after Jackson was an adult, the two hovered around each other with anxious unease. Fred Wesley: "I saw them together one time, it was the most amazing thing you ever saw. Michael was looking at James as if he was looking at God, and James was talking fast 'cause he was nervous because Michael Jackson was in the room with him. I couldn't believe it! I thought, here are two of the greatest entertainers in the world and they affect each other this way. But I think insecurity is inherent in all stars . . ."

A full-page ad appeared in *Variety* in June 2003, announcing that, "Due to Mr. James Brown and Mrs. Tomi Rae Brown's heavy demanding tour schedule, they have decided to go their separate ways. There are no hard feelings . . ." One thing that made it strange was that the couple was touring together, so conflicting work schedules shouldn't have been a problem.

Whatever the matter, they were together again by the end of the year when Brown received a Kennedy Center Award in Washington, D.C. It was an auspicious evening: the fellow awardees (Carol Burnett, Loretta Lynn, Mike Nichols, and Itzhak Perlman) and dignitaries working their way through a ceremonial Washington reception line. When Brown made his way to General Colin Powell, the two slapped palms.

A month after that career-capping moment, another. James and Tomi Rae were arguing in the bedroom. There was a struggle and she called the police. She had scratches and bruises on her right arm and hip and told officers that he had threatened to hit her with an iron chair. There was a scuffle with the police, in which Brown's green terrycloth robe was ripped. The mug shot that the police passed out to the public that January 2004 day showed a disoriented-looking man with thickly matted hair, unshaven, the pallor of exhaustion across his face. The image was picked up by countless newspapers and magazines around the world.

Every day of his life since 1956, before Brown stepped out of his house, he asked himself a single question: Do I look like someone people would pay money to see? His hair had been so lovingly tended over the years, soaked in relaxer, that he invited people to touch it, bragging that it felt "just like hospital cotton." When he stepped out his teeth gleamed, his face was imperial. He was expoobident. The infamous mug shot brought mocking laughter, as well as frank amazement that a seventy-year-old man was living the wild life. Eight days later, he and Tomi Rae were on the stage at B.B. King Blues Club & Grill in New York, and he serenaded her with "You Send Me."

Still a rigid disciplinarian, Brown kept his band, now called the Soul Generals, tight and alert. When you did something he didn't like, his judgment was swift. "Sometimes for punishment he would make you sit on the side of the stage in full uniform. He'd tell you to just sit there and the whole audience would know," said Tomi Rae. "Then he'd say, 'You learned your lesson?' And we would say we had."

Musical director for the band was Keith Jenkins, a redheaded

Georgian whose feet were solidly on the ground. "My attitude was, we were the last James Brown band, so we ought to be the most comprehensive," said Jenkins. "We're probably not going to have any hits of our own, not going to be known for ourselves, so we ought to be the most thorough." Jenkins and the band learned dozens and dozens of less-played Brown tunes, and sought to get them back into the show. Brown would listen to them play, but if this was tribute he wasn't much feeling it.

He would bark, "What are you playing on such and such a number?" and Jenkins would offer a guitar part. "Naw," Brown would say dismissively.

"I'm playing the way they cut it, Mr. Brown."

"Well they *cut* it wrong."

One day Brown came in as they were rehearsing "Cold Sweat," and he had a lemon-sucking look on his face, yelling out, "What key are you playing it in?" "D, Mr. Brown," came the answer. "No wonder you playing it wrong," he said triumphantly. " 'Cold Sweat' is in G."

"But Mr. Brown, the record is in D."

"They cut it wrong!"

So the band spent a whole rehearsal re-voicing "Cold Sweat" into a new key. "Do you know how hard that is, especially for the horns?" said Jenkins. In the dressing room before a show they nervously held a meeting, because the transposed "Cold Sweat" still wasn't quite working. Throwing caution to the wind, they played it that night the old way, in the regular key.

Halfway through the song, a smiling Brown turned around and gave the band the thumbs-up, and kept right on singing.

He had just finished a two-week tour through Canada in fall of 2004 when a visit to the doctor revealed a growth on his prostate. He had surgery in December, which he declared a success. After three weeks at home, he was back on the road. At a press conference for the Live 8 concert in Edinburgh, Scotland, the following summer, Brown was asked how the cancer had affected him. He acted liked this was another hypothetical. "When I'm ripping and running, I don't have time to worry about the situation," he barked back. "A lot of people have the same thing and I pray for them." Next question.

The Augusta airport is not such a big place, and he was easy to spot whenever he passed through. A kid was waiting for his mother's plane to arrive when he saw Brown. He began talking to the singer, and then talking some more, and, when his mother finally walked off her plane, there was Brown, holding up a sign reading, "Welcome Home Mom." He told her Augusta had survived all right in her absence, but was even better now that she was home.

He acted like that in other places. But Augusta was a city full of such stories, and they can't all be attributed to public relations—Augusta *mattered* to him. He wanted the respect of his neighbors, and wanted to be loved when he went out in the streets. But it was complicated. Brown had a reputation around town for not paying his bills, for promising things he forgot to deliver. And there were plenty of folks who were never going to like him because he was the most famous black man in town.

In downtown Augusta, there is a statue commemorating Georgia's colonial founder, a confederate memorial, and the so-called "cursed pillar," an obelisk that legend claims was a whipping post for slaves. As Brown was turning seventy, mayor Bob Young tried to get the city to agree to a privately funded statue on Broad Street that would place Brown among these monuments. Young was a pop DJ in the mid-'60s, and had flown helicopters in Vietnam with "Mother Popcorn" stenciled on his helmet. Now he was arguing with segments of the citizenry about whether Brown was worthy of the honor.

The singer sat for a sculptor, and the piece had been sent down in Florida to be cast, when his mug shot got in all the papers. "I just about had a stroke. I thought, who's going to give money for a statue to somebody who just got arrested," remembered Young. He waited for Brown's case to work its way through court–Brown did not go to jail–before discussing a date to dedicate the statue. Meanwhile, he discovered that he needed $18,000 more to finish the work, and the mayor felt a need to raise it soon, before anything else bad happened.

Finally, in May 2005, three days after Brown's seventy-second birthday, Reverend Sharpton made a benediction not far from where Brown had shined shoes six decades before. After they unwrapped the statue, invited guests went around the corner to the Old Governor's Mansion for a reception. "We got out and walked together," remembered Sharpton. "He said, 'Reverend, I appreciate that you came.' I said, 'You *know* I was coming. Man, it's a huge debt they repaid.'

"'Yeah.'

"'I never thought they'd have a statue of you in Augusta–and facing a confederate marker!'"

He touched Sharpton on the arm. "And don't forget what I told you–I did it on my own terms," he said. "I never conformed to Augusta; they had to conform to me."

In his last years, Brown had a new management team, an actively involved group of people controlling his money and booking him on the road. In 2000, he formed a trust to protect his assets, and then, in signed documents, he turned over management of his assets to the group. The three trustees were attorney Buddy Dallas, business manager and accountant David Cannon, and Alford "Judge" Bradley, who first met Brown in 1990 as his designated legal "sponsor" upon release from South Carolina prison. The trust worked in tandem with "SuperFrank" Copsidas, a New York agent, and Joel Katz, Atlanta entertainment lawyer, when it came to booking shows and making certain business decisions.

In 2006, Brown had a remarkably draining schedule for a man

in his seventies. According to one account of his tour schedule posted on a fan site, the singer did eighty-one shows that year. He performed eighteen in July alone, did four dates in four days on a trip through Europe in November, and played Morocco, Tokyo, Estonia, Turkey, and all over the United States.

The longtime fans in the audience for the 2006 shows said they were as good as they'd seen in the past two decades. "I'm telling you, they were some of the best shows I have ever done with him," declared trumpeter Hollie Farris. "He was already sick at this point, we could tell, he was losing weight, but they were great shows. They would actually roll him out sometimes to the edge of the stage in a wheelchair, and he'd get up and do the show.

"One time we were in South America, maybe Argentina, he was so sick and had just flown in from the States and the doctor had to come to his hotel room to give him some shots and put a catheter up in him. He got up off the bed, took the catheter out and did the show, came back and put the catheter back in. They said he was really close to death, but then he did a full hour and a half show. It was incredible what that guy could do . . . but he was way sicker than we knew, obviously."

Some say the only one overworking Brown was himself. According to Dallas, nobody could make him do anything he didn't want to do. Roosevelt Johnson, a valet and assistant, said, "If he wanted a break they booked it that way. He wasn't gonna let anybody overwork him."

He had picked up a rattling, cavernous cough, one that did not go away. "The last tour was completely ridiculous," said Amy Christian, a singer with the show. "We were in Europe for twelve days and did ten shows in nine different countries—we went from Scotland to Moscow to London to Thessalonica to Helsinki to Latvia.

"It wasn't just bebopping around. The last show we were playing in Croatia, and staying in Prague, just traveling to it by private jet then flying back, it was hot in this club and it was packed, and I remember by the end Mr. Brown, he just handed me the mic and said, 'Here.' He was shaking his head, like, 'That's it, I'm done.'

"It was obvious. I'm half his age and *I* was exhausted. But my god, there was so much money to be made. And they just kept adding on more and more shows . . .'"

In Tbilisi, Georgia, in the former Soviet Union, they played an Olympic-style swimming facility. A twelve-foot-high stage had been built on the edge of the pool. The audience sat across the pool on the far side.

The band called this night "Georgia out of my mind." At sound check, Brown kept walking up to the edge of the stage and looking down at the water. He laughed that cackle, and would ask, "Who's going in? Who's going in with me?"

They played their show, a good one, finishing with "Sex Machine," and just as the song was reaching a climax, Brown took a running leap and jumped into the deep end of the pool. "Now, he's fully clothed, he's got his cowboy boots on, and he sunk like a rock. Some of us just about had a heart attack," remembered Keith Jenkins. Hollie Farris was the first to get to him. "He starts trying to swim, but he doesn't make it ten feet before he sinks," said Farris. "I leapt in and dragged him back to the edge of the pool–I almost made it back until . . . then *I* sank. But I tossed him off to somebody else and they got him and drug him out of the pool.

"He had a look of terror on his face. Two of the dancers, me and the saxophone player, five or six of us all jumped in. He was a sinking man, on his way down."

He came back onstage, soaking wet with his hair totally flat. The rhythm section was still playing, and Brown finished the song.

Everybody who jumped in got a two hundred dollar bonus.

Returning home in the latter part of November 2006, Brown had little time to relax. There was his annual Thanksgiving turkey giveaway to plan, and a toy giveaway in December. He had meetings with local promoters of a charity benefit.

As was standard procedure in his down time, Brown was going to doctors, getting things taken care of. "He was having some difficulties. He was just so sick," recalled Leon Austin. "He said, 'I'm tired. I'd like to retire, but I can't. I don't know if I'll ever be able to retire, because I'm making money, and people are needing me to work.' He said to me, 'My knees hurt . . . my knees hurt. I don't know how much more I'll be able to do.'" That was on the day before the toy giveaway, December 22.

Hair and teeth, the man said: If you had those you had it all. He had an appointment to see his dentist in Atlanta. But when he went, after the toy giveaway, the dentist took one look at the woozy, semi-coherent patient, and summoned a doctor. After a brief examination, Brown was sent to Emory Crawford Long Hospital in Atlanta, where by Saturday he had been diagnosed with congestive heart failure and pneumonia.

That night Sharpton called Brown from New York, not knowing he was in a hospital. He could instantly tell he was sick by the tone of his voice. Still, Brown wanted to talk and was in an expansive mood. He was all but berating Sharpton on the topic of profanity in rap music.

A little later, while Sharpton prepared for an imminent South African trip with Oprah Winfrey, an associate said, "Sorry about your pops, Reverend."

"What do you mean?" Sharpton asked. The aide explained he'd just seen on the CNN news ticker that Brown had been hospitalized.

Sharpton called the singer's daughter Deanna, and asked about the report. She knew nothing of it.

Later that night, after he'd fallen asleep, Sharpton's cell phone started ringing. He thought it was a family member wishing him a merry Christmas, and let it ring. But it kept up, and when he answered, it was Bobbit:

"He's gone. Your pops is gone."

"What?"

"James Brown is dead."

"What are you talking about?"

"Reverend, James Brown is dead."

Sharpton lay down like he was having a bad dream.

Somebody who had embodied invincibility, who he knew to be fixing to play New York City on New Year's Eve . . . it didn't make sense.

Calling Bobbit back, Sharpton asked him again: "What did you say?"

Tomi Rae had spoken to him on the phone that Saturday from the Southern California treatment center where she was fighting an addiction to painkillers. Bobbit calmly did what he'd been doing for decades: He managed the situation. He called band members, current and former wives, members of the trust. In New York, Sharpton got on a plane to Atlanta, and headed to the house of Brown's daughter Yamma, where ex-wife Deidre and Deanna were waiting. It was a sorrowful time, but the reverend brought up the need to plan a service.

One thing Sharpton grasped immediately: They had to take him to the Apollo. Deanna agreed, but she felt there needed to be a private service in Augusta, and somebody else spoke up that a public service was needed there, too, for all the years he had lived in Augusta and sung about the place. Thus, an improbable, exhausting plan was hatched for three services in three places to send off the Godfather of Soul.

The daughters, Sharpton, and longtime family friend and funeral director Charles Reid Jr. viewed the man, laid out peacefully. "He looked in a strange way like he had just done a show and hadn't done his hair yet," Sharpton recalled. Only now was it sinking in that the man was really gone.

The Apollo was contacted and arrangements made for an event on the stage he had dominated for decades. At some point, Reid called the reverend, saying the family had changed their mind about the choice of casket, wanting a solid gold one. Fine, he said, they had the money for it. But there was a problem, explained Reid— the 500-pound box was too heavy for the Learjet Sharpton had ready to fly to New York. Sharpton called Donald Trump, but his jet was being repaired. Attorney Willie E. Gary's jet was in Los Angeles, and Delta's last flight out of Atlanta had left for the evening.

Reid, however, was placid. The daughters had picked out three changes of clothes for him to take with Brown's body. The funeral director loaded the gold casket and the man into one of his vans, picked up Sharpton and two others, and started a drive from Georgia to Harlem. There really was no other way. James Brown had a commitment to keep.

"The feeling was, you can't miss a date at the Apollo," said Reid.

"The ride was, it was long. It wasn't tiring, though," he said. "We rode all night."

As they went up I-95, the signs and markers flashed before them. Sharpton read them off silently, many with special meaning. There was Greenville, South Carolina, where Brown produced Sharpton's single; and Raleigh, Charlottesville, and Baltimore, where Brown owned the radio station Sharpton had been on; Washington, D.C., and the Howard Theatre—each place its own sense memory. Night train.

"I had my hand on him most of the time," said Sharpton. "I didn't want to leave him."

They stopped for coffee and gas, and folks would recognize the reverend, but before they grasped what was going on, the men were back in the van, on the highway. They chatted in the car, and Reid started messing with the reverend, saying, "Shh, I think James has something he's trying to tell you." They joked about what Brown would say to them then if he could. But most of all, they slurped down coffee and looked at their watches.

When they approached New York City the party turned on the

radio and heard a newscaster say crowds were lining up all night at the Apollo Theater to say good-bye.

In November, Sharpton had taken on the case of Sean Bell, a black man from Queens who was shot fifty times by New York police officers. Calling the funeral home he'd used for Bell, Sharpton explained he needed a hearse and a horse-drawn carriage *now*. The carriage reflected the gravity of the event; the hearse was to get Brown to the carriage, because if Brown *could* have spoken to them he would have said no way was he going to be sent off in public from the back of this old drafty van.

The hearse drove to Sharpton's home on 145th Street, and the carriage, pulled by two plumed Percheron horses, steered the body down Malcolm X Boulevard to 125th Street. Friends, fans, and musicians all made their way past the singer on the Apollo stage. The service was held that evening, but with so many lined up to see Brown, the Apollo stayed open until eleven that night.

After the event was finished, they loaded Brown back into the van and Reid did a return drive all the way to Augusta, getting in around 11:30 the next morning. They brought him in, changed his clothes, and then headed to the service in North Augusta for family and immediate friends.

The private family service was at the tiny, red-brick Carpentersville Baptist Church, just across the border into South Carolina. Sharpton delivered the eulogy, telling the gathered, "When he started singing, we were sitting in the back of the bus. When he stopped singing, we were flying Learjets." Squabbling over money and decades of hurt feelings had spilled over in the days after Brown's heart stopped beating, with wives and children and trustees all taking shots at one another in the media. From the pulpit at Carpentersville Baptist, Sharpton made a statement ostensibly directed to all who were waging battles before the cameras, but he fixed his gaze on Tomi Rae as he spoke.

"If you really are all that you say you are, you don't place yourself in the story, the story puts you in your place," said Sharpton. "We don't want to hear your story or your mess; we're here because of James Brown."

The man everybody at Carpentersville was remembering had an old, unswerving practice: Wherever he was, before he went on the stage, he made a point of getting paid. His head peeking out of his dressing room, Brown would find whoever was designated the carrier of the cash, and ask, "You got my money?" Meaning, are we ready to proceed? At the end of the service, Sharpton slowly made his way down the center of the church, the casket pushed along behind him. Spotting Fred Daviss sitting in the back of the church, Sharpton leaned over as he passed, and whispered into his ear his best Brown imitation: "Fred, you got my money?"

"I almost expected Brown to rise from his casket and laugh," said Daviss.

The show could now go on.

"It was like being on the road with Dad," said Deanna Brown. "Hitting and quitting it in different cities. I tell you, when we sat down and looked at the whole thing it was really amazing. I know it was nothing but God that gave us the strength to get through it. We just needed our legs and hands to make it happen."

The public service was booked for Saturday night in the Augusta venue just recently renamed James Brown Arena. Brown got his third costume change and was placed on the stage before more than 8,500 fans from around the country.

In the wings, in the seats, everywhere one cared to turn, there was drama at hand. Between Buddy Dallas and Deanna Brown, warring over who should control the estate; between Deanna and Tomi Rae, over who represented "the family." Tomi Rae delivered a quizzical, emotional version of "Hold On, I'm Coming" before the cameras, and Brown's son, Darryl, flexed his muscles in the band that would carry his legacy forward, the Soul Generals. And everybody trying to act like they were not looking at Michael Jackson as he cried.

Farris had the sobering task of writing the last ever set list for a James Brown gig, and the Soul Generals sent him off. Veterans of the band were all around: Bootsy Collins and Bobby Byrd, Johnny Terry and J. C. Davis. As the Soul Generals played, Farris looked down at the body before him, and beyond Brown, he saw Jesse Jackson, Don King, Michael Jackson, and the rest in the seats. It just did not seem real.

The night Brown died, Bobbit called Marva Whitney, once a featured singer in the show, and told her that Brown wanted her to be the last singer on the last ever bill. At the funeral Whitney walked over to the casket and quietly said, "You're *still* dictating to me," and then she sang "Kansas City."

> I'm gonna pack my clothes
> Leave at the break of dawn
> I'm gonna pack my clothes
> Everybody will be sleeping
> Nobody will know where I've gone

AFTERWORD

J ames Brown was obsessed with Elvis Presley. In conversation he made much of the few times they met, until it appeared the two were confidants. It was said Brown's wife Adrienne once dated Elvis, and it might have been Brown who spread the story: It put him in the proper company. Maybe they recognized something of each in the other: dirt-poor Southerners with rural roots who moved to the big city and did not disappear.

But it wasn't the man he liked. Not really. It was the crown. And if he'd come along a few decades later, Brown might have been spreading rumors his wife had once dated Michael Jackson. They called Elvis the King, and Brown tracked his reign from early on, for Brown planned on supremacy himself. As artists, they were only comparable to each other. Elvis alone put more singles on the *Billboard* charts than Brown during their lifetimes. It was on the black list, called the "rhythm & blues" charts, that Brown ruled in his lifetime. They were King and cape, separate and unequal.

Elvis died August 16, 1977, and the moment Brown heard the news he rolled into action. Chartering a Learjet, he took Fred Daviss and Danny Ray to Memphis, where police escorted them to Graceland. The three were brought in a side entrance for a private viewing of Presley. "Elvis, you rat," Brown wailed as he leaned over his body. "I'm not number two no more . . ."

"I went to the funeral, you know, and I touched his body," Brown said a few weeks later. "It was hard to believe it was him. I saw him five years ago in Hawaii and he looked great. I kept saying, 'What happened? What happened?' They never let him alone. They never understood." Only Brown understood, went his thinking, and now he was alone. Number One.

For the rest of his life, he would measure himself against Elvis, gauging how much the public loved each. In a spoken introduction to his cover of "Love Me Tender," posthumously dedicated to Presley, Brown addresses his listeners like a country lawyer appealing to a jury: "I want to talk about a good friend I've had for a long time and a man I still love, Brother Elvis Presley. You know, if he was here right now, I'm sure he would say the same thing for me. I loved the man because he was truly the King of Rock and Roll. We've always had kind of a toss-up between Elvis and I, The King of Rock And Roll and I'm the King of Soul. So I want to sing this to the people, for Elvis and myself . . ." *The King is gone, and I am your only King. Now your love is mine.*

On a prison phone in 1989, Brown told a caller that his real crime was his fame, that America tried to bring him down because he was so big. He thought back to seeing Elvis in his coffin, and said, "Well, now I'm catching *his* flack and mine."

Touching his dead body was as close as Brown would get to something he wanted desperately. He wanted the adoration people reserved for their King, but the best he could do was reap the celebrity attention, the kind that ripens to jealousy, then to hate. He hungered for the love, but he prepped for the jury's sentence. "If America can stand to have James Brown in prison, James Brown can stand it," is how he put it.

"I know what madness is. It's not knowing how another man feels," wrote María Irene Fornés. Unable to put himself in another person's place, Brown was desperate to connect the best way that he could, by bringing others into his world. It made his art a total experience, the opposite of crossover pop–the *audience* crossed over, to a world that hadn't existed until he made it so. We are still not near the bottom of his music. The songs of Elvis or Motown or most of the music of his peers, however great, tend to sound finished to our ears. It has arrived at its destination. But James Brown's music still mystifies, and we have yet to get to the bottom of it. His music still sounds alive.

As an artist, as a conductor of American energy, as a master of a nerve-control technique that makes the whole body tremble, Brown was simply greater. He just could never make America love him like we love Elvis. He was who he was, and America was what it was.

Money won't change you, but time will take you out: He said it, and boy did he mean it. You make the most of whatever you have right now, a steak one day and fatback the next, because enjoyment is all you get. The rest of life was forces messing with you, chaos you had to meet with more chaos or be washed down the Augusta canal.

The art was one part of his legacy. The chaos was the rest. The singer had once declared to his drummer that when he died, it would take another lifetime for anybody to figure out where all the money had gone. He might have had a smile on his face when he said it. "Mr. Brown was an exceptionally slick, conniving, brilliant man. And he made sure–*made sure*–he was misunderstood," his closest associate, Charles Bobbit, told a journalist. In death the misunderstandings started shaking loose.

In a courtroom in South Carolina lined with paintings of celebrated South Carolina judges of the past, lawyers have been gathering. They came out of the woods to speak for Brown, against him, and speak for and against the money he had left behind. They came from Savannah and Atlanta, New York and beyond. Their teeth and hair were impeccable.

In 2000, Brown wrote out a will, with the assistance of H. Dewain Herring, one of his many lawyers. Herring was later best known for murdering a strip club employee, for which he received a thirty-year sentence in 2006. Assisting Brown in this period was probate attorney Strom Thurmond Jr., best known for being Strom Thurmond Jr.

The will divided the singer's personal effects among a small set of his children. The real wealth, however—the bank accounts, royalties, the rights to his image and songs—was controlled by two trusts, one to benefit his grandchildren and one to benefit needy children of the region. These trusts were managed by three men appointed by Brown: Aiken county magistrate Alford Bradley, attorney Buddy Dallas, and accountant David Cannon. They had managed Brown's finances in his last years, putting him on a monthly salary of $100,000. The trio had worked in those later years with a New York-based agent calling himself "SuperFrank" Copsidas and entertainment attorney Joel Katz, to send Brown out on the road. And they had overseen his finances while he was gone.

Copsidas was responsible for one of the more colorful statements of the funereal moment. When asked what he would do now that Brown was dead, SuperFrank said that, from his perspective, nothing had changed. "We're still managing him," the agent said. "There's lots to do."

Whether it was Brown's true wish to create these trusts rather than giving all his money to his heirs is at the heart of an ongoing battle. The trustees' opponents suggest that Brown was not in his right mind when he created the trusts. Buddy Dallas heartily disputes the claim.

"To even make a statement like that . . . the obvious answer would be, obviously you did not know James Brown, the Godfather of Soul," he said. "To quote Mr. Brown, 'Papa don't take no mess! Papa didn't cuss and papa didn't raise a fuss! But if we did wrong, papa beat the hell out of us!' Mr. Brown was his own counsel when it came to his business. Mr. Brown made his own decisions, okay?"

Over the months and then years following his death, lawyers billed large sums trying to explain how Brown's wealth should be spent. Much of the legal wrangling took place in the courtroom of South Carolina Judge Doyet A. Early III, a native of the same region to which Brown was born. Early yelled at the trustees, and he ultimately encouraged them to remove themselves from control of Brown's estate, which they did. But for all his peppery tirades and vainglorious courtroom antics, Early struggled to get to the bottom of one essential question that concerned his court: Exactly how much money did Brown leave behind?

The bookkeeping Brown left behind was hard to follow. When trustee David Cannon testified to his role in the trust for six hours, he was repeatedly asked how much he had made from his association with Brown. Alas, explained the accountant, he must take the Fifth Amendment on this and other questions. Early placed Cannon in jail for six months for failing to heed his order to pay back over $300,000 to the estate.

What would Brown have thought of his longtime friend being sent to jail after misappropriating his money? It seems that Brown did not trust honest men. "James Brown liked the thieves," said Bob Patton. Whether it was because he understood them better, or because such people were easier to control, who can say. But at least when he was not high, Brown was alert to the business, and for that reason it's hard to believe he didn't know, or at least expect, any and all shenanigans.

"He dealt with that his whole career," said Hollie Farris. "I think how he rationalized it was, as long as they didn't come up and actually take the money out of his pocket, it was okay with him. That was his mentality growing up as a thief, living any way he could. Everybody he knew was a thief—so being a thief to him was kind of all right."

Family and friends who gathered in Early's courtroom were focused on money, and how much might come their way, but the arguments strayed far from that bottomless topic. Lawyers representing the state of South Carolina argued against lawyers from Georgia, and then there were the parties who felt they had been stiffed by Brown. They sent representatives to Aiken just to keep some skin in the game. On some days there were more than thirty attorneys in Early's courtroom–so many that the judge allowed them to fill up the jury box, the only available seats in the house.

After Brown's trustees resigned from his estate in November 2007, Early selected new trustees to make sense of his accounting and steer his estate forward. The big asset there is the licensing of his music and image, worth millions. Since then, Early has replaced that second team of court-appointed trustees with a new appointee, and proceedings have slouched toward an ending.

Children have come forth claiming Brown was their father. Velma Brown, Brown's first wife and still living in Toccoa, filed notice with the court that Brown had never legally divorced her. That development briefly rippled the waters, until divorce papers she filed in 1969 were dug out of a Georgia file.

There is more. There will be more. In the wake of Brown's death, it is as if all the discord and rupture he had created among those closest to him had now been liberated. These demons could finally shake themselves free, and dance around the stuffy Aiken courtroom. Perhaps, as they do the mashed potato before the painting of Strom Thurmond hanging on Judge Early's wall, they take turns doing a quick floor-smacking split, each after the other, every ghost hitting on the One.

Before Early released them, his two appointed trustees succeeded in doing one big thing: emptying out a portion of Brown's Beech Island home. They suggested a way to help cover their growing bill while paying some of the creditors waiting in line for Brown's money. They would auction off valuable objects in Brown's house.

So, accompanied by representatives of Christie's auction house in Manhattan, they cherrypicked his Beech Island home. They auctioned off capes, trophies, gold records, clothing, letters, and furniture, reaping a disappointing $857,688 from the sale of over three hundred items. After the auction, Brown's wish to have a museum dedicated to his memory seemed far less possible. (The bullet-riddled pickup truck, at least, remains parked on the grounds.)

Meanwhile, the house he left behind stays guarded and locked tight. Rumors abound: that dozens of holes have been dug up around the sixty acres, as visitors search for loot; that a compartment behind a picture on one wall yielded several hundred thousand to the child lucky enough to find it.

The record albums James Brown left behind at Beech Island:

- Wildman Steve's *The Six Thousand Dollar Nigger*
- Isaac Hayes's *The Isaac Hayes Movement*
- The Hollyridge Strings' *The Nat King Cole Song Book*
- Kermit Schafer's *All Time Great Bloopers*
- *Magic Moments with Johnny Mathis and Ray Conniff*
- Jimmy Smith's *Back at the Chicken Shack*
- Memphis Slim's *Messin' Around With the Blues*

This is what he listened to when he wasn't on duty. Almost as revealing is the reading material found in Brown's house after he died:

- *The Autobiography of Malcolm X*
- *How to Speak Southern*, a joke book
- *Legend Dies*, the special issue of the *Augusta Chronicle* commemorating Strom Thurmond's passing
- Dee Brown's *Bury My Heart at Wounded Knee*
- "State Laws and Published Ordinances–Firearms," a guide to gun law by the Bureau of Alcohol, Tobacco, Firearms and Explosives.

Cultural scholars will be pondering this material for years. Even more interesting, in the end, are other things Brown left scattered throughout his home. They weren't there for strangers to appreciate; few strangers ever got near them.

One was a heavy set of leg irons, an artifact of the slave trade that he brought back from Senegal. Thick, corroded fetters that linked chattel together, oxidized restraints tethered to weights. This was for *him* to see.

Also arrayed on the premises, something more approaching the festive: cotton in every room. Sprigs in a vase arranged like trillium, balls settled in bowls, and stalks left on flat surfaces. It was a part of the South's past, and part of Brown's, too, for he picked it as a boy. He used cotton as decoration in his home, but really, it wasn't so different from the irons. In the end they amounted to the same thing: a remembrance of who he was.

"I want to say one thing about the world," Brown rasped. "Christ asked for justice and he got death. I want mercy, and I want to live like Moses, happily ever after.

"If we ask for justice, we'll die right then. If we ask for mercy, we can live a while. Christ got us mercy. He paid the debt of justice."

Everything in life was measured by what it could be traded for. The boxes of money went around and around. Here he was in a fine house, with his wife busy somewhere, his mistress in another room, his Viagra ready, and the Playboy Channel on. The boxes stayed in motion, and maybe they will forever, but when Brown came to rest, here he was, alone with his cotton and his irons.

"They can kill my body but they can't kill my soul. God got that," he once said. "I'll serve humanity well, and I'm not angry about nothing. But I don't want nobody to bother me. That's not asking too much, is it?"

LIST OF INTERVIEWEES

Haji Ahkba, Steve Alaimo, Jeff Allen, Tony Allen, Emma and Leon Austin, Afrika Bambaataa, Amiri Baraka, Jack Bart, Toni Basil, Bobby Bennett, Steve Binder, Big Black, Cody Black, Darren Blase, Solomon Blatt Jr., Jerry Blavat, Chuck Brown, Ray Brown, Tomi Rae Brown, Tommy Brown, Young James Brown, Chris Burgan, David Butts, Emily Carder, James E. Carter, Devin Christy, Larry Cohen, Newton Collier, Bootsy Collins, Catfish Collins, Charles Connor, Albert Dallas, Gloria Daniel, Billy Davis, J. C. Davis, Ofield Dukes, Hollie Farris, Anthony Fillyau, Clayton Fillyau Jr., Sarah Byrd Giglio, Robert Gordon, Steve Halper, Erik Hargrove, Lee Hay, Roy Head, Stan Hertzman, Martha High, Hermon Hitson, Orangie Ray Hubbard, James Hudson, Keith Jenkins, Mack Johnson, Roosevelt Johnson, Leroy Jones, Willie Mae Keels, Gwen Kesler, Ronald Laster, Allyn Lee, Alan Leeds, Lola Love, Frank McCrae, Khalid Abdullah Tariq al-Mansour, David Matthews, Hal Neely, Betty Jean Newsome, Lunetha Nolen, Bob Patton, Philip and Juanita Paul, Danny Ray, Jimie Railey, Levi Rasbury, Charles Reid, Roy Rifkind, Bobby Roach, Chuck Seitz, Ron Selico, Al Sharpton, James Shaw aka the Mighty Hannibal, Clay Smith, Charles Spurling, Henry Stallings, Frank Stanford,

Ralph Stanley, Seymour Stein, Henry Stone, Reppard Stone, Clyde Stubblefield, Bob Sullivan, Hamp Swain, Deanna Brown Thomas, Shawn Thomas, Robert Thompson, Frankie Waddy, Charles Walker, Melvin Webb, Fred Wesley, Otis Williams, Tony Wilson, Bob Young

OTHER INTERVIEWS USED

Bobby Byrd, conducted by Portia Maultsby, Archives of African American Music and Culture, Indiana University, Bloomington, Indiana

Bobby Byrd, Emily Acree, Jim Andrews, Sarah Byrd Giglio, M. Carter, Sylvester Keels, Willie Mae Byrd Keels, J. C. Lawson, M. Perry, Nafloyd Scott, Johnny Terry, M. Tabor, conducted by Fred Hay, the Center for Appalachian Studies at Appalachian State University, Boone, North Carolina

Bobby Byrd, Richard Kush Griffith, Danny Ray, conducted by Howard Burchette

Henry Glover, Colonel Jim Wilson, conducted by John Rumble, Frist Library, Country Music Hall of Fame, Nashville, Tennessee

Hal Neely, conducted by Jeff Yaw

Jim Deak, conducted by Jon Hartley Fox

NOTES

INTRODUCTION

Stono Rebellion: "General Oglethorpe to the Accoutant, Mr. Harman Verelst," Oct. 9 1739, in Candler, Allen D., etc., *The Colonial Records of the State of Georgia, vol. XXII, pt. 2* (Charles P. Byrd, 1913); Dena J. Epstein, *Sinful Tunes and Spirituals: Black Folk Music to the Civil War* (University of Illinois Press, 1997); Mark M. Smith, ed., *Stono: Documenting and Interpreting a Southern Slave Revolt* (University of South Carolina Press, 2005); Richard Cullen Rath, "Drums and Power: Ways of Creolizing Music in Coastal South Carolina and Georgia, 1730-1790," in *Creolization in the Americas*, David Buisseret and Steven G. Reinhardt, eds. (TAMU Press, 2000).

South Carolina slaves marching into Augusta: Edward J. Cashin, *The Story of Augusta* (Richmond County Board of Education, 1980).

A Barnwell corn-shucking: William Cullen Bryant, *Letters of a Traveller; or, Notes of Things Seen in Europe and America* (Putnam, 1850). For drums and dance in South Carolina, see also, Henry William Ravenel, "Recollections of Southern Plantation Life," *Yale Review* 26, June 1936.

"The 'One' is derived from the Earth itself." James Brown and Marc Eliot, *I Feel Good: A Memoir of a Life in Soul* (New American Library, 2005).

Chapter One: A CERTAIN ELEMENTAL WILDNESS

James Brown: James Brown and Bruce Tucker, *James Brown: The Godfather of Soul* (Macmillan, 1986); Geoff Brown, *The Life of James Brown: A*

Biography (Omnibus Press, 2008); Don Rhodes, *Say It Loud!: My Memories of James Brown, Soul Brother No. 1* (The Lyons Press, 2008); James Sullivan, *The Hardest Working Man: How James Brown Saved the Soul of America* (Gotham, 2008); Nelson George and Alan Leeds, eds., *The James Brown Reader: Fifty Years of Writing About the Godfather of Soul* (Plume, 2008); Cynthia Rose, *Living in America: The Soul Saga of James Brown* (Serpent's Tail, 1991). Also, chapters on Brown in Peter Guralnick, *Sweet Soul Music: Rhythm and Blues and the Southern Dream of Freedom* (Perennial, 1994); Gerri Hirschey, *Nowhere to Run: The Story of Soul Music* (Southbank, 2006).

"Muddying for fish": "The Red Sea," in *Barnwell County Heritage* (Barnwell County Heritage Book Committee, 1994); Mamie Garvin Fields, *Lemon Swamp and Other Places: A Carolina Memoir* (Free Press, 1970); William A. Owens, *This Stubborn Soil* (The Lyons Press, 1999).

Bella Vista plantation: Michael J. Heitzler, *Goose Creek: A Definitive History vol. 1* (History Press, 2005). There were so many Behlings in the area, the *Atlanta Constitution* reported in 1901 that an effort was made to establish a colony for those with the name near Augusta, where they would make cheese and wine. Alas, it was never finished.

James Brown's family tree: comes from Brown and Tucker, *The Godfather of Soul*; Bruce Tucker files; Deanna Brown Thomas interview.

"I was a stillborn kid." *Godfather of Soul*; for another interpretation of the term, see Phillip Gourevitch, "Mr. Brown," *The New Yorker*, July 29, 2002.

A Chosen One: Tucker files; Fred Daviss interview.

"I been dead all my life anyway." Vernon Gibbs, "James Brown is Super Bad," in *The James Brown Reader.*

"He was a personal person and some things he didn't want out." Roosevelt Johnson interview.

"Something in the milk may not be clean." Brown interview, Tucker files.

"She lived down in Smoakes." Deanna Brown Thomas interview.

Living in a shack: Phillip T. South and Wesley Drotning, *Up From the Ghetto* (Washington Square Press, 1972).

Barnwell and the Barnwell District: *Barnwell County Heritage*; Tom Downey, *Planting a Capitalist South: Masters, Merchants, and Manufacturers in the Southern Interior, 1790-1860* (Louisiana State University Press, 2005); John Caldwell Guilds ed., *Simms: A Literary Life* (University of Arkansas Press, 1995); Richard David Brooks and David Colin Crass, *A Desperate Poor Country: History and Settlement Patterning on the Savannah River Site, Aiken and Barnwell Counties, South Carolina* (University of South Carolina, 1991); Margaret Spann Lawrence, *The History of Bamberg County, South Carolina, Commemorating 100 Years 1897-1997* (The Reprint Company, 2003); F. Stuart Chapin et al., *In the Shadow of a Defense Plant: A Study of Urbanization in Rural South Carolina* (University of North Carolina, 1954); Steve Gaither, William Henry, J. W. Joseph, Mary Beth Reed, and Mark T. Swanson, *Savannah River Site at Fifty* (U.S. Government Printing Office, 2002); Lucius Sydney O'Berry, *Ellenton, South Carolina: My Life...Its Death* (University of South Carolina, 1999); Tonya A. Browder and Richard D. Brooks, *Memories of Home: Reminiscences of Ellenton* (University of South Carolina Press, 1996); Stephanie McCurry, *Masters of Small Worlds: Yeoman Households, Gender Relations, and the Political Culture of the Antebellum South Carolina Low Country* (Oxford University Press, 1997); Jean Martin Flynn, *A History of the Barnwell First Baptist Church and Antebellum Barnwell* (Barnwell First Baptist Church, 2002); "Court Orders New Trial For 17-Year-Old Farmer in S.C.," *Pittsburgh Courier*, July 16, 1942.

South Carolina landscape: Walter B. Edgar, *South Carolina: A History* (University of South Carolina Press, 1998); Edgar, *The South Carolina Encyclopedia* (University of South Carolina Press, 2006); Downey, *Planting a Capitalist South; The WPA Guide to the Palmetto State* (University of South Carolina Press, 1988).

Newcomers known as "crackers": Cashin, *The Story of Augusta*; Cashin, "Paternalism in Augusta," in *Paternalism in a Southern City: Race, Religion and Gender in Augusta, Georgia*, Edward J. Cashin and Glenn T. Eskew, eds. (University of Georgia Press, 2001); Charles Woodmason, *The Carolina Backcountry on the Eve of the Revolution: The Journal and Other Writings of Charles Woodmason, Anglican Itinerant* (University of North Carolina Press, 1969); William Bartram, *The Travels of William Bartram* (University of Georgia Press, 1998).

A South Carolina tradition of violence: Michael Stephen Hindus, *Prison and Plantation: Crime, Justice and Authority in Massachusetts and South Carolina, 1767-1878* (University of North Carolina Press, 1980); Jack Kenny Williams, *Vogues in Villainy: Crime and Retribution in Ante-Bellum South Carolina* (University of South Carolina Press, 1959); Fox Butterfield, *All God's Children: The Bosket Family and the American Tradition of Violence* (Alfred A. Knopf, 1995); John Hammond Moore, *Carnival of Blood: Dueling, Lynching, and Murder in South Carolina, 1880-1920* (University of South Carolina Press, 2006); Orville Vernon Burton, *In My Father's*

House Are Many Mansions: Family and Community in Edgefield, South Carolina (University of North Carolina Press, 1987); C. Vann Woodward, "District of Devils," *New York Review of Books*, October 10, 1985; Elliot J. Gorn, "Gouge and Bite, Pull Hair and Scratch: The Social Significance of Fighting in the Southern Backcountry," *The American Historical Review*, vol. 90, February 1985; Mark M. Smith, " 'All Is Not Quiet In Our Hellish County': Facts, Fiction, Politics, and Race–The Ellenton Riot of 1876," *South Carolina Historical Magazine*, vol. 95 no. 2 (April 1994).

"We live in the fields among the growing cotton and the green corn." Ben Robertson, *Red Hills and Cotton: An Upcountry Memory* (University of South Carolina Press, 1983).

The Lynching at Broxton Bridge: "An Ugly Lynching," *Atlanta Constitution*, December 6, 1895; "The Colleton Horror," *Atlanta Constitution*, January 11, 1896; "Letting Light on a Lynching," February 21, 1896; "They Were Dumb," February 24, 1896; "White Men May Hang," *Atlanta Constitution*, October 18, 1896; "Rose Told the Story Again," *Atlanta Constitution*, October 29, 1896; "Two Negroes Beaten to Death," *The New York Times*, December 6, 1895; "A Failure of Justice," *The New York Times*, March 1, 1896.

Eight lynched in Barnwell: "Eight Men Lynched by Maskers," *Atlanta Constitution*, December 29, 1889: "Eight Hanging Bodies," *The New York Times*, December 30, 1889; "Negroes Shot to Death," *Chicago Daily Tribune*, December 29, 1889.

African Americans in South Carolina: I. A. Newby, *Black Carolinians: A History of Blacks in South Carolina From 1895 to 1968* (University of South Carolina Press, 1973); George B. Tindall, *South Carolina Negroes 1877-1900* (University of South Carolina Press, 1952); Richard Zuczek, *State of Rebellion: Reconstruction in South Carolina* (University of South Carolina Press, 2009); Philip G. Grose, *South Carolina at the Brink: Robert McNair and the Politics of Civil Rights* (University of South Carolina Press, 2006); Kari Frederickson, "'The Slowest State' and 'Most Backward Community': Racial Violence in South Carolina and Federal Civil-Rights Legislation, 1946-1948," *South Carolina Historical Magazine* 98, April 1997; Paul Lofton, "The Columbia Black Community in the 1930s," in *The Proceedings of the South Carolina Historical Association*, 1984; Robert W. Bagnall, "Light and Shadows in the South," *The Crisis*, April 1932; Edwin D. Hoffman, "The Genesis of the Modern Movement for Equal Rights in South Carolina, 1930-1939," *Journal of Negro History* 44, 1959.

Turpentine: Robert B. Outland, *Tapping the Pines: The Naval Stores Industry in the American South* (LSU Press, 2004); George Brown Tindall,

The Emergence of the New South, 1913–1945 (LSU Press, 1992); William Powell Jones, "Cutting through Jim Crow: African American Lumber Workers in the Jim Crow South, 1919-1960" (PhD diss. University of North Carolina at Chapel Hill, 2000); Cassandra Y. Johnson and Josh McDaniel, "Turpentine Negro," in *To Love the Wind and the Rain: African Americans and Environmental History*, Dianne D. Glave and Mark Stoll, eds. (University of Pittsburgh Press, 2006); Josh McDaniel, "Pulling Streaks: Voices from the Turpentine Woods," *Southern Quarterly*, vol. 46, (Fall 2008); "Faces of the Piney Woods: Traditions of Turpentining in South Georgia" is an impressive website established by Valdosta State University that features oral histories, explanations of techniques, and much more: www.valdosta.edu/turpentine/index.htm; Zora Neale Hurston's interviews with turpentine workers, conducted for the WPA, are preserved by the State Library and Archives of Florida, www.florida memory.com/onlineclassroom/zora_hurston/lesson_2.cfm.

The overfarming and agricultural economy of Barnwell: Melanie A. Cabak and Mary M. Inkrot, *Old Farm, New Farm: An Archaeology of Rural Modernization in the Aiken Plateau, 1875-1950* (University of South Carolina, 1997); Chapin, *In the Shadow of a Defense Plant*; Brooks and Crass, *A Desperate Poor Country*.

Poverty in Barnwell region: Tonya A. Browder, Richard D. Brooks, and David C. Crass, *Memories of Home: Dunbarton and Meyers Mill Remembered* (University of South Carolina, 1993); *Annual Report of the Barnwell County Department of Public Welfare*, fiscal year ending June 30, 1938.

Chapter Two: **THE TERRY**

"A region of the Savannah River Valley." Strom Thurmond, *Congressional Record*, vol. 142, no. 7 (January 22, 1996).

Augusta, Georgia: Edward J. Cashin, *General Sherman's Girlfriend and Other Stories About Augusta* (Augusta College History Department, 2001); Cashin, *The Quest: A History of Public Education in Richmond County, Georgia* (R. L. Bryan, 1985); Cashin and Eskew, eds. *Paternalism in a Southern City*; Cashin, *The Story of Augusta*; Cashin was the great historian of the city, and I'm sorry I never got to meet him. Also useful were "Cashin's Notes," a bound set of citations from the *Augusta Chronicle*, on file at Reese Library, Georgia State University; Federal Writers' Project, *Augusta* (Tidwell Printing Company, 1938); Vicki H. Greene, Scott Loehr, and Erick D. Montgomery, *An Augusta Scrapbook: Twentieth-Century Memories* (Arcadia Publishing, 2000); Don Rhodes, *Entertainment in Augusta and the CSRA* (Arcadia Publishing, 2004);

Curt Samson, *The Masters: Golf, Money, and Power in Augusta, Georgia* (Villard, 1999); James C. Cobb, "Politics in a New South City, Augusta, Georgia, 1946-1971," (Ph.D. diss., University of Georgia, 1975).

"A town with a fascinating case of schizophrenia." Dorothy Kilgallen, "A Big Night in Augusta," *Good Housekeeping*, May 1953.

African Americans in Augusta: Carl Lavert McCoy, "A Historical Sketch of Black Augusta, Georgia, From Emancipation to the *Brown* Decision: 1865-1954," (master's thesis, University of Georgia, 1984); Cashin, *Old Springfield: Race and Religion in Augusta Georgia* (Springfield Village Park Foundation, 1995); *WPA Guide to Augusta*; Sean Joiner and Gerard Smith, *Black America Series: Augusta Georgia* (Arcadia Publishing, 2004); Lucius Harper, "I Go Back Home After Thirty years," *Chicago Defender*, June 18, 1949; "Hooded Georgia Mob Tries to Abduct Negro After He Applies for Job on Police Force," *Los Angeles Sentinel*, September 16, 1948.

The Terry: Diane Harvey, "The Terri, Augusta's Black Enclave," *Richmond County History*, Summer 1973; John Mills, "Black Businesses Thrived in City's Golden Blocks," *Augusta Chronicle*, April 24, 1995; *Augusta Chronicle*, August 7, 1941. "The Terry" was a term sometimes defining the larger community of African Americans in Augusta, and other times a much smaller geographic area. Nobody ever formally established its boundaries.

Lenox Theater: "Lenox Theater Gives Blacks Seat up Front, Opens Door to Growth," *Augusta Chronicle*, February 5, 1990; James Carter interview.

Brown's early years in Augusta: Rhodes, *Say it Loud!*; Hirshey, *Nowhere to Run*; South and Drotning, *Up From the Ghetto*; Gourevitch, "Mr. Brown"; Simon Witter, "James Brown," *Sky*, September 1990; interviews with Carter, Allyn Lee, Emma Austin, Leon Austin, Henry Stallings.

Susie Brown living in Augusta: Assorted city directories by R. L. Polk & Co.; Don Rhodes, Emma Austin interviews.

"People were real bad there." Tucker files.

"If you want to be a man, you got to fight to get respect." Butterfield, *All God's Children*.

Silas X. Floyd School: "Augusta: City Whose Negro Leaders Point the Way," *Augusta Chronicle*, Nov. 26, 1939; see also *Chronicle*, Aug. 26, 1934; Butterfield, *All God's Children*; Laura Garvin interview in Tucker files; Henry Stallings interview.

"Augusta is a good place to live." *Augusta Chronicle*, April 19, 1936.

"A poor waif on the streets of Augusta." "Response to 'James Brown Editorial'," *Augusta News-Review*, Nov. 22, 1973.

Swanee quintet and gospel in Augusta: Carrie A. Allen, " 'When We Send Up the Praises': Race, Identity, and Gospel Music in Augusta, Georgia," *Black Music Research Journal*, Fall 2007; "Gospel Group 'Walked in the Light' for Half a Century," *Augusta Chronicle*, Dec. 29, 1990; "Lord Provides All, Gospel Singers Say," *Augusta Chronicle*, Oct. 5, 1985; "Singing the Gospel," *Augusta Chronicle*, Oct. 4, 1997; Percy Griffin interview.

Arthur Lee Simpkins: "Arthur Lee Simpkins Sings," *Augusta Chronicle*, Aug. 1, 1934; "Foster Tops Revue," *Los Angeles Times*, Dec. 6, 1947.

Camp Gordon: "Augusta May Get Cantonment of 20,000 Draftees," *Augusta Chronicle*, Oct. 11, 1940; "Pay Roll Totals $190,000 As Camp Work Nears Peak," *Augusta Chronicle*, Oct. 12, 1941.

Cremona Trio: "Singer's Career Launched in Augusta," *Augusta Chronicle*, May 3, 1993; Brown interview, Tucker files.

Vice and panic in the Terry: "Night-Sticks Come Into Own in Quelling Negro Soldiers," *Augusta Chronicle*, August 7, 1941; "Blame for Spread of Disease Denied by Negro Civic Group," *Augusta Chronicle*, November 8, 1941; "Defends Race Women From Insulting Rap," *Pittsburgh Courier*, November 15, 1941; "White Soldiers Override Social Lines in Augusta," *Chicago Defender*, November 22, 1941; "Georgia Cops Nab Women With Soldiers," *Pittsburgh Courier*, October 24, 1942.

Secret plans for subduing the Terry: "Army Service Forces–Distr. 4, Fourth Service Command–Racial Disturbance Plan, Augusta, 9 Oct 1944," Defense–Adjutant General–Misc. Files, Georgia Archives, Morrow, Georgia.

"If nobody else loved him, *he* loved him." Stanley Booth, "James Brown 1933-2006," *Georgia Music*, Spring 2007.

The air compressor incident: Willie Glenn interview, Tucker files; Fred Daviss interview.

"I knew one thing - that I was different." Rose, *Living in America*.

Chapter Three: THE BLACK SATCHEL

"The Bon Air gazes, like the Sphinx, upon Augusta." Dan Jenkins, "Augusta: Where Georgia Retaliates for Sherman's March," *Sports Illustrated*, April 6, 1964.

The Bon Air: Stan Byrdy, *Augusta and Aiken in Golf's Golden Age* (Arcadia Publishing, 2002); Jeanne M. McDaniel, *North Augusta: James U. Jackson's Dream* (Arcadia, 2006); Samson, *The Masters*; Picturing Augusta: Historic Postcards from the Collection of the East Central Georgia Regional Library; "Brighter Days Fill History of City Landmark," *Augusta Chronicle*, June 11, 2011.

Battle royals: Geoffrey C. Ward, *Unforgivable Blackness: The Rise and Fall of Jack Johnson* (Knopf, 2004); Andrew M. Kaye, *The Pussycat of Prizefighting: Tiger Flowers and the Politics of Black Celebrity* (University of Georgia Press, 2004); "The Milk-Ice Fund FIGHT," *Pittsburgh Courier*, July 14, 1923; "Fighters, Keep Out of Those 'Battle Royals'," *Pittsburgh Courier*, Feb. 11, 1928.

Brown the boxer: "Bax Hardy to Weigh 160 Pounds for Bout," *Augusta Chronicle*, January 26, 1946; "Hardy Captures Decision," *Chronicle*, January 29, 1946; "Buddy Rose After Knockout," *Chronicle*, Feb. 12, 1946; "Soul Searching," *Chronicle*, May 3, 1969.

"Mr. Brown liked to have idols." Emma Austin interview.

Beau Jack: "Stork Club Champ," *Time*, November 23, 1942; "Beau Jack Kayoes Tippy Larkin," *Augusta Chronicle*, December 19, 1942; Grantland Rice, "Concerning Beau Jack," *Chronicle*, Jan. 20, 1943; "Crack O' Dawn," *Chronicle*, Feb. 15, 1943; "Dan Burley's 'Confidentially Yours,'" *New York Amsterdam News*, Dec. 26, 1942, and May 29, 1943; "Beau Jack Learns to Read and Write," *Chronicle*, Oct. 7, 1944; "The Tragic Case of Beau Jack," *Pittsburgh Courier*, Jan. 29, 1955; Gary Smith, "Still Fighting Old Wars," *Sports Illustrated*, Feb. 15, 1988; "Beau Jack, 78, Lightweight Boxing Champion in the 1940s," *The New York Times*, February 12, 2000; "Jack Always Packed Exciting Punch," *New York Daily News*, February 13, 2000; Carter interview.

Daddy Grace: Marie W. Dallam, *Daddy Grace: A Celebrity Preacher and His House of Prayer* (NYU Press, 2007); Sherri Marcia Damon, "The Trombone in the Shout Band of the United House of Prayer for All People," (Ph.D. diss., University of North Carolina Greensboro, 1999); Federal Writers Project, *Augusta*; "Negro 'Bishop Who Cures both White and Black' Tells Judge of his Troubles From the City," *Augusta Chronicle*, April 28, 1927; "Order House of Prayer Reopened," *Atlanta Daily World*, August 5, 1932; "Bishop Grace Hailed by His Augusta 'Children'," *Chronicle*, April 25, 1934; "Owner of 'Harlem Heaven' to Insist on 'Good Rent,'" *Chronicle*, March 11, 1938; "Thousands See Daddy Grace Ride," *Atlanta Daily World*, Sept. 27, 1938; "Is He Charlatan or Saint?," *Augusta Herald*, September 26, 1956; "Marching, Music and

Memories," *Charlotte Observer,* January 3, 1990; "Sweet Soul Music: The Trombone-Drive 'Shout' Sound," *Charlotte Observer,* July 4, 1993; Al Sharpton interview.

Cracker Party: Cobb, "Politics in a New South City"; James C. Cobb, "Colonel Effingham Crushes the Crackers: Political Reform in Postwar Augusta," *South Atlantic Quarterly* 78, Autumn 1979; "Negroes Indorse McDonald...," *Augusta Chronicle,* December 19, 1932; "How Augustans Lost Their Democratic Government," *Chronicle,* Jan. 25, 1939; "Campaign 'Pay-Off' System is Revealed in Probe Testimony," *Chronicle,* May 16, 1934; "Ninety Arrested as Federal Men Descend on Augusta Liquor Dives," *Chronicle,* May 23, 1931; "Municipal Race Not Necessary," *Chronicle,* Nov. 4, 1937.

"He'd steal anything that wasn't tied down." Carter interview.

Brown's 1949 prosecution: Record of Indictments Superior Court Richmond County Book 11, Augusta records storage facility.

1949 corruption trial: "Two Police Commissioners Arrested on Bribe Charge," *Augusta Chronicle,* May 4, 1949; "Bitter Court Battle is Indicated...," *Chronicle,* June 12, 1949; "Bribe Trials Delayed Till July 18," *Chronicle,* June 14, 1949.

"Tell daddy, try to get me out." Willie Glenn interview, Tucker files.

Chapter Four: **TOCCOA**

Herman Talmadge: Donald L. Grant and Jonathan Grant, *The Way It Was in the South: The Black Experience in Georgia* (University of Georgia Press, 2003); "Springfield Spectacle," *Time,* February 24, 1936; "Georgia: Death of the Wild Man," *Time,* Dec. 30, 1946.

Eugene Talmadge and prison reform in Georgia: William Anderson, *The Wild Man from Sugar Creek: The Political Career of Eugene Talmadge* (Louisiana State University Press, 1975); Harold P. Henderson, *The Politics of Change in Georgia: A Political Biography of Ellis Arnall* (University of Georgia Press, 1991); "Prisons - Director's Office - Director's Subject Files, 1940-1975," Georgia Archives; *Augusta Chronicle,* April 23, 1948 and Dec. 16, 1948.

Talmadge speech in Rome: "Speech by Governor Herman Talmadge, 1949," folder, Prison Director's Subject Files, Georgia Archives.

The Rome facility: "Juvenile Training Institute Formed," *Augusta Chronicle,* Nov. 20, 1946; "Statewide Search Launched for 'Honor Roll'

Escapees," *Chronicle,* November 25, 1946; "Battey General Hospital Transferred to State," *Chronicle,* February 11, 1947; "Battey Expansion is Well Underway," *Chronicle,* November 20, 1949; "Georgia Juvenile Training Institute Rome 1950-51" and "Speech by J. B. Hatchett," folders, Prison Director's Subject Files, Georgia Archives.

Camp Toccoa: *Toccoa Record,* January 31, 1952; *Rome News-Tribune,* April 6, 1953; *Toccoa Record,* April 23, 1953; "Memo from Walter Matthews," folder, Prison Director's Subject Files, 1940-1975, Georgia Archives.

Johnny Terry: Bobby Roach interview; Roach interview, Hays; Brown and Tucker, *Godfather of Soul*; Brown, *The Life of James Brown.*

Toccoa: *Stephens County, Georgia: Its People,* vol. 1 (Stephens County Historical Society, 1996); Wilber W. Caldwell, *The Courthouse and the Depot: A Narrative Guide to Railroad Expansion and Its Impact on Public Architecture in Georgia, 1833-1910* (Mercer University Press, 2001); Fred J. Hay, "Music Box Meets the Toccoa Band: The Godfather of Soul in Appalachia," *Black Music Research Journal,* vol. 23, no. 1-2 (Spring-Autumn, 2003); "Another Large Liquor Still Cut in Gum Log Last Friday," *Toccoa Record,* June 12, 1952; "Liquor Car Nabbed By Officers Yields Over 100 Gallons in Wild Chase," *Toccoa Record,* May 7, 1953; "Godfather of Soul Attends Local Funeral," *Toccoa Record,* January 6, 2004; "Georgia (Mountains) On My Mind," *Washington Post,* May 16, 1993.

Music in Toccoa: The entire issue of *Black Music Research Journal* volume 23, no. 1-2, 2003, is devoted to African American music of the region, and has shaped my thinking about the music made in Toccoa.

James Brown in Toccoa: Hay, "Music Box Meets the Toccoa Band." Fred J. Hay captures the time and place that Brown entered upon his release from prison. It's a region he knows better than most. Brown, *The Life of James Brown*; Cliff White, "The Roots of James Brown, Part One," *Now Dig This,* May 1993; interview with James Shaw, Sarah Byrd Giglio, Willie Mae Keels; interviews with Bobby Byrd conducted by Hay, Howard Burchette, and Portia Maultsby were invaluable. Much of what we know of Brown's musical progress in Toccoa, and of the groups he joined, comes from Byrd. He was generous with his time and stories of Toccoa times, and, sometimes, the stories and dates changed. Memories are fungible.

Velma Brown: interviews by Hay; Rhodes, *Say It Loud!*

"At the time we didn't really care," Byrd Giglio interview.

"They didn't have no band, they was just patting their legs." James Shaw, aka The Mighty Hannibal, interview.

Chapter Five: A NEW ORLEANS CHOO-CHOO

Macon: Candice Dyer, *Street Singers, Soul Shakers, Rebels With a Cause: Music From Macon* (Indigo, 2008); Andrew M. Manis, *Macon Black and White: An Unutterable Separation in the American Century* (Mercer University Press, 2004); *Macon's Black Heritage: The Untold Story* (Tubman African American Museum, 1997); Preston Lauterbach, *The Chitlin Circuit: And the Road to Rock 'n' Roll* (W. W. Norton & Company, 2011); Scott Freeman, *Otis! The Otis Redding Story* (St. Martin's, 2001); Douglass Theatre collection, Middle Georgia Regional Library, Macon; James Brown folder, Middle Georgia Regional Library.

Clint Brantley: Clint Brantley folder, Middle Georgia Regional Library; Scott Freeman, "James Brown: Soul Brother No. 1," *Creative Loafing Atlanta*, Jan. 10, 2007; Scott Freeman, Newton Collier interview.

Charles Connor: unpublished manuscript, the Charles Connor Collection, Archives of African American Music and Culture (AAAMC), Indiana University; Connor interview.

The Upsetters: *Home of the Groove* blog, posted April 20, 2008 ("Tracking Lee Diamond"), and December 3, 2004; Connor interview; Grady Gaines interview, Alan B. Govenar, *Texas Blues: the Rise of a Contemporary Sound* (TAMU Press, 2008).

Little Richard: David Kirby, *Little Richard: The Birth of Rock 'n' Roll* (Continuum, 2009); Charles White, *The Life and Times of Little Richard* (Da Capo Press, 1994); "Little Richard Penniman" folder, Middle Georgia Regional Library, booklet to *Little Richard: The Specialty Records Sessions* (Specialty, 1990); "I've Quit Show Business," *Puget Sound Observer*, Dec. 25, 1957; "Rappin' With a Rock 'n Roll Pioneer," *Pittsburgh Courier*, January 19, 1985; "Little Richard Touched Macon," *Charlotte Observer*, Sept. 4, 2005; Connor interview.

Tent show queen tradition: Esquerita interview, *Kicks* (1983); Marybeth Hamilton, "Sexual Politics and African-American Music; or, Placing Little Richard in History," *History Workshop* 46, Autumn 1998.

Billy Wright: The Hound Blog, entry posted June 15, 2009; liner notes and interview found in *Billy Wright: Stacked Deck* (Route 66, 1980); Tommy Brown interview.

"I've never seen a man work so hard in my whole life." Brown, *The Life of James Brown*.

Funk: Tony Scherman, *Back Beat: Earl Palmer's Story* (Da Capo, 2000); Robert Farris Thompson, *Flash of the Spirit: African and Afro-American Art and Philosophy* (Vintage, 1984); Connor interview.

"Please, Please, Please" in Macon: "James Brown" file, Middle Georgia Regional Library; "Radio History 'Pioneer' WIBB," and "WIBB Founders Faced Uphill Battle," *Macon Telegraph*, May 31, 1998; Hamp Swain, Satellite Papa interview.

"Oh man, that's more like it." Byrd interview, AAAMC.

"A sort of seventh son, born with a veil." David Levering Lewis, ed., *W.E.B. Du Bois: A Reader* (Holt, 1995).

The conjure woman: Terry interview, Hay; Brown, *The Life of James Brown*.

Ralph Bass and the signing of the Flames: Lauterbach, *The Chitlin Circuit*; Michael Lydon, *Boogie Lightning* (Dial Press, 1974); Norbert Hess, "I Didn't Give a Damn If Whites Bought It!," *Blues Unlimited* 119, May/June 1976; Brantley file, Middle Georgia Regional Library; Henry Stone, Gwen Kesler interviews.

The first recording session: Jon Hartley Fox, *King of the Queen City: The Story of King Records* (University of Illinois Press, 2009); Hal Neely interview, conducted by Jeff Yaw; Philip Paul interview; Sylvester Keels, Nafloyd Scott interviews, Hay.

"It took so long for it to finally come out." Byrd interview, Burchette.

Chapter Six: TOP BANANA

King Records: Fox, *King of the Queen City*; Richard Kennedy and Randy McNutt, *Little Labels, Big Sound: Small Record Companies and the Rise of American Music* (Indiana University Press, 2001); John Broven, *Record Makers and Breakers: Voices of the Independent Rock 'n' Roll Pioneers* (University of Illinois Press, 2010); Brian F. X. Powers, *A King Records Scrapbook* (Terra Incognita Press, 2008); Steven C. Tracy, *Going to Cincinnati: A History of the Blues in the Queen City* (University of Illinois Press, 1993); Darren Blase, *King Records: The Story* (undated, Cincinnati Public Library); Colin Escott, *Tattooed On Their Tongues: A Journey Through the Backrooms of American Music* (Schirmer Trade Books, 2000); John W. Rumble, "Roots of Rock & Roll: Henry Glover at King Records," *Journal of Country Music*, vol. 14, no. 2 (1992); Larry Nager, "The King is Dead, Long Live the King," *Cincinnati*, March, 2008; Billy Vera, "The Henry Glover Story," *Blues & Rhythm*, Oct. 2008; "Cincinnati

Manufacturer Proves that Integration Will Work," Cincinnati Ed. of *Cleveland Call and Post*, Dec. 13, 1947; "Records Are Biscuits," *Pittsburgh Courier*, June 19, 1948; "Strummin' 'Geetar' is Music to Millions," *Cincinnati Enquirer*, Nov. 27, 1948; "Standout – In Business," *Cleveland Call and Post,* March 26, 1949; "King, Apollo Denounce Wax Race Tags," *Pittsburgh Courier*, May 14, 1949; private files of Steve Halper; Cincinnati Music file, Cincinnati Public Library; oral histories of Henry Glover and Colonel Jim Wilson, conducted by John Rumble, Country Music Hall of Fame; interviews with Darren Blase, Steve Halper, Lee Hay, Orangie Ray Hubbard, Leroy Jones, Philip Paul, Ralph Stanley, Marion Thomson, Otis Williams; several publications on King by Brian Powers at the Cincinnati Public Library, and Powers's ongoing research and advice, have been indispensable.

Syd Nathan: Nelson Burton, *My Life in Jazz* (Clifton Hills Press, 2000); Tommy Scott, *Snake Oil, Superstars and Me* (Author House, 2007); Darren Blase, "The Man Who Was King," *CityBeat*, March 19, 1997; "King of King's 25th Year," *Cincinnati Post and Times-Star*, July 21, 1967; "Rock and Roll Hall of Famer Syd Nathan Brought R&B, Country to Cincinnati," *The American Israelite*, July 25, 2002; Seymour Stein interview.

"This morning I was a kike, tonight I'm an elegant Jew." Interview with Hank Penny, *JEMF Quarterly*, Spring/Summer 1982.

The chitlin circuit: I have adopted the colloquial "chitlin," rather than the formal "chitterling." Lauterbach, *The Chitlin Circuit*; Steven Roby and Brad Schreiber, *Becoming Jimi Hendrix: From Southern Crossroads to Psychedelic London* (Da Capo, 2010). A circuit story waiting to be told is the rise and fall of Charles Sullivan, sold into servitude in his Depression boyhood, only to become a West Coast nightclub kingpin until his mysterious death in the late 1960s.

James Brown and the Famous Flames on the chitlin circuit: Cliff White, "The Roots of James Brown Part Two," *Now Dig This*, June 1993; Opal Louis Nations, "Louis Madison and the Famous Flames," *Now Dig This*, March 2004; Dante Carfagna, "The Journeyman: Saxman J. C. Davis," *Wax Poetics* 28, 2008; Bobby Roach, J. C. Davis interviews. For an indelible picture of the sometimes complicated racial politics of these clubs in Brown's South Carolina backyard, see Frank Beachum's *Whitewash: A Southern Journey Through Music, Mayhem and Murder* (Beacham Story Studio, 2007).

"I knew the struggle." Byrd interview, AAAMC.

"I done been through it." Liner notes, *The Singles Volume One: The Federal Years 1956-1960* (Hip-O Select, 2006).

Nat Kendrick: Davis, Lee interviews. "He is an OG," Ahmir ?uestlove Thompson says of Kendrick. "He was highly effective in those songs. Deceptive, awesome swing."

"Oh that was devastating." Byrd interview, Hay.

"James was different from us." Scott interview, Hay.

"The best time we *ever* had." Byrd interview, Hay.

"He didn't record anyone's songs unless he got a rate." Glover interview, Rumble.

"Give me the *song*." Bootlegged recording of in-house sales staff meeting at King.

"Playing behind Sam Cooke was like playin' for people in a convalescent home." Connor manuscript, AAAMC.

The Apollo debut: Frank Schiffman Apollo Theater Collection, Smithsonian; Bobby Bennett, Davis, Connor interviews; Byrd interview, AAAMC. The fable of Brown's talent show triumph in the mid-1950s seems to have first emerged in articles in the New York press lauding the Apollo's significance, decades after Brown and the Famous Flames' real debut.

Chapter Seven: **THE TRAVELER**

Birmingham Trailways station: Tucker, *The Godfather of Soul*; Raymond Arsenault, *Freedom Riders: 1961 and the Struggle for Racial Justice* (Oxford University Press, 2006); David J. Garrow, *Birmingham Alabama 1956-1963: The Black Struggle for Civil Rights* (Carlson, 1989); Bobby Roach interview. For a thoughtful examination of black mobility and how it was contested on the open road, see Cotten Seiler, " 'So That We as a Race Might Have Something Authentic to Travel By': African American Automobility and Cold-War Liberalism," *American Quarterly*, vol. 58, no. 4 (December 2006). At a time when whites used restrictions on black mobility as a way to curtail other freedoms, it is possible to view Brown's travel through the South, with his name emblazoned on the side of the car or bus, as a symbolic challenge to impediments placed on African American freedom.

Tough times for black musicians traveling the South: Peter Guralnick, *Dream Boogie: The Triumph of Sam Cooke* (Little, Brown & Co., 2005); Brian Ward, *Just My Soul Responding: Rhythm and Blues, Black Consciousness, and Race Relations* (University of California Press, 1998); "How Dixie Race Tension is Killing Mixed Shows," *Jet*, Dec. 22, 1960, and June 8, 1961; "The Strange, Flaming Death of Jesse Belvin," *Sepia*, June 1960.

The role of the black DJ: Magnificent Montague with Bob Baker, *Burn, Baby! Burn! The Autobiography of Magnificent Montague* (University of Illinois Press, 2009); Richard E. Stamz and Patrick A. Roberts, *Give 'Em Soul, Richard! Race Radio and Rhythm and Blues in Chicago* (University of Illinois Press, 2010); Shelley Stewart with Nathan Hale Turner, *The Road South: A Memoir* (Grand Central Publishing, 2002); Lee, Bob Patton, Swain, Satellite Papa interviews.

Ben Bart and Universal Productions: "Tiny Bradshaw's New Ork Hailed as Season's Greatest Swing Find," *Pittsburgh Courier*, June 19, 1937; "Four Scottsboro Boys Starting Theatre Tour," *Pittsburgh Courier*, August 21, 1937; "They Traveled 10,000 Miles in Eight Weeks," *Pittsburgh Courier*, April 2, 1938; "'Nevermore,' Quoth Ravens," *Pittsburgh Courier*, July 26, 1947; "One Night Stands Get Barnum Touch," *New York Amsterdam News*, Feb. 26, 1949; "Packages Among the Things Fans Liked Best," *Chicago Defender*, Jan. 24, 1953; "Well, Oh Well! Tiny Bradshaw Very Much Alive," *Pittsburgh Courier*, March 12, 1955; Jack Bart, Steve Alaimo, Stone, Patton interviews.

"An older white guy who, with a big .45 on his hip." Etta James and David Ritz, *Rage to Survive: The Etta James Story* (Da Capo, 2003).

"Jimmie is dying!" *Jet*, Nov. 16, 1961.

"Another Jackie Wilson incident." *Pittsburgh Courier*, Nov. 4, 1961.

The 5-4 Ballroom incident: 1995 interview with Brown, AAAMC; Taylor Branch, *Pillar of Fire: America in the King Years 1963-65* (Simon & Schuster, 1998).

Chapter Eight: STAR TIME

Apollo Theater: Douglas Wolk, *James Brown's Live at the Apollo* (Continuum, 2004); Ted Fox, *Showtime at the Apollo: The Story of Harlem's World Famous Theater* (Holt, Rinehart and Winston, 1983); *New York Amsterdam News*, Oct. 26, 1974; Apollo Theater Collection, Smithsonian.

Brown's intentions to record at the Apollo: Brown, *The Life of James Brown*; Wolk, *Live at the Apollo*; Chuck Seitz interview.

"Didn't nobody believe in us." Byrd interview, AAAMC.

"They're talking about...James Brown's 'secret' project." *Pittsburgh Courier*, July 28, 1962.

The Apollo show: *Live at the Apollo 1962* (Polygram, 1990).

"How do you define soul, James?" *David Frost Show*, March 30, 1970.

Lewis Hamlin: Tonya Taliafierro and Rosa Pryor-Trusty, *African American Entertainment in Baltimore* (Arcadia Publishing, 2003); liner notes to *James Brown, Soul Pride: Instrumentals 1960-1969* (Polygram, 1993); Devin Christy, Reppard Stone interviews.

Clayton Fillyau: Jim Payne, *Give the Drummers Some! The Great Drummers of R&B, Funk and Soul* (Face the Music Productions, 1996); Clayton Fillyau Jr., Anthony Fillyau, Jim Payne, Melvin Webb interviews.

New Orleans funk drumming: Scherman, *Backbeat* is a well-told tale narrated by a true pioneer, though, listening to Earl Palmer, you'd think he invented all of New Orleans. Antoon Aukes's *Second Line: 100 Years of New Orleans Drumming* (C. L. Barnhouse, 2003) does a great job of breaking down the area's history and styles for nonmusicians. Stanton Moore's rich *Groove Alchemy* (Hudson Music, 2010) and interviews with Ahmir ?uestlove Thompson and Moore were also drawn upon.

Fillyau's musical upbringing: Has another surprising element. In high school in Tampa, Fillyau was a student of Reynold Davis, and through Davis he learned the drum cadences pioneered at Florida Agricultural and Mechanical University. Known as FAMU, this school's great marching band drum section would play its fabled "death cadence," during which the 100-plus marchers would move one step every three seconds, and then explode into a cadence requiring six steps per second. FAMU had a reputation for bringing jazz and then R&B rhythms into the marching band format from the 1940s on, and they performed in Tampa. Schoolmate Melvin Webb recalled, "We played a lot of jazzy stuff. Reynold Davis would keep up with all the songs at the time. Even at parades we would stop and do special steps – say a record came out that was very popular. What Davis would do was write the song out, arrange it for the band, and we would perform that in a parade along with your marches – and we would stop and do a dance step as we were marching when we played those tunes." Not just in New Orleans, but in various Southern enclaves, marching, drumming, and dancing were folding into one another.

"I've Got Money": *James Brown, The Singles Volume Two: 1960-1963* (Hip-O Select, 2007).

Aftermath of the *Live* recording: Wolk, *Live at the Apollo*; Blavat, Lee and Seitz interviews.

"I became a big city thinker." Cliff White, "The Man Who Never Left," *Black Music*, April 1977.

Chapter Nine: KEEP ON FIGHTING

Club 15 shoot-out and the feud with Joe Tex: Freeman, "Soul Brother No. 1"; Freeman, Satellite Papa, Allyn Lee interviews.

The house in St. Albans, Queens: "Cootie Williams, Queens" in "Know Your Boroughs," *New York Amsterdam News*, April 30, 1949; Doon Arbus, "James Brown is Out of Sight," in Leeds and George, *James Brown Reader*; Betty Jean Newsome, Roach interviews.

"James Brown, who is grossing more than a half million this year." "New York Beat," *Jet*, Sept. 19, 1963.

"When you are a child who is unwanted." Marlon Brando and Robert Lindsey, *Songs My Mother Taught Me* (Random House, 1994).

"It's the ultimate hustle." Shana Alexander, "The Grandfather of All Cool Actors Becomes the Godfather," *Life*, March 10, 1972.

"Hair and teeth." Brown and Tucker, *The Godfather of Soul*. Interestingly, in the original transcript, the quote is a little different: "You got implants on the hair and implants on the teeth and that's the end of it. A man got those two things, he got it all." Booker T. Washington's dental avidity is spelled out in *Up From Slavery* (Penguin Classics, 1986), where he says of the toothbrush, "I am convinced that there are few single agencies of civilization that are more far-reaching." See also Robin D. G. Kelley, "Nap Time: Historicizing the Afro" (*Fashion Theory*, vol. 1 no. 4, Nov. 1997), where the author goes so far as to rank the comb with the drum as "an essential part of African culture."

"There is a close relation between bad teeth and dyspepsia." Richard Carroll, "The Negro Church as the Guardian of Public Health," in James Edward McCulloch, *Democracy in Earnest: Southern Sociological Congress, 1916-1918* (BiblioLife, 2009).

Expoobident: Pianist and gentleman's gentleman Babs Gonzales is said to have coined the term, perhaps in the 1950s. An interpretation in the *Jazz Journal* defined it best: "All is well. It is here." See also: *Expoobident*, a good album by trumpeter Lee Morgan (Vee-Jay, 1960).

"You got to be like an act, so therefore you cannot mingle." Byrd interview, AAAMC.

The surrounding circle of roughnecks: Henry Stallings, Alan Leeds, Frank McCrae, Al Sharpton interviews.

The argument over "Oh Baby Don't You Weep": Alan Leeds, liner notes to *The Singles Volume Two*; Leeds interview.

"He couldn't read music, but he knew exactly what he wanted." Fillyau in Payne, *Give the Drummers Some!*

"You don't know why one day you want steak, the next day you want fatback." Markus Schmidt, interview with James Brown, *Wax Poetics* 21, Feb.–Mar. 2007.

Fair Deal and the Smash deal: Brown and Tucker, *Godfather of Soul*; Leeds liner notes to *Singles Volume Three: 1964-1965*; "King Wins Brown Suit," *Billboard*, October 24, 1964; Leeds interview.

"Papa's Got a Brand New Bag": "First Recording of Papa's Bag was in Charlotte," *Charlotte Observer*, Feb. 25, 1992; "Give Him a Little Thanks for a Great Song," *Charlotte Observer*, January 3, 2007; "'Guitar Boogie' Launched Legend," *Charlotte Observer*, April 8, 2007; Clay Smith, Levi Rasbury interviews.

"I was just trying to be different." Payne, *Give the Drummers Some!*

"When Maceo plays, it's almost like an extension of me." Sarah Bryan, interview with Parker, for the North Carolina Arts Council, posted at www.ncarts.org/elements/project_specs/MaceoParker.pdf.

"There is nothing so personal as the sweat from your eyebrow." Schmidt interview, *Wax Poetics,* Feb.–Mar. 2007.

"It was the beginning of a new world." Unpublished interview conducted by Christina Patoski.

Raid on a dope den: "Bronx Raid," *New York Amsterdam News*, Nov. 13, 1965.

Tammi Terrell: Ludie Montgomery and Vickie Wright, *My Sister Tommie: The Real Tammi Terrell* (Bank House Books, 2005); TV documentary series *Unsung*, produced by TV One, program on Terrell aired Sept. 20, 2010; David Butts, Lee, Bennett interviews.

Chapter Ten: **THE CAPE ACT**

The Rockland Palace show: Stella Comeaux, "The Amazing Power of James Brown," *Sepia*, Jan. 1961.

"No one made a remark." "Interview With Edward Bishop," Box 4, folder 84, Mura Dehn Papers on Afro-American Social Dance, circa 1869-1987, Jerome Robbins Dance Division, New York Public Library.

Ostyaks and shamanism: V. M. Mikhailovskii, Oliver Wardrop translator, "Shamanism in Siberia and European Russia, being the second part of 'Shamanstvo.'" Essay from *The Journal of the Anthropological Institute of Great Britain and Ireland, vol. XXIV* (London, 1895); Fridtjof Nansen, *Through Siberia: The Land of the Future* (Yokai Publishing, 2010); *Encyclopedia Britannica, Eleventh Edition* (Cambridge University Press, 1910).

"Perhaps the most outlandishly shamanistic performer of all." Rogan Taylor, *The Death and Resurrection Show* (Frederick Muller Ltd., 1983).

Gorgeous George: John Capouya, *Gorgeous George: The Outrageous Bad-Boy Wrestler Who Created American Pop Culture* (Harper Entertainment, 2008).

Danny Ray: Ray David Hoekstra, "James Brown's Cape," *Chicago Sun Times*, Dec. 25, 2006; Danny Ray interview. Guitarist Keith Jenkins says Ray would save up a perfect, glorious suit for the final days of a long tour; when the rest of the band was down to dirty laundry, Ray would emerge from the bus in a shining cream-colored coat, defying all understanding.

TAMI Show: *The T.A.M.I. Show Collector's Edition* DVD, essay by Don Waller (Shout! Factory, 2010); Greil Marcus, "Rock Films," in *The Rolling Stone Illustrated History of Rock & Roll*, Jim Milled ed., (Random House/Rolling Stone Press, 1980); "Star-Studded TAMI Rock n' Roll Show Thrills Teens" and "The Inside Story," *Los Angeles Sentinel*, Nov. 5, 1964; Steve Binder, Toni Basil, Lee, Bennett interviews.

"It's a Holiness feeling - like a Baptist thing." *Soul Illustrated*, Summer 1968.

Other men in capes: Opal Nations, "The Story of His Grace King Louis Narcisse," *Blues and Rhythm* 150, June-July 2000; For Brother Joe May, see Guralnick, *Dream Boogie*.

"I am lost for words to speak about this man." Buster Brown letter, Dehn Papers.

"His emphasis on ego breaks all bounds." Mura Dehn, *Sounds & Fury*, June 1966.

"I danced so hard my manager cried." Rose, *Living in America*.

Chapter Eleven: MAN'S WORLD

James Meredith: Meredith, *Three Years in Mississippi* (Indiana University Press, 1966); Charles W. Eagles, *The Pride of Defiance: James Meredith and the Integration of Ole Miss* (University of North Carolina Press,

2009); Meredith, "Black Leaders and the Wish to Die," *Ebony*, May 1973; Paul Hendrickson, "The Dilemmas and Demons of James Meredith," *Journal of Blacks in Higher Education* 40 (Summer 2003).

The March Against Fear: Taylor Branch, *At Canaan's Edge: America in the King Years, 1965-68* (Simon & Schuster, 2006).

Carmichael and Black Power: Chester Higgins, "Divided on Tactics, Leaders Agree March A Success," *Jet*, July 14, 1966; Robert E. Johnson, "Black Power: What it Really Means," *Jet*, July 28, 1966. For interpretations of the Black Power movement, see William L. Van Deburg, *New Day in Babylon: The Black Power Movement and American Culture, 1965-1975* (University of Chicago Press, 1992); Peniel E. Joseph, *Waiting 'Til the Midnight Hour: A Narrative History of Black Power in America* (Henry Holt and Co., 2006); and Joseph, ed., *The Black Power Movement: Rethinking the Civil Rights Black Power Era* (Routledge, 2006).

"The 'Negro' should not return." Dick Gregory, *Up From Nigger* (Stein and Day, 1977).

"I'm sorry, y'all. James Brown is on. I'm gone." Jonathan Rieder, *The Word of the Lord Is Upon Me: The Righteous Performance of Martin Luther King Jr.* (Belknap Press, 2008).

Brown at Tougaloo: newsreel clips; *Jet*, July 14, 1966.

The Canton, Mississippi, workers and "Papa's Brand New Bag": Marty Jezer, *Abbie Hoffman: American Rebel* (Rutgers University Press, 1992); "Mississippi Woodworking, Leather Cooperatives Formed," *The Movement*, Nov. 1965.

"James Brown's got more musical genius than Bach, Beethoven, and Mozart put together." Clipping from *Newark Evening News*, Aug. 26, 1966, in the Mississippi State Sovereignty Commission online files, mdah.state.ms.us/arrec/digital_archives/sovcom/.

"There was no doubt that he was addressing this plea to the Freedom Marchers." "Brando Shouts 'Black Power,' James Brown Cries on Miss. Stage," *Philadelphia Tribune*, June 28, 1966.

"It's a Man's, Man's, Man's World": *James Brown, The Singles Volume Four: 1966-1967* (Hip-O Select, 2007); Michael Clancy, "It's A Woman's World," *Village Voice*, Dec. 18, 2007; Betty Jean Newsome, Carl Kaminsky interviews. Years after pressing her case, and after numerous court dates, Newsome did get her name listed as a cowriter of the song.

Frank McRae: Mainstem column, *Philadelphia Tribune*, Feb. 19, 1966; "Singer James Brown Sues Phila. Process Artist for Million," *Philadelphia Tribune*, July 19, 1966; *Tribune*, July 23, 1966; *New York Amsterdam News*, July 23, 1966; Masco Young, "The Notebook" column, *Philadelphia Tribune*, July 30, 1966; McRae interview.

Sex change rumors: *Houston Forward Times*, Nov. 13 and 27, 1965; "James Brown Sex Shift Denied in Houston," *Philadelphia Tribune*, Dec. 21, 1965; *Michigan Chronicle*, Oct. 26, 2005; Brown and Tucker, *Godfather of Soul*; Stallings, Fred Wesley interview.

"'Race music' is perhaps at last becoming interracial." "The biggest cat," *Time*, April 1, 1966.

Jackie Wilson feud: Brown interview, Tucker files; McRae interview.

"Being a mulatto, he didn't have the energy or strength I had." Brown, Tucker files.

King Records in transition: Fox, *King of the Queen City*; Darren Blase, Leeds interviews.

"James had his way then." Glover interview, Country Music Hall of Fame.

Brown builds a staff at King: Charles Spurling, Leeds, Patton interviews; Jim Deak interview.

Bud Hobgood: David Matthews, Patton, Spurling interviews.

The El Dorados: Leeds, Patton interviews.

Kansas City riot: "Sexy Dance Triggers Wild Riot," *Philadelphia Tribune*, Oct. 1, 1966; "James Brown Dance Broken Up as 8,000 Riot," *Jet*, Dec. 8, 1966.

Rockefeller, Javits and Hampton visit the Apollo: Theatricals Column, "Campaign Sidelights," *New York Amsterdam News*, Nov. 12, 1966; Brown interview, Tucker files.

Chapter Twelve: **GHOST NOTES**

John "Jabo" Starks: Payne, *Give the Drummers Some!*; Ken Micallef, "Stubblefield & Starks: The Funkiest Men Alive," *Modern Drummer*, September 1999; "Funk Equation = Starks + Stubblefield no. 2," *Wax Poetics* 5, Summer 2003; "Red Bar Drummer Plays With the Best of Them," *Walton Sun*, Sept. 3, 2009; Susan Kepecs, "Cue Up the Funk," *Isthmus*, July 13, 2007; *Soul of the Funky Drummers* DVD (Rittor Music, 2004).

"Mardi Gras started in Mobile. I used to watch the marching band." Starks, *Wax Poetics*, Summer 2003.

"In the holiness churches they didn't have sets of drums." Payne, *Give the Drummers Some!*

The shuffle and what followed: Alexander Stewart, " 'Funky Drummer': New Orleans, James Brown and the Rhythmic Transformation of American Popular Music," *Popular Music*, vol. 19, no. 3 (October 2000); Home of the Groove blog, May 10, 2007 ("Funky to a Fault"); Geoff Brown, "Slave to the Rhythm: Earl Palmer Invented Rock Drumming," *Independent*, London, June 18, 1999; John Broven, "Charles 'Hungry' Williams – An Appreciation," *Juke Blues* 7, Winter 1986-87.

Clyde Stubblefield: Payne, *Give the Drummers Some!*; "Funkiest Men Alive," *Modern Drummer*, Sept. 1999; "Funky Drummer is Home to Stay," *Wisconsin State Journal*, April 16, 1995; "Funk Equation = Stubblefield + Starks," *Wax Poetics* 4, Spring 2003; Ben Sisario interviews Ahmir ?uestlove Thompson, Crimes Against Music blog, charmi carmicat.blogspot.com/2011/03/questlove-on-clyde-stubblefield.html, March 29, 2011.

"Cold Sweat" and the story of its making: Aaron Cohen, "James Brown's Musicians Reflect on His Legacy," *Down Beat*, February 15, 2007; Stanton Moore interview.

The second Apollo recording: *Live at the Apollo Volume Two*, CD and liner notes (Polydor, 2001); Leeds, Stubblefield interviews.

"There Was a Time": *Down Beat*, Feb. 15, 2007. For an amazing breakdown of this piece of music, see Manthia Diawara's "The 1960s in Bamako: Malick Sidibe and James Brown," in *Black Cultural Traffic: Crossroads in Global Performance and Popular Culture*, ed. Harry J. Elam Jr., and Kennall Jackson (University of Michigan Press, 2005). Along with work by Mura Dehn, it is the best writing anybody has done on Brown.

"I used to just try to play and keep my rhythm going as much like a drum as I possibly could." Lee Hildebrand and Henry Kaiser, "Jimmy Nolen: A Rare Interview with James Brown's Longtime Sideman," *Guitar Player*, April 1984.

"Combine the applejack, the dolo, which is a slide, almost like the skate, and the scallyhop." Scott Cohen, *Yakety Yak: Midnight Confessions and Revelations of 37 Rock Stars and Legends* (Fireside, 1994).

"Have you ever been embarrassed because of prejudice?" *Philadelphia Tribune*, April 26, 1966.

"In 12 hours after leaving the US for Europe, I became a man," "Treated Like a Man in Europe," *Jet*, Oct. 19, 1967.

Donald Warden: Sullivan, *The Hardest Working Man*; Donna Jean Murch, *Living for the City: Migration, Education and the Rise of the Black Panther Party in Oakland, California* (University of North Carolina Press, 2010); Thomas Barry, "The Importance of Being Mr. James Brown," *Look*, Feb. 18, 1969; *The New York Times*, May 21, 1963; interview with Al-Mansour.

Brown and radio: Wolfman Jack with Byron Laursen, *Have Mercy!: Confessions of the Original Rock 'n' Roll Animal* (Warner Books, 1995); *Los Angeles Sentinel*, Oct. 6, 1966; Clay Smith interview.

"His mother died when he was four years old." "James Brown Stands Alone," *New York Amsterdam News*, May 20, 1967.

Playing sick, rumors of retirement: "People Are Talking About...," *Jet*, Aug. 11, 1966; "James Brown's 'Retirement,'" *Jet*, March 30, 1966. For Sarah Bernhardt's coffin on wheels, see Bernhardt, *My Double Life* (State University of New York Press, 1999).

"How on earth am I going to sell this to redneck distributors in the South?" Glover interview, Country Music Hall of Fame.

Chapter Thirteen: AMERICA

Life on the road: Alan Leeds, "James Brown and His First Family of Soul," *Wax Poetics,* February–March 2007; Leeds, Rasbury, Patton, Alaimo interviews.

"Somebody that's thin, they can only be my sister." Brown interview, Tucker files.

Charles Bobbit: Leeds, Patton, Daviss, Sharpton, Roach interviews; Tim Drummond interview with Bruce Tucker, Tucker files.

"I am afraid of what lies ahead of us. We could end up with a full-scale race war in this country." David J. Garrow, *Bearing the Cross: Martin Luther King Jr., and the Southern Christian Leadership Conference* (William Morrow & Co., 1986).

The concert at Boston Garden: David Leaf and Morgan Neville, *The Night James Brown Saved Boston* DVD (Shout! Factory, 2009); Sullivan, *The Hardest Working Man*; J. Anthony Lukas, *Common Ground: A Turbulent Decade in the Lives of Three American Families* (Knopf, 1985); the clip of Brown performing "I Can't Stand It," often viewable on YouTube, alone is worth a book. And, during all of this life-changing intensity, another moment: With politics and lives on the line, Brown hears something he doesn't like, thinks, smiles to himself, and signals to drummer Clyde Stubblefield that he's gonna owe a fine. The coolest head in the house.

Washington, D.C., riots: "National Dateline," *Pittsburgh Courier*, June 22, 1968; "The Wreckage of a Dream," *Washington Post*, Aug. 24, 2004.

America is My Home: *James Brown, The Singles Volume Five: 1967-1969* (Hip-O Select, 2008).

Brown's desire to play Vietnam: memos and letters written by Ofield Dukes, folders marked by month and year, in Hubert Humphrey papers, Minnesota Historical Society, St. Paul, Minnesota; "'Want to Take Soul to Vietnam,' Says James Brown," *Jet*, Nov. 30, 1967; "So This is Washington," *Pittsburgh Courier*, Dec. 16, 1967; "James Brown Tunes Up For Vietnam," *Los Angeles Sentinel*, May 16, 1968; "Lack of Negroes in USO Shows Hit," *Los Angeles Times*, June 25, 1968; "Despite Criticism, State Department Road Blocks, Brown Set to Go," *Jet*, June 6, 1968; Ofield Dukes interview.

"I've been trying to get to Vietnam for the past 18 months." *Jet*, Nov. 30, 1967.

"With a throbbing beat that is primitive and somewhat savage." Press release, James Brown Clipping File, New York Public Library, Lincoln Center.

Antiwar pressure on black entertainers: "Dr. King's Views Keeping Negro Entertainers Out of Vietnam?" *Soul*, Nov. 13, 1967; "Charge Negro Entertainers Won't Go to Vietnam," *Soul*, Oct. 26, 1967.

"Our black entertainers have been attacked in the white press." *Jet*, June 6, 1968.

Brown in Vietnam: James Maycock, "Death or Glory: James Brown in Vietnam," *Mojo*, July 2003; "James Brown Entertains the Troops," *Ebony*, August 1968; Michael C. McDonald, "James Brown Comes Home for his First Farewell," *Village Voice*, June 27, 1968; "James Brown Runs Into U.S. Bias on Vietnam Tour," *Jet*, July 4, 1968; *The Night James Brown Saved Boston*; Marva Whitney, interview with DJ Pari (www.wefunkradio.com/extra/marva); Danny Ray, Stubblefield interviews; Drummond interview, Tucker files.

"We didn't do like Bob Hope. We went back there where the lizards wore guns!" "James Brown, the Sultan of Sweat and Soul," *Washington Post*, Dec. 7, 2003.

"A lot of blacks thought they didn't have a real reason to go there because they wasn't getting their rights here." Christian G. Appy, *Patriots: The Vietnam War Remembered From All Sides* (Viking, 2003).

Chapter Fourteen: HOW YOU GONNA GET RESPECT?

"I am a soul brother." *Washington Afro-American*, May 7, 1968.

Humphrey's courting of African Americans in his 1968 campaign: "Humphrey Visits Cleveland Bearing Gifts for Ghetto," *Cleveland Call and Post*, July 6, 1968; an editorial in the *Chicago Defender*, May 18, 1968, noted approvingly how Humphrey had attacked prejudice in a recent address in Chicago; *Jet*, May 30, 1968, pointed out that Humphrey was the first candidate to visit Resurrection City in D.C., a community erected on the Mall by the Poor People's Campaign, Martin Luther King's final project; the vice president's 1968 trip to Africa, accompanied by Supreme Court Justice Thurgood Marshall, was widely covered in the black press.

Robert Kennedy as the "blue eyed soul brother": Thurston Clarke, *The Last Campaign: Robert F. Kennedy and 82 Days That Inspired America* (Henry Holt & Co., 2008); in her political column, syndicated in the African American press, Ethel Payne praised Kennedy for receiving the endorsement of Rosey Grier and Rafer Johnson, two prominent black athletes.

Brown at Yankee Stadium: *Village Voice*, June 27, 1968.

"What about our negro entertainers?" July 16, 1968, memo from Humphrey. Box two, folder titled "Vice President Hubert Humphrey; Presidential Campaign, July 1968." Ofield Dukes Papers, Reuther Library, Wayne State University, Detroit, Michigan.

The deal to keep the peace in Watts: Ofield Dukes interviews. Baraka disputes Dukes's account, calling it "Mother Goose tales" that "have no validity." Complicating the picture is a memo dated Jan. 8, 1969, from Dukes to Humphrey. It's an evaluation of Humphrey's unsuccessful campaign, in which Dukes tells him: "It is also inconceivable to me that we should start thinking in terms of 'black political sinners,' when in your campaign we had lots of 'bad guys' 'risky, unpredictable people,' according to white standards, 'doing their thing' for your election . . . black militant Ron Karenga, who made certain your visits to Newark, Harlem and Watts were not disrupted. Even Leroi Jones cooperated." (Jones had changed his name to Baraka in 1967; folder "Hubert Humphrey; corres., Dec. 1968-Jan. 1969," in Dukes papers, Wayne State University).

Humphrey booed in Watts: "Humphrey in 'Hoot Out'," *Los Angeles Sentinel*, Aug. 1, 1968.

Brown endorses Humphrey: memo from Dukes to Humphrey, dated July 24, 1968, Folder "Dukes. By date: July 1968," Humphrey papers; "Singer James Brown Endorses HHH," *Washington Post*, July 30, 1968; "Humphrey Joins in but Rock Singer Steals the Show," *Los Angeles Times*, July 30, 1968; " 'Soul Brother No. 1' in Watts," *Los Angeles Sentinel*, Aug. 1, 1968; "HHH Bares His Soul in Watts," *Jet*, August 15, 1968.

"James Brown will be black power." Carmichael interview in *Baltimore Afro American*, May 11, 1968.

"America is My Home": Jordan Kessler, "The Political Impact of James Brown, 1967-1972," unpublished paper; "James Brown Waxes Tune Aimed at Uniting Blacks, Whites," *Jet*, May 23, 1968; *Muhammad Speaks*, July 19, 1968; Byrd interview, AAAMC; Byrd interview, Tucker files.

"We hope this record, if handled right, will provide a public service." *Jet*, May 23, 1968.

"Everybody got on us about [the song]." Byrd interview, AAAMC.

"Roy Wilkins of the music world." *Look*, Feb. 18, 1969.

"What record could possibly follow 'America'?" *Muhammad Speaks*, July 19, 1968.

"You got a white man playing with you, a black man needs a job." Drummond interview, Tucker files.

Brown and the cultural conflict over hair style: Bobbit interview in *The Night James Brown Saved Boston*; Leeds interview. Also see a series of columns Brown wrote for *Soul* magazine in this era, in which he passionately and suddenly champions the Afro.

"If James Brown is so soulful why does he still wear that konk in his hair?" *Baltimore Afro American*, May 25, 1968.

Fake bomb left outside hotel door: Brown and Tucker, *Godfather of Soul*; Patton interview.

"The Black Panthers were putting the heat on us." Panel discussion with Bobbit, David Leaf, and others in Boston, March 31, 2008.

"Say It Loud–I'm Black and I'm Proud": *James Brown, The Singles Volume Five: 1967-1969* (Hip-O Select, 2008); *The Night James Brown Saved Boston*; Wesley interview, Red Bull Music Academy posted at redbull musicacademyradio.com/shows/1402/; Matt Rowland, "For Sweet People From Sweet Charles," *Wax Poetics* 5, Summer 2003; C. L. Franklin Papers, Bentley Historical Library, University of Michigan; two full-page ads, *Los Angeles Sentinel*, Aug. 29, 1968; "California, Here I Come?," *Cleveland Call & Post*, Oct. 5, 1968; "Black Deejay Quits Station In Fuss Over Record," *Jet*, Oct. 25, 1968; *Jet*, Oct. 31, 1968; "Singer Explains 'White and Proud' Song," *Baltimore Afro American* Dec. 20, 1975; "Say it Loud: Black Anthem Turns 40," *South Florida Sun-Sentinel*, Aug. 10, 2008; Wesley, Patton interview.

"A violent struggle in which black people would stand up on our feet and die like men." Steve Estes, *I Am a Man!: Race, Manhood and the Civil Rights Movement* (University of North Carolina Press, 2005).

On self-identifying as "black": "*Jet* Opinion Survey Reveals What Names That Readers Want to be Called," *Jet*, Jan. 11, 1968; "Thurman: The Word 'Black' has Changed its Meaning," *Muhammad Speaks*, June 21, 1968.

"After I heard the words to it, it kind of frightened me." *Wax Poetics*, Summer 2003.

Ben Bart's passing: Jack Bart, interview.

Black promoters trying to keep a hold on Southern turf: "James Brown Cancels, Not Due to 'Soul Power'," *Jet*, July 18, 1968.

Fair Play Committee in Philadelphia: *Philadelphia Tribune*, December 14 and 21, 1968.

Brown plays Nixon's inauguration: "James Brown, Lionel Hamp Headline Inaugural Gala," *Jet*, Jan. 23, 1969; "P.S.," *New York Amsterdam News*, Jan. 25, 1969; "Hamp's Harlem, Brown's Soul Score!," *Jet*, Feb. 6, 1969.

The most important black man in America?: *Look*, Feb. 18, 1969.

Chapter Fifteen: COLOR TVS AND DASHIKIS

Nixon, Black Power, and black capitalism: Manning Marable, *Dispatches From the Ebony Tower: Intellectuals Confront the African American Experience* (Columbia University Press, 2000); "Nixon on Racial Accommodation," *Time*, May 3, 1968; Alex Poinsett, "The Economics of Liberation," *Ebony*, Aug. 1969; Robert Weems Jr., and Lewis A. Randolph, "The Ideological Origins of Richard M. Nixon's 'Black Capitalism' Initiative," *The Review of Black Political Economy*, vol. 29, 2001; Earl Ofari, "The Dilemma of the Black Middle Class," *Ebony*, Aug. 1973.

Carl Stokes onstage with Brown in Cleveland: "People Are Talking About," *Jet*, April 17, 1969.

Nixon secret meetings with black activists: Robert Weems, *Business in Black and White: American Presidents and Black Entrepreneurs in the Twentieth Century* (NYU Press, 2009).

"I learned to do[...] what Mr. Brown called 'on the one.'" Marva Whitney interview with DJ Peri, posted at www.wefunkradio.com/extra/marva.

Brown's concept of the One deepens: Brenda Danielsen, *Presence and Pleasure: The Funk Grooves of James Brown and Parliament* (Wesleyan, 2006); *Soul of the Funky Drummers* DVD, in which Jabo Starks shows Brown expanding on the concept–now it could be felt even in its absence. "Even though you may play a *silent* one," said Starks, "he always had you hit it on the one, make sure you hit it. Always had to be dominant."

The Popcorn: Douglas Wolk, "Popcorn Unlimited," an essay posted at wfmu.org/LCD/25/popcorn.html, is a thing of beauty. For "popcorn" being Brown's way of referring to a female's backside, I draw on remarks made by Pee Wee Ellis at "Ain't That a Groove: the Genius of James Brown" symposium, Princeton, Nov. 29-30, 2007; Payne, in *Give the Drummers Some!,* feels that Stubblefield basically came up with a whole new beat on "Mother Popcorn."

Mayor Yorty proclaims James Brown Day in Los Angeles: "Singer James Brown in 'Mixup' at City Hall," *Los Angeles Times*, July 12, 1969; "Hear This: Brown Won't Accept Citations From Aides," *Jet*, July 31, 1969. Yorty staffers expressed perplexity, saying it had been Brown who requested the day in his honor.

Black & Brown stamps: *Los Angeles Times*, March 23, 1969; *Los Angeles Sentinel*, July 24, 1969; *Atlanta Daily World*, May 10, 1970; ad in *Jet*, March 25, 1971; Al-Mansour interview.

Gold Platter: "Singer Has Food for Thought," *Los Angeles Times*, Jan. 10, 1969; "Inside Story," *Los Angeles Sentinel*, Jan. 16, 1969; "Soul King in Restaurant Venture," *Chicago Defender*, Feb. 24, 1969; "Retailing: Soul Stamps," *Time*, July 11, 1969; Gold Platter scrapbook, exhibited in "Preserving the Legacy," Stanback Museum and Planetarium, South Carolina State University, Orangeburg, South Carolina, Feb. - Sept. 2009.

"This is pioneer, like Daniel Boone and Davy Crockett." *Philadelphia Tribune*, Sept. 2, 1969.

"It's a little like the black capitalism Mr. Nixon is stressing." *Los Angeles Times*, Jan. 10, 1969.

Nixon and the Southern Strategy: Rick Perlstein, *Nixonland: The Rise of a President and the Fracturing of America* (Scribner, 2008); Garry Wills, *Nixon Agonistes: The Crisis of the Self-Made Man* (Cherokee Publishing Company, 1990).

"My understanding of black power is of a man owning his own." Kessler, "The Political Impact of James Brown, 1967-1972."

"Once upon a time if a Negro got out of line, they either put him in jail or made him a Judge." *Philadelphia Tribune*, Feb. 15, 1969.

African American business: Robert C. Kenzer, *Enterprising Southerners: Black Economic Success in North Carolina, 1865-1915* (University of Virginia Press, 1997); A'Lelia Bundles, *On Her Own Ground: The Life and Times of Madam C. J. Walker* (Scribner, 2002); Weems, *Business in Black and White*; Bayard Rustin, "The Myth of Black Capitalism," *Ebony Special Edition*, 1970; Linda Horton, "Pilgrim's Progress," *Black Enterprise*, June 1983.

Mary Florence Brown's suit: "Lawyers Will Bring Baby to Court in Brown Paternity Hearing," *Sacramento Bee*, Sept. 13, 1969; "Paternity Case Hearing is Told of $25,000 Payment," *Sacramento Bee*, Sept. 15, 1969; "James Brown's Accuser Tells of Tryst in Motel," *Baltimore Afro-American*, Sept. 20, 1969; "Senator Negotiates Paternity Settlement for Brown," *Jet*, Oct. 16, 1969.

Problems with Black and Brown stamps: "Black Stamp Firm Seeks $10.4 Billion in Suit Against 21 White Companies," *Jet*, Aug. 5, 1971; *Los Angeles Times*, June 27, 1972.

Gold Platter flounders: "Jim Brown's Chain Fading," *Baltimore Afro-American*, Feb. 21 1970; "It Takes More Than a Star to Sell Goods," *The New York Times*, Oct. 25, 1970.

The Philadelphia show: David Matthews interview.

Chapter Sixteen: **THE OTHER FURTHER**

Bud Hobgood's death: "Record Exec Hopgood Dies of Cerebral Hemorrhage," *Jet*, August 13, 1970; Dennis Wholey, "Thinking About Bud Hobgood," *Cincinnati Enquirer*, August 9, 1970. Rumors persist to this day that he met foul play in Kentucky; his death certificate indicates a cerebral hemorrhage.

King sells to Starday: Blase, *King Records: The Story*; Fox, *King of the Queen City*; Colonel Jim Wilson interview, Country Music Hall of Fame; Hal Neely interview.

The Pacesetters: Dave Marsh ed., *George Clinton and P-Funk: An Oral History* (Avon Books, 1998); Bootsy Collins, Frankie Waddy interviews.

Brown's band falls apart in 1970: "Maceo & All The King's Men," *Blues & Soul* 78, Feb. 1972; Maceo Parker BBC interview available at time of writing at YouTube.com/watch?v=nvY5ZYzQOqw&feature= related; Starks interview in Payne, *Give the Drummer Some!*; Stubblefield, Wesley interviews.

"He opposed us trying to solve the problems as a group, I suppose, because as a group we were stronger." Maceo Parker, BBC interview.

The Cincinnati crew arrives: Waddy, Bootsy Collins, Wesley, Patton interviews; Byrd, AAAMC; Starks in Payne, *Give the Drummer Some!*; "Bootsy Tells Life Story to TV's 'Unsung,'" *Cincinnati Enquirer*, Nov. 5, 2009.

"That's when the funk moved." Melvin Parker interviewed in Payne, *Give the Drummers Some!*

The JBs: "The Life and Soul," *Evening Herald* (Ireland), June 26, 2008; "Inside the World of a P-Funk Time Lord," Kash Waddy interview, posted online at www.hollywoodfiveo.com/exclusive/funk/kash_waddy.shtml; Catfish Collins, interview; Terri Gross, *All I Did Was Ask: Conversations With Writers, Actors, Musicians and Artists* (Hyperion, 2004); Craig Charles, "Funk & Soul Show," BBC, aired April 23, 2011; "James Brown's Bassists," *Bass Player*, March 2005.

Sex Machine: *James Brown, The Singles Volume Seven: 1970-1972* (Hip-O Select, 2009); Byrd, AAAMC.

"Combining the free expression of the oldest 'Shouts' . . . the sound of the other further!" From "What You Mean, Du Wop?," Amiri Baraka, in *Digging: The Afro-American Soul of American Classical Music* (University of California Press, 2009).

Augusta riot, May 10, 1970: News program on the riot, prepared by WJBF, videotape at Augusta State University, special collections; two scrapbooks of riot related news clippings, Augusta State University; John M. Smith, "The Riot of May 1970: A Humanistic Perspective," *Richmond County History*, Summer 1975; Steven Tuck, *Beyond Atlanta: The Struggle for Racial Equality in Georgia, 1940-1980* (University of Georgia Press, 2003); Lester Maddox oral history, interviewer John Allen, Georgia Governors Series, Georgia State University.

"Governor, I'm from Augusta, Georgia. The black people here don't have equality." *Atlanta Constitution*, May 13, 1970.

"You don't think it could happen in Augusta." WJBF documentary footage.

WRDW's politics and accusations of incitement: *Baltimore Afro-American*, May 23, 1970; Gordon and Carter interviews; undated *Atlanta Journal-Constitution* clipping in riot scrapbook, Augusta State University.

Chapter Seventeen: MASTER OF TIME

Marriage to Diedre Jenkins: "Soul Brother No. 1 in Surprise Wedding," *Jet*, Nov. 12, 1970; "James Brown Wed to Baltimore Girl," *Washington Afro-American*, Oct. 27, 1970; Brown Thomas interview.

Moving back to Augusta: *Augusta News-Review*, Nov. 11, 1971.

The House on Walton Way: "$116,000 Mansion is James Brown's Gift to Bride," *Baltimore Afro-American*, Nov. 7, 1970; Rhodes, *Say it Loud!*

"Augusta has gotten a little more civilized since when I was a child." Frank Yerby, *Augusta Chronicle*, March 11, 1975.

The trip to Nigeria and Zambia: Bootsy Collins interview in Tony Bolden, ed., *The Funk Era and Beyond: New Perspectives on Black Popular Culture* (Palgrave Macmillan, 2008); "James Brown Returns From Tour of Nigeria," *Atlanta Daily World*, Dec. 25, 1970; "James Brown Tours Africa," *Soul*, March 22, 1971; "A Soulful Welcome for Brown in Africa," *Augusta News-Review*, Aug. 19, 1971; Matthews interview.

Fela Kuti: Jay Babcock, "Bootsy Collins on Fela Kuti," *Arthur*, Oct. 1999; Trevor Schoonmaker, ed., *Fela: From West Africa to West Broadway* (Palgrave Macmillan, 2003); Michael Veal, *Fela: The Life and Times of an African Music Icon* (Temple University Press, 2000).

"You have your pride. You possess your culture. The white man couldn't rob you of it." Mike Ogbeide, "James Brown Speaks to 'Observer,'" *Nigerian Observer*, Dec. 13, 1970, in *The James Brown Reader*.

"He did that so fast and forcefully, I tell you what, he *levitated*." Waddy interview.

The last months of the Cincinnati crew: Tiger Martin interviewed in Payne, *Give the Drummers Some!*; Waddy, Collins interviews.

The Collins crew exits: Starks interviewed in Payne; Bootsy Collins in "James Brown: Say it Proud," 2007 CNN documentary; "Funk & Soul Show," BBC, April 23, 2011; Bootsy and Catfish Collins, Waddy interviews.

"To put a tie on Bootsy was like to put a bridle on a wild horse." Brown, Tucker files.

A new band is assembled: Fred Wesley, *Hit Me Fred: Recollections of a Sideman* (Duke University Press, 2002); Wesley, Red Bull Academy interview; interview with author.

Turk's tale: Matthews interview.

"Control I must have of everything, of myself." Brown interviewed on *Detroit Black Journal*, 1978, available online at abj.matrix.msu.edu/videofull.php?id=29-DF-22.

The Philadelphia Spectrum show: Leeds interview.

"Here was a quarterback." Colonel Jim Wilson interview, Country Music Hall of Fame.

Leaving King, Polydor enters: Randy McNutt's *Little Labels, Big Sound* has a good thumbnail sketch of Brown's departure; Russell Sanjek's *American Popular Music and its Business, Vol. 2* (Oxford University Press, 1980) and Fredric Dannen's *Hit Men: Power Brokers and Fast Money Inside the Music Business* (Crown, 1990) sketch Polygram's creation of Polydor.

On the Polydor signing: "Soul Brother No. 1 Signs $910,000 Record Deal With New Disc Company," *Jet*, Aug. 5, 1971; "Brown to Polydor in 5-Yr. Pact: Buys Pub," *Billboard*, July 24, 1971: "James Brown Signs with Polydor Records," *New York Amsterdam News*, Oct. 21, 1971; Tucker files; Roy Rifkin, Daviss, Leeds, Stone, Neely interviews.

"King Heroin": liner notes to *James Brown, The Singles Volume Eight: 1972-1973* (Hip-O Select, 2009); "Brown to Give Third of Sales of Record to Fight Drug Abuse," *Jet*, March 2, 1972.

Donated to Jimmy Carter's drug treatment program: *Augusta Chronicle*, July 13, 1972.

Chapter Eighteen: **SOUL POWER**

White radio ejects after "Say It Loud": Rickey Vincent, *Funk: The Music, The People and the Rhythm of the One* (St. Martin's Griffin, 1996); Charley Gillett, in *Record Mirror* (September 6, 1966), said the song was played precisely once on the BBC, then filed.

Black Arts Movement confronts Brown: Stephen E. Henderson, "Inside the Funk Shop," in *African American Literary Theory: A Reader*, Winston Napier, ed. (NYU Press, 2000); Cecil Brown, "James Brown, Hoodoo and Black Culture," *Black Review* 1 (1971); Larry Neal, "And Shine Swam On," in *Black Fire: An Anthology of Afro-American Writing*, Amiri

Baraka and Larry Neal, eds. (Black Classic Press, 2007); Neal's "Suppose James Brown read Fanon," from "The Social Background to the Black Arts Movement," *The Black Scholar* 18, no. 1 (1987); Amiri Baraka's poem "The Funk World," in Baraka, *Digging*; "The Changing Same (R&B and New Black Music)," *The LeRoi Jones/Amiri Baraka Reader* (Basic Books, 1999); "James Brown," The Last Poets, on *Right On!* CD; Mel Watkins, "The Lyrics of James Brown: Ain't It Funky Now, Or Money Won't Change Your Licking Stick," in *Amistad 2: Writings on Black History and Culture*, John A. Williams and Charles F. Harris, eds. (Random House, 1971).

"I'm a racist when it comes to freedom." "James Brown Goes Through Some New Changes," *Jet*, Dec. 30, 1971.

Soul City: Devin Fergus, "Black Power, Soft Power: Floyd McKissick, Soul City and the Death of Moderate Black Republicanism," *Journal of Policy History*, no. 2 (2010); "McKissick's New Town for Blacks Called 'Soul City'," *Jet*, Jan. 30, 1969; "Soul City Makes Changes: Receives Federal Help," *Jet*, March 9, 1972.

Floyd McKissick: Oral History with Floyd B. McKissick Sr., Wilson Library, University of North Carolina at Chapel Hill; *Cleveland Call & Post*, July 5, 1972; *California Voice*, Aug. 31, 1972; letter from McKissick to James Brown, dated Jan. 3, 1973, McKissick Papers, Chapel Hill.

"This black man who used to style himself a super-militant" and "political prostitutes." Carl Rowan syndicated column, Aug. 16, 1972.

"I can't throw you a rope until I save myself. It's slippery around the edge of the bank." *Newsweek*, July 1, 1968.

Sammy Davis Jr. embraces Nixon: Wil Haygood, "The Hug," *Washington Post*, Sept. 14, 2003; the picture appeared in *Jet*, Sept, 7, 1972.

"If you've seen one city slum, you've seen them all." Agnew quoted in Perlstein, *Nixonland*.

"There are people in our society who should be separated and discarded." Agnew in the *Chicago Tribune*, July 1, 1970.

Robert Brown: interview with Bruce Tucker, Tucker files; "Robert Brown Puts Black Consciousness in the White House," *Jet*, March 4, 1971; "Nixon Shines at Brown's Bash," *New York Amsterdam News*, Feb. 12, 1972; "Testimonial for Brown Benefits Sickle Cell Anemia Drive," *Jet*, Feb. 17, 1972.

Nixon meets with James Brown: White House recording made on Oct. 10, 1972, conversation 7958, National Archives, College Park, Maryland.

Brown Endorses Nixon: "Brown Urges Nixon to Help Blacks and Endorses President," *Jet*, Oct. 26, 1972; "Black Entertainers Say Every Voter Has the Right to his Opinion," *Atlanta Daily World*, Nov. 5, 1972.

The endorsement fallout: "Brailey Accuses James Brown of Soul Sell-Out for Backing Nixon," *Baltimore Sun*, Oct. 12, 1972; "Black Supporters of President Under Fire," *The New York Times*, Oct. 17, 1972; "Brown Says Nixon Backs King 'Day,'" *Augusta Herald*, Oct. 20, 1972; "Stars for Nixon Camp Assailed," *Chicago Defender*, Oct. 23, 1972; "White House Delegation Meets With James Brown," *Atlanta Daily World*, Oct. 24, 1972; Charles Green, "The People Speak" *Newark Afro-American*, Oct. 28, 1972; "Down the Big Road," *Cleveland Call & Post*, Oct. 28, 1972; "Say James Brown is no Soul Brother," William Marable, *New York Amsterdam News*, Oct. 28, 1972; "Has James Brown Sold Black People Out or Sold Them In?" *Jet*, Nov. 2 1972; "Angela Calls Sammy Traitor to Black People," *Cleveland Call & Post*, Nov. 18, 1972; "Davis and Brown Prod President Nixon to Help Blacks," *Jet*, Nov. 23, 1972; "Right On by Pamala Haynes," *Pittsburgh Courier*, Dec. 2, 1972.

Election night in Washington: Ethel Payne, "So This is Washington," *Pittsburgh Courier*, Nov. 25, 1972.

Knoxville beating: *Knoxville Sentinel*, Dec. 11, 1972; also Dec 12, 13, 27, and 28. Daviss interview.

"He found out this country is not as free as he thought." Letter, *Jet*, Jan. 11, 1973.

Nixon's inauguration: "The Nixon Inauguration," *Ebony*, March 1973.

"Don't *make* me equal. I can't survive on equality." *Newsweek*, July 1, 1968.

Chapter Nineteen: FOLLOW THE MONEY

"There's a lot of money here." Brown interview, Tucker files.

The Third World: *Augusta Chronicle*, April 17, 2008, Sept. 9, 1973; *Augusta News-Review*, Oct. 18, 1973; Charles Reid interview.

"You never seen a Brink's truck follow a hearse to the graveyard." Danny Ray interview.

James Brown Motor Inn: *Baltimore Sun*, June 6, 1970; *Baltimore Afro-American*, May 30 and June 6, 1970; March 27 and April 3, 1971.

James Brown film projects: *Jet*, July 25, 1968, March 13 and Oct. 5, 1972; *Philadelphia Tribune*, March 26, 1969; "People, Places 'n' Situwayshuns," *Los Angeles Sentinel*, April 26, 1973.

Blaxploitation Cinema: Darius James, *That's Blaxploitation!: Roots of the Baadasssss 'Tude* (St. Martin's Griffin, 1995); David Walker, Chris Watson, Andrew J. Rausch, *Reflections on Blaxploitation: Actors and Directors Speak* (Scarecrow Press, 2009); Richard Simon, "The Stigmatization of 'Blaxploitation'," in *Soul: Black Power, Politics and Pleasure*, Richard C. Green and Monique Guillory, eds. (NYU Press, 1997); "Isaac Hayes and the Volatile Black Image," *Soul*, Jan. 25, 1971; "Sara Speaking," *New York Amsterdam News*, Aug. 7, 1971; "College Marching Bands Get 'Shaft Theme' Sheet Music," *Jet*, Dec. 23, 1971; "Isaac Hayes, Sammy Davis and 'Shaft' Steal Oscar Show," *Jet*, April 27, 1972; James Brown on Blacula: "New York Beat," *Jet*, Oct. 5, 1972.

"We shall forget morality and grade this on effort and Blackness." "Superfly, New Super Flic," *Soul*, Sept. 11, 1972.

Black Caesar: *Black Caesar*, MGM (1973; 2001 DVD); Wesley, *Hit Me Fred*; Leeds, liner notes to *James Brown, The Singles Volume Eight: 1972-1973* (Hip-O Select, 2009); Rhodes, *Say it Loud!*; " 'Black Caesar,' Inverted American Dream," *Pittsburgh Courier*, June 30, 1973; Larry Cohen, Wesley interviews.

"The Godfather of Soul": Bobbit, interviewed in 1978 British documentary, *Soul Brother Number One*.

Bob Marley and Brown: John Masouri, *Wailing Blues: The Story of Bob Marley's Wailers* (Omnibus Press, 2010); Christopher John Farley, *Before the Legend: The Rise of Bob Marley* (Harper Paperbacks, 2007).

The King presses sold to Jamaica: Colonel Jim Wilson interview, Country Music Hall of Fame.

Brown in Brazil: Anna Scott, "It's All in the Timing: The Latest Moves, James Brown's Grooves and the 70s Race Consciousness Movement in Salvador, Bahia-Brazil," in *Soul*, Green and Guillory, eds.; Livo Sansone, "In Bahia and Rio," in *Brazilian Popular Music and Globalization*, Charles A. Perrone, Christopher Dunn, eds. (Routledge, 2001).

"There was no band from Benin who didn't have something in their repertoire influenced by James Brown." *Wax Poetics*, no. 39, 2010.

Get on the good foot and beginnings of hip-hop: Michael Holman, "Breaking: The History," in *That's the Joint!: The Hip-Hop Studies Reader*, Murray Forman and Mark Anthony Neal, eds. (Routledge, 2004); Frank Owen, "Back in the Days: Most of What You Know About the Old School is Wrong," *Vibe*, December 1994.

"James Brown Nixon's Clown": *New York Amsterdam News*, May 26, 1973; *Baltimore Afro-American*, June 2, 1973.

Nixon assisted Brown: Daviss, Leeds interviews.

James Palmer: Martha High, Wesley, Leeds interviews; Leeds email.

Brown and Watergate: "You Can Have Watergate Just Gimme Some Bucks and I'll Be Straight," the J.B.'s, on *James Brown: The Singles Volume Eight: 1972-1973* (Hip-O Select, 2009); "Brown Calls $94,000 Tax Case A Fraud 'By a White Man's Nigger'; Discusses His Views On Nixon Since Watergate," *Augusta News-Review*, Jan. 24, 1974.

The IRS spies on Brown: "Top Blacks Among Persons Spied On by Tax Officials," *Jet*, Oct. 23, 1975; *Augusta Chronicle*, Oct. 3, 1975; *Time*, Oct. 13 1975.

Teddy Brown: "James Brown's Son Killed; Star Goes on With His Show," *New York Amsterdam News*, June 23, 1973; Roach, Danny Ray, Daviss, Patton, Sharpton, and Leeds interviews.

Slaughter's Big Rip-off: DVD, 2001 (MGM, 1973); Rhodes, *Say it Loud!*; Wesley, *Hit Me Fred*; Wesley Red Bull Music Academy interview.

"The Payback": Adam White and Fred Bronson, *The Billboard Book of Number One Rhythm & Blues Hits* (Billboard Books, 1993); Leeds liner notes, *James Brown, The Singles Volume Nine: 1973-1975* (Hip-O Select, 2010); Byrd interview, AAAMC; High, Wesley, Cohen interviews.

Chapter Twenty: **EMULSIFIED**

Life at Walton Way: Brown Thomas, Daviss, Sharpton, Austin, Roach interviews.

The death of Poojie: Daviss interview.

Al Sharpton: Sharpton, *Go and Tell Pharaoh* (Doubleday, 1996); "The Gospel According to James Brown and Reverend Al Sharpton," *Jet*, Aug. 26, 1991; Sharpton interview.

Secret submarines in the Savannah River: Daviss interview. The region that Brown was born in was wiped off the map by the federal government in the 1950s and turned into the Savannah River Nuclear Reactor Site, a high-security facility where uranium is enriched for nuclear weapons.

"They were looking up to me like a god." M. Cordell Thompson, *Black Stars*, Oct. 1972. In this article Brown makes a point of defining, while putting borders around, his feelings for Africa. "We're spiritual brothers and they even want to strengthen these ties even more," he said of blacks in America and Africa. "But we're still from another country, three hundred years did that, and even the Honorable Elijah Muhammad says this. America is going to be our home. That's why I'm a constitutional man myself, 'cause that's the only stick we have."

Zaire: *Soul Power* documentary DVD (Sony Pictures Home Entertainment, 2010); Hugh Masekela and D. Michael Cheers, *Still Grazing: The Musical Journey of Hugh Masekela* (Crown, 2004); Gary Steward, *Rhumba on the River: A History of the Popular Music of the Two Congos* (Verso, 2000); James, *Rage to Survive*; Wesley, *Hit Me Fred*; James P. Murray, "A Look at Zaire '74," *Amsterdam News*, Sept. 21, 1974; "Festival in Zaire," *Blues & Soul*, Nov. 5 1974; Roach interview.

Ali & Brown: The poem appears in the catalog to the Christie's auction of the James Brown Collection, July 17, 2008; for the two competing to stop traffic in Manhattan, see Hirshey, *Nowhere to Run.*

Senegal: *Soul Brother Number One* documentary; Wesley, *Hit Me Fred*; Lola Love, Daviss interviews.

Omar Bongo: "African President Pays $160,000 for James Brown Concert," *Augusta News-Review*, Jan. 23, 1975; Love, Patton, Stone interviews.

"Star-Spangled Banner" sung in Cleveland: *Augusta Chronicle*, March 26, 1975.

George Clinton and P-Funk: Greg Tate, *Flyboy in the Buttermilk: Essays on Contemporary America* (Simon & Schuster, 1992); Dave Thompson, *Funk: The Essential Listening Companion* (Backbeat Books, 2001); Marsh, *George Clinton and P-Funk*; Vincent, *Funk*; Joe McEwen, "Funk," in *The Rolling Stone Illustrated History of Rock & Roll*, Anthony DeCurtis, James Henke, Holly George-Warren, eds. (Random House, 1992); Archie Ivy, "We'll Just Keep Doin' What Comes Funky," *Soul*, June 9,1975; JA, "Countdown on Parliament, From Launchpad to Mothership Connection," *Blues & Soul*, June 29, 1976; Steve Ivory, "If All Else Fails...Funk It," and Mike Terry, "Funkadelic," *Soul*, Feb. 5, 1979; Barry Michael Cooper, "The Gospel According to Parliament," *Village Voice*, Jan. 14, 1980; "Stuffs + Things: A Motorbooty Rap With George Clinton," *Motorbooty*, 1989; Hank Bordowitz, "The Three Funkateers," *American Visions*, December 1993; Collins, Waddy interviews. And the work and memory of David Mills.

"We called him the grandfather of soul." Clinton in *Blues and Soul*, June 29, 1976.

"His music has primal rhythm..." Clinton in *Soul*, Feb. 5, 1979.

Chapter Twenty-one: **THE HUSTLE**

Disco: Alice Echols, *Hot Stuff: Disco and the Remaking of American Culture* (W.W. Norton & Co., 2010); Tim Lawrence, *Love Saves the Day: A History of American Dance Music Culture, 1970-1979* (Duke University Press, 2004); Peter Shapiro, *Turn the Beat Around: The Secret History of Disco* (Faber & Faber, 2005).

James Brown and disco: Alice Echols, "The Land of Somewhere Else: Refiguring James Brown in Seventies Disco," *Criticism*, vol. 50 no. 1 (Winter 2008); Steve Blush, interview, *Soho News*, June 28, 1979; "Funky Godfather is Disco's Daddy," *Amsterdam News*, June 30, 1979; Joe McEwen, "James Brown Scales the Mountain," *Village Voice*, July 9, 1979; "Pop Beat," *Los Angeles Times*, Aug. 25, 1979; "People, Places 'n' Situwayshuns," *Los Angeles Sentinel*, June 19, 1980.

Disco as "a cottonfield": Brown, interviewed on *Detroit Black Journal*, 1978, available online at abj.matrix.msu.edu/videofull.php?id=29-DF-22.

"James Brown is being left out and he feels it." Vernon Gibbs, "Is James Brown Obsolete?," *Village Voice*, July 28, 1975.

"Get Up Offa That Thing": *James Brown, The Singles Volume Ten: 1975-1979* (Hip-O Select, 2011); Hollie Farris interview.

Copying other records: Wesley at Princeton symposium; Wesley, *Hit Me Fred*; Siddhartha Mitter, "Capturing the Cameroon Sound," *Boston Globe*, June 26, 2009.

"He was stumbling through the dark." Byrd, AAAMC.

"If I had to go to work today, I would have *no* job." Brown, *Detroit Black Journal.*

Sweet Charles hijacks Brown's band: *Wax Poetics* 5, Summer 2003.

Problems arise with Polydor: Brown, *The Life of James Brown*; Daviss, Leeds, Stone interviews.

"The Jews wanted me to make it and the Germans didn't." Brown interview, Tucker files.

Jimmy Carter and Brown: Brown's 1977 letter to the president was part of an exhibition devoted to Brown's life at the Stanback Museum and Planetarium, South Carolina State University, Orangeburg, South Carolina, in 2009. Correspondence records in the Carter Library indicate Carter did not respond to Brown's letters, but instead forwarded Brown's appeal to his legal staff. Brown also sent a telegram to Carter offering to help with unrest in Africa, and reached out to Senator Sam Nunn for help making a connection with Carter; Daviss interview.

Frankie Crocker: Dannen, *Hit Men*; *Amsterdam News*, July 31, 1976, and March 5, 1977; "Brown in Court: 'No Crocker Pay,'" *Billboard*, Dec. 25, 1976; "N.Y. DJ Frankie Crocker Found Guilty of Perjury," *Jet*, Jan. 13, 1977; Cynthia Kirk, "Payola vs. the Power of 'Trust': Frankie Crocker," *Soul*, Dec. 19, 1977; Sharpton interview.

Problems at Brown's radio stations: For J.B. Broadcasting taken to court for failing to air commercials, see *Augusta Chronicle*, April 15, 1972. Regarding the IRS lien filed against Brown's stations for $94,000 in unpaid payroll taxes, *Chronicle*, Dec. 14, 1973.

For the FCC giving evidence in Circuit Court that WEBB had more than 100 rules violations, *Baltimore Afro-American*, Jan. 19, 1974. In the wake of the ASCAP suit, WEBB is revealed to lack even the proper license to play copyrighted music: See *Baltimore Afro-American*, July 5, 1975 and *Amsterdam News*, July 16, 1975. Action against WEBB slows, due to the station's ongoing bankruptcy proceedings: *Baltimore Sun*, May 6, 1978. Regarding the station's sale in 1980 in order to pay off debts, see *Atlanta Daily World*, Jan. 31, 1980. For sale of the Augusta station at public auction, after owners defaulted on a $268,000 loan, see *Baltimore Afro-American*, April 12, 1980.

"I don't know that Mr. Brown ever paid any money on that station." Percy Sutton in Artbeat, *Village Voice*, Nov. 13, 1979.

"Now Mr. Brown, dumb you're not." *Baltimore Afro-American*, Oct. 21, 1978.

William Kunstler teaming up with Brown: David Hershkovits, "James Brown: I Was Robbed," *Soho Weekly News*, Nov. 15 1979; "Art Beat," *Village Voice*, Nov. 13, 1979; *Augusta Herald*, Nov. 2, 1979; *Augusta Chronicle*, Nov. 2, 1979; Sharpton interview.

Webb Pierce's guitar-shaped swimming pool: "Row's Guitar Pool Strums Swan Song," *Nashville Banner*, March 2, 1979.

Porter Waggoner goes Disco: "He's the Same Porter But With a Disco Beat," *Banner*, February 1, 1979.

Brown conquers Music City: "Fiddle Before Politics Senator's Preference," *Nashville Tennessean*, March 3, 1979; "'Soul' Spot Angers Opry Regulars," *Banner*, March 5, 1979; "James Brown Subject of Protest by Some at Grand Ole Opry," *Atlanta Daily World*, March 8, 1979; "Opry Discord Has a Familiar Note," *Banner*, March 9, 1979; letter, "'Soul'

Music Doesn't Belong With 'Country'," *Banner*, March 9, 1979; "James Brown at the Opry," *Tennessean*, March 10, 1979; "Brown Fails to Stir Audience," *Banner*, March 12, 1979; Daviss, Farris interviews.

Chapter Twenty-two: I CAN SEE THE LIGHT!

Beech Island: *Augusta Chronicle*, May 30, 1988; photographs in "Preserving the Legacy," Stanback Museum, 2009; Sharpton interview.

Studying the Koran: Hermon Hitson interview.

"You can trust a Southern white man, you are always gonna know where he's coming from." Daviss interview.

Blues Brothers: *Blues Brothers* (Universal Studios, 1980; DVD 2009); Tom Shales and James Andrew Miller, *Live From New York: An Uncensored History of* Saturday Night Live, *as Told by its Stars, Writers, and Guests* (Little, Brown & Company, 2002); Pauline Kael, *Taking It All In* (Holt Rinehart and Winston); Gayle Wald, "Soul's Revival: White Soul, Nostalgia, and the Culturally Constructed Past," in *Soul*, Green and Guillory, eds.

Brown's influence on hip-hop and go-go: Jeff Chang, *Can't Stop Won't Stop: A History of the Hip-hop Generation* (St. Martin's Press, 2005); Angus Batey, "DJ Kool Herc DJs His First Block Party," London *Guardian*, June 13, 2011; Kip Lornell and Charles C. Stephenson, Jr., *The Beat! Go-Go Music From Washington DC* (University Press of Mississippi, 2009); Afrika Bambaataa, Chuck Brown interviews.

"The man looks great. He could still act if he wanted to." Brown on Reagan, in *Los Angeles Times*, Jan. 31, 1982.

Nov. 4, 1981 letter from Reagan: "Preserving the Legacy," 2009 exhibition at South Carolina State University.

"Rabble-soother." Garry Wills, *Reagan's America* (Doubleday, 1986).

"Singer James Brown has found he can no longer perform those wild athletic leaps he did as of yore." *Los Angeles Sentinel*, April 23, 1981.

"He really did give *more*, unleashing a series of inspired moves." *Los Angeles Times*, Feb. 2, 1982.

PCP: Brown, *The Life of James Brown*; Barney Hoskyns, *Ragged Glories: City Lights, Country Funk, American Music* (Pimlico, 2003); Michael Goldberg, "Wrestling With the Devil: The Struggle for the Soul of James Brown," *Rolling Stone*, April 6, 1989; Clayton Fillyau Jr., McRae, Rasbury interviews.

Adrienne: Thomas Brown, Sharpton, Daviss, Love interviews.

"Our souls met a long time ago." Brown, Tucker files.

Jimmy Nolen: Lunetha Nolen, Ronald Laster, Keith Jenkins interviews.

Island Records Deal: Leeds and George, eds., *James Brown Reader*; Sly Dunbar and Wally Badarou interviews, Red Bull Music Academy (redbullmusicacademy.com).

Afrika Bambaataa and "Unity": Gavin Martin, "James Brown (and Afrika Bambaataa): Sex Machine Today," *NME*, September 1, 1984; Bambaataa interview.

Rocky IV and "Living in America": *Rocky IV* (MGM 1985; 2004 DVD); Ethlie Ann Vare, "Brown's Career Has Punch Thanks to Stallone," *Billboard*, Nov. 8, 1986.

Dan Hartman: Robert Hilburn, "James Brown's Godson of Soul," *Los Angeles Times*, Oct. 19, 1986; Linda Kelly, "License to Chill," *Spin*, November 1989; Larry Flick, "Dan Hartman Dies at 43," *Billboard*, April 9, 1994.

"James Brown has made a lot of good records, but it was that purist James Brown thing." Hartman in *Los Angeles Times*, Oct. 19, 1986.

Playing "Living in America" to big, new crowds: "James Brown: The Godfather's Back, With a Bullet!," Ben Fong-Torres, *Not Fade Away: A Backstage Pass to Twenty Years of Rock & Roll* (Backbeat Books, 1999); *Chicago Sun Times,* March 30, 1986; *Chicago Tribune*, Nov. 20, 1986; Laster interview.

Chapter Twenty-three: AN UPROAR ALL THE TIME

"We met visually on Solid Gold. But we was already really together because we're Third World people." Brown interview, Tucker files.

Jealous of Dan Hartman watching his wife: "Full Force discuss James Brown on angel dust," YouTube.com/watch?v=E8C_TytrtRc.

Domestic violence and other encounters with the law: "James Brown: Troubled Times in Augusta," *Atlanta Journal and Constitution*, April 11, 1988; Steve Dougherty and Victoria Balfour, "After Allegedly Beating His Wife and Shooting Her Car, James Brown May Have to Face the Music," *People*, April 25, 1988; "James Brown Arrested on Drug and Assault Charges," *Jet*, June 6, 1988; Ivan Solotaroff, "Pleas, Pleas, Pleas: The Tribulations and Trials of James Brown," *Village Voice*, Feb. 21, 1989; "Wrestling With the Devil," *Rolling Stone*, April 6, 1989.

Sept. 1987 chase through an IHOP parking lot: *Augusta Chronicle*, September 13, 1987.

Alfie pulled over in a Lincoln Town car: *People*, April 25, 1988.

Careening through Todd's Shop N Go: *Augusta Chronicle*, Nov. 9, 1987.

A bloody Easter weekend, 1988: *Augusta Chronicle*, April 8, 1988.

Alfie arrested at Bush Field: "James Brown's Wife Arrested On Drug Charge Third Time," *Jet*, June 6, 1988.

Alfie arrested for setting his clothes on fire in New Hampshire hotel room: *Augusta Chronicle*, May 10, 1988.

"Everybody loves the Godfather of Soul...America is the Godfather of Soul." *Augusta Chronicle*, May 14, 1988.

Brown spends a night in jail, and wants a divorce: *Augusta Chronicle*, May 20, 1988.

"Diplomatic immunity": "Lawyer Seeks 'immunity' For James Brown's Wife," *Jet*, June 20, 1988.

"My nose, my ears, my eyes, my rectum, my privates, those are parts of my body that I don't want to fool with. And my arm." Brown interview, Tucker files.

The bathroom incident and penultimate chase: Michael Vitez, "James Brown, Up and Down," *Philadelphia Inquirer*, Feb. 9, 1989; Rhodes, *Say It Loud!*; Solotaroff, *Village Voice*.

"I've been in slavery all my life, ain't nothing new." *Rhythm and Business*, May 1989.

"He thinks his fans would have seen it as a greater weakness to admit he has a drug problem." *Rhythm and Business*, May 1989.

"God said, 'boy, go home.'" Solotaroff, *Village Voice*

Zsa Zsa Gabor's bust: "'I Can't Believe It,' She Says: Zsa Zsa Gabor Convicted of Slapping Police," *Los Angeles Times*, Sept. 30, 1989; "Judge Sentences Gabor to Three Days in Jail," *The New York Times*, Oct. 25, 1989.

Columbia judge displays Brown in his chamber: "Judge Summons James Brown to Court to Sign Autographs," *Spartanburg Herald-Journal*, April 28, 1989.

FAMU marching 100 represents America: Jacqui Malone, *Steppin' on the Blues: The Visible Rhythms of African American Dance* (University of

Illinois Press, 1996) has a transcendent chapter on this band, at home and abroad.

Cash and checks found in Brown's cell: "James Brown Sent to Another Prison for Having $48,000 in Checks in His Possession," *Jet*, Aug. 14, 1989; Renee D. Turner, "The Ordeal of James Brown," *Ebony*, July 1991.

Brown's presidential gold card: Herb Kent and David Smallwood, *The Cool Gent: The Nine Lives of Radio Legend Herb Kent* (Lawrence Hill Books, 2009).

"They went way back with this, before civil rights, before Martin Luther King." Tucker's notes, Tucker files.

Photographs of Adrienne's bruises passed on to the *National Enquirer*: "Singer James Brown's Battered Wife Tells Her Own Shocking Story: How He Tried to Kill Me," *National Enquirer*, April 26, 1988.

Adrienne called the FBI, demanding they investigate the racially motivated arrest of her husband: FBI files, released shortly after James Brown's death. There are *many* more files, from the FBI and other government agencies, in the National Archives, awaiting declassification.

"Where are his friends? They're as far away as they can get." Bobby Byrd, quoted by Michael Vitez, "James Brown, Up and Down," *Philadelphia Inquirer*, Feb. 9, 1989.

One rare visitor was Lee Atwater: Eric Alterman, "G.O.P. Chairman Lee Atwater: Playing Hardball," *The New York Times*, April 30, 1989; Sharpton interview.

"You start out in 1954 by saying 'Nigger, nigger, nigger.' By 1968 you can't say 'nigger'–that hurts you." Atwater quoted in Jack Bass and Marilyn W. Thompson, *Strom: The Complicated Personal and Political Life of Strom Thurmond* (PublicAffairs, 2005).

Atwater, Brown, and South Carolina politics: John Brady, *Bad Boy: The Life and Politics of Lee Atwater* (Da Capo Press, 1996); Jerry Shriver, "Lee Atwater: A Blues Bash is Republican Leader's Ideal Grand Old Party," *USA Today*, March 13, 1989; In Roxanne Roberts's "The Very Senior Senator," *Washington Post*, March 10, 1993, Brown sings "Happy Birthday" at Strom Thurmond's 90th birthday celebration; "Generational Change Coming to South Carolina in Graham," *Atlanta Journal-Constitution*, Nov. 4, 2001, describes Brown singing "God Bless America" at an event where the 98-year-old Thurmond gave his senatorial blessing to Lindsey Graham.

A furlough to sing for the troops: "James Brown Gets Release From Work Center to Entertain Troops in S.C.," *Jet*, Jan. 14, 1991.

Brown's 1991 parole: Rhodes, *Say It Loud!*

"We'll do more bonding now, and I'm gonna just eat his face." "James Brown Talks about What's Ahead Now That He Has Been Paroled," *Jet*, March 18, 1991.

The pay-per-view return: Chris Smith, "A Conversation With the Godfather," *New York*, June 3, 1991; Jon Pareles, "James Brown Returns, on Pay-per-View Cable," *The New York Times*, June 12, 1991; Jeff Niesel, "Soul Brother No. 2," *Cleveland Scene*, September 15, 2010; Sharpton interview.

Problems with Adrienne: "James Brown Faces new Assault Charges; Says, 'I Never Touched' Wife," *Jet*, Dec. 26, 1994; "James Brown's Wife Says He Didn't Hit Her," *Jet*, Dec. 4, 1995.

Adrienne Brown's death: Rhodes, *Say It Loud!*; "Adrienne Brown Mourned After Mysterious Death Following Liposuction," *Jet*, Jan. 29, 1996; "James Brown's Wife Died After Taking PCP and Prescription Drugs, Autopsy Report Says," *Jet*, Feb. 26, 1996.

The 1998 gun incident: Hoskyns, *Ragged Glories*.

Committed to a mental facility: "Family Members Hospitalize James Brown," *Augusta Chronicle*, Jan. 16, 1998; "Soul Singer James Brown Hospitalized," *Chronicle*, Jan. 17, 1998; "James Brown Released From Hospital," *Chronicle*, Jan. 22, 1998.

Further troubles: "Police Arrest James Brown," *Augusta Chronicle*, Jan. 28, 1998; "James Brown Sentenced to Drug Treatment or Jail," *Chronicle*, March 14, 1998; "Singer Attacked Woman, Suit Says," *Chronicle*, March 20, 1998; "James Brown Ordered to Undergo Drug Rehab After Firing Rifle at His Home," *Jet*, April 6, 1998; "Ex-backup Singer Sues Brown," *Chronicle*, Aug. 8, 2000.

"Well, you reach out for help if you need it. If I needed it, I'd probably reach out for it." Hoskyns, *Ragged Glories*.

"It's going to be an uproar all the time." Letter to President Clinton, March 26, 1998, "Preserving the Legacy," South Carolina State University.

Pullman Bonds: Craig Rosen, "Bonds...James Brown Bonds," *Yahoo Music*, May 4, 1999; "Singer Intends to Issue Bonds," *Augusta Chronicle*, May 5, 1999; Ann Brown, "Royalties 'R' Us," *Black Enterprise*, June 1999; "Brown Bags $30 Million Bond," *Chronicle*, June 17, 1999;

Stephen Gandel, "False Notes: Banker to Music Legends More Myth Than Reality," *Crain's New York Business*, June 11, 2001; Jeff Allen interview.

Deanna and Yamma sue their father: "Singer's Daughters Sue Over Royalties," *Augusta Chronicle*, September 18, 2002; Emma Austin interview.

Brown's 2003 pardon: "Godfather of Soul is Granted Pardon," *Augusta Chronicle*, May 20, 2003.

"I'm getting very tired, and I'd love to quit yesterday." "James Brown Keeps Up the Pace," *Augusta Chronicle*, May 22, 2003.

Chapter Twenty-four: THE DANCER

James Brown and dance: James Brown thought about dancing all the time; interviewers just didn't ask him about it much. In October, 1991, the PBS series *Great Performances* aired "Everybody Dance Now," a program on street dance styles, and featured an interview in which Brown says many deep things about his art. Perhaps the whole interview will some day be shared. Brenda Dixon, in "James Brown: Godfather of Dance," *Dance Magazine,* August 2000, asks a number of dancers for their thoughts on Brown. This is barely a start.

"I realized dancing was gonna be a way of life for me." "Everybody Dance Now."

Future Shock: Russell Simins, "Future Shock Cannot Be Stopped," *Grand Royal* no. 3. A sacramental 30-minute suture of some of what has survived: blog.wfmu.org/freeform/2008/02/post-2.html.

"Dynamic suggestion." Zora Neale Hurston, "Characteristics of Negro Expression," in *Signifyin(g), Sanctifyin', and Slam Dunking: A Reader in African American Expressive Culture*, Gena Dagel Caponi, ed. (University of Massachusetts Press, 1999).

"Rhythm is everything in boxing." Sugar Ray Robinson and Dave Anderson, *Sugar Ray* (Da Capo Press 1994).

Chapter Twenty-five: HIT IT AND QUIT IT

Tomi Rae and their marriage: "James Brown Weds Sweetheart," *Jet*, Jan. 21, 2002; Rhodes, *Say it Loud!*; "Brown's Wife Gets Clean Slate," *The State*, April 18, 2004; Tomi Rae Brown interview.

Life at Beech Island: Tomi Rae Brown, Roosevelt Johnson, Gloria Daniel interviews.

"Everything in this world disappears and vacates." Curt Sampson, *Chasing Tiger* (Atria Books, 2002).

The duet with Pavarotti: Amy Christian, Keith Jenkins, Farris interviews; Lou Reed quote from *Daily Telegraph*, London, May 26, 2007.

A museum installation: Michael Marriott, "Project Virtual Funk: The Digitizing of James Brown," *The New York Times*, April 13, 2000; "Artist's Journey catapults riders into psychedelic world," *Seattle Times*, June 20, 2000.

"I'm gonna stop when George Burns comes back and be born again." Hoskyns, *Ragged Glories*.

Michael Jackson and James Brown: J. Randy Taraborrelli, *Michael Jackson: The Magic, The Madness, The Whole Story, 1958-2009* (Hachette, 2009); "Michael Jackson praises James Brown as inspiration," *Reuters*, Dec. 30, 2006; Wesley interview, *New Funk Times*, 1991.

Full page ad in *Variety*: July 21, 2003. The divorce announcement is illustrated with a photo of Brown, Tomi Rae, and James Brown Jr., posing at Disneyland with Goofy.

Events leading up to the mugshot: "James Brown Busted in Spousal Spat," *US*, Jan. 29, 2004; "James Brown Released From Jail on Domestic Violence Charge," *Jet*, Feb. 16, 2004; "Singer James Brown Files for Annulment," *Jet*, Feb. 23, 2004; "Holding It Down," *Vibe*, May 2004.

The growth on his prostate and the Edinburgh press conference: Rhodes, *Say it Loud!*

Brown and Augusta: "Editorial: Black and Proud," *Augusta News-Review*, Oct. 21, 1971; "Editorial: James Brown Loves Augusta," *News-Review*, November 15, 1973; Frank Christian, Bob Young interviews.

The statue: Jonathan Lethem, "Being James Brown," *Rolling Stone*, June 29, 2006; Young, Sharpton interviews.

Brown designates trustees to run his career: Irrevocable Trust Agreement of James Brown, August 1, 2000; Bill Torpy, "James Brown's Road to Wealth Was Rocky," *Atlanta Journal-Constitution*, Jan. 7, 2007; "Further Disputes Are on the Way," *Augusta Chronicle*, May 7, 2007.

The grueling final tour: itinerary posted on James Brown fan website, www.greatest-jamesbrown-videotradinglist.com/JB_09/; Jenkins, Amy Christian, Farris, Buddy Dallas, Leon Austin, Johnson interviews.

Final days: Sean Flynn, "Papa," *GQ*, April 2009; Austin, Emily Carder, Brown-Thomas interviews.

The drive: Sharpton, Charles Reid, Brown Thomas, Rhodes interviews.

The final Apollo bill: "A Loud, Proud Sendoff for an Icon of Soul," *The New York Times*, Dec. 29, 2006; "James Brown Laid Out in 24-Karat Gold Coffin," *People*, Dec. 29, 2006; Sharpton, Reid interviews.

The small service in Augusta: "Private Service Held for James Brown," *USA Today*, Dec. 30, 2006; Daviss interview.

Augusta's public sendoff: "Hardest Work is Done," *Augusta Chronicle*, Dec. 31, 2006; Farris, Leeds, Gordon interviews.

Afterword

Brown and Elvis: Woody Marshall, "Perry Man Remembers Visit to Graceland After Death of Elvis Presley," from *The James Brown Reader*; Don Rhodes, "The Godfather and the King," *Augusta Chronicle*, Dec. 23, 2007; Patton interview.

"I went to the funeral, you know, and I touched his body." *Columbia Record*, Sept. 10, 1977.

"Now I'm catching *his* flack and mine." Brown interview, Tucker files.

"I know what madness is. It's not knowing how another man feels." Maria Irene Fornes, *Promenade*, 1965.

"Mr. Brown was an exceptionally slick, conniving, brilliant man." "Papa," *GQ*, April 2009.

H. De Wain Herring: "Last will of James Brown," Aug. 1, 2000; "Herring Guilty, Murderer Gets 30 Years in Prison," *The State*, May 22, 2007.

Brown's probate attorney, Strom Thurmond Jr.: "Will is On File," *Augusta Chronicle*, Jan. 19, 2007.

"We're still managing him. There's lots to do." Torpy, *Atlanta Journal-Constitution*, Jan. 7, 2007.

The trust examined in court: I attended about ten court dates in South Carolina in 2008 and 2009, and my reporting there has shaped this section. Also: "A Legacy in Limbo," *Augusta Chronicle*, Dec. 23, 2007; "Trustee accused of misconduct," *Chronicle*, Aug. 2, 2007; "Brown Trustee Pays Up, Quits," *Chronicle*, Aug. 11, 2007; "Brown Team Quits, Judge Hints at Jail for Former Adviser," *Chronicle*, Nov. 21, 2007.

The messy bookkeeping Brown left behind: "Brown Estate Shows Disorder," *Augusta Chronicle*, June 14, 2007; "Brown's Wealth Targeted by Claims," *Chronicle*, Sept. 1, 2007; "Brown Trustee is Mum on Pay," *Chronicle*, Nov. 16, 2007; "Brown Auction Will Pay Legal Bills, Estate Taxes," *Chronicle*, Feb. 28, 2008; "Tortured Soul," *Portfolio*, Aug. 2008.

"Christ asked for justice and he got death. I want mercy, and I want to live like Moses, happily ever after." Tucker files.

ACKNOWLEDGMENTS

It's only just to break a sweat while on the trail of the Hardest Working Man in Show Business. During three years of researching and writing this book, I crawled around a South Carolina cemetery as it sank into the swamps, reading tombstones in the dark with my hands. I got run off the road by an 18-wheeler near Macon, caught pneumonia twice, and lost my job. In Newport, Kentucky, I heard a couple of soulful King Records veterans sing karoake. In Augusta, Danny Ray showed me the world's most beautiful black velvet painting, depicting James Brown and his loyal friend. And a local fixed me a serving of wienie stew. In Kinston, North Carolina, I received a faith healing in the parking lot of an Outback Steakhouse. Needed it, too. Beautiful people like Martha High, J. C. Davis, Ralph Stanley, and dozens more took me into their homes and buses and shared with me the history that they had lived. Don Rhodes and I were the last journalists to interview Leon Austin, Brown's boyhood friend, before he died. Bob Patton, a hipster Santa who believed in this project, died while I was making plans to come to Atlanta and talk to him again. I thank everybody who showed me kindness along the way.

I am grateful to Rhodes for his tour of Augusta, the map of James Brown's 1989 car chase, and for his own very fine book. Fred

J. Hay from the Center for Appalachian Studies at Appalachian State University in Boone, North Carolina, was kind enough to not just discuss his terrific essay on James Brown's Toccoa, but share with me the interviews he did for that study, including a number of conversations with long-deceased members of the original Flames. The first autobiography Brown wrote, 1986's *James Brown: The Godfather of Soul*, is crucial to understanding the man; Brown's co-writer on that project was Bruce Tucker, who came to know Brown better than most. I learned much from my conversations with Tucker, and my understanding was immeasurably aided by access to his files, notes, and interviews, which Tucker gave me.

Alan Leeds is a human archive on Brown, King Records, and more; I am lucky he shared with me a fraction of what he knows, and lucky to have his rigorous liner notes to Hip-O Select's towering series of James Brown's singles. At the I. P. Stanback Museum and Planetarium at South Carolina State University in Orangeburg, South Carolina, Ellen Zisholtz curated a sweeping exhibition dedicated to Brown's life. Conversations with drummers were crucial to *The One*, and I am fortunate to have had Charles Connor, Clyde Stubblefield, Ahmir Questlove Thompson, Stanton Moore, and Tony Wilson to talk to. Anything I have gotten wrong in the book is despite their best efforts to make me see the light.

So many folks shared their ideas, research, and music, and helped make this book what it is. All the flaws are mine, all praise be to them: Jim Payne, Ned Sublette, Carrie Allen, James C. Cobb, Darren Blase, Oliver Wang, Steve Oney, Dr. Ike Padnos. A great big bucket of lowdown popcorn to Bob Pfeifer, Douglas Wolk, Phil Jones, Howard Burchette, Peter Afterman and Inaudible Productions, Eric Mercado, The Hound, Kembrew Mcleod, Lee Hay, and, damnit, David Mills. Alan Leeds, Fred Daviss, and Harry Weinger all took the time off from their own projects to help me with mine. Look for their books and labors ahead, because they will be huge.

A chunk of *The One* was researched at the Richard J. Riordan Central Library in downtown Los Angeles, and most of the rest of it would have been impossible without the public libraries in almost every town I visited. At a time when a political assault is being waged against the public institutions we all share, we need to give the librarians some. Thanks to: Ellen Zisholtz and the entire staff of the I. P. Stanback Museum and Planetarium, South Carolina State University, Orangeburg, South Carolina; Christine Miller-Betts and Corey Rogers, Lucy Craft Laney Museum of Black History, Augusta, Georgia; Brian F. X. Powers and everyone at the Public Library of Cincinnati and Hamilton County, Cincinnati Ohio; Portia K. Maultsby and Brenda Nelson-Strauss at the Archives of African American Music and Culture, Indiana University, Bloomington, Indiana; John Rumble at the Frist Library and Archive, Country Music Hall of Fame, Nashville, Tennessee; Christopher Harter at the Amistad Research Center, Tulane University, New Orleans, Louisiana.

I am indebted as well to the staffs of: The Library of Congress, Washington, D.C.; Smithsonian Institution, Washington, D.C.; National Archives, College Park, Maryland; the Schomburg Library, Harlem, New York; Jerome Robbins Dance Division and the Billy Rose Theater Division, New York Public Library for the Performing Arts, New York, New York. In South Carolina: The South Carolina Historical Society, Charleston; South Caroliniana Library at the University of South Carolina, Columbia; the Strom Thurmond Institute and Department of Special Collections, Clemson University, Clemson. In Georgia: The Augusta-Richmond Public Library, Augusta; Department of Special Collections, Reese Library, Augusta State University, Augusta; Jimmy Carter Presidential Library, Atlanta; Auburn Avenue Research Library, Atlanta; Georgia Newspaper Project, University of Georgia Main Library, Athens; Georgia Archives, Morrow; Toccoa–Stephens County Public Library, Toccoa; Washington Memorial Library, Macon.

Other collections essential to this book: Southern Historical Collection and the Southern Folklife Collection, Wilson Library,

University of North Carolina, Chapel Hill, North Carolina; Minnesota Historical Society, St. Paul, Minnesota; Walter P. Reuther Library, Wayne State University, Detroit, Michigan; Bentley Historical Library, University of Michigan, Ann Arbor, Michigan.

"The one thing that can solve most of our problems is dancing," Brown said. For everything else, a good editor is the solution, and I am lucky to have a great team at Gotham Books: William Shinker believed in *The One* from the first, and my editor Jessica Sindler helped me stay on the good foot. I'd also like to thank Anne Kosmoski and Lisa Johnson for putting together an outstanding publicity campaign for the book. Charles Rappleye got this ball rolling, and I properly owe him another drink. Paul Bresnick is a master of rapid response, an excellent sounding board, and one fine agent, too.

Grits and gratitude to the friends and family who helped me and made this book possible. Thanks to Harold and Sally Burman; Bill and Rita Mangione-Smith; Linda Breggin and Michael Vandenbergh; Leann Van Wyck McLeod and Geary McLeod; Mark Schone; Brandi Beck; Carol Mangione. Peter Herdrich is a true patron of the arts and one of the good guys; Dan Spector and Richard Goff continue to help me find where the first beat is. Madeleine Echo showed me the right way to dance.

Most of all, thanks to my partner and wife, Jenny Burman. She kept me on the road, and when I was lost in Georgialina, she guided me home. I can't repay all her help and sacrifice. It's a good day when I can live up to her love.

INDEX

Palmer, Earl, 68
Palmer, James F., 268, 284-285
"Papa's Got a Brand New Bag,"
  135-137, 155, 162, 322, 323
Parker, Colonel Tom, 103
Parker, Maceo, 134-136, 173, 197,
  231, 232, 304, 311, 345
Parker, Melvin, 134, 136, 236
Parliament, 305
Patton, Bob, 102, 164, 188, 203, 287,
  316, 332, 385
Paul, Philip, 74, 75
Pauling, Lowman "El," 55
Pavarotti, Luciano, 364-365
"Payback, The," 290-291, 295
Payne, Jim, 117
Payola, 101, 102, 316
PCP (angel dust), 332-333,
  340-345, 350, 351, 353,
  363-364
Pearl, Jack, 104
Pelé, 280
Penny, Hank, 84
Perry, Hubert, 87, 115, 118
Perry, Lee "Scratch," 281
P-Funk, 305-308, 311
Pickett, Wilson, 195
Pinckney, St. Clair, 106, 116, 251,
  252, 334, 336
"Please, Please, Please," 69-76, 79,
  81, 82, 88, 103, 120, 132, 140,
  141, 143, 147, 150, 156, 169,
  248, 347
Podell, Jules, 250
Polydor, 257-260, 313-314, 318, 320,
  329, 336, 349
Polygram, 257, 259
Poojie (dog), 293-294
"Popcorn, The," 220
"Popcorn Charlie," 221
Powell, Adam Clayton, Jr., 115
Powell, Art, 224
Powell, Colin, 368
Presidential elections
1968, 202-206, 225
1972, 265-271
Presley, Elvis, 94, 103, 333, 339,
  381-383
"Prisoner of Love," 119,
  121, 147
Pryor, Richard, 241

Prysock, Arthur, 231
Pulliam, Fred, 54
Pullman, David, 353

"Rapp Payback," 328
Rasbury, Levi, 134-136, 188,
  215, 333
Rath, Richard Cullen, 2-3
Ravens, the, 103
Ray, Danny, 144-145, 148, 149, 187,
  197, 245, 255-256, 275, 280,
  288, 294, 299, 332, 335, 346,
  367, 381
Reagan, Ronald, 260, 269, 329-330,
  337
Redd, Gene, 130, 131
Redding, Otis, 116, 123, 124, 179
Red Hills and Cotton (Robertson), 11
Reed, Lou, 364, 365
Reed, Waymon, 197
Reid, Charles, Jr., 375-376
Reuther, Walter, 204
Rhodes, Don, 23
Richards, Keith, 146
Roach, Bobby, 48, 84-85, 87, 89-92,
  94, 99, 125, 187, 288-289,
  314-315
Robertson, Ben, 11
Robinson, Jackie, 124, 268
Robinson, Sugar Ray, 361
Rochereau, Tabu Ley, 301
Rock and Roll Hall of Fame, 339
Rockefeller, Nelson, 165
Rocky IV (movie), 337-339
Rolling Stones, 146, 262
Rosen, Manny, 260
Ross, Diana, 203
Rowan, Carl, 266
Rubber Band, 305, 307

Sanders, Gertrude, 129, 249, 346
"Santa Claus Go Straight to the
  Ghetto," 232
Saturday Night Live, 327, 328
"Say It Loud," 210-215, 219, 232,
  247, 261
Schiffman, Frank, 108
Schoenbaum, Jerry, 258
Scott, Melvin, 22

Printed in the United States
by Baker & Taylor Publisher Services

Printed in the United States
by Baker & Taylor Publisher Services